Therapy Gone Mad

Therapy Gone Mad

THE TRUE STORY OF HUNDREDS OF PATIENTS
AND A GENERATION BETRAYED

Carol Lynn Mithers

ADDISON-WESLEY PUBLISHING COMPANY
Reading, Massachusetts   Menlo Park, California   New York
Don Mills, Ontario   Wokingham, England   Amsterdam   Bonn
Sydney   Singapore   Tokyo   Madrid   San Juan
Paris   Seoul   Milan   Mexico City   Taipei

Author's Note

With the exception of Konni Corriere, the identities of all Feeling Therapy patients (including "junior" therapists and clinic counselors) have been disguised. Names have been changed, as have physical descriptions, minor background detail, and current occupations and cities of residence.

Many of the designations used by manufacturers and sellers to distinguish their products are claimed as trademarks. Where those designations appear in this book and Addison-Wesley was aware of a trademark claim, the designations have been printed in initial capital letters (i.e., Band-Aid).

Library of Congress Cataloging-in-Publication Data

Mithers, Carol Lynn.
    Therapy gone mad : the true story of hundreds of patients and a
generation betrayed / Carol Lynn Mithers.
        p.   cm.
    ISBN 0-201-57071-8
    1. Feeling therapy.   2. Center for Feeling Therapy.   3. Hart,
Joseph Truman,—1937-   4. Corriere, Richard.   I. Title.
RC489.F42M58   1994
616.89'14—dc20   93-30571
                                                                      CIP

Jacket design by Jean Seal
Text design by Karen Savary
Set in 11-point Palatino by Impressions, a division of Edwards Brothers, Inc.

1 2 3 4 5 6 7 8 9-MA-97969594
First printing, March 1994

Contents

Acknowledgments

This book could not have been written without the assistance of some forty-eight former patients at the Center for Feeling Therapy. These men and women talked to me—some repeatedly and for many hours; they shared diaries, notes, and audiotapes, tirelessly helping me piece together the story of the Center, even though that meant returning to a time and place most had spent years working to leave behind. Because all felt strongly about maintaining their privacy, I can't thank them by name here. But I hope they know much I've appreciated their generosity and valued their intelligence, eloquence, and insight—and how deeply I wish them nothing but happiness in the future.

I also owe a big thanks to attorney Paul Morantz, and to the members of my writer's group, Frank Clancy, Sue Horton, and Joe Domanick, for their comments on early manuscript drafts and much-needed support. Thanks too to my editor, Nancy Miller, for all her help, and for her continued faith in this project. For astute editorial guidance when it was needed most, I owe an enormous debt to Alexia Dorszynski. And from the start, David Black has been the kind of agent most writers only dream about—both staunch advocate and constant cheerleader.

Jonathan Tasini was a continual source of telephone reassurance. Encouragement also came from Joel, Gloria, and especially Joan Mithers, and from my other "family" as well—Leslie Spanier-Wyant, Scott Wyant, Bob Gillies, Bill Nail, Bob Mann, Mary Frei, Marty Borko, Teri Wolfe, Jerome Cummings, Eric Stodder, and above all, Cathy Goodman Robin, who traveled with me through the seventies, then beyond, and whose love has been an enduring anchor.

Finally, I would be nowhere were it not for my husband and comrade, Bill Gibson, who taught me all I know about obsessive researching, and gave this project countless hours of his time—sometimes reading, editing, and taking care of prose, often just taking care of me.

Beginnings

June 1974

"Man, you really sold yourself out," the therapist blasted the twenty-three-year-old patient crouched on the floor of the dimly lit small room. "... You're just lying! You're a fraud, you're a phony, you're a fool. ... Half the time you don't know what's going on—90 percent of the time you don't know what's going on. So talk about what you did know and what you didn't do about it."

"Uh, I played, uh, chess with Dan," the man stammered. Center for Feeling Therapy patients always hesitated at moments like this, wanting to speak honestly, but no longer sure what that meant. The therapy made everything so confusing. "I played a good game. I beat him. ... He told me I set him up and I told him I didn't set him up. I didn't think I played chess that well. ... But I did tell Dan—"

"What?" the therapist demanded.

"Uh, that I didn't set him up. I just told him that I didn't think I played chess that well. ...

"Boy, you are such a fool," sneered the therapist. That

tone—it always told a patient he'd said or done something wrong. Now the therapist would show him just how crazy and sick he was. "You get that innocent little voice. . . . OK, let's play innocent. Now, did you set him up or didn't you?"

"No, I didn't set him up."

". . . Now here's that fucking voice!" shouted the therapist. "Stop it." His arm drew back, then struck. The blow made a muffled, thudding noise. "Don't do that again! One more fucking time and I'm going to rip you apart. Now I'm not fucking around. I mean it."

"I know you do, God . . ." The patient's voice rose, higher-pitched, trembling. Another blow.

"Goddamn it, you want to play innocent right now? . . . Let's hear that innocent voice. Let's hear it. . . ."

"Stop it!" The patient sounded frantic. Anything could happen in this room, anything.

"I'm not going to stop it"—now there were loud, scuffling, thrashing noises—"until you get that fucking voice out of you."

"Stop it. Goddamn it!" the patient panted. "Stop it!" More blows. Bruises bloomed on his arms and thighs. "Stop it!" His legs shot out.

"Don't kick me, you asshole, or I'll knock the shit out of you," hissed the therapist.

"I know you will. Stop it!"

"Do you want to play innocent?"

"No. . . ."

"Then you start talking . . ."

"Uh, you scared me. . . ." The patient's voice shook like a child's. ". . . I'm afraid you're going to kill me."

"Ah, fuck." The therapist sounded disgusted. "You're not afraid I'm going to kill you. Stand up. Now talk."

"Nothing's coming out. I'm afraid."

". . . Oh boy, there's the innocent voice."

"I *am* afraid, goddamn it. You really hit me. You really hurt me."

"I really hurt you. I really hurt you. Because *I* don't take setups. You set people up. If you set me up, you pay for it. You got it?"

"Yeah, I got it. . . ."

"Now," the therapist commanded, "you talk about all the setups you went through yesterday. Start with Dan. And cut the innocent shit. You're not innocent. You're a devious, devious little snake. Now start."

"I was . . . ," The patient trailed off, then began again. "OK," he gave in. "I set Dan up. I set him up. I set him up. . . . "

It was a long way from the back rooms at the Center for Feeling Therapy's Los Angeles headquarters to New York City, where two of the therapy's founders flew one day in 1976 to make an appearance on Tom Snyder's immensely popular "Tomorrow" show. At 1:00 A.M., 6 million American viewers tuned in.

"Our first guests tonight are two really interesting people, and they have a new thing which is called Feeling Therapy," Snyder announced, his eyebrows shooting up in their trademark high arch. "Richard Corriere, and Joseph Hart. . . ." He turned to the men sitting opposite him in burnt orange easy chairs. "We've never done a thing called Feeling Therapy, and I want to know what it is. I'm sure you experienced it yesterday as you stepped off the plane here in New York City. . . . What was the first thing that happened to you?"

Joe Hart gave a broad smile, his teeth flashing in the light. He was a good-looking man of forty-two, tall and lean, with brown eyes, silky red hair that brushed his shirt collar, and a face one reporter would liken to actor Robert Redford's. "Someone wanted to threaten us to share a cab. We had to call on all our feeling to say no."

Snyder chuckled at that. People always liked Joe. It

wasn't just his looks—a palpable benevolence radiated from him, an aura of wisdom that was deep but not intimidating. And his voice was extraordinary, smooth and resonant—the way a child might imagine the voice of God.

"We're professionals, so we've studied lots of different therapies." This voice was harsh and crackling, and the camera zoomed in on Richard "Riggs" Corriere. Riggs was ten years younger than Joe, and equally attractive, though he was as dark as the other man was fair. Thick black hair cut in a then-fashionable "shag" framed an olive-skinned face with a strong nose and full, sensual mouth. Intense brown eyes gleamed behind aviator glasses. As much as Joe emanated calm, the air around his colleague seemed to whirl and burn. He spelled excitement, with an edge of danger. "We kept coming to one conclusion," he said. "None of it worked. So we got a group of professionals together and said, 'Let's follow that old maxim: Physician, heal thyself *first*.' And that was the birth of Feeling Therapy."

"Therapies work to a point," Joe said. "They all do a certain amount of repair work. . . ."

"It's like Band-Aid therapy," said Riggs. There was an ease between the two men, the comfortable give-and-take of two people who'd spent years together and practiced their rap till they got it down just right. "You put one Band-Aid on your head and before you know it"—he clapped his hand to his face—"your cheek's bleeding! We've talked to thousands of people who say, 'I've been to an analyst, and the main thing he did was sleep for forty-nine minutes of the hour.' We don't think that's the way therapy should be. It should change your entire life. Otherwise, why go through it?"

"We did two things that were very different," said Joe. "One, we made sure the therapists got therapy. . . . Each week, I'll have an individual session with one of my friends who's a therapist, . . . then I'll have a group session. I can talk about anything that's affecting me. . . ."

Snyder was puzzled. "But do you tell how you feel about things?"

"You start with that," Joe said smoothly. "And then you tell about those little upsets of feeling that get you off the track—those times when you'll be feeling something but don't really show it. . . ."

"So the people who come to the Center for Feeling Therapy do the same thing?" Snyder wanted to know.

"Yes," Joe said.

Three thousand miles away, in Hollywood, the 350 young men and women who lived in the community that had formed around Feeling Therapy sat in their communal living rooms and nodded, their faces shadowed in blue-and-white television light.

"And then we take it further," Joe continued, "because we think anyone smart enough to get help should be smart enough to give it. After a year, we train all our patients to be therapists for each other. We don't want to have 3,000 patients apiece. We don't want them to be dependent on us forever. . . ."

"It drives other therapists *wild*," said Riggs.

"Well," Snyder said drily, "you probably don't have a lot of friends in the American Psychiatric Association."

At that, Joe smiled, then leaned back, clasping his hands around one knee. "We're called," he said, drawing out the line, to make sure it got the proper attention, "the Butch Cassidy and Sundance Kid of American psychology."

Butch and the Kid! As Snyder laughed in appreciation, he couldn't have realized that despite the line's glib cleverness, it wasn't meant as a joke. Maverick cowboys who were close as brothers and rode into town like conquering heroes—in their patients' minds and their own, that *was* Joe and Riggs. Only a few years ago, they'd been virtual nobodies. Now millions would know of them and the therapy they'd founded—and tonight was only the beginning. Through the seventies, Joe and Riggs would capture a national urge toward self-exploration and improvement and ride it to fame. They would publish books and research articles, be profiled in dozens of newspapers and popular magazines, lecture to overflow crowds throughout the United States and Canada, appear on hundreds of radio and TV shows. They would turn Feeling Therapy into nothing less than a psychological empire whose heart was a Hollywood neighborhood where a passionately committed group of young men and women devoted their lives to therapy. And at the time, no one would know that Feeling Therapy had two sides. The world saw charismatic leaders speaking of a bold new psychotherapy that offered followers happiness, fulfillment, and utopian community. Hidden from view, in the therapy rooms and houses of its Los Angeles community, were 350 patients who were hit, humiliated, controlled—trapped for years in what an administrative law judge would later call an "almost gothic maelstrom."

———————

"Are you one of *them?*" an old woman with a shopping cart asked me as I moved into a house in the Feeling Therapy neighborhood one February day in 1976.

"No," I answered. There was no question who "them" might be.

"Thank God," the woman said, then stopped and shot me a look: If you aren't, why are you moving *here?*

It was a good question. Just over a year before, the man I'd loved through college, a student of Joe Hart's, had become a Feeling Therapy patient. I'd known nothing about the Center's program, and my introduction to it didn't come easy. My lover spent his first three weeks in therapy living in a hotel near the Center, doing nothing but seeing a therapist daily. During that time, we weren't allowed to get together or even speak; afterward, once we did I found him completely, radically changed. Nothing seemed important to him anymore but Feeling Therapy. Former concerns over career and future were dismissed as irrelevant. Old friends were rebuked as "crazy" and "dead"; in fact, he was leaving the apartment he shared with some buddies and moving fifty miles north to Los Angeles, to live with seven people from the Center who made up what he called his "Group." They were his best friends, he said, almost like family and the people with whom he wanted to spend all his time.

Feeling Therapy, I quickly grasped, bore about the same resemblance to traditional therapy as becoming a missionary did to occasionally going to church. It was no once-a-week counseling, but a complete way of life. Center patients all lived together in Hollywood; they worked together, played and went out together, and spent all their time trying to remake themselves into people who lived with the spontaneity and emotional honesty of children. The quest was so central and important that it left no room for anything else.

Although for a while I'd suspected that my boyfriend and I were living on borrowed time and that our relationship would probably end as we made the transition from student life to the real world, under the Center's influence, it broke down immediately and dramatically. New expressions that meant nothing to me filled my lover's speech—"spacing out," "having thoughts." When he wasn't crying over pains I didn't quite understand, he was speaking with an "honesty" I thought was brutal—telling me, for instance, when he'd slept with a Center woman or that he thought I looked fat—and shouting furiously if I objected: The behavior I was rejecting, he said, was his true self, and everything I'd seen before an image, a pose. Before long, we couldn't touch or connect at all, and the feeling was painful and terrifying. It was as if overnight, someone I'd loved had simply disappeared, leaving only his body behind. Worse, the stranger who inhabited it was telling me that the man I mourned had never really existed.

Our breakup should have ended my contact with the Center. But anguished as one can be only after a first major heartbreak, and trapped in the malaise and aimless drift common to those who became adults in the mid-1970s, I found myself drawn to the Center—or rather, to the Hollywood community that formed its core. Admittedly, the initial pull was that it offered a way to maintain a semblance of contact with my old lover. But that wasn't all. The place felt familiar to me, comfortable. Most of its inhabitants were just like me—they'd grown up in the same era, read the same books, listened to the same music, and done the same drugs. They lived communally, as I always had. Most of all, I loved the area's small-town feel, the way everyone was welcome in everyone else's house and no one was a stranger. It seemed to offer what I (and everyone else I knew) wanted most right then: a place to belong. For eighteen months, I lived in the neighborhood I dubbed "Therapyville," and the Center people got to know and accept me as much as they ever did any outsiders. I dated a number of Feeling Therapy men, played on their ragtag ice hockey team, went to a number of parties. And I listened to stories about the therapists around whom people's lives seemed to revolve, men like Joe and Riggs.

I never seriously considered Feeling Therapy for myself. For one thing, it cost $2,500, a small fortune at the time. It wasn't just the money, though. I never learned of the therapy's dark side—not one person I knew then ever told me what went on at the Center behind closed doors—but even so, patients' lives struck me as terribly monochromatic: Hearing hours of conversation focused solely on whether or not someone was "feeling" often bored me to despair. And there was a creepy sameness to the words Center people all used to express themselves, as if their personal vocabularies had been erased. Ultimately, for all I came to care for Feeling Therapy's people, I found what they were doing absurd. After I moved out of their neighborhood in 1977, first to another part of Los Angeles, then to New York, most of the Center stories I told were jokes.

"I'm having a lot of feeling talking to you," my boyfriend

once said to me after we'd had a fight on the telephone. "I have to hang up. I have to talk to someone and find out what I'm feeling."

I have to talk to someone and find out what I'm feeling. Everyone laughed.

The afternoon I visited the Center community while on a trip home in 1979, I stopped laughing about Feeling Therapy. In only two years, everything about the place had changed. The men and women I'd last seen wearing bell-bottom blue jeans, T-shirts, and clunky platform clogs were now decked out in stylish, obviously expensive clothes. There was a disconcerting smell of hustle in the air when they talked to me about programs the Center was offering the general public. "It's so *good* to see you again!" I heard over and over, while familiar faces broke into smiles that were a little too warm and wide. "Have you heard what we're doing now? It's really exciting!" And most remarkably of all, people who'd once been obsessed solely with "feelings" now talked only of *money.* Even my old boyfriend, a quasi-hippie whom I'd last seen driving a battered VW bug, showed off a brand-new, luxuriously appointed silver van. "I've become a dirty capitalist!" he told me, repeating the words again and again, as if they delighted him. "I'm a dirty capitalist! I *like* making money!"

I was revolted. Even more, I was mystified. How had the offbeat, utopian quest I'd known come to *this?* The question haunted me for years—haunted me after my last connection with the Center was finally severed, haunted me after I heard that the place had self-destructed, sparking an avalanche of civil lawsuits and psychotherapy malpractice charges against, among others, Joe and Riggs. But it wasn't until the late 1980s, when I finally learned the full story of what had gone on at the Center, that I understood the answer.

On one level, that story was simply a nightmare, a bizarre tale of intelligent and well-meaning men and women doing unspeakable things in the name of self-improvement. To someone who'd known and liked the people involved, it was excruciating to hear. But in a deeper sense, it was something more. When I looked at the Center for Feeling Therapy between the years 1971 and 1980, then at America during that same time, I realized I was seeing a mirror image.

At first glance, claiming a parallel between a radical therapy and "ordinary" American culture seems a stretch. But psychology is a perfect window to a country's soul. Although the discipline presents itself as a "science," its entire history is one of a series of new techniques and schools of thought, each profoundly influenced by the culture in which it flourished: Every "sickness" therapy has defined, then sought to heal, has been the spiritual complaint of its age, whether nineteenth-century hysteria or twentieth-century angst and anomie. Psychological theory also shapes culture, for its discoveries and prescriptions reach beyond individual patients to teach the wider community—as religion and mythology taught more primitive societies—who they are, what made them that way, and what to do about it.

The spiritual complaint that defined the 1970s was numbness, an inability to "feel." The cause, said the Center—and the hundreds of other popular and quasi-professional therapies that also flourished at the time—was not oppressive social conditions but that people had become estranged from their "real" selves. The "cure" was to reach those selves by stripping away socialization and defenses until everyone was as unintellectual, instinctual and "open" as children. The promise had been the creation of a new, superior kind of human. The ultimate outcome of the effort, however, was the creation of millions of infantilized adults.

It was that realization which finally helped me understand not only what had happened at the Center but the time in which I was then living, one in which the prevailing ethos was get-and-spend; in which there was little outcry over a growing Third World–like gap between rich and poor; in which millions embraced a president clearly indifferent to the complexities of governing, because he told comforting stories in a soothing voice. And it explained how America, as a nation, had gotten there. The journey was customarily presented as a mystery, as if recent history contained some "Twilight Zone" abyss. One minute the country had been quivering with the possibility of social revolution; then boom!—we'd all awakened to find the lucky making millions on Wall Street while the unlucky lived off their garbage.

The abyss, of course, was the 1970s. That time, according to common belief, was a joke, a forgotten decade in which the excitement of Vietnam, Watergate, and reborn feminism faded into the vacuousness of disco, platform shoes, and years in which nothing much happened.

But something *did* happen during those "forgotten" years. In the 1970s, millions of Americans set out on a path that promised to help them "grow." Instead, they—and the country—were led *backward*, into regression.

The story of the Center for Feeling Therapy was played out along that path.

PART ONE

Joe's Kids

1

One could not imagine a more incongruous birthplace for a "gothic maelstrom" than the University of California, Irvine, but all that happened at the Center for Feeling Therapy began there, in the late sixties, with the remarkable popularity of Joe Hart. Some UCI students said that the young assistant professor of psychology was a genius. No student with a mystical bent graduated without taking his course "Psychology of Awareness," and the class was always jammed, 100 students, 130, in a school whose total population was only around 6,000. During his office hours, there was always one kid with him, while three or four more waited in the hall.

"Student guru" wasn't a role anyone would have predicted for Joe. He grew up in a working-class family in Portland, Oregon, the eldest of three, and was a self-described "tennis bum" who for years played in junior championships all up and down the West Coast. Off-court, though, he was a serious student, a thinker and voracious reader. After graduating summa cum laude from local Lewis and Clark College in 1958, he and his new wife, Gina, also from Portland, set off for the University of Wisconsin, where Joe had been accepted to do graduate work in psychology.

It was a smart career choice, for at the time, the mental health field was expanding wildly. Only three years before, the executive secretary of the American Psychological Association had told a congressional commerce committee that "if [our organization's] present rate of growth continues, we will have, by simple arithmetic, 60 million members 100 years from now." Equally important for the man Joe would become, psychology was changing. For the past fifty years, two schools of thought had dominated the field. One, of course, was Freudian psychoanalysis. Born in blood-soaked, nineteenth-century Europe, its vision of the psyche was a gloomy one, emphasizing repression, resistance, and the murderous impulses of the Oedipus complex. To be human, it said, was to be filled with inner conflict, and the best any therapy could do was help a patient cope with the turmoil. The second was behaviorism, promoted by men like B. F. Skinner and John Watson, which categorized observable acts in terms of stimulus and response. Behaviorists studied people the same way they did animals; they seemed more interested in predicting behavior than understanding it.

By the 1950s, however, a "third force," quintessentially American in its optimism, was being put together by a number of prominent U.S. psychologists, including Erik Erikson, Rollo May, and Abraham Maslow. Behaviorists' emphasis on simply studying what people did did nothing to advance human understanding, they said; people were more complex than lab rats. And Freud's vision of the psyche was unreasonably dark because he based his theories on analysis of dysfunctional people. "The study of crippled, stunted, immature and unhealthy specimens can yield only a cripple psychology and a cripple philosophy," Maslow pointed out. Why not instead study healthy, successful individuals to find out why their lives worked?

The way Maslow and his colleagues, who became known as humanist psychologists, saw it, human beings' true nature wasn't conflict at all; it was wholeness. Beneath every neurotic exterior there existed a healthy self that could be found, led out, and allowed to flourish. Moreover, such an act of liberation was not just for the "sick." Certainly psychotherapy could help individuals get past the problems that tormented them, but it could also improve the lot of humankind as a whole. With hard work, every person could realize his or her full human potential, could become what Maslow called "self-actualized." As it happened, in 1958 one of the seminal figures of the humanist psychology movement was teaching at the University of Wisconsin—Carl Rogers.

The therapy Carl Rogers had developed was called client-centered therapy. It stressed the therapeutic relationship as a growth (rather than healing) experience, and emphasized the "feeling" aspects of a situation over the intellectual ones. At the time Joe Hart met him, Rogers was studying the use of client-centered therapy as a treatment for schizophrenics. Joe soon became involved in the work, first doing research that attempted to measure subjects' personality change, later with what was called "psychophysical correlates of psychotherapy": During a therapy session, a patient would be attached to a polygraph machine so researchers could determine how therapy affected the body as well as the mind. In 1961, Joe wrote his master's thesis on Rogers's work, and Rogers served as his adviser. He seemed to genuinely care for Joe, and other graduate students thought that made sense, for in some ways the two men were alike, both intellectually demanding yet quiet and gentle.

Some students also had other, more mixed feelings about Joe. He still looked like an all-American jock, tall and lean, his red hair worn in a crew cut, and he was an easygoing, unpretentious guy. But anyone who tried to get to know him quickly came up against an aloofness that let him know he'd never get too close. At an age when most young men were obsessed with the struggle to break away from their families, Joe never even talked of his. And unlike most graduate students, who relieved the tension of tight budgets and endless studying with occasional blowouts, Joe never acted silly or publicly let go. He and his wife, Gina, a tall, pale woman with ash-brown hair, were like a tight, private unit, locked away together behind a wall of propriety and rigid reserve. Once Joe drank too much at a student party, and had to be put to bed. A classmate who knocked on the bedroom door looking for him found Gina blocking the way.

"Is Joe OK?" he asked.

"Of *course* he is!" she said angrily. "What makes you think he's not?"

In the bedroom, Joe snored on. And that was as much as anyone at the University of Wisconsin ever saw him cut loose.

After Wisconsin, the Harts moved to Northern California, where for four years Joe worked for his Ph.D. at Stanford. He did extremely well there. His dissertation, which examined what happened in the brain during the common experience people had of feeling sure they knew something yet being unable to get to the information, was supported by grants from the National Science Foundation and the National Institutes of Health. The dissertation itself won a prize for creativity. Then, in 1965, Joe got his doctorate and a job offer, and the Harts moved south to Laguna Beach, a short drive from the raw, just-opening campus of UCI.

―――――――――

Nineteen sixty-five was a great year to be educated and young and just starting out, especially in Southern California. The middle of the decade was a fat, smug time. U.S. ground troops had recently been sent to stop the spread of communism in a nowhere country called Vietnam, but few doubted that the effort would end soon and well. At home, the whole country was high on four straight years of economic boom, with Southern California the wildest, giddiest place of all. Population was exploding, and every region was growing, especially Orange County. Not the old county, the inland, blue-collar towns known as the home of John Birchers and reactionary cranks: Close to the coast, near the rich, blond enclaves of Newport Beach and Corona del Mar, the Irvine Company was building a whole new glittering suburb of homes, offices, and shopping malls. Irvine was to be a different kind of city, wholly planned from the start. It would have airy, bright houses, just the right number of greenbelts and "lakes," a population that was educated, attractive, wealthy and white. There would be no surprises in Irvine, no repeats of past urban mistakes. The new U.C. campus there—one of two opening that year—had risen from acres of cow pasture like the very embodiment of American confidence, all modern concrete-and-glass towers and manicured lawns. President Lyndon Johnson himself presided over its opening ceremonies. Any 28-year-old assistant professor who played the academic game right at UCI could look forward to a predictable, pleasant existence there—teaching, writing, tenure by 35, regular salary increases funding a house in some local development with a name like Turtle Rock or Spyglass Hill.

At first, Joe Hart was the very image of a promising new professor doing everything by the book. On his own, he went to local businesses and talked executives into donating tens of thousands of dollars worth of equipment so he could set up a campus research laboratory. "Joe could have been a banker," another social science professor remarked to a colleague, not entirely approvingly. Then, with grants from the U.S. Public Health Service and National Institute of Mental Health, he continued his psychophysical research. The new experiments, on the connection between brain waves and hypnotic susceptibility and the use of biofeedback techniques to help people control their own brain waves so they could become more susceptible to positive hypnotic suggestion, were in the vanguard of what would become a major field of research. Quickly, Joe published an impressive number of articles. And he and a former colleague from the University of Wisconsin started work on a book about client-centered therapy.

But a part of him was beginning to rebel. At the time, most academic psychologists viewed their discipline as a "hard" science, like physics: What they considered important was taking measurements and quantifying results. Although it was what he'd been hired to do, that goal had begun to strike Joe as contemptibly predictable and narrow. "What most psychologists study," he told a student, "are anal droppings." In 1966, he passed the state exam required to get a clinical psychologist's license (at the time, no additional training was required), and started a tiny private practice. And he became increasingly fascinated with the study of altered states of consciousness—drugs, dreams, visions, mystical experiences—and the role they played in shaping personality and perception. He started studying Transcendental Meditation, a still-esoteric Eastern discipline (though it would soon be popularized by celebrities like the Beatles and Mia Farrow); he read mystic Georges Gurdjieff and rebel psychoanalyst and political radical Wilhelm Reich, who studied with, then rejected Freud, arguing that sexual energy was the criterion for healthy human functioning. He delved into William James's *Varieties of Religious Experience* and the work of mythologists Joseph Campbell and Mircea Eliade.

Intellectually, Joe's new explorations were a natural extension of his brain wave research. But they also seemed to express an emotional need for some kind of transcendence in his own life. Some who knew Joe sensed a void at his center, a hungry loneliness as if he'd never really settled in at Irvine, or found friends and intellectual comrades among the social science faculty. He and Gina were as close as ever and now had a child. But the Harts were always on the move, changing yearly from one rented house to another. It was almost, a student who knew him said later, as if Joe were continually looking for a place where he might feel at home. During one unhappy period, the Harts lived in Mission Viejo, a quintessential white-bread Orange County suburb, where neighbors' kids constantly threw things against their garage. Joe wasn't mad at the kids, though. "They're just acting out their parents' unconscious thoughts," he said. "They know I don't belong here." The statement was matter-of-fact, but there seemed sadness beneath it. Joe Hart was young, with a passionate and intense intellectual life, and a desire for something spiritual. He was on a quest, and he wanted to share it.

His students were only too happy to join him. The more Joe explored "alternate consciousness," the more far-out his classes got. While other social science professors in too-tight tweed jackets droned on about statistics and neurons, Joe, in his jeans and sandals, talked about magic: What were the different ways that existed of seeing the world? Were there limits on what a human being could become? His lecture subjects danced from hypnosis to LSD to the Senoi Indians, a Malayan tribe who lived communally and sought personal power and mystical visions in their dreams.

"We can do this too," he told his students. "We can learn to harness the powers of our dreams."

The kids ate it up. But it wasn't just Joe's lectures they loved; there were also the hours before or after class when they could sit in Joe's small office, amid bookshelves crammed with volumes on psychology and philosophy, talking. As usual, Joe didn't share much about himself, but the removal his fellow Wisconsin graduate students had found disconcerting his UCI kids read as wisdom. And he had a naturally slow, deliberate way of speaking that made for a compelling personal style; each of Joe's words was chosen so carefully that whatever he said carried extra weight. There was nothing self-aggrandizing about Joe—in fact, other faculty members thought his first response to attracting a following was discomfort—but before long, he accepted the role of sage and settled into it, letting his students know he was available to listen and advise, to help them with their lives.

"Write down your dreams and bring them to me," he told one young man. "You can learn from them, and I'd like to help you." Later, he pored over the scribbled notebooks, making sense of dinosaurs and car chases and tidal waves. "You see?" he pointed out. "You're frustrated. You're finding it hard to work and get yourself going. But you really do have talent. You just have to find a way to cultivate it."

The boy glowed. "I'm frustrated with my job," he confessed. "I need the money to pay for school, but I wish I could do something more with my life."

There was the typical Joe pause, then the measured, deliberate words. "Well . . . I need someone to run my lab. Would you like to do that?"

"I felt *chosen*," the man later recalled. "Joe became a hero to me. I thought he was an extraordinary intellect and I wanted to be everything he was."

Soon a small group of student followers were going to dinner at Joe's home, chattering excitedly about the Senoi. A core crowd that was mostly male spent hours at Joe's office or around his lab, four rooms in a temporary building a short walk off campus that was improbably shared by the social science and art departments. New experiments were getting under way, one an attempt to see if brain waves could be artificially pushed to the same frequency reached by advanced meditators. Art students in paint-spattered overalls peered in to see people wired to electrodes and staring at flashing lights while noise blared, and even they shook their heads in wonder and admiration.

Everyone knew that Joe was going somewhere big, and being around him was like entry into a glamorous world of famous names and therapy pioneers. "When I was talking to Carl Rogers last weekend . . . ," Joe might say, and kids' hearts would stutter and jump. And as 1967 became 1968, then 1969, Joe's popularity kept growing. UCI was no Berkeley—few of its students were hippies or lefties in any true sense of the word—but by the end of the decade, that didn't matter. As the "limited" war in Vietnam grew into a monster that killed hundreds of thousands of Americans and Vietnamese; as Robert Kennedy and Martin Luther King were gunned down; as ghettos exploded and police went on murderous rampages, a kid didn't have to be hard-core to have learned to feel nothing but contempt for "straight" society and adults in general, with their hypocritical, racist, money-grubbing, warmongering ways. Like most American kids, UCI students had no intention of turning out to be like their parents. Instead, the sons and daughters of doctors and mechanics were seeking spiritual wisdom like Herman Hesse's *Siddhartha* and peyote visions like Carlos Castaneda and the telepathic mind-merge called "grokking" practiced by *Stranger in a Strange Land*, Valentine Smith. Kids of teachers and salesmen were engrossed in the heroic struggles of *Lord of the Rings*, cheering Hobbit Frodo Baggins's attempt to keep the One Ring of absolute power from the Dark Lord, Sauron, and were caught up in Arthur C. Clarke's *Childhood's End*, the story of a generation born with supernatural powers who ultimately board the ships of outerspace "Overlords" and leave the planet. Kids from Central Valley farm towns and Southern California freeway suburbs weren't sitting up late worrying about their résumés; they were tripping and watching the earth breathe and the universe bend. A sense of absolute possibility was in the air, and when you were out on the empty Irvine campus at night, ripped on $10-a-lid Mexican weed with the hot wind blowing and the smell of sage everywhere, it was easy to feel on the cusp of something entirely new, as if your mind was opening so far you could understand things there weren't even words for yet.

Joe Hart didn't call that kind of thinking nuts, and his students loved him for it. There was a secret most people didn't know about late sixties kids, with their wild hair and ripped jeans: Beneath their loud disdain for conventional authority lay a desperate craving for someone they *could* trust. There was one word that came to their minds when they looked at Joe: *father*. The father they all wished they had.

Richard "Riggs" Corriere knew all about the appeal of surrogate fathers. When Riggs (the name was a childhood nickname) was eighteen, he would later tell a friend, he informed his own Roman Catholic father that he wasn't going to go to church anymore. His father beat him. Riggs had been born in Chicago and grown up in Phoenix, the only boy in a family of six, and through the years and cities, the Corriere home was not a happy one. Riggs's father was hardworking and harshly authoritarian; hitting was no one-time event. His mother, Riggs said, also went after him physically, and his four older sisters kicked and scratched and brutalized him so much that for years he didn't feel at ease with women. (At twenty-three, Riggs would record a dream in which one of his sisters fights with him and his father burns him with a hot coffeepot. Riggs then hits his father with a strap and eventually kills the entire family.)

Early on, he'd learned to look outside home for emotional support. In Phoenix, he'd found solace in friendship with a local family whose life together was fun, not a constant battle. And he'd gotten close to one of his parochial high school teachers, a Jesuit who treasured the spirited smart kid who sat in class firing question after question at him. Even after the Corrieres moved to Orange County, where they ran a Mexican restaurant, Riggs and his teacher kept in touch. By the time he entered UCI as a freshman in the fall of 1965, Riggs was ripe for finding a new mentor.

When he took his first course from Joe Hart, it changed both their lives. "Joe really knows about people," Riggs raved to other students. "He's brilliant!" Another class followed, then another—by Riggs's senior year, one social science department professor guessed that 80 percent of the courses Riggs had taken had been taught by Joe Hart. There was nothing unusual about a student being captivated by Joe, of course; what was different was that this time Joe felt the same. The shaggy-haired teenager, in his jeans, flannel shirts, and heavy black-framed glasses, was someone with whom Joe Hart— there were no other words for it—fell in love. Almost certainly part of Riggs's appeal was his wit and quick verbal intelli-

gence; he offered Joe the kind of intellectual sounding board
Joe hadn't yet been able to find. And unlike Joe's UCI colleagues, Riggs was ready and willing to share Joe's spiritual
explorations.

But there were other compelling aspects to Riggs's personality, ones that stayed in the memory of everyone who met
him. Brash, energetic, and loud, the young Riggs had an extraordinary and absolute self-confidence. He told jokes with
the assurance of someone who never doubted he was funny;
although neither classically handsome nor well dressed and
smooth, he seemed to expect women to find him attractive.
(Many did; during Riggs's sophomore year, shocked social
science faculty passed the rumor that he was having an affair
with a department secretary, a woman of forty.) And he had
a breathtaking directness.

"I know you like me," he informed one plump girl who'd
made it clear she wanted to date him. "But you're overweight,
and that tells me you're unhappy about something. I don't
know if I can take that on."

Such blunt honesty was painful—but also strangely al-
luring. The girl fled to her dorm room to cry, but later sought
Riggs out again and became his friend; no one had ever spoken to her so candidly before. And something in Riggs's expressiveness and spontaneity seemed to pull at the removed,
deliberate Joe Hart, to suggest the possibility of another way
to be.

Before long, the two men's lives and interests were so
intertwined that it was hard to tell who was leading whom.
In 1968, Joe went to Zurich to study at the Jung Institute; that
same year, Riggs began writing down all his dreams. Around
the time Riggs spent a month studying Transcendental Meditation with the Maharishi, Joe's research focused on brain
waves and meditation. Riggs was at the center of the knot of
students who hung out at the lab and dined at Joe's home—
whenever he walked into the room, Joe's face would light up.
By his senior year, Riggs was helping Joe run his biofeedback

experiments; by the time he graduated from UCI with a B.A. in psychology in the spring of 1969, he'd already decided to reenroll as a psych graduate student. And it was around the same time that Joe made the final shift away from his promising straight academic career. Although he continued to do laboratory experiments, he was ready to move from studying psychology to using it to improve and expand people's lives—including his own. It was a crucial decision at a crucial time. Even as academic psychologists continued to scratch out their charts and graphs, outside the university walls the practice of therapy was being transformed.

———————

Around the time Abraham Maslow and Carl Rogers were first formulating their theories, a number of people—both social scientists and lay workers—were experimenting with effecting behavioral change in individuals via group activity. "Sensitivity training," born at National Training Laboratories in Bethel, Maine, and also practiced at the Western Training Laboratories at UCLA, was teaching groups of white-collar workers to explore their emotional relationships with each other so they would be better executives and managers. An organization called Alcoholics Anonymous was proving that being part of a supportive group helped alcoholics stay sober. And an AA alumnus named Chuck Dederich had begun holding "free-association" discussion groups with drug addicts in his apartment in the hope of keeping them off drugs. Of course, the emphasis of such groups was behavior change, not self-fulfillment. But by the early sixties, the two movements began to merge.

As the boxed-in 1950s gave way, the conviction that there was more to life than adapting and conforming, that it was time to break out, was exploding all through America. Psychedelic pioneer Timothy Leary was holed up in a Victorian mansion in Millbrook, New York, leading an ever-changing flow of stoned guests in an attempt "to create a new paganism and a new dedication to life as art." In Michigan, a small group of college students met to give birth to a new political movement, a "New Left" that would not only tackle economic and racial injustice but inject an emotionally comatose society with passion and meaning. A few years later, hippies would start an alternative society based on people loving each other and being "real." And a growing segment of the middle class, caught in the euphoria of the prosperous times, was embracing the idea that it was time to attend to matters of the soul. In 1963, a young man with mystical leanings named Michael Murphy founded the Esalen Institute on the green cliffs of Big Sur, California. It was to be, he said, "a center to explore and expand and enhance the human potential." Esalen's weekend retreats offered communal massage, naked hot tub bathing, and exercises that taught openness, sensitivity, and trust, and the place was an immediate success.

By 1967, the same year as the hippie Summer of Love and Abraham Maslow's election as president of the American Psychological Association, tens of thousands of Americans were attending workshops or seminars at one of the fifty "growth centers" that had sprung up across the country; some 25,000 a year were going to Esalen alone. And enormous numbers were taking part in "encounter groups," small gatherings in which people closeted themselves for hours or even days, and, guided by a leader, confronted each other until they broke through to some higher level of "realness." Some people were even making encountering a way of life: In Los Angeles, Chuck Dederich had turned his apartment discussions with drug addicts into Synanon, a small rehabilitation community. Now it was expanding into a whole alternative society, where ex-addicts, alcoholics, and "squares" strived to become superior humans by playing "the Game"—a group encounter where people confronted and attacked one group member for up to twenty-four hours at a time.

The kind of inner searching, confession, and self-discovery that went on in such places was labeled "growth." In practice, though, it often was quite a lot like *therapy*—but a new kind. Until now, therapy usually meant something ongoing and formal, weeks of hourly sessions in which a patient talked and a therapist listened, taking care to keep his own personality out of the equation. Because it was terribly expensive, it also was reserved almost entirely for the wealthy. But there was nothing exclusive about the new growth experiences. Anyone with twenty or thirty bucks and a free weekend could join in. And there was nothing at all formal about them. People didn't just talk; they howled, screamed, cried, touched, took off their clothes. Leaders—who might or might not have any conventional training—talked about themselves, shared their own feelings, and actively pushed others to make changes. Unlike that of analysts, their goal was not to lead people to a new understanding of themselves but to *force* them to it.

In this therapy, change always came via group effort, and it came *fast*. "Face-to-face therapy is a luxury," Abraham Maslow himself would tell a reporter. "It's too slow and too expensive. It's not the right answer if you think, as I shamelessly do, in terms of changing the whole world." Most important, it came without therapy's old stigma. People who went to growth centers knew they weren't sick. They were well people who wanted to become *better*. Trying to improve was considered not only acceptable but admirable. Even Joe Hart's old mentor, Carl Rogers, was now leading encounter workshops at the Western Behavioral Institute in La Jolla, California; a film of one of his sessions had won an Academy Award for Best Documentary in 1968. Intensive group experiences, said Rogers, were "perhaps the most significant social invention of this century," teaching people that "security resides not in hiding oneself but in becoming more fully known."

All through 1969, Joe and Riggs sampled the experimental banquet that was being called the "human potential movement." They tried Gestalt and Rolfing, a painful, deep-tissue massage supposed to release tension and "realign" the body, and took part in encounter groups at Kairos, a growth center near San Diego. They thrilled at an introduction to bioenergetics, a therapy developed by Wilhelm Reich student Alexander Lowen that used special exercises like kicking out and yelling to exhaust the defenses and free "physical blocks" in the body. "We've been looking for something with power like this!" Joe exulted. And soon, they began running groups of their own. During the winter of 1969–70, Joe brought his fascination with dreams to Kairos, leading workshops that taught students traditional and modern interpretation, as well as ways to use their dreams to alter their waking lives. Riggs even had a job there, living on the grounds as Director of Facility, and leading encounter groups for students, singles, and the overweight. That school year, the two men turned the "Psychology of Awareness" class into an encounter group. Out in the lab's big room, its floors covered with mattresses, students went on "trust walks," where they closed their eyes and allowed friends to lead them, and played "the Bullshit game"—one person would sit in the center of a circle speaking about himself, and if the group felt he was being manipulative or evasive, everyone would shout, "Bullshit!" Or sometimes Riggs—who by now was always Joe's teaching assistant—led students into a bioenergetic frenzy.

"Come on!" he'd push. "Breathe deep! Kick your legs! I want to hear you *yell!*" If coaxing didn't work, maybe needling would. "Look at you!" Riggs would shout. "What's that grin on your face? You're a piece of shit! Let me hear you! You're mad at your folks? Let's hear it!"

"I hate you, Dad!" students screamed, their legs flailing and fists smashing into pillows. "Fuck you, you shithead!"

After the yelling, Joe did more quiet individual work. "Get under this mattress," he told one boy. "Talk to me from there. You see how muffled you sound? That's the way you are in the world. That's how cut off you are."

The sessions were heady stuff if you were at an age when questions like "Who am I really?" could wake you, heart pounding, in the middle of the night. Sure, the sessions could be hard, but it felt daring to risk such exposure. And there was a high that came afterward, a feeling that was raw and earthy, as if emotions had been turned up until they vibrated with a force most people felt only occasionally, such as when newly in love. Kids came away so wired they couldn't sleep.

Yet if the groups changed the students who took them, they also changed Joe and Riggs. Through their own participation in new therapies, the two men had begun confronting the parts of themselves that prevented them from experiencing life fully. For Joe, that meant struggling to break through his reserve and control. Riggs, for all his directness and candor, seemed to feel cut off from others, unable to really connect. ". . . i cannot speak," he wrote in 1969, "and the words / of my soul crowd into my mouth / and i choke on loneliness. . . . "

At the same time, both men were learning they could make others feel the kinds of breakthroughs toward which they themselves strove. In fact, the twenty-two-year-old Riggs was proving to be a therapist of astonishing power. He had incredible intuition, an uncanny insight into how people worked, always seeming to know exactly how they had constructed their defenses and what buttons to push to dismantle them. At Kairos, he brought one young woman to orgasm through a bioenergetic pelvic exercise; he made others break down in anguished tears, then gently comforted them.

But Riggs's power went beyond the therapeutic moment. The sense of personal freedom he exuded, of not caring what others thought of him, was irresistible, especially to anyone who was young or had a few self-doubts. And just by being his natural, unabashed self, he perfectly epitomized the honest, open, human potential movement ideal. High school kids who went to his weekend workshops at Kairos came away babbling about the man who wouldn't close the top button on his jeans because it was too "confining," who burped without

covering his mouth, and who even farted loudly and abso-
lutely without shame. "He was the most magnetic personality
I've ever met in my life," one recalled, even two decades later.
"He became my god."

Soon, Riggs had a following as devoted as Joe's, kids who
came back to Kairos again and again for his encounter
groups—including one lovely seventeen-year-old girl who
eventually ended up in the graduate student's bed. But if the
idea of leading others had at first troubled Joe, it gave Riggs
no pause: He took to it as if it were what he'd always been
meant to do. His other interests, like music and camping, fell
away before the importance of helping people change. *All* men
and women, Riggs seemed to believe, needed to live honestly,
to be fully themselves. It was his job to make sure that
happened.

"I've always wanted to be a singer," one girl confessed
to him during an encounter group at UCI. "But I don't think
my voice is good enough."

"Bring your guitar next time and sing for us," Riggs ordered, and when she did, he listened intently. "Something
came out in you just then that I've never seen before," he told
her when she finished, "something deep. It's a way you have
of communicating with people that's different from words.
You don't have to have a big powerful voice to do that." Then
Riggs went further. "I've talked to my brother-in-law about
you," he told the girl not long afterward. "He has a restaurant,
and he's willing to hire you to sing."

Just like that, a girl who'd hardly dared to dream of singing was doing it professionally. Even at twenty-two, Riggs
Corriere had the power to make people see that anything was
possible—and that he could make their deepest wishes come
true.

By the spring of 1970, there had been two important additions
to Joe and Riggs's partnership. One came with the appearance

in Orange County of the former high school parochial school teacher with whom Riggs had stayed in touch for so many years. By now, thirty-one-year-old Dominic Cirincione, shortish and balding, with a round, genial face, had left Phoenix and his Jesuit order and embarked on a new search for spiritual fulfillment that had already included regular stays at Esalen, experiments with mysticism and drugs, and pursuit of a master's degree. The other had occurred when a twenty-three-year-old graduate student named Werner Karle, tall, slender, and athletic, with brown hair and a thin, sharp face, took over running Joe's lab experiments. Although meticulous and research-oriented, he too was a searcher. As the two men, half colleagues, half followers, joined the group that hung out with Joe and Riggs, its core strengthened and its focus changed. Increasingly, talk turned from "consciousness" to therapy and founding an alternative community—doing something that would change the world.

"We'll get a bus and go around grabbing people and doing therapy on them!" one boy shouted giddily.

"Someday," said Riggs, "Joe and Dom and I are going to go off and live together."

"Wow! I'd like to be a part of that," one of Joe's other followers said.

There was a pause, while Riggs considered. "I guess," he said, "there'd probably be a place for you."

In the midst of the excitement, Joe was hard at work writing. He'd recently gotten tenure at UCI and been promoted to associate professor, so his future there was secure. And his own theories about what psychology could and should do were gradually becoming clear. Most existing therapy, he now thought, concentrated on repairing people without telling them what to do next. But therapy needed to go beyond that— to become more like religion. Religion, after all, provided externally imposed moral guidelines and ideal images of what a human being could be. Psychology could teach people to look inside *themselves* for those same things. It could help people tap into their own inner wisdom and values, turning these into forces that guided their lives. Making that change, Joe was thinking, required a whole new school of psychology, one that combined the best of everything—science, the experimental therapies now in vogue, mysticism, myth. He would be the one to pull the pieces together and create it.

"We are trying . . . to bring together disciplines and ideas that have been artificially separated," he wrote that year in a paper introducing a concept he called "integrative psychology." ". . . To facilitate growth toward wholeness we must see the variety and fullness of human existence in the round. Nothing relevant can be excluded, even if it overlaps science into religion, medicine into magic, therapy into art. . . . "

He seemed to feel that he was onto something, that he and Riggs were moving fast toward a goal they could sense but not yet name. And then they made a discovery that changed everything.

———————

The fall of 1970 blasted into Southern California with a week of Santa Ana winds, zero humidity, and brutal heat; every hill and mountain in three counties was in flames. At Irvine, the campus Bank of America burned down, "Oink of Amerika" spray-painted on its walls. And on the first day of class, Joe Hart informed his students that this year, "Psychology of Awareness" would be covering something completely new. There would be no more Senoi, no more bioenergetics, no more encounter groups. Instead, they would study a revolutionary theory of how people were made sick—and how they could be cured. It had produced a therapy so good and so important that he and Riggs were going through it themselves.

The kids sucked on their pens, looking at the two men, wide-eyed.

Riggs stared back. You'd better start paying attention, he said, in his challenging way. "Because every one of you . . . every one of you . . . "—now everyone was listening—"Every one of you is *insane.*"

2

Insane? Russell Gilbert sat in a front-row seat staring at his teachers in worship and confusion. This was his second class with Joe, though he didn't look like a typical follower. He was twenty-six, older than most students, and already had a college degree—a B.A. in mathematics. He was neater as well, clean-shaven, his blond hair trimmed, his jeans clean and shirt pressed. He looked like the kind of nice young man who shows up at suburban doors selling cleaning supplies. But what was most out of place was his manner. Usually, Joe's kids were obvious seekers whose wild dreams virtually leapt out of their eyes. Everything about Russ was flat and subdued. His face was so without spark or radiance that even his good looks became bland, forgettable. Russ knew how he looked. He hated it. That was why he was here.

For years, Russ had felt as if he lived in a world apart from other people. He knew when the feeling had begun—when he was around four and the older brother he idolized had left him behind to start school—but he didn't know why or what to do about it. All through his childhood, he'd been unable to manage the most minimal interaction—couldn't even joke or carry on a casual conversation—without feeling scared and off-balance. Throughout the middle-class Southern California suburb in which he'd grown up, other kids spent their afternoons playing baseball in the street or throwing basketballs through driveway hoops. Russ stayed inside, in his room, alone. It was as if there was something physical between himself and others, a wall that kept him from reaching out. Through high school and his first two years at a small private college, he'd been so withdrawn he barely spoke. Then he fell in love. Sensation, intimacy, overwhelmed him; he was stunned by how much it was possible to feel. He and the girl got married too fast and too young, and only a few years later it was over.

As his marriage ended, Russ felt the old wall rise up around him, icy and impenetrable, and realized he couldn't bear to return to his former isolation. He left the apartment he'd shared with his wife and moved in with a younger brother who lived in Orange County. His brother had turned out differently. He was having a great time, smoking dope and fucking lots of different girls. There were constant parties at his house, joints and cheap wine, the Stones blasting on the stereo. Russ didn't want *that* life, but seeing its vividness was like glimpsing the promise of another world. He and his wife had gone to see a counselor when things started getting bad between them. The visits hadn't helped keep them together, but therapy had been the first time Russ had ever stepped back to examine who he was and to consider what had made him that way. Now he wanted to go further, to leave everything he'd known and been behind. For the past five years, he'd worked in a dull, safe job as an engineer for an aerospace firm. He decided to quit, go back to school, and study psychology.

"What I'm interested in is therapy," he told the UCI social science graduate adviser.

"Then you want Joe Hart," the man said.

Russ had never met anyone like Joe. He sat still as a Buddha as Russ talked, so relaxed and quiet he might have been asleep, but Russ quickly saw that every word he said registered.

"I guess I want to study psychology because of my own experience," he tried to explain.

"I understand," Joe said, as if he really did. That voice!

"One of the things I'm really interested in is dreams."

"Mmmm." Joe nodded. He reached into a file drawer, began pulling out copies of scholarly articles—dream analysis, dream interpretation, dream therapy.

"I'd also like to learn about therapy in groups."

"Mmmm." Joe's hand dipped into the drawer again, came out with yet more relevant material. Russ knew he'd found his professor, and his first class with Joe sealed the conviction. "Psychotherapy and Meditation" met out at the lab, and concentrated on the same kinds of brain wave control theories Joe was exploring in his research. It was great stuff, Russ thought. And one day, Joe and his teaching assistant, Riggs, took a break from theorizing and led the students in a bioenergetic therapy group.

Standing in a "stress" position, his trembling legs bent as if he were skiing, Russ found himself unable to take his eyes off Riggs. The guy looked like some unenlightened Marlboro Man, but as he moved quickly around the room, pushing students to flail their arms, kick, and yell, intelligence and energy pulsed from him. "We get taught to hold ourselves in," he told one student. "It keeps you from being who you are." Immediately, he was on to the next. "Yeah!" he cheered. "Now you're standing like a primitive animal!" There was something quick and incisive for almost everyone, and it wasn't always nice. "I don't *like* what you're doing," he told one boy flatly. Russ held his breath. What if the guy got pissed at Riggs? Or what if his feelings were really hurt? Riggs's eyes kept boring in. "I don't *like* it!" he told the boy again.

Riggs didn't care what happened, Russ realized with slow amazement. He was just going to do and say whatever he wanted. Russ, who as a child had had no interest in music but dutifully practiced piano everyday for six years because he was afraid to say no to his mother, was hit with a wave of pure longing. He wanted to learn from Joe, but Riggs was who he wanted to *be*.

Even though he was a graduate student, he'd decided to take this quarter's undergraduate "Psychology of Awareness" class. Almost as soon as Joe and Riggs started speaking that first day, he knew what they were talking about. The previous spring, Joe had suggested that his students read a new book called *The Primal Scream*, by a therapist named Arthur Janov. Russ had bought it but never gotten beyond a glance at the cover. Now he went home, took it off the shelf, and didn't leave his apartment until he'd read it through.

Forty-six-year-old Arthur Janov, graying and craggily attractive in his book jacket photo, was a therapist who for twenty years had had a fairly conventional private practice. Then, in 1967, his world exploded. He'd been working with a young patient he called "Danny," but getting nowhere. One day, Danny mentioned hearing of a performer whose act consisted of wearing a diaper and calling for his parents. He seemed curiously fascinated by it. On a hunch, Janov had him do the same.

"Mommy!" Danny called out. "Daddy!" Emotion crossed his face and his voice rose. "Mommy, daddy! Mommy, daddy!" As he continued to shout, his agitation grew. He fell to the floor, writhing and screeching. The writhing turned to convulsions, then suddenly he released a "piercing deathlike" scream that "rattled the walls" of Janov's office. And when Danny came to a few moments later, his entire life had changed. "I made it!" he told Janov. "I don't know what, but I can *feel!*"

The "what" that had happened, Janov said, represented nothing less than the cure for neurosis. This was how Janov's new theory worked: Babies came into the world as relatively happy, simple creatures. Their impulses pointed them toward what felt good; they made straightforward efforts to satisfy basic needs for food, dry diapers, warmth, attention, and love. Then parents went to work on them. They weaned children before they were ready; they didn't cuddle them enough; they criticized, mocked, hit, withheld praise. Over and over, kids looked to their mommies and daddies for unconditional love and acceptance and were disappointed. One day, a horrifying realization hit: They would never be loved for who they were. The despair that followed was overwhelming. In order to survive it, the child became neurotic, splitting off from his or her real feelings and needs and trying to disavow them, doing instead whatever would please Mom and Dad. Yet for all the disavowal, and even though these kids usually grew up to become functioning adults, deep inside the hurt—and damage—remained. Some spent their lives numb and shut-down. Others tried endlessly to soothe their old wounds—children weaned too early, for instance, later "sucked" cigarettes; those denied cuddling became promiscuous. But none of these tries for comfort worked, because no action taken in the present could affect what had occurred in the past. Nor could traditional therapy do much, for it just provided an intellectual *adult* understanding of what had happened.

Janov's therapy was completely different. During daily marathon sessions over a three-week period, therapists worked nonstop to force patients to regress to infancy, relive the original trauma, and feel the pain *exactly* as they had first felt it as children. At that moment, a series of uncontrollable, heartrending wails would erupt—what Janov called the "primal scream." "Mommy!" the children who hid within adults howled in anguish. "Why don't you love me? Oh Mommy, love me, please!"

Afterward—after enough regression and "primaling" that the pain of the past was fully exposed and healed—people's lives were changed forever. Post-Primal people no longer acted in neurotic ways, for neurosis no longer served a need. They didn't try to please Mommy and Daddy or anyone else but themselves. What *felt* good was their only guideline for action. Deep inside, they knew who they were and what they wanted, and that was enough.

––––––––––

The book seemed to smash Russ in the heart. He found himself weeping as he read. Long-buried scenes from his own past kept coming up. The tension he'd felt at age three, when his father came home from World War II; how terrified he'd been of his own dad. His mother's rigid reserve; the desperate, always futile attempts he'd made to please her. The terrible aching loneliness that even now sometimes made him feel despairing enough to think of suicide. He finally understood that he hadn't been born isolated—he had *learned* to become that way. That meant he could unlearn it.

In class, Joe and Riggs taught him that primal therapy was the only way to do that. "If you really want to change, you need primal therapy," Riggs emphasized. "It's the only way to get whole." Russ studied the two men. There seemed a new depth to them, knowledge that hadn't been there before. Almost certainly, part of that was projection—anyone who read *The Primal Scream* was likely to see those who'd felt primal pain as pioneers who'd traveled to an unknown land and returned, their eyes burning with fantastic visions. But Joe and Riggs were also genuinely being swept along by some powerful force. Both were spending vast amounts of time at Janov's Primal Institute; Riggs had even moved to Los Angeles to be near it. Sometimes their faces had a reddened, ravaged look that spoke of hours of crying. One day, Joe showed a film of Riggs having a primal, a stark, frightening scene in which he wailed and wept and rolled on the ground. Another time, it was Joe himself who broke down. He'd been trying to draw a map of something on the blackboard, couldn't get it to come out right, stopped, and in front of everyone began to cry. "I can't draw maps," he told Riggs, sobbing.

The class tittered with nervous laughter, and Riggs

whipped around in a fury. "Look, he has a *feeling*," he told them angrily. "It's his feeling, and it's very important." The laughter turned to awe. All through the semester, being around Joe and Riggs was like setting foot on new ground. There were no books but Janov's to study in class and no formal lectures, just talk of birth and childhood and going where feelings led: One day, Joe and Riggs took everyone outside to celebrate someone's birthday by eating cake with their hands on the lawn, like free little kids. And there was endless talk of pain.

"You've got to feel your pain," Riggs emphasized again and again.

"I've been remembering what it was like when I was a kid—" a student blurted out, then started to cry.

"That's good," Riggs said encouragingly. "Feel the pain."

Now someone else broke down. "Last night, when I was reading the book . . . "

"Just feel it."

Sobbing. "But what do I *do*?"

"You need primal therapy," Joe said.

"It's the most powerful therapy that's ever come along," Riggs broke in, his voice strong and sure. As usual, Russ noticed, Joe didn't even react to the interruption. Traditional teacher-student hierarchies meant nothing to him. "It's more powerful than Gestalt or Rolfing. It's more powerful than analysis—which is so far removed from real experience that it's a joke. If you're doing drugs as a way to figure out who you are, forget it." He looked at Russ and it was as if he were speaking directly to him. "All you need in this world is to have your own feelings."

By December, it was clear that Joe and Riggs weren't the only ones who believed in primal therapy. That month, John Lennon released his first album since the breakup of the Beatles. "Plastic Ono Band" was an astonishing record, passionate, raw, shockingly intimate. On it, the arrogant man who'd once declared himself more popular than Jesus was transformed into a frightened little boy howling with grief over the loss of his Daddy and Mummy. And soon, in an interview so long it ran through two issues of *Rolling Stone* magazine, he revealed what had changed him: John Lennon and his wife, Yoko Ono, had gone through primal therapy. "Janov showed me how to feel my own fear and pain, therefore I can handle it better," Lennon proclaimed. "We primal almost daily. . . . I think Janov's therapy is great."

The revelation might not have meant much had "Plastic Ono Band" been a less powerful and less popular album. (It became a million-seller only six weeks after release.) Or if it had come from someone else. But Lennon wasn't just any celebrity or even just any ex-Beatle. He was the smart and artistic Beatle, the visionary radical. The fact that it was he who spoke for primal therapy gave it a legitimacy and cachet it had never had before. Now getting into primal therapy was all the students around Joe Hart's office could talk about.

"I hurt so much," they told each other. "I'm in such pain." Russ Gilbert started hanging around them, listening. As usual, he didn't say much, but his brain was buzzing. There was such magic to the primal idea. One burst of emotion, and he'd break through the wall around him to clean, open air. Everything he hated most about himself would just melt and fall away. He would be so changed he might not even remember his own name.

That winter, Russ took a leave from school, borrowed money from his father, and applied and was accepted as a patient in primal therapy.

———————

The Primal Institute was on South Altmont Drive in Beverly Hills. Its reception room was dimly lit, the walls covered with wood paneling and the floors with dark red carpet. Russ had never been in a whorehouse, but this was exactly what he'd always imagined one would look like. He was a little dazed. Because primal patients spent their first three weeks in daily, open-ended sessions, they had to leave home and check into motels near the institute—the sleazier the better, Janov said. Russ hadn't slept well the night before; he'd been too scared about what was going to happen to him.

When he found out that he'd be seeing the same therapist who'd worked with both Joe and Riggs, he felt a little better. The man turned out to be utterly nonthreatening, warm and accepting. He talked about his own feelings in sessions, as if he and Russ were already close friends. And no matter how crummy a patient Russ was, how absurdly he tried to *have his feelings*, imitating the tormented outbursts he'd read in *The Primal Scream*, the therapist worked to bring him back to what was *really* happening inside. He saw right away that Russ had never had a chance to mourn the collapse of his marriage, and for days all Russ did was bring in records that reminded him of his wife, listen to them, and weep.

After that, he got stuck. He couldn't seem to "let go." One afternoon, after a few hours his therapist simply cut off the session, sent Russ back to his motel, and told him to stay there, then not sleep all night. Russ sat there in the depressing room for what felt like an eternity. He wasn't supposed to watch TV, read, listen to music, or do anything else that might distract him from thoughts of himself. Midnight passed, then 2:00 A.M., 3:00. Outside, the pinkish night sky of L.A. slowly lightened. He could hear traffic noises. The rest of the world was waking up. Other people were alive. Not him. He'd never be able to feel. He'd always be alone. Nothing would ever change.

By the time the sun rose, he felt crazy and desperate, so distraught he started crying in the shower. He tried to cancel that day's session at the Primal Institute, but his therapist said no. And that morning . . . Jesus. Russ was talking about his grade school years. Suddenly, an image came into his mind, less a memory than a movie being played in his head, every detail excruciatingly exact. He was about five. His mother was in a chair, darning socks. The light was dim. His father was leaving for work. And somehow the pain of this scene—his father was leaving. His father was going away again. There was no hope. *He* had no hope. His whole childhood whirled, compressed itself into this one moment: anguish, terror, a child's despair without bottom or end. Suddenly, something took hold of his body. It was like having a seizure; he was out of control, writhing, shrieking, screaming. The pain was worse than anything he'd ever known, but he could feel something inside him breaking open and he didn't ever want it to stop.

When the primal ended, Russ felt drained and light. All he wanted was to see his dad. He picked up a new copy of *The Primal Scream* and drove fifty miles to the golf course where he knew his father played each afternoon. By the time he got there, it was almost dark. His father and two partners, similarly conservative, prosperous businessmen, were on the last green. He walked up to them, shaking. He felt like a little boy again. He longed to be in his daddy's arms. "I want you to read this," he said holding out the book, his voice trembling.

"OK," his father said. Russ waited for more—a smile, a hug—but none came. His eyes filled with tears, and as they rolled down his cheeks, the three golfers just stared at him, blank-faced and embarrassed, not knowing what the hell was going on, not knowing at all what to say.

3

Twenty-year-old UCI junior Mary Farrell heard of Russ Gilbert's entrance into primal therapy with hopeless jealousy. Someone else, she thought, was getting the one thing she wanted—needed. She was being left to live with herself. To live with the knowledge that she was hopelessly insane.

Before she took Joe Hart's class, *insane* wasn't a word most people—including she herself—would have applied to Mary. She was a good student, with a methodical, organized mind, and essentially a "good girl" as well, polite, conscientious, and responsible. She may have dressed like a hippie, in overalls and Mexican peasant blouses, her pretty, high-cheekboned face free of makeup and long curly red-blond hair pulled back in a leather thong, but she always came to class on time, listened quietly, and took careful notes. And although she was tall and slender, almost delicate, there was no hint of the ethereal about her. Mary's parents had five kids, and she'd put in plenty of time doing child care, especially for the little brother who'd been only four when she left home and whom she adored as if he were her own son. She also knew about working hard. On top of a full courseload, she did clerical work to help pay tuition. Since sixteen, she'd never been without a part-time job.

Perhaps a better word to describe Mary was *sad*—since childhood, she'd struggled with periodic depression. Or *scared*. From the outside, the Farrell family had looked like an ideal one, middle class and devoutly Catholic, with a hard-working father, stay-at-home mother, and children who all attended parochial school and showed up for mass each Sunday. But though it usually went unmentioned in the 1950s and 1960s, bad things happened behind the walls of "ideal" suburban homes. Mary's father drank. He never let it affect his work, but at home he fell into violent, unpredictable rages. He tore at Mary with vicious words, and sometimes with his fists. Her life shaped itself around his moods, and she was always slightly afraid, for although she did her best to please him, she never knew when something would set him off.

Going away to school was the start of a different life— new friends, even a boyfriend. While her older sister married and immediately started bearing good Catholic kids, Mary tried to let religion slide away, instead, like half the kids around her, seeking some vague notion of "enlightenment" via studying Eastern philosophy, smoking dope, and taking acid. But the transition into free spirit was only partly successful. Drugs were one thing, but leaping from the shelter of an all-girls' school to the sexual feeding frenzy that was college life in the late 1960s was another. She managed sex once, and badly; her boyfriend "understood." Then, the summer before junior year, he started having problems of his own. Mary never grasped their seriousness, shrugged off his complaints about depression, even declarations like "I've found the perfect way to kill myself." She felt lousy sometimes too, and people who were serious about suicide didn't make announcements. One night, after a fight, she told him she didn't want to see him anymore. A month later, he was dead. The guilt she felt was almost worse than the grief. With a friend, she escaped to the Sierras, a few hits of LSD in her backpack.

Acid had always been benevolent, but this trip was pure terror.

She was agitated and on edge as she started school. In a later decade, she might have found her way to the student health service and a counselor who would have recognized her years of depression and fear as typical of the child of an alcoholic, then carefully worked through that painful legacy, as well as tackling her sexual problems and guilt over her boyfriend's death. Instead, primal therapy hit her like a shovel to the gut. *Look back and feel the pain,* Riggs said, and when she did, it was as if a door opened inside her that she couldn't close again. There was her father, her mother, the church, screaming at a little girl, turning her into someone who couldn't relax, couldn't love, couldn't even fuck—the enormity of it all swept over her each time she reread *The Primal Scream*. It seemed as if every chapter had been written just about her. She was damaged, almost beyond repair. *Unless you have your feelings, you're wasting your life. Go with your feelings. Look back and feel the pain. . . .* After a while, it was all she could do.

Primal therapy was everywhere around her that quarter. In a complete coincidence, she'd also signed up for a class called "Consciousness and Communication," which was being taught by Dominic Cirincione, whom Joe had gotten a temporary teaching position at UCI. He too was in primal therapy. Dominic's graduate student teaching assistant was Joe's lab technician, Werner Karle. He had gone into primal therapy as well. It was all any of them talked about.

One afternoon, when Mary was hitchhiking home from campus, Dominic picked her up. "Why don't you come visit me tomorrow?" he said. "Just to talk."

That seemed like a decent idea to Mary. She'd heard her teacher was an ex-Jesuit; talking to him might be like being with a kind of hip priest, and he seemed nice. So the next day, she hitched to Laguna Beach, where he lived. They smoked some dope together, and Mary found herself recounting the story of her boyfriend's death and how it had hurt, and how scary she found life now, with guys at school constantly trying to get in her pants when she was just a Catholic schoolgirl who didn't really know what to do. . . .

"I'd never do that," Dominic said, but then somehow the conversation changed and *he* was urging her into bed, this ex-priest, this man who was balding, *old*.

"Uh-uh," Mary said. She said, "I don't want to." She said, "I can't." And then, twenty years before the phrase "sexual harassment" became part of the national vocabulary, in a time when the ultimate uncoolness was a woman who insisted on saying no, she ran out of options. This man was her teacher—she couldn't insult him. It seemed easier just to shut her eyes and get it over with. When they were done, she fled as fast as she could, her teeth clenched in disgust. Afterward, her despair deepened. In class, Riggs always talked about the importance of having lots of sex and enjoying it. What was wrong with her?

Joe had his office hours on Tuesdays, and Mary started going to school early to meet with him. The aggressive Riggs both attracted and scared her, but she purely loved talking to Joe. Being in his office, high in the social science building, felt like being in a different world, someplace safe and serene. And Joe was so peaceful and gentle, the dead opposite of her own father. Joe listened to everything she said, and she could tell he really cared about her—not just about her grades and plans for the future but about how she felt inside.

"I feel so awful," she told him. Sometimes she started to cry.

"That's good," he encouraged. "You're getting into your feelings. You need that."

It was new to Mary to have someone just be there for her without asking anything in return, to feel that someone simply cared. She knew Joe was talking from that caring. And from his special knowledge. In *The Primal Scream* it said that primal therapists could *sense* it when other people weren't really feeling. If Joe said she needed primal therapy, he had to be right.

But the more convinced Mary became that therapy was

her only answer, the more desperate she grew. Primal therapy cost $4,500—more than the cost of a new car, twice the price of four years of undergraduate tuition at UCI. There was no way she could get that kind of money. Then the institute announced that its admittance policy had changed: Because it was primarily interested in training professionals, from now on it would not accept anyone under the age of twenty-six! What were she and the rest of Joe's students supposed to *do* for the next six years? How were they supposed to *live*?

One of Riggs's older sisters was married and lived on a farm in the Pacific Northwest, and he said in class that going there could be the answer: Kids could form a kind of community, be in nature, and work on their feelings together until they had primals. Some of Mary's classmates were dubious. Forget college, just pick up and move? "I'm into the *theory*," one of them told Mary. "But I don't know about the *therapy*."

Mary was disgusted. "What a lightweight," she thought. "If you really believe a theory, you *do* it. Otherwise, you're just talking." She was no talker.

By late November, she and a boy from Joe's class had decided to make the 1,500-mile drive north at Christmas. One weekend, they drove up to Los Angeles to buy sleeping bags and on impulse decided to visit Riggs, who lived in Beverly Hills, not far from the Primal Institute. Mary felt a little shy about showing up without an invitation, but Riggs seemed glad to see them. He even cooked dinner. Afterward, they all sat around and talked. It got late. Mary's friend wanted to go. Riggs turned to Mary. "You could stay . . ." he said.

Mary was excited, flattered. She hadn't even expected Riggs to remember her name. But this time too was bad. Sex was awkward and painful, and Riggs barely spoke to her. Then the next morning, he took off for the institute, leaving her stranded without a car. For hours, she roamed aimlessly through the apartment. Why had Riggs asked her to stay? He didn't really care. She felt rejected and lost.

When Riggs finally came home, Dominic and Joe were

with him. Dominic looked at Mary and began to cry. "I never would have left you alone," he sobbed.

Riggs started to cry too. So did Joe. Mary didn't know what to do. She wanted to cry herself, to say how alone she'd felt, but she was too scared. Everyone was older than she and knew things she didn't. What if she reacted wrong and showed just how unfeeling she was? She stood stiffly, just watching. Finally, Dominic gave her a ride back to Orange County. Riggs never called. In class, he acted as if he didn't even remember what had happened between them, which confused Mary even more. Was all this going on because she was so crazy?

It had to be. OK, she would go to the farm. That would be a start. But the trip turned out to be a disaster. The farm was in the middle of nowhere, a dark green landscape pelted by an endless cold rain. Its primitive house was heated by a single wood stove whose heat never reached the bedroom where the two students huddled, shivering, in sleeping bags. Riggs's sister was pregnant and overworked; although she'd agreed to have them, she really didn't want guests. Riggs had predicted that her husband would be negative about what Mary was doing, and he was. He said some awful things. Mary and her friend spent their days alternately helping out with chores and trying to make each other cry. They didn't have a clue what they were doing, Mary quickly realized. She was cold, homesick—if anything was crazy, *this* was. Another student from Joe's class was supposed to come to the farm soon. Mary called him. "Don't bother," she said.

By January, she was back in class at UCI, reenrolled in Joe's class, right where she started. In a strange way, the trip changed her relationship with Riggs. He respected her for having gone, and in class listened seriously to what she had to say. But that pleasure couldn't override a desperation that grew daily. She couldn't stop looking inside herself, and everywhere she saw dark, monstrous shadows. She had to primal. Had to.

"What kind of mother were you that you wouldn't even breast-feed your child?" she screamed when her mother called.

"What?"

"Did you ever think of anyone but yourself? Do you realize what you did to me?"

"Mary, what's the matter?" her mother pleaded.

She hung up. *Mommy didn't love me.* The pain mounted, demanding release. One afternoon, she and a girlfriend decided they would *force* themselves to primal. They took LSD— a *huge* dose of LSD. Mary never remembered exactly what happened that day, only screaming and screaming, and looking down at her hands to see they'd become infant-size. . . .

The next day, her brain felt shorted-out. She couldn't think or drive, barely made it to Joe's class. There was a guest lecturer, a tall, attractive black-haired man of twenty-nine. His name was Lee Woldenberg, and he was a doctor, the Primal Institute's medical director. Lee's talk had barely begun when sirens went off—someone had called the school to say he'd planted a bomb in the lecture hall to protest the war. This happened all the time—it was the kind of sixties stuff no one took seriously anymore—but Mary listened to the alarms and their wails sounded like the inside of her head exploding. She lost it, just started shrieking and crying uncontrollably.

"What's the *matter* with you?" Joe asked, when everyone had dutifully evacuated and was outside.

"I couldn't feel enough and I knew I had to start feeling, so I took a lot of LSD," Mary told him.

"We didn't tell you to do that," Joe said carefully. He and Riggs backed off, their hands raised in negation until they were at their cars in the parking lot. "We never said you should do that to feel." They drove off.

Lee stayed behind. He listened to Mary's estimate of how much acid she'd taken, whistled, and phoned a drugstore for the traditional anti-bad-trip drug, Thorazine. Then he stuck around—it seemed he liked Mary's girlfriend and wanted a date. Mary couldn't make sense of anything that was happening. It never occurred to her to feel betrayed by Joe and Riggs; her sole concern was that she'd made them angry when she'd only wanted to please them. And now she felt worse than ever. Despite another dose of Thorazine, she couldn't stop crying for weeks, and lost her job. Twice she drove up to L.A. to the Primal Institute and, weeping, *begged* to be let in. It was impossible, and she drove back to Irvine, her hands white around the steering wheel. Anything else she'd ever planned to do with her life was forgotten. Nothing mattered now but finding some way to get primal therapy. Until she did, she would simply survive.

4

All through the early months of 1971, primal therapy fever spread across the United States. John Lennon left the Primal Institute when his immigration visa expired, but other celebrities, like Dyan Cannon and James Earl Jones, followed, which meant reporters weren't far behind. Most found Janov a dream of a source—journalists who came for interviews got copies of a slick color promotional film demonstrating the therapy's success—and life at the institute was so wild that stories practically wrote themselves. "The patients—predominantly youthful middle-class men and women—came dressed for physical freedom, like a Beverly Hills exercise class," Lennon biographer Albert Goldman reported. "They assumed various positions about the room, standing, sitting or lying on the carpeted floor. Janov, dressed in shirt and slacks, would say: 'Who's got a feeling?' Somebody would speak up, recounting a disturbing scene from his childhood. As if on cue, the other patients would swing into their primaling rituals. Where, a moment before, an exercise class had been about to begin, now there was Marat/Sade!

"On one side of the room a couple of husky guys, raging

and crying, would start punching holes in the Sheetrock wall with their bare fists. Over there, in the corner, a mature woman in leotard and tights would curl up in the fetal position and start sucking her thumb. A paunchy middle-aged man would scream out his pain so violently that he made all the fat on his body vibrate. As the uproar mounted, with cries of 'Daddy! Mommy!' rending the air and tears streaming down faces contorted by sobbing and gasping, Janov would move about the room, working quietly and efficiently, like a doctor in an emergency clinic.

"He might make one patient go further into her fit. To another he would flash a sign that meant: 'Hit the deck!' His assistants went about wiping tears and offering cues to generate fresh outbursts. The screaming, the crying, the violent physical behavior would continue without letup for two hours, until the room resembled a nursery or day-care center filled with oversize infants throwing tantrums—an illusion heightened by the introduction of a man-size crib and huge teddy bears and baby dolls."

Clearly, to some outsiders much of what went on at the institute wasn't therapy as much as madness. To more mainstream psychologists and psychiatrists, it was something even worse: pure quackery. Janov's theories, after all, weren't exactly new. The idea that patients could gain full psychic relief merely by reliving past trauma (a process called abreaction) was one Freud himself had proposed but later abandoned. Almost fifty years ago, Otto Rank had suggested that some adult anxiety was merely a screen for the original "primal" anxiety of being separated from the mother at birth. That notion too had been mostly discredited. Meanwhile, Janov had the audacity to claim that in less than a year, primaling could cure *everything*—not only generic "neurosis" but homosexuality (which, like most therapists of his day, he considered a sickness), drug addiction, alcoholism, and psychosis, *plus* physical ailments like headaches, ulcers, and asthma. All this, based on sixty case studies with no long-term follow-up.

But maybe most of all, those who thought about it worried about Janov's therapeutic methods, which seemed to put a lot of emphasis on dismantling people and very little on putting them back together. Only recently, Drs. Irvin D. Yalom of the Stanford Medical School and Morton A. Lieberman of the University of Chicago had published, in a psychiatric journal, the first study of psychological dangers associated with encounter groups. The report was ominous. Sixteen of the 170 college students studied, the men said, could be considered "casualties"—people who'd had enduring and significant negative outcomes to their group experience. And the type of encounter group leader most likely to cause such damage was someone who was aggressive, charismatic, and highly intrusive, and who believed that everyone needed the same kind of help. If contact with such a leader over the course of a weekend was destructive, what might one do if he dominated a patient's life for three full weeks?

But Yalom and Lieberman's study received little publicity. And when tens of thousands of ordinary Americans read *The Primal Scream*, many found themselves hooked by its uncanny ability to touch the soft place inside where everyone felt infantile, alone, unloved, and afraid—and by its promise to make those feelings go away. Soon, Janov was appearing on television talk shows. He was the subject of a feature article in *Vogue*. The Primal Institute began receiving some 3,000 applications for therapy *each month*.

This success didn't go unnoticed. Suddenly, therapists who'd never even met Janov were offering "primal" therapy. Across the nation, programs promising happiness via radical self-change blossomed. On the Upper West Side of New York, which was declared to contain "more people prepared for reality than previously seen," a three-month, $3,000 program called Arica promised disciples they could reach "a natural internal equilibrium." In California, a forty-year-old former car and encyclopedia salesman named Werner Erhard experienced a moment of revelation that "what is, is and what isn't, isn't" while driving his Mustang. Soon, thousands of people across the country were paying $250 for a weekend of "Erhard Seminars Training," in which they sat locked in a hotel ball-room for sixteen-hour stretches, forbidden to eat or use the bathroom, listening to "trainers" lecture them on the nature of reality and call them "assholes" whose lives weren't working.

The Primal Institute began expanding. Janov himself had trained five people, including his wife, Vivian, to do primal therapy. The five produced a second generation of therapists and now were at work on a third. Joe and Riggs were among them, and moving up fast in the primal hierarchy. Although still teaching at UCI, Joe had been named the institute's re-search director, and Riggs and his fellow UCI graduate stu-dent Werner Karle were completing experiments proving that primal therapy resulted in physical changes in patients, in-cluding lowered body temperature, slowed pulse and altered brain waves. The practical importance of this finding, they wrote in a chapter for Janov's second book, *The Anatomy of Mental Illness*, was immense. Post-Primal women, for instance, could rely on natural birth control because their "temperature changes [were] not contaminated by alterations in tension lev-els. . . . It is when women are unnatural, neurotic, that they cannot rely on natural bodily rhythms for internal indica-tions. . . . Primal man [*sic*] is truly a new kind of person on this earth." On a more personal level, Arthur Janov seemed to consider Werner one of his therapeutic success stories. Since the age of sixteen, Werner had suffered from epilepsy, and his testimony, that he now understood his grand mal seizures to have been repressed primals and that Janov's therapy had cured him, was also being included in *The Anatomy of Mental Illness*. "The day I started my therapy, I stopped taking my medication," wrote the patient Janov called "Simon," "and I haven't taken any since then. There is simply no more need to take the medication because there is no more need to have seizures."

Yet for all the professional success the Irvine group enjoyed at the institute, they were growing restive. What had attracted Joe and Riggs to primal therapy was its promise of fast change—Janov had said he could cure people of neurosis in six to nine months. But nearly a year had passed, and Joe and Riggs didn't think their lives had improved at all. Maybe they'd even gotten worse: When you spent all your time in the past, you lost the present. In fact, they were beginning to think, focusing on childhood pain could be its own defense. It was something that kept you from facing what you were feeling (or not feeling) in your current life. Even primaling was losing its emotional power—after a while, even screaming got routine and gave only a dull release, like bad sex. And Janov's talk-show appearances and quest for fame seemed to them the opposite of what therapy was supposed to be about. "Art's blowing it by going so public," Joe and Riggs told their UCI class. "The whole feeling side of the therapy is deteriorating."

Dissent started brewing at the Primal Institute, and a rebel group formed around Joe and Riggs. Some members were the men's friends—Werner Karle; Dominic Cirincione, Riggs's former teacher; Lee Woldenberg, who'd lectured Joe's class. But soon two others joined as well, a significant addition, for while Joe and Riggs were only *training* to do primal therapy, these men were among the few Arthur Janov had certified to *practice*.

Stephen Gold, twenty-seven, short and slightly chubby, with reddish curly hair and a baby face, and Gerald Binder, a year older, with dark curly hair, brown eyes, and rounded features that sometimes evoked the description "teddy bear," were best friends. They were different kind of men from Joe and Riggs, less charismatic, less studied and flashily intellectual. Neither had more than a state college master's degree, Steve's in psychology and Jerry's in adult education. Though Steve had tried some Synanon Game-playing while a student, they were also far more conventional. They dressed neatly, in suits and ties. Both were married. (Their wives were in primal therapy too, and Linda Binder was training to become a therapist herself.) Before primal therapy, both had held "straight" jobs at the Economic Youth Opportunity Agency, a job training program. And unlike Joe and Riggs, they had come to primal therapy looking not for transcendence but for help dealing with personal problems.

Steve, from a middle-class San Fernando Valley family, believed that the life had been squeezed out of him by a domineering mother. He even had a physical manifestation of his inner torment—he stuttered. Jerry had grown up poor and angry, a Boston street-fighter who was still filled with rage. (In 1970, the Primal Institute had thrown a "come-as-your-sickness" Halloween party, and Jerry had carried a toy sword with which he hit people, because he was a "bad boy.") Now that they'd completed their therapy and training, they wanted to *do* primal therapy because they wanted new careers.

Still, something in what Joe and Riggs were saying pulled at them. Maybe they too had some doubts about primal therapy theory and technique. Maybe they'd started to realize they would always be minor figures in what was essentially a one-man show. For weeks, even as Russ Gilbert threw his life into primal therapy and Mary Farrell went on her desperate farm pilgrimage, the rebels—Joe, Riggs, Dominic, Werner, Lee, Steve, Jerry, Linda—held secret meetings at Steve's apartment to discuss their grievances.

Later, Joe and Riggs would claim that the group had confronted Arthur Janov with their unhappiness and told him they thought patients needed to move beyond past pain to change their present lives. Janov would deny that, comparing any attempt by Joe and Riggs to improve his theory with interns correcting a senior surgeon's technique. Interns, moreover, who were really interested only in power, who he'd pegged as "abreactors"—people who had emotional outbursts without truly feeling anything—and who were about to be fired anyway.

By spring, everything blew and the rebels quit—or were

thrown out of—the Primal Institute. Around twenty-five patients went with them. Some had personal ties to the group—one, for instance, was Riggs's new girlfriend; another was twenty-five-year-old Konni Pederson, a strikingly beautiful divorcée who was the mother of a two-year-old girl and who was involved with Dominic. For the rest, the decision to go was impulse—all the rebels had been great primalers; perhaps they seemed like therapeutic "winners."

Russ Gilbert was torn. He'd been helping with research at the institute, and through the work had gotten close to Werner. He was still devoted to Joe and worshiped Riggs. But his primal had been so intense, had felt so real and right, that turning his back on primal therapy went against all his instincts. He went to lunch with Joe, Riggs, and the others, and sat without speaking as they made their plans. Suddenly, Riggs turned to him.

"What are *you* going to do?" he asked.

"I don't know," Russ said honestly.

"You don't have any choice," Riggs said. "We're taking you with us."

His second year in college, Russ had been asked to join a fraternity. He'd been flooded with amazed joy. Someone liked him! Wanted him! He had the same feeling now, and it overwhelmed everything else. "OK," he said, trying not to grin too widely. "Sure."

———————

The building the primal rebels found for their new center was in mid–Los Angeles, on South La Brea Avenue. It was a long fall from Beverly Hills. The neighborhood was crummy, a bleak landscape of fast-food joints and auto shops. The building itself was a graceless, two-story box painted a lurid orange-and-blue with a facade of cinderblocks. The interior was bare of anything so genteel as paneling or plush carpet. But it was affordable and spacious, both important. Despite the group's quarrel with Arthur Janov, the therapy they planned to offer was essentially primal therapy. (The major difference was that their program would cost only $2,500 and would accept patients as young as twenty-one.) Downstairs at the La Brea building were a reception room and some offices that could be used for therapy sessions. Upstairs were two rooms big enough to accommodate "Laydown," the weekly en masse primaling. Some renovation was needed—office walls had to be padded, for instance, so patients' shrieks wouldn't upset the neighbors. There wasn't much money for that, so the rebels hired Russ Gilbert and a few other ex-primal patients who'd defected with them. They also did a lot of work themselves, hammering, scraping, taking time off only to go to special soundproof rooms at USC they'd gotten through a professor Joe knew, so they could primal in peace.

Construction went on for two months—burnt-orange carpet was laid down, clean-lined modern furniture installed, double-thick cork attached to second-story walls, and mattresses scattered about the floor. It was a strange, slightly surreal time. No one could tell what was going to happen; they were a group of people who'd joined lives without knowing each other very well, who'd given up a sure thing (and the prestige and salaries that came with it) for a seriously iffy enterprise. And no one was fully in control. They were all coming off weeks, months, spent in states of profound regression. All boundaries were loose and nerve endings exposed. Emotion came in great flooding bolts; there was always someone crying. Ice cream and cookies tasted great. The smallest things—like Riggs lisping "I'm just two years old!"—was enough to crack everyone up.

But despite the craziness, Joe, Riggs, and their new comrades met regularly to work out the necessary details of what they planned to do. The first decision to be made was who among them should be considered ready to practice. Between them, they'd tried virtually every growth movement of the sixties, but only half had conventional training or any kind of professional license. Joe, of course, had been a licensed clinical psychologist for five years. Dominic had obtained a Marriage, Family, and Child Counselor license nearly a year before; Steve Gold also had an MFCC. Lee Woldenberg's M.D. entitled him to practice psychiatry, although his training was in surgery. And around the time the building renovation was completed, the group was joined by another Primal Institute defector, Carole Suydam, twenty-eight, a tall, big-boned blond who was a licensed social worker. But in the antiauthoritarian spirit of the times, none of them seemed to care about legalities like state licensing—nor, they probably figured, would equally radical prospective patients, who knew that "official" approval meant nothing. Since they were offering primal therapy, that was the training that mattered. It was decided that once the new business got under way, Jerry Binder and Steve Gold—both certified primal therapists—and Joe Hart and Linda Binder, who'd nearly completed their primal therapist training, would be the only therapists to actually see individual patients. The others would continue training, just as they'd been doing at the institute.

Meanwhile, although they'd be following Janov's program, they would keep exploring ways to go beyond it. They already knew two things for sure: They would avoid the narcissism that had claimed Janov, by sharing the therapy's leadership. All decisions would be made collectively; that way, no one person's theories or ego would dominate. Even more important, all therapists would continue to get treatment from their peers. That way, the therapy would grow as they did. Eventually, they would find a way to help patients move beyond past pain to actively change and transform their present lives. Until then, every step would be on new ground.

Later, the hope of those early days was what those who were there would remember, the joyous excitement of being part of the great changes of their time and—though perhaps none even realized it—of a great American tradition. Again and again, especially in periods of great social change, men and women had broken away from mainstream society in search of something more. And, as Joe, Riggs, and the rest looked at the ugly new building that housed what they'd named the Center for Feeling Therapy, the feeling that shot through must have been the same one their predecessors had known: thrill at catching that first glimpse of a distant but reachable utopia, a brave new world where everyone would be happy and free.

———————

Just before the school year ended, Joe made an announcement to his UCI class. Mary Farrell and the rest of the would-be primalers listened, riveted to his words.

"You don't have to wait on the Primal Institute anymore," Joe told them. "We're opening our own center. And all of you will be able to come."

PART TWO

Brothers and Sisters

5

August 1971

Through the early and middle seventies, twenty to thirty students who took Joe Hart's classes at UCI sought treatment at the Center for Feeling Therapy. The first was Mary Farrell. Two days after she turned twenty-one, Mary borrowed $2,500, packed three weeks' worth of clothes, and drove to Los Angeles as if toward salvation.

"Twenty-four hours before your therapy begins, check into a motel near the Center," read the Center's sheet of "Instructions for New Patients," echoing the directions the Primal Institute gave its clients. Whereas Arthur Janov believed patients should stay at sleazy places to prompt introspection, the two motels the Center usually recommended were merely bleak.

"Forty-eight hours before your therapy begins, stop all smoking and drinking of alcoholic beverages, coffee and tea," the instruction sheet continued. *"Stop taking all drugs such as painkillers, aspirin, sleeping pills, tranquilizers, mood elevators, stimulants, or any other drug that may affect your state of being. . . ."*

The night before therapy started was a long one. No dis-
tractions were allowed. *"You already know what you do to relieve
tension,"* the instruction sheet said. *"Stop doing it! This means
giving up compulsive eating and snacking, keeping busy and on the
go, biting nails, gum chewing, over-sleeping, compulsive sex and
masturbation, etc. . . . Do not make phone calls, chat with people, see
anyone, watch television, read, listen to the radio, or go to the movies.
If you want to, you may keep a diary. Try not to leave the motel
room except for your meals until your therapy hour the next day."*

Alone in the room, it was hard for Mary not to be afraid.
Three weeks of intensive daily sessions lay before her, and
anyone who read *The Primal Scream* knew the sessions would
involve a face-to-face confrontation with immeasurable anguish. Yet exactly what would take place was frighteningly
mysterious. Arthur Janov had been deliberately vague about
what therapists said and did to induce primals, explaining
that primal therapy techniques were too powerful to chance
their fall into unskilled hands. Whenever Mary had had therapy fantasies, they had been not of specific words or scenes
but of feelings—pain that was almost voluptuous in its intensity, hours of weeping with Joe or Riggs.

When Mary arrived for her first session at the Center,
though, neither of the two men was there. Her therapist was
someone she'd never seen before, a man in a suit—a suit!—
named Steve Gold.

"You're just a *teenybopper,*" he said when they were alone
in a small therapy room. He looked her over, taking in the
wild hair and patched jeans, then shook his head. "You don't
even know why you're here. I'm going to have to undo everything Joe and Riggs have done to you and get you in touch
with your real feelings. What you're having now are the feelings you think *they* want you to have."

It went on from there. Therapy was interminable, three-
to seven-hour sessions that ended only when Steve decided
they should. And the whole first week, it seemed to Mary that
all he did was "bust" her—the primal therapy word for chal-

lenging a statement or behavior as a defense (in essence, calling "Bullshit!"). She was busted for being a hippie. She was
busted for wearing overalls, for being "a cute little neuter."
None of her responses to what Steve said was right. None of
her feelings was "real." Nothing she'd thought about herself
or her life was true. Her whole personality was built on craziness and had to be chipped off and swept away.

Day after day passed in the small room at the Center,
night after isolated night in the motel, where sometimes, per
Steve's orders, she stayed awake till dawn, so the defenses
that kept her from feeling would be weakened to break more
quickly. Especially when she was so exhausted she could
barely think, the onslaught on her sense of self was overwhelming; it was like being picked up by the feet and shaken
violently. With each day, she found herself growing less and
less certain of *anything*. If she wasn't who she'd always
thought, who was she? Confusion and uncertainty kept her
constantly on the edge of hysteria. She couldn't stand Laydown, the sessions just like those at the Primal Institute, where
patients primaled as a group. Dozens of people gathered in
the Center's big upstairs room, screaming "Mommy!" and
thrashing around on the floor; the chaos and noise made Mary
so frantic that finally even Steve saw a problem. Simply getting hysterical wasn't getting in touch with oneself. Lee, as the
Center's doctor, prescribed Valium for Mary. If she could just
calm down a little, she might be able to really feel *something*.

Nothing about therapy was turning out as Mary had expected. She barely saw Joe, and the one time she said hello to
Riggs, he acted so aloof and superior that she wanted to slink
off. But even as she entertained the awful notion that maybe
she'd made a mistake, she began catching glimpses of what
she had come to the Center for. As Steve kept pushing at her,
it was as if something inside her cracked. The past rose to
wrap around her, the terror of childhood unbearably real, and
suddenly she was wailing "Daddy!" and beating her fists
against a mat until she was so hoarse and tired she could

barely lift her arms. *"Feel the pain,"* Joe and Riggs had said. This was what they'd meant. If she continued, surely the sadness that had plagued her for so long would fall away.

And she found herself growing powerfully attached to Steve. She hated the busts that broke her down, but once she was in the past, sobbing out her fear of her father's fists, Steve became heartbreakingly tender, a man who could hear a little girl's cries and protect her. She came to crave seeing him; once, when he was away and she had to work with Jerry Binder, she was flooded with loss.

The initial three-week period of Feeling Therapy was called the "Intensive," and during it patients were asked to put their lives on hold and not do anything but attend individual sessions and Laydown. After that, although like primal therapy patients, they were still expected to attend nine months of weekly Laydowns, they could go home, return to work, and resume their normal lives. Instead, Mary rented an apartment and moved to Los Angeles. She shocked her parents with the announcement that she wasn't going back to school. Oh, she'd graduate—she'd already met nearly all the requirements for a bachelor's degree in social science, and had arranged to do independent studies under Joe to take care of the rest. But there was nothing and no one left for her at Irvine. Here, it was different. There was a palpable bond between all the men and women who sat on the floor of the big upstairs room each week after Laydown, as Joe or Jerry led them in talk about what they'd experienced that night. It was almost like those magic days of the late sixties, when an exchange of peace signs on the street was all it took to turn strangers into comrades. All the men and women at the Center had come for the same reason. They wanted to do what few had the courage to try—to search out the hidden, closed-off places in themselves, to face and share with each other the pain and ugliness they found there.

The doubts that had troubled Mary through the first days of her Intensive faded, and conviction took their place. After a fearful childhood and the confusion and loneliness of her time at Irvine, she was finally where she belonged.

For months, Arthur Janov's shadow hung over the new Center. The therapists never missed a chance to mock the weeping they'd done at the institute. Jerry Binder shocked patients by saying that he'd been one of the case studies in *The Primal Scream*—and that a lot of what had been said was a lie. When Lee and Riggs mentioned their former mentor, their voices had a sarcastic edge. The "cured" Werner was having seizures again.

There was, of course, jealousy beneath the antagonism. The Center was still a makeshift enterprise, fledgling, unglamorous. "Improving" the building's gaudy orange-and-blue exterior, for instance, had meant repainting it a bilious brownish yellow. Outside those yellow walls (and UCI), no one had ever heard of the Center therapists. In contrast, by now Janov had published not only *The Anatomy of Mental Illness* but a new book as well, *The Primal Revolution*. Meanwhile, some 200,000 copies of *The Primal Scream* remained in print, and the book continued to exert an enormous influence. It was said that some people had primals just from *reading* it. The institute was still getting tens of thousands of requests for therapy.

Yet the therapists' jealousy of primal therapy's success had to have been accompanied by an uneasy awareness that they themselves couldn't have survived without it. Here and there, they'd managed to bring new patients into the Center— some of Joe's and Riggs's followers from Kairos signed on; so did students who took a nighttime extension course the two men taught at UCI. But more than anything else, it was the Primal Institute's decision not to meet the huge demand it had created that was putting the Center on its feet. The rules governing admittance to the institute had gotten even more restrictive: Patients now had to have the intent of practicing therapy themselves *and* be able to afford an entrance fee that had risen to a heart-stopping $6,000, enough for a down payment on a modest house. Each week, dozens of would-be primalers flocked to Los Angeles as if to some latter-day Vienna, only to be turned away from the Primal Institute. A number of them ended up at the Center—some, surprisingly, referred by the institute itself. In February 1972, the magazine *Psychology Today* ran a feature on primal therapy that mentioned the Center and gave its address. After that, requests for information began coming directly. In responding, the Center always played up its primal connection to the hilt, reporting that staff members were "either certified primal therapists or trainee primal therapists" and offering a course of therapy that, like the institute's, could be completed in a year.

But even as the Center therapists continued to need Arthur Janov, they were working hard to leave him behind. Steve, Jerry, Joe, and Linda were taping all the Intensives they did, then using the tapes to train Riggs, Werner, Dominic, Lee, and Carole to be therapists. Once that training was done, the Center could accept nine new patients each month instead of four. (Because doing an Intensive was so time-consuming and emotionally draining, a therapist saw only one patient at a time, and afterward took a week off to recuperate.) All of them paired up weekly to work on each other, trading off who was therapist and who patient. And they met often to thrash out ideas about therapy and theory. The brainstorming went on behind closed doors, so none of the Center's patients knew what happened or why, but in early 1972 the therapists made a major ideological shift.

Arthur Janov's theory that adult neurosis was the product of distinct moments of childhood trauma was abandoned. Instead, the Feeling Therapists now asserted, neurosis was the result of years of undramatic but destructive emotional "disordering" that ultimately robbed children of their natural feelings. One morning, at a pancake house in Santa Monica, a few of them had witnessed an encounter between a seven-year-old girl and her father that to them said it all:

"I want some candy, Daddy," the girl had announced, pointing at peppermint sticks in a glass jar near the cash register. Her father ignored her. "Daddy!" This time she was louder. "Daddy! I want some candy!" Still no response, so the girl changed her tack. "What's that?" she demanded, pointing. "What *is* that?" Now she was tugging at her father's sleeve. "What *is* that?"

The man pulled away. "You've had enough sweets today."

"But what *is* it?" Again the girl pointed at the peppermint.

"It's licorice."

"What's lickrish?"

"Where's your mother?" the father asked suddenly. "Did she go to the ladies' room again?"

"I want one!"

"Oh all right," the man said impatiently. "But it's bad for your teeth."

The incident was so illustrative of how disordering occurred that over the years, the therapists would repeat the story again and again. True human feelings, the analysis began, were simply body sensations that had meanings. When someone heard a loud *bang*, for instance, his stomach might tighten. The meaning of that sensation was *I'm scared*. Or, in the case of the little girl in the pancake house, the sight of striped candy made her mouth water. The meaning was simple: *I want that*.

The little girl had acted on her feelings, saying clearly and simply, "I want some candy." Her father's response, however, was to ignore her. She'd persisted, trying to touch him— he'd pulled away. She'd asked, "What *is* that?" and he'd blatantly lied that peppermint was licorice. And when she demanded, "What's lickrish?" he'd changed the subject with irrelevant questions about his wife.

After a thousand similar exchanges, this little girl would learn—as most children did—that the meanings *she* attached to her body sensations were wrong. Her *feelings* were wrong.

And so she would give them up and instead adopt words and behaviors to which her parents (and later society) responded. Ultimately, she would become so estranged from her original impulses that she wouldn't even know what she really wanted or felt. Because she had no internal compass, she would look outside herself for guidance in how to behave. She'd adopt a socially recognized *image*, whether it was "good girl" or "brain" or "slut," and any sensations that rose in her would be filtered through it. (Now if the sight of candy in a glass jar made her mouth water, she might think it meant *sugar is bad for you*.) She would live in what the therapists called a state of *reasonable insanity*—functioning, coping, looking good to the rest of the world, but dead inside. She wouldn't do what she felt; she wouldn't say what she meant; she wouldn't be guided by her own body sensations or heart. She couldn't be. Her true feelings—and self—were so deeply buried that even she didn't know what they were.

Of course, the point of primal therapy had been to restore what had been lost. But Joe Hart, who had taken the role of the Center's chief visionary and theorist, said that claiming cure via a few screams was a cruel hoax. In fact, Joe now believed that primals didn't even exist. When Center therapists worked with patients who'd been at the Primal Institute, "we found that most had been *faking* their primals," he would tell an author writing a critical analysis of psychotherapy five years later. "It's hard to say if they were consciously faking, but they had learned to do what their therapist wanted." Reexperiencing the pain of the past *was* important. But it was simply the first step toward change. Far more important was learning to feel in the present.

How exactly was *that* to be accomplished? The Feeling Therapists had no idea. And so, in private and among themselves, they began an experiment. They understood that people learned to attach false meaning to their body sensations out of self-protection—once the girl in the pancake house realized her assertion "I want that" meant nothing to Daddy, each time she felt "I want that" she'd be reminded of that pain. It hurt far less to dismiss a watering mouth with "Sugar is bad for you." That false meaning was a *defense*. To get to any true feeling, then, required dismantling the defenses that covered it.

Together, the therapists decided to commit what they later called "image suicide": they would purposely tear down all their own "reasonably insane" images to see what lay beneath. Using what they'd learned about their pasts, they began to pinpoint the ways old pain led to present-day defending. As a kid, for instance, Carole Suydam had felt huge, graceless, and dumb; ignored by her parents; and so fundamentally *wrong* to her peers that at one point she'd made a list of ways to change so people might like her more. She'd survived the pain of feeling unaccepted by others by telling herself that she really preferred to be alone. And now, when she was feeling vulnerable or needy, she covered up by retreating into isolation. As a kid, Riggs had felt abandoned by parents who didn't seem to have the patience to teach him anything; the lack of guidance made him feel hopeless. Sometimes now, when he was overburdened with work, similar feelings rose in him. His defense was to tell himself, "I'll show them!" and do even more.

Such defenses had to be *counteracted*, stopped. That could happen in one of two ways. Each time Carole started to withdraw or Riggs to "act big," they could catch themselves and become aware that they were defending. They could then try to find out what they were really feeling by doing what they hadn't been able to do in the past—admit they needed help and reach out for it. Or, if Carole and Riggs weren't aware of what was happening to them, their colleagues would force them to be. "Hey, just a minute, what's going on here?" someone could say as Carole headed for home. "You say you want to be alone, but I don't think that's what's really happening. Are you feeling afraid?"

Giving up familiar behavior was hard, even frightening.

There were times all the therapists felt confused, lost, even literally insane—"I began to feel the disintegration of me—the me I had carefully constructed," Steve Gold later wrote. "At times. . . . I wanted to kill and tear. . . . And then at other times I was totally afraid. . . . " But sometimes each of them had what were undeniably *feelings*: sensations and impulses that were simple, clear, and very real. *I like you. I hurt. I want to touch you and be close.* Because this time they were not with disordering parents but trusted friends, those feelings could be expressed. And the more the therapists said and acted on their feelings, the more they felt at peace with themselves— as if for the first time since early childhood, their inner and outer selves matched. "What was at first a dim awareness of a forgotten me," Riggs wrote, "has become clear and vivid."

Finally, all that primal theory had missed was apparent. It wasn't dramatic screams but small, quiet awareness of one's everyday feelings that moved people out of the craziness of living from symbols and roles and back into who they really were. Such awareness could never be produced overnight; nor was it possible in the traditional setting (which even primal therapy had used) of a patient spending time alone with a therapist, dealing with his problems, then returning alone to the world he'd left. Undoing disorder was a constant chipping away of layers, a constant struggle; living from feeling meant being forced to see your own defenses and break through them again and again. It required the ongoing help of others engaged in the same effort, the kind of communal social structure that Joe Hart had found so appealing in the Senoi Indians.

And with that understanding, Feeling Therapy moved in a direction more radical than that of even the other new therapies of its time. It said that therapy wasn't something one went through alone and finished; it was a lifetime activity to be done with others. Bound together in struggle now, dependent on each other's help to know what was real, the Feeling Therapists no longer considered themselves nine professionals in practice together. They were a therapist *community*.

In the spring of 1972, the therapists decided to expand their experiment of dealing with present-life feelings to a select group of patients. There were about ten who seemed ideal. They were young and aimless, kids who'd come into therapy without having lived a whole lot first. They desperately needed to be taught about living in the present—present lives were exactly what they didn't have. Russ Gilbert was one of those chosen. Mary Farrell was another. And one was an old patient of Jerry's from the Primal Institute, a tall, skinny twenty-one-year-old with curly black hair and a perpetual look of frightened confusion on his angular, high-cheekboned face. His name was Kevin Fitzgerald.

Through childhood, Kevin Fitzgerald had been almost any parent's idea of a good kid. Though not the greatest student in the world, he was personable and sweet, easy to be around. The year he turned nine, his parents separated. His mother was left with both a ranch house in the dry scrub of a new San Fernando Valley suburb and the job of raising four children alone. Kevin took on the responsibility of being a substitute father. But in 1967, he turned sixteen and adolescence came on like a boiling rage. There were terrible fights at home, teacher complaints and plummeting grades at school. Overwhelmed, his mother sent Kevin to live with his father in Pasadena.

That arrangement wasn't so great either. After all the years of separation, Kevin and his father were hardly best friends. And the man, as stolid and unemotional as most of his generation, had absolutely no idea what to do with an overwrought kid who was either exploding in defiance or screaming "You don't love me! I need you to love me!" Still, for two years they coped. Then Kevin, like most of the guys in his high school, started playing around with psychedelics and weed. For a while, it was fun. Then one weekend, he dropped some acid, went way up—and never quite came down. He felt stoned all the time. He couldn't think straight. He never knew when the world around him would dissolve into a trip-landscape's shimmering flow. The official description of what was happening was "acid flashbacks"; Kevin knew only that something in him had gone out of control. There was a tight, paranoid feeling that never left him. He had violent fantasies filled with death and blood. He was terrified. He thought he was losing his mind.

Like most parents faced with a kid in such obvious trouble, the Fitzgeralds decided it was time to seek professional help. As it happened, Kevin's mother knew exactly where to turn. Some years back, she herself had gotten traditional counseling from a therapist she'd thought was great—Arthur Janov. She'd heard he was doing something new, and reading *The Primal Scream* convinced her that primal therapy was just the thing to cure Kevin.

Kevin was accepted into primal therapy just days before its no-one-under-twenty-six policy went into effect. He had no idea what it was all about but was scared enough to try anything. He was immediately taken with his therapist, Jerry Binder. He'd never had a man in his life who just sat and listened to him. The mere act of talking brought such intense release that he was certain Jerry could make whatever was wrong with him go away.

He was far less comfortable with the Primal Institute itself. Kevin was years younger and far less worldly than most of the other patients; he always felt intimidated around them. Mostly, he kept to himself. He rented an apartment not far from his father's home, got a night job as a janitor, and occasionally saw a few old drug buddies who understood he wasn't getting high anymore because he was into a new scene that had something to do with John Lennon. Then he waited to be cured.

But nine months of spending endless hours focused on infancy left Kevin feeling more spaced-out than ever. And there were times when group Laydown sessions at the institute were so crowded and zoolike that he thought the whole primal business might be a ripoff. In the summer of 1971, when he learned that Jerry was leaving to start the Center, he knew right away that he was going too.

But Kevin's first year at the Center was a big disappointment. He still lived in the same apartment, still held the same job, still felt crazy. Once a week, he drove into L.A. for therapy; he spent the rest of his free time thinking about his primals, crying, and wondering if he would ever get well. He knew that other people in their twenties went to school, got married, and established careers, but he was unable to imagine any such normal future for himself. All he wanted was to feel better. When the therapists said they wanted him to try something new, he was thankful. Finally, someone had a plan.

―――――――――

The new group Kevin joined was led by Riggs and met weekly at the Center. It was called "Reality Group." Riggs told everyone that in it, there would be no primaling or trips to the past. The group would be talking only about reality—about what was going on in their lives here and now. No one knew what to make of that. In fact, focusing on childhood had become so habitual that the order didn't even sink in. At the group's very first meeting, a former primal patient immediately started to weep about her mother. Riggs cut her off.

"Hold on," he said. "Don't cry. Tell me what you had for breakfast today."

"Breakfast?" The young woman was taken aback. "I don't know. Eggs."

"Eggs," Riggs said. "Fine. What kind of eggs were they?"

"Scrambled."

"Did you use cheese?"

"No."

"No cheese! Fine. How long did you cook them?"

As the gentle interrogation continued, the group members looked at each other in confusion. What was therapeutic about a blow-by-blow account of someone cooking eggs?

"Was anyone else in the room while you cooked?"

"No."

"Did you eat the eggs by yourself?"

"Yes."

The talk went on in the same vein, eggs, toast, a knife and fork. Finally, it narrowed to a new question: While the woman ate her eggs, what had she felt? Happy? Sad? Lonely? Gradually, the group glimpsed what Riggs was after. Crying about Mama being mean would teach them nothing about living as adults. But if they could know how it felt to have one true feeling, however small—*I was eating eggs and I felt sad*—then in the future, they could tell the difference between when they were feeling and when they were not. That knowledge could change their lives.

Once a week, through spring, the twenty-four-year-old Riggs led the group over the same ground he and his colleagues had explored with an almost paternal air. Over and over, the group discussed their daily lives, identifying moments when each of them had failed to recognize or express a feeling; they made huge charts, tracking how and why they'd adopted defenses in the past, and how those defenses still warped their lives. Some people numbed themselves through drinking or overeating. Some got dull and inattentive; they "spaced out." Kevin Fitzgerald got scared; Mary Farrell grew rigid and "Catholic" (a word Riggs used as a synonym for "repressed"); Russ Gilbert got passive.

But these defenses could be broken. Each patient could fight to break his or her own patterns. "Approach people and talk to them about anything at all," Russ Gilbert wrote to himself. "Play tennis, run, walk, bicycle. Begin doing the tasks I usually put off 'til later. Just say feelings—don't back them up with extraneous verbiage. . . . Talk to people I have feelings about."

But because, as the therapists had learned, people

weren't always aware when they were defending, the group also needed to keep watch over each other, to speak up when they saw a problem, to move strongly to "counter" it. Like the therapists, they would get well by working together.

"Look around you," Riggs told Russ, Kevin, Mary, and the others. "These people will be your best friends for the rest of your life."

Most Center patients were still doing primal therapy and couldn't make sense of what Reality Group was about.

"What do you *do* in there?" one man asked Kevin Fitzgerald.

"We talk about our jobs and dates and stuff," he said.

"What do you mean? Don't you have primals?"

"No," Kevin said. "He won't even let us cry."

The man's mouth hung open, and Kevin understood his incredulity. By primal therapy standards, what Riggs was doing was *weird*. But what was weirder was that Kevin thought it was helping him. It was emotionally steadying to talk about something as concrete as what he'd felt and said during a trip to the store, to be able to see a movie without bursting into tears or order lunch in a coffee shop without feeling obliged to think how the waitress reminded him of his mother. Through the group, he was becoming friendly with new people for the first time in years—a couple of the guys, and Mary Farrell, who he thought was a really cute, fun girl. Sometimes they'd get together, watch football on TV, drink beer, and laugh.

The eight other therapists seemed to agree that Riggs had done great things. Unlike other Center patients, the people in Reality Group didn't cry all the time, and they seemed more focused and clear. Soon Dominic's girlfriend, Konni, was sent to join them. So was Carole Suydam, even though she was a therapist herself. Therapist Linda Binder came to observe once, and Riggs said, "I think *you* need this." Linda too joined.

In October 1972, the therapists divided the whole Center into Reality Groups; every therapist led one. From now on, participating in a Reality Group would be an essential part of Feeling Therapy. Every nine patients who started therapy at the same time would form the core of a new group; ultimately, they'd merge with several other batches of nine to form a larger, permanent group.

The therapists began two other new programs as well. One was selecting a small number of patients whom Jerry and Steve would train to be a second generation of Feeling Therapists. The other was called "co-therapy" and was the logical expression of the Feeling Therapists' new belief that getting well required friends working together. After nine months in therapy, every patient would learn to be a "co-therapist" who had regular one-on-one sessions with a peer, with no other therapist present.

The new programs, together with the Center's philosophy that therapists, like patients, needed constant help staying sane, crossed many of the boundaries traditional psychotherapists erected to establish professional distance between themselves and their patients. They were meant to. As with licenses, the therapists seemed to see such boundaries as another way to pretend that some people were "better" than others—which Feeling Therapists emphasized they were not. "In helping relationships," Joe Hart had written in a 1970 essay, "there are no professionals; there are only people." At the Center, everyone was part of one world. True, the therapists led and the patients followed, but if they all worked hard, one day the patients would catch up and the distinction between the two groups would disappear entirely.

"I want you all for *friends,*" Riggs told his Reality Group. "I want you to get in touch with yourselves so we can be friends and equals."

One day we will all be equal. With that core myth in place, it was as if the *real* Center for Feeling Therapy was being born. Unlike the Primal Institute, it had no sleek buildings or Hollywood gloss, no autocratic leaders or stars. "You've got your pain and I've got mine and that's all there is," proclaimed

Dominic in a three-day seminar on Feeling Therapy that he, Joe, and Riggs ran at Esalen that fall. "There's no rooster on top of the henhouse and everybody else pecking around on the ground. To me, that's probably the most beautiful part of our therapy. You become just people who have feelings. And you go on from there."

6

The Center's new structure and emphasis changed a lot of things. At the top, positions shifted. It wasn't exactly that Carole and Linda fell in status. They were still acting therapists. But because they were in a Reality Group with patients, their weaknesses became more public than those of their seven colleagues, making them seem more flawed and vulnerable. And it wasn't exactly that Steve and Jerry lost authority. They had the vital job of training the patients who were to be therapists, just as they themselves had been trained by Vivian Janov. But as the Center's program veered away from primal therapy, the fact that they were certified primal therapists mattered less.

Riggs's success with Reality Group, on the other hand, added to his stature. And a number of the new directions taken at the Center clearly bore the stamp of Joe Hart. For all the contempt for academic psychologists Joe had long expressed, his consistent record of experiments and publications suggested he also wanted their approval. Now the Center therapists began playing similar standard academic games. Though neither Steve nor Jerry had ever expressed a desire for more schooling, by 1972 both had joined Riggs and Werner as Ph.D. candidates at UCI, working under Joe. The study Joe, Riggs, and Werner had done at the Primal Institute, showing how tension reduction led to physiological changes in primal therapy patients, had been published in the prestigious journal *Psychotherapy*. Now, under Joe's overall guidance and Werner's direct supervision, the Center formed its own non-profit, educational, tax-exempt research arm, the Center Foundation, and began studies that would take those experiments a step further: They would show that the present-life changes Feeling Therapy encouraged were leading to even greater reductions in levels of tension. "We're finding that your blood pressure is going down," Joe Hart told patients as research got under way. "What we're doing is completely new. You're all really lucky to be part of it."

But the biggest change was in the practice of Feeling Therapy itself. Before, patients had developed powerful connections to their Intensive therapists. Reality Group created an equally strong bond with whichever therapist was the Group's leader. Before, patients had spent only one night a week at the Center, going to Laydown. Now, weekly Laydowns were still scheduled—the therapists thought it important that everyone continue to explore his or her past—so the addition of Reality Group meant going to the Center twice. And the current emphasis on living from feeling in the present made every aspect of patients' lives open to therapeutic intervention. If, according to theory, most people lived reasonably insane lives, then everything they normally did, believed, said, or thought was probably a defense.

Those defenses had to be broken down, "normality" thrown off-balance. Reality Group—soon just called "Group"—started getting wild. "You don't fuck any different than you do anything else," Riggs told his people one night. "Use your hands as models. Show me how you fuck." One man's fingers flew back and forth in his fist. "Like a rabbit," Riggs said. "That's just like you. That's just like you live the rest of your life. . . . "

Every Group, there was something new. One week, the

therapists would give life-changing take-home exercises, called "assignments." A woman so cheap she denied herself pleasure might be told to go to the most expensive restaurant in L.A. and order a huge meal. A man who'd passively accepted being lonely might be ordered to call four different women and ask them all for dates. Other sessions would be devoted to bioenergetic body theory: Since children reacted physically to hurt and rejection—their metabolisms speeded up, their muscles got chronically tense—people's bodies were shaped as they were for a *reason*. Patients took off their clothes to poke and examine each other, commenting on underdeveloped physiques that spoke of repression, frowning at fat from overeating that made it clear feelings were being suppressed. Sometimes the therapists took pictures. Or Groups might be held nude or part-nude, no matter what was being discussed, just to heighten people's feelings of vulnerability. "Women!" a clothed therapist would order from his or her chair. "Take off your tops!"

But Group didn't stop at self-exploration. In fact, its true aim was nothing less than complete resocialization: Patients were meant to learn—as the therapist had been learning—a new way of living, interacting, *being*. Traditional therapists' image of the ideal posttherapeutic patient was of an even-keeled adult able to cope with life's vicissitudes. Arthur Janov saw a kind of perennial infant. The Feeling Therapists' model, on the other hand, was like an adult four-year-old. His reactions to everything that happened were clear and immediate, his feelings uninfluenced by social "shoulds," shame, or self-censorship. And he never hesitated to express those feelings or worried that what he said would hurt someone else: It was his responsibility to be true to what he felt, and that of others to care for themselves. Each week, in Group, patients learned to report what was going on inside them literally moment by moment. "I really like you," one Group member might say to another. "Saying that made me a little afraid. Then I could feel myself spacing out a little. I'm getting sad now, telling you this. . . ." Each week, they analyzed in excruciating detail everything they had or hadn't dealt with on the job, at home, even in bed. "When I was fucking, I tried to stay with feeling good," a man might confess. "But I didn't ask for everything I wanted, and I started to worry whether or not it was too soon to come, and I know that took away from fully feeling myself. . . ."

For anyone with an even vaguely counterculture past, none of what was happening was inordinately strange. All over America, people were still "sharing" in encounter groups, bouncing in and out of each other's bedrooms, taking off their clothes in various public settings. Still, there were times—like when one was standing, naked, before a dozen pairs of scrutinizing male and female eyes—that Group could feel scary, even a little humiliating. And even when Group wasn't frightening, it was intense, a constant weekly stripping of self. Group members were gaining powerful, private knowledge about each other: who ate compulsively; who was impotent; who had perverse sexual fantasies; who was afraid to love.

Some of the Center's older patients, people who were in their thirties, with careers, families, and outside lives, started finding the new program a bit much. They'd come to the Center looking for a therapy that would help them exorcise the pain of the past. They were *not* looking to have their lives examined and judged by twenty new "best friends." One by one, they began to drift away.

But what drove some patients away pulled those who were younger—and more needy—even closer. To them, growing involvement with the therapists and other Center patients was not a burden but an opportunity. Many had had little in their lives before therapy, and the new connections the Center offered promised so much: friends willing to love them for who they *really* were; therapists who—unlike parents—took the time to listen.

As their own interdependence increased, the therapists

had begun seeing each other outside the Center, socializing, double-dating. Riggs and his colleague Lee even lived across the street from each other, on Norwich Avenue in West L.A. In contrast to traditional therapists, who actively discouraged fraternizing among their patients, the Feeling Therapists encouraged theirs to get together too. During the day, Center patients were the messengers, secretaries, pathologists, attorneys, nurses, and teachers they'd been before therapy. But at night and on weekends, they met for picnics and volleyball games, gatherings where they also could practice the expressiveness and honesty they were learning in Group. Some single patients even became roommates, sharing houses and apartments in cheap, funky communities like Venice, Echo Park, and Silverlake.

Settled in an old L.A. house with a roommate who'd also defected from the Primal Institute, Russ Gilbert reveled in the new swirl of activity around the Center. He was finding therapy itself incredibly hard: In months of Reality Group, Russ had never had a moment when he felt as completely in touch with himself as he had during what he still secretly believed had been a true primal. In fact, the more he tried to follow his feelings, the more elusive they became. Whenever he went to the grocery store, took a shower, or even had sex, he was always monitoring himself so carefully that half the time he didn't know *whether* he was feeling, much less *what*.

But if the Center hadn't yet "cured" Russ, it had given him one of the things he'd wanted most: a place to belong. He'd cashed in a life insurance policy and with the money had reenrolled at UCI, where he was now part of Joe Hart's inner circle, one of the guys who hung around his office telling wide-eyed undergrads all they were missing in their lives. He'd also gotten involved in the Center Foundation's research experiments—he was planning to use some of the data as the basis for a doctoral dissertation—and through the work had gotten even closer to Werner Karle. And he felt more drawn than ever to Riggs. Sometimes in Group, his heart ached for the therapist when he talked about his own life, about the way the lively, curious little boy he'd been had been squelched by an authoritarian father. Then, in Laydown, when Russ was exploring his own past, it was Riggs who cared for him.

"I remember feeling confused . . . and alone . . . ," he'd stammer.

"That little boy must really have needed his daddy right then," Riggs would say softly, his tone so gentle and loving it almost made Russ cry with pure pleasure.

But maybe the best times were when he and Riggs were doing research work together. It was as if the therapist burned with excitement. He was going far and moving fast, and he wanted all his friends to come with him. After so many years of isolation, Russ found the call "Join me!" irresistible. It didn't matter if he didn't quite get the therapy yet; it didn't matter if he still felt lost. All he had to do was follow. The realization gave him a happiness he hadn't known in years. He'd started to feel cut off at four, when his older brother left him behind and entered school. And now, it was as if he'd come back again.

Going on her second year in Feeling Therapy, Mary Farrell was more committed to the Center than ever. And just as was true for Russ, part of the reason was Riggs.

It was so strange. Her first months of therapy, she'd felt only anger toward Riggs—for how badly Joe's and his teaching had upset her as a student, for snubbing her when she came to the Center. For the one night of sex Riggs had still never mentioned. Gradually, though, she'd come to understand that these were *feelings*. Experiencing them fully mattered more than what they were about. And then, to Mary's surprise, around the same time she was picked to be in his Reality Group, Riggs began reaching out to her, as if he wanted to be her friend. That was flattering, of course—as the success of the Reality Group idea made Riggs a more important person at the Center, any patient who hung around him also gained prestige. But what Mary couldn't understand was why Riggs wanted to be with *her*: She knew she was still very, very crazy. Sure, there were ways in which she was useful to him. She was earning money cleaning houses and doing odd jobs for the Center itself, and usually had plenty of free time. She'd always had good organizational skills, and spent hours helping Riggs put data in order for his Ph.D. dissertation, which was already hundreds of pages long. She also brought notes from the early days of the first Group to Riggs's house, and there the two of them made up outlines that would help the other therapists get the members of newly formed Groups to bond and cohere.

But Riggs wasn't just using her. It was true that being with him never felt quite like being with an equal. Because he'd been her teacher and was her Group leader, Mary still looked up to Riggs in a way she never would another patient. Still, they did what ordinary friends did—play Ping-Pong; walk Riggs's Doberman pinscher, Heidi; go to the movies; or just talk. Riggs could listen to her in a way no one else did, with his whole soul and being, as if nothing else mattered to him. And there were times when he let his own guard down as well, when his cockiness disappeared and what was exposed was sadness and pain. He'd get a distant look in his eyes, a stare, almost as if he weren't there anymore. If he and Mary were watching TV, an hour might go by before he said anything. He seemed *lonely*. He and his current girlfriend weren't getting along well, and his relationships with the other therapists were mixed. Sometimes he joked that none of them even liked him. Mary knew he'd never gotten close to Steve or Jerry, and from the way he talked about the wiry, assertive Linda Binder, it was clear he couldn't stand her. But even the therapists who were his friends had other things going in their lives and weren't always around. Dominic was living with Konni and her young daughter. Werner was madly in love with a young patient who was lovely but street-tough, and she and Riggs had taken an instant, passionate dislike to each other. Even Joe retreated to spend time alone with his family; his wife, Gina, wasn't involved in Feeling Therapy at all.

Hours would go by there at the house on Norwich. There was a peace, a sweetness to the time. And yet . . . Although Mary always felt comfortable at Riggs's home, she was always afraid of him in Group. When Riggs did therapy, he changed before her eyes from an easygoing friend into someone powerful and relentless. He wanted perfection from his patients, and if Mary was anything less, their friendship offered no protection.

"Talk about your favorite sex act," he ordered the Group one night.

Mary's heart pounded. Sex again—always her weakest point! When her turn came, she had nothing to say.

"What are you," Riggs shouted in disgust, "a sexual *midget*?"

It was hard to describe how she felt inside when Riggs came after her like that. His warm attention could make her feel like the most important person in the world, but beneath his crushing disapproval, she would shrink and disappear. Everyone in the Group looked on as she was defined as stupid, crazy, not even worth being here. . . .

Mary never questioned the judgment. She had been scared and unhappy much of her life. When she was nineteen, Riggs and Joe had convinced her they knew how to change that, and from there, accepting whatever they said or did was but a small step. If nothing else, Catholicism had taught her about faith. Nor did she realize, as one day she glowed in Riggs's affection and the next withered under his scorn, that something even stronger than faith had begun to tie her to

him and to the Center. It was all so familiar. It was like returning to a place she had inhabited since childhood, where
love coexisted with punishment, the latter making the former
seem infinitely more precious.

Kevin Fitzgerald also found himself drawn into the tightening
knot of connection at the Center. One night after Laydown,
Steve Gold talked about how everyone was scattered across
Southern California and that it would be nice if they lived
closer together so they could see each other more. That made
sense to Kevin. He gave up his Pasadena apartment and
moved to Los Angeles.

Finally, it seemed that he was progressing. The fog was
lifting from his mind. And then, like a miracle, for the first
time since his bad LSD trip, he stopped being afraid. At that
moment, he knew with utter certainty that he'd been right to
leave the Primal Institute. One night, he and another ex-primal
patient talked privately about how grateful they were for what
they'd found at the Center, then wrote a poem about their
feelings, a takeoff on the Lord's Prayer. The next week, they
read it in Group. Other therapists might have heard their
words and risen from their chairs in alarm. But Riggs Corriere,
unlicensed, untrained in any but the most radical new therapies, firm in his conviction that he and his colleagues had
found the one way, simply listened to what his patients had
to say.

"Our father, who lives on Norwich," Kevin and his
friend intoned, "Hallowed be thy name: Riggs."

7

May 1973

In Paris, France, the governments of the United States and the Democratic Republic of Vietnam, at war since 1965, announced the signing of a peace treaty. Finally, American troops would withdraw from Southeast Asia. Finally, America's part in a war that had caused so much death, destruction, grief, and rage was over. But no one was celebrating. There was nothing to cheer about, for the war's end brought home all that had been lost during it: Gone was the unwavering belief in America's claim to morality and goodness; gone was the assurance that there was nothing the most powerful country in the world couldn't do. Facing such losses meant acknowledging that a national mythology had been damaged beyond repair; terrified, the country tried to patch over the fracture and forget it. The soldiers returned and the war disappeared from the newspapers, TV news, public debate. Yet its burial brought no relief, for other cracks in the social fabric were appearing everywhere. In 1971, the publication of the Pentagon Papers had made it clear that the U.S. government lied to its people. Now, an even more serious scandal was unfolding in Washington, D.C.: A special Senate panel had been assembled to investigate just who had been behind a 1972 burglary at the Democratic party's national headquarters, and each day it became more obvious that President Nixon himself—a man recently reelected by the largest landslide in history—was implicated.

The spring of 1973 could have been a moment of long-delayed triumph for the counterculture—the war had ended just as activists had said it must; the government in power was proving even more venal than they'd always insisted it was. But that culture had been splintering and shrinking for several years; now, with its one unifying issue gone, it frag-mented completely into a mass of aging kids veering in wildly different directions. Some fled mainstream America com-pletely, dropping out to grow dope and organic vegetables; some raced back in, in a desperate effort to make up for lost time, cutting their hair and applying to law school. And some, not drawn to either extreme, found themselves living in an unhappy limbo: Their old dreams of living heroic, meaningful lives were as strong as ever, yet without widespread cultural and political change, how could they ever come true?

Increasingly, those who wanted more out of life turned toward the maze of programs that made up the human po-tential movement, their desire for fulfillment translated to a need for psychological help. The move in this direction wasn't entirely new. In the early 1970s, some radicals had started turning toward self-reflection, in the belief that in their ab-sorption with politics, they'd ignored human needs. "The new mode of relationship on the campus, in the commune and the political collective, is the heavy encounter in which it becomes possible, even obligatory, to confess and 'get into' one's fear, pain, instability," wrote one former member of Students for a Democratic Society in a magazine article praising John Len-non. Arthur Janov had made participating in primal therapy sound like joining a heroic moral struggle. "I believe the only way to eliminate neurosis is with overthrow by force and violence," he wrote in *The Primal Scream*. And some of the unhappiness people suffered *was* rooted in genuine psychological pain: Anyone who'd grown up in a 1950s or 1960s nuclear family had at best parents with no understanding of their own psyches, much less their children's, and at worst had contended with alcoholism, domestic violence, and/or incest—problems whose existence no one even acknowledged.

But perhaps more to the point was that if you wanted to improve your life, psychological growth—as opposed to revolution—at least seemed *possible*. Each day, some former counterculture hero announced he'd discovered that the best way to change the world was to change himself. Former Chicago Ten defendant Rennie Davis was publicizing his devotion to a fat, fifteen-year-old guru named Maharaj Ji, whom he called "the Divine Master." An ex-speechwriter for liberal presidential candidate Eugene McCarthy was promoting the "Be Here Now" philosophy of a former Harvard professor and LSD experimenter who'd traveled to Katmandu and been reborn as Baba Ram Dass. And yippie Jerry Rubin had announced in *Psychology Today* that he was "going back to his body," where "the real wars of liberation were taking place."

The changing American landscape didn't bring a sudden flood of people into the Center—Feeling Therapy still lacked the Primal Institute's celebrity aura and drawing power. At the same time, its $2,500 fee was far too steep for weekend dabblers who patronized programs like est. But the change meant that a market existed for the brochures the Center had begun to send out. A market existed for the lectures Joe, Riggs, and Dominic gave at UCLA and the National Institute for the Psychotherapies. And as word of the Center spread, slowly but steadily envelopes began arriving from around the country, in them the desperately sad four-page "autobiographies" prospective patients were required to write, describing their childhoods, their lives, and their reasons for wanting therapy.

"I want to grow emotionally, instead of holding back. . . ."

"The sick me is depressive and bisexual. . . . I hear voices in my head saying 'You can't do it; you're stupid.' "

"Nothing has ever seemed 100 percent real to me. . . . I've always lived in a continual state of temporary. Being around my parents drives me crazy. There is so much hate and yelling and hurting. . . ."

Not everyone who applied to the Center was accepted. Joe Hart loved to shock lecture audiences by telling them that because they didn't live from their feelings, he considered them insane. "And not 'I'm OK, you're OK' neurotic insane," he'd declare. "Out-and-out psychotic." In reality, though, the Center was not looking to treat people who talked to lampposts. Through the spring and summer of 1973, as the Senate Watergate hearings captivated the nation and a bizarre, unheard-of event, an oil shortage, raised the price of gas to an unbelievable 37¢ a gallon, nine patients a month started therapy at the Center. Some were people even traditionalists would have recognized as disturbed, men and women sexually and physically abused as kids, Vietnam vets haunted by violent memories, heroin junkies. (The addicts had to kick their habits before they would be admitted; the Center wanted to treat craziness itself, not what they considered a symptom.) But most were classic cases of "reasonable insanity," men and women who were in their twenties, white, educated, middle class, and materially privileged, but the products of unhappy families, newly out of school and drifting, recently single, friendless, alienated: for one reason or another, miserable.

The Center's three-week Intensives had gotten harder. They retained primal therapy's heavy emphasis on parents as the source of all grief. "Goddamn you, Dad! You lied!" patients were pushed to scream, as every childhood wound was exposed. "You don't care! You motherfucking bastard! Fuck you! Fuck you!" But though they'd always had some busting of patients as well—shouting accusations like "You're a fraud! A loser!" was the primal therapy way to crack tough adults until the damaged children within them emerged—with the new emphasis on breaking present-life defenses, that got more intense. In theory, the therapists' self-work had enabled them to "intuit" whether whatever a patient said was a true feeling or a defense. (Arthur Janov had made the same claim for primal therapists.) And once they sensed a defense, it was imperative to go after it.

"*You're* not talking!" one therapist blasted a patient. He pulled the man to his feet, then pushed him hard against a wall. "*You're* not talking." When the man tried to speak, he pushed again. "*You're* still not talking."

"Get out!" shouted another, throwing his patient out of the therapy room. "Do what I say, or don't come back here!"

Over and over, the therapists lashed out: "You're all intellect, no emotion, you're dead, you're like the Pillsbury Doughboy!" "Jewish kid! You're a wimp!"

The traditional notion that therapy should provide patients with a "safe haven" to explore their inner selves fell away; there was no safety in Feeling Therapy's Intensive rooms. Every tactic to unnerve was used: mockery, name-calling, racial slurs. Every secret shame revealed in the application autobiography was turned into a weapon to smash defenses.

"You *are* a failure; you can't even make it with men!" one therapist yelled at a twenty-six-year-old who'd confessed that she'd tried sex with a woman.

Later, it would be almost impossible for Center patients to describe or even reimagine the transforming power of those weeks. It wasn't any one thing that took place; it was the unremitting assault, the yelling, screaming, confrontation, the denigrating of every old emotional connection, the being stripped—sometimes psychically, often physically—all of it happening over and over, and all of it taking place in absolute isolation: Through the Intensive, patients were forbidden to contact friends or family, and although they saw others leaving therapy rooms looking tear-stained or distraught, no one knew what was happening to anyone else.

The therapists had a reason for doing what they did. All problems, they believed, stemmed from the same root cause: lack of feeling. Learning to feel required breaking defenses. That meant that in therapy, patients needed to be made child-like, dependent, for people loved their defenses and, if they felt any adult strength, would cling to them in moments of doubt. When a man or woman felt truly broken and lost, how-ever, he or she would turn to a mother or father surrogate, the therapist, for guidance. And since defenses, not patients' "real" selves, were what was being "busted" in a therapy ses-sion, there was no harm in going all-out.

It was testimony to the naïveté of the era that it never occurred to anyone that there might be some danger in—as one patient later described it—"stomping through the uncon-scious with cleats." But even at the time, the feeling the Inten-sive evoked was of one's innermost self invaded, brutalized, left raw. "It was like being stripped naked," one man would recall, "and being left on the corner of Wilshire Boulevard in a rainstorm." And the therapists' busts, which often seemed inexplicable and random, were made more terrifying because there was no fighting back against them. When it came to deciding what constituted truth or true feeling, the therapist was *always* right, and attempts to contradict him or her were labeled "resistance."

Still, few patients walked away. Young, confused, ready for something extreme, and utterly uninformed about the ac-ceptable bounds of psychotherapy, most gave their therapists the benefit of the doubt. It was a given that the therapists knew something they didn't—that was why they were therapists. Besides, all the awful things they said *could* be true. Anyone with an elementary understanding of psychology knew that defenses were tricky, deceptive. Anyone who'd tried psyche-delic drugs (as perhaps the majority of Center patients had) and watched seemingly solid objects melt and flow knew that nothing was necessarily as it appeared.

Moreover, the therapists weren't *always* cruel. There were moments in every session—when a woman was sobbing and a therapist reached out to gently touch her face; when a man who'd always secretly felt alone heard the words "I can see how lonely you've been"—when it was as if they reached deep into patients' hearts and souls. "At their best," one man would later recall, "the therapists were brilliant. Probably Riggs more than anybody could spot things you'd think only a psychic would know. I think every one of us wants to be understood. And when you're sitting there and someone like Riggs is saying things that only you have known about your life—it's so emotionally rewarding."

And some of the therapists' harsher methods seemed to produce almost instantaneous results. One young man who told his therapist he was afraid of the dark was left alone to scream in a pitch-black room. The man had complained that he hadn't been able to weep since childhood; that day, he cried. A young nurse who came to therapy to break through severe emotional numbness left by childhood battering was terrified when her therapist pinched her legs so hard it hurt— but to her, feeling *anything* was progress. In between the confusion and fear, patients had moments of "breakthrough" that produced utter exaltation.

"I'm afraid of becoming a person I don't know," one man pleaded after his therapist busted him for not being more aggressive in trying to rent a house. "If I say what I feel, I won't know anybody. My old friends won't like me."

"How does it feel to come and go, to fluctuate between being you and not you?" the therapist asked.

". . . It just seems so hard . . ." he said. "It seems crazy."

"Be crazy."

"I want to talk, but I'm afraid. I keep letting it all go by." Now the man was shouting, beating a mat. "I *do* want that house! Goddamn it! I want that house! I want a woman to love! I want good sex!"

High, low, approval, bust—the fact that some of what therapists said to patients was true made it hard to dismiss what seemed not to be. Soon, it was as if nothing were sure, as if none of one's feelings, thoughts, desires, reactions, or impulses could be trusted. "My therapist is really an asshole," the twenty-one-year-old called "Jewish kid" and "wimp" wrote after his third day of therapy. "I think my therapist is an asshole," he wrote on the fifth day. "But that may be my old defense system operating."

Then, over that uncertainty came a reassuring flood of information. Whether by outright instruction or through the behavior they rewarded, the therapists let the patients know there were specifically "sane" ways to act and react. Sane people, for instance, expressed their desires as directly, vehemently, and immediately as the little girl who craved peppermint candy. When they wanted something, they said "I WANT THAT." They didn't use complicated metaphors or subtle innuendo; they didn't feel, "Hmmm, a little depressed today"—they FELT REALLY BAD. They didn't shrug, "That's OK," when someone pissed them off—they bellowed, "I DIDN'T LIKE THAT!"

People who were sane said and acted on what they felt right away, so they had no need for symbolic gratifications. They didn't smoke cigarettes or dope or drink alcohol or caffeine to numb themselves. They didn't stuff down feeling by overeating. They were at ease with their bodies and felt no shame in nakedness. People who were sane didn't concern themselves with politics, for being able to feel turned everyone into natural democrats. They didn't follow traditional gender restrictions. Men weren't afraid to show vulnerability and tenderness; women could be strong, not coy—they didn't hold in their farts or hesitate to ask for what they wanted in bed. Sane men and women adored sex, without feeling the need to attach the act to marriage or even love. Sane people liked exercise, particularly team sports, and played with the exuberant joy of children. Most of all, sane people were intensely social, for they knew that old defenses arose when one was alone: it was the continual presence and efforts of friends that kept people straight.

The new guidelines went right to the confusion inside, and it was as if they soaked in, for suddenly they became conviction in a way that bypassed rational thought or question. Friends and family of new Center patients often saw something spooky about the change the Intensive effected in their loved ones. Men and women with different histories and personalities all emerged similarly furious at their parents, denouncing their past lives and speaking the same loud phrases with the same peculiar lilting cadence: "God, I just know that when I saw her, I WANTED her. I didn't say anything, and I started having these crazy thoughts, and now I fuckin' feel BAD."

"What's *happened* to you?" family and friends sometimes asked post-Intensive patients. But the patients paid no attention. Their first three weeks of Feeling Therapy had showed them just how deeply damaged they were, and who was responsible. And it had convinced them that only more Feeling Therapy could save them. If many still had one foot in their old lives, working the same jobs, married to the same men and women, from now on their main energy would go toward moving beyond that. And when patients started feeling confused or lost, they didn't turn to their old friends or ways of coping. They turned to the only people who really knew how to feel, the people whose behavior they'd been told should serve as a model for their own. They turned to their therapists.

After the Intensive, Group was the core of Center life. Each met weekly for three to four hours. The time was free-form, unstructured. "Who's got a problem?" the therapist who was leader would ask. "Who wants to talk?" There might be an awkward silence, then someone would bring up a problem at work, a date, a small setback or triumph. There could be a sweetness to it, men and women trustingly admitting the kind of need or weakness that was impossible to share in the outside world.

"I went out over the weekend and . . . actually made it with a girl," a man might announce. "It was unbelievable—I didn't go soft. I stayed hard. I didn't come fast. . . ."

"I've never felt important," another could confess. "I just want to like myself." Tears began. "I'm afraid people will leave me."

A woman opened her arms. "No one in *here* is going to leave you."

But Groups also had a ferocity to them. Each member had a responsibility to the rest, to be totally honest. That meant admitting any lapses, drinking, overeating. It meant admitting any time one had "thoughts" that were clearly a defense against some emerging feeling. (Thinking "I don't like anyone here," for instance, was "crazy"; the true feeling beneath it was fear over how vulnerable it made one to really need friends.) Even more important, when someone didn't see or admit her own defenses, other Group members absolutely had to call her on them, to stay with her, pushing, berating, and not stopping until she "came through" to her real feeling.

"I feel bad," one man said after his friend yelled at him for being withdrawn. "I feel like I *am* bad, a bad person. That there's something wrong with me. . . ." Tears started. ". . . I don't always say what's happening with me. Things pile up. . . . Pretty soon I start falling apart—and then everything I do is fucked. And all the while I'm just waiting for someone to see that *I* really need help. I can't help—I've got nothing to give."

"That sounds too pat," a Group member snapped.

Another man nodded. "You've said that before, lots of times."

"Say some more about that," the therapist prompted them.

"Well, like you were told that you don't help enough. So you cry about being bad, a bad person, then you wind up saying you have nothing to give. . . . I don't believe it."

"What don't you believe?" asked the therapist.

"That he—you—have nothing to give. That's crap. . . . Why don't you say what's really going on with you?"

"Harry?" said the therapist. "Say something."

"I don't know. . . ."

"Oh shit!" shouted a woman. "You say all the right therapy phrases . . . and you cry, but you just wind up justifying that you have nothing to give. . . . You're lying."

"Damnit!" screamed a man. "Say something! Cut out this 'hurt little boy' shit."

". . . And stop that fucking whining! It's an act and you know it!"

". . . You fucking blob—TALK! Come on, Goddamnit. Every fucking week it's like this—you fuck around and everyone goes nuts trying to get you to come out and show some feeling. I hate it! I hate it! I HATE YOU. You're fucked. Either put out or get the fuck out of here. . . ."

". . . I know I do this stuff," Harry finally choked, breaking. "I know I'm dead. I hate when I get this way, I HATE IT! . . ."

Through the end of 1973 and into 1974, with each week the Groups' intensity grew. Any failure or pulling back made the therapists wild with urgency. It was as if having explained what needed to be done, they couldn't understand patients' failure to follow, especially when the stakes were so high. What they were doing here was no game! Not living from feeling was *dying*. Something new had to be done—and when the first move to try it came, inevitably it was in Riggs's Group. The power that encounter groups had begun to unleash in Riggs was reaching full force at the Center. Unlike his friend Joe—whose Group once busted *him* for being too held-back—Riggs was the perfect feeling behavior "model," spontaneous, outspoken, quick to spot retreat in others, and never afraid to hurt someone if doing so was for his or her own good.

On this night, he was seething. Kevin hadn't been speaking up. Russ had been procrastinating with his schoolwork, letting his old passivity take over. Mary Farrell had backed away from sex—again. What had they all been *doing*? he wanted to know. Half the people in the Group were throwing their lives away, and the other half didn't care! It was too easy for complacency to set in—he'd even seen it happen among the therapists. It was easy to get numb and sleepy and "dead."

"I've let Joe go to sleep!" he said, his voice rough with passion. "I've let Dom go to sleep! And you guys are letting each other go to sleep!" Then he introduced the Group to a new technique the therapists were trying among themselves. They called it "sluggo" therapy. It was simple. When someone was really spacing out, just give him a slug in the shoulder. BAM! That would wake him up.

With the therapists' encouragement, over the next few months sluggo started catching on, a slap here, a BAM! on the shoulder there. There was a gratifying release to it. When you were trying to get through to someone, there was always a point when he or she kept resisting, the stubbornness became unbearable, and mere words didn't seem like enough. "You're fucking *dead*!" emphasized with a punch brought home the reality of what was happening. It forced people to pay attention.

"Wake up!" BAM. No one was asleep anymore. Center patients were spending more and more time with each other. (Sometimes therapists even made togetherness an assignment—hanging out with one's Group members was considered therapeutic.) Those who worked in the same part of L.A. met at lunch hour; on evenings and weekends, patients now shared not only volleyball games but beds. It was inevitable. Many patients were young and single, and the Center was like a huge social pool. Even single therapists used it, for outright condemnation of sex between therapist and patient was still years away. In 1971, for instance, a panel at the annual meeting of the Association for Humanist Psychology had seriously discussed whether therapists should go to bed with patients if the two parties were mutually attracted. A year later, the American Psychological Association convention featured a session on the wisdom and ethics of therapist-patient sex. The Feeling Therapists' compromise was that it was OK for a therapist to date a Center patient so long as it wasn't someone whose Intensive he or she had done. Among the increasingly close crowd, the atmosphere grew feverish, charged. The emphasis on being absolutely honest meant that every interaction was unpredictable; the need to act on every feeling and report the outcome publicly in Group made friendships and romances form, deepen, then quickly blow apart.

"I can't BELIEVE you asked my boyfriend to sleep with you!" a woman screamed at a Group friend. "I *HATE* YOU!"

"Um, I have to tell you that I don't like the hair on your legs," Kevin Fitzgerald informed the young woman he'd just taken to bed. That was the last date *they* had.

Even relationships among the therapists were in continual flux. Steve Gold and his wife had divorced around the time the Center began (she remained in Feeling Therapy); now he and Carole Suydam had fallen in love and moved in together. Riggs's romance was on the rocks. Konni was unhappy with Dominic, and Riggs often pushed her to explore her dissatisfactions in Group. (Konni had also decided to send her four-year-old daughter to live with the child's father; she said being a mother made it hard to concentrate on helping herself.) Even Joe and Gina Hart, who'd been married more than fifteen years, had split up.

But the most dramatic breakup was that of Jerry and Linda Binder. None of the patients knew exactly what had happened, but some heard rumors that Jerry had cheated on Linda with two female patients. After the split though, it was *Linda* who the other therapists said was "having trouble." She wouldn't be working as a therapist anymore. For a while, the men and women who'd gone through their Intensives under Linda had trouble dealing with that. They'd accepted being shouted at by Linda, having their lives ripped apart, because they knew she could feel and they couldn't. Now, it seemed, she was crazy, just like them. But their misgivings didn't last, because soon they grasped that Linda's demotion actually proved the beauty of the whole Center system. Even a therapist couldn't get away with acting crazy—her friends would step in and stop her.

Group just kept getting more intense, all busting, a frenzied passion that pushed sluggo beyond hits on the shoulder to real force, violence.

"I want *more* from you!" a woman screamed, slapping her friend across the face.

"Harder!" the Group yelled. "Do it again!"

"You're *out* of it!" a therapist shouted. His fist crashed full-force into a patient with an audible *whack*; the man flew clear across the room and fell to the floor.

There was no question what anyone felt at such moments—it was terror. But it was a special kind of terror, necessary to the pursuit of a cause. And it made the struggle to change feel more important, more real.

"Can you imagine acting like this with your parents?" the therapists would ask. "Can you imagine being this open with your old friends?"

Of course, no one could, and mixed in with the tears and fear—often subduing them—was a powerful pride. At the Center, patients were leaving the kind of dull, half-lives with which most people were content in pursuit of a fulfillment most couldn't even imagine. Abraham Maslow had described what he called "peak experiences," moments in which people were lifted out of ordinary consciousness into an ecstatic oneness with self and the world. Anyone who'd done drugs had had a fleeting glimpse of them, but Feeling Therapy promised much more: When each second was fully felt, "peak experiences" need not last only a moment. They could be for life.

8

Kevin Fitzgerald was feeling more and more lost. Group scared him. He couldn't feel the difference between the times therapists or friends told him he was "there" and the times they said he'd "gone dead," which meant that his feeling level had dropped dangerously low. He couldn't feel the difference between when he was "breaking through"—moving from nonfeeling to feeling—and when he was "resisting." He often didn't spot it when someone else "spaced out." Others did— he'd watched them turn on Group members with a savage clarity he never could manage. Even those few times when he did know people were "in their shit"—reverting to old defenses—he had real trouble busting them hard. There was a look people got on their faces when the whole Group was descending on them, screaming and mocking the fucked-up way they were behaving: They looked destroyed. It made him feel sorry for them.

But obviously these feelings were all wrong, for even patients who'd been at the Center less time than him seemed to have no trouble getting along. He was failing. The realization was not only painful but terrifying. Feeling Therapy was the only thing that could save him, but if he didn't get with the program, he might not be allowed to stay. "Get out!" he'd heard therapists scream at patients who clung stubbornly to their craziness. "Don't come back until you want what we offer here!"

If he was kicked out of therapy, where would he go? Back to the father who could barely speak to him? To the mother responsible for fucking him up? He had nothing—Riggs had told them all that repeatedly in Group. "You're here because you have to be," he said. "You're here because you've tried everything else and it doesn't work."

Then, always in the fore, Riggs upped the Group ante again, by starting to take everyone for weekends away. Out of the city and by themselves, he said, they could truly concentrate on what they were doing. The trips were supposed to be a privilege—not that anyone could choose whether or not to go—but they petrified Kevin. In early summer, he, Mary Farrell, Russ Gilbert, Dominic's girlfriend, Konni, Carole Suydam, and about twenty others headed out to the Anza Borrego desert. It was a long way from L.A., east through smoggy inland cities, south past the dull gleam of the Salton Sea and glossy groves of date palms and orange trees to a vast open emptiness of sharp, varicolored rock. Saturday was brutal, all confrontation; the whole Group clustered around a campsite, sweat-slicked and half-naked in the heat, screaming at each other. By nighttime, Riggs was furious. Nothing anyone said was right. Everyone was fucked. Everyone was dead. "Maybe you need more stimulation," he said, abruptly. "Come on." A number of them crowded into his Land Rover. Riggs veered out into the desert, then stopped.

"Get out," he said to Konni. She looked stunned, but obeyed. "I'm going to let you off one by one and leave you until you can feel something," he said. He gunned the motor and drove away.

There were no lights anywhere. Even the yellow of Konni's hair was lost in the immense silent blackness. As she disappeared, one woman broke. "She could get lost; she could die out there, you asshole!" she shrieked, then burst into tears. Riggs whipped the car around. It took only a minute to reach Konni, but she too was screaming. Everyone was shaking, freaked. They were *feeling*—back at the campsite, Riggs seemed pleased. They could go to bed now; they'd start again in the morning. People unrolled their sleeping bags. Riggs set up his bed atop the Land Rover. Then he had a private conversation with Konni. And when Riggs went to bed that night, she went with him.

The next day, the whole group was on edge. For hours, they confronted each other until one by one, people "broke through." Triumphant and intent, those who were "feeling" went after those who were not. There was a pause for a game of basketball, then everything began again. Russ broke through; so did Mary. "I don't feel you!" they screamed at their friends. The day passed; the sunlight thinned; evening came with the cool smell of stones. "All you guys are all right," Riggs finally told the group. "Except *him*." He pointed to Kevin. "And no one's going anywhere until *he's* made it."

Kevin felt the eyes on him. He panicked, searching inside himself for—*what*? He wanted to do the right thing, but what was it? *What did the others get that he didn't?*

"I—"

It was too late. Mary Farrell strode toward him. She drew back and hit Kevin across the face as hard as she could. Someone else followed, smashing with his fist.

Kevin fell on his face in the sand. Blood poured from his mouth. Everyone froze. Slowly, he pulled himself to his hands and knees and peered up at Riggs. The therapist winked. The attack was over, though Kevin didn't understand why. His insides felt twisted with shame. He was a failure. He would do nothing after this but try to change that. He would do nothing but work to get well. He would watch himself carefully,

every thought and feeling, every instinct. He would become
the best patient at the Center. He would never let this happen
again.

––––––––

Because he was honest, Riggs told his good friend Dominic
about what had happened between him and Konni in the desert. Shortly afterward, Riggs and his girlfriend broke up.
Konni and Dominic separated, and within months, she was
living with Riggs. Neither Konni nor the two therapists ever
said anything about the matter publicly, but sometimes Dom
got tears in his eyes when Riggs kissed Konni while he was
watching, or even fondled her breast.

"I think it's fucked you do that in front of me," he said
once.

Riggs looked impatient. "That's just a feeling," he said.

––––––––

Once a week, Laydown. Once a week, Group. Through July,
the Watergate scandal filled the newspapers; enormous head-
lines blared words like *criminal* and *impeachment*. In August,
President Richard Nixon resigned from his office in disgrace.
The shock waves that shook America missed the Center community. If the rest of the country saw Watergate as a disillu-
sioning national crisis, at the Center it was just more confir-
mation of what they already knew: Everybody in the
"straight" world was crazy.

And through the summer of 1974, then into the fall, the
Center kept growing. The therapists hired a longtime female
patient to work as a full-time secretary, and registered with
the state of California as a psychological corporation. As a
result, patients with health insurance were entitled to reim-
bursement for their $200 a month post-Intensive therapy bills.
Those therapists who were actually licensed, like Joe and Lee,

signed claims for therapists who were not. (No matter how little Center therapists and patients cared about licensing, the truth was, this was fraud.) A new effort to train patients to become full-fledged therapists began as well; everyone who'd started working with Jerry and Steve several years earlier had found it so difficult to bust people as hard as they were asked to that they'd all failed the program.

Other attempts at legitimization were continuing. Joe and Riggs contributed an essay to an academic anthology, and Riggs completed and turned in a 500-page doctoral dissertation arguing that participation in Feeling Therapy resulted in a new kind of dream, one that completely changed patients' lives. Most important, Joe, Jerry, and Riggs were hard at work writing a book that would explain Feeling Therapy to the world and finally free them from the ghost of Arthur Janov. (After all this time, patients still showed up at the Center expecting to primal.)

When the Feeling Therapists wrote and talked about their theories, they openly admitted that their methods were radical. Nor did they hide an outright arrogant belief in themselves: Riggs's dissertation simply dismissed Gestalt dream interpretation, as well as Freudian free association and Jungian amplification, as old hat. And the bulk of proof for the therapist's argument that Feeling Therapy created a whole new kind of dream was based on experiments done on a few Center patients and on a single, extremely detailed case study of an individual described as "very likeable and well adjusted . . . a hard worker and very excellent thinker" who apparently was Riggs himself. (This less-than-rigorous scholarship didn't seem to bother anyone at UCI—Riggs's three-man dissertation committee, naturally chaired by Joe, awarded him a Ph.D.)

Still, in public the Feeling Therapists didn't talk about practices like naked Groups or sluggo, and for the most part their talk of therapy theory—descriptions of personality structure and the way disordering led to defenses—was a remarkable contrast to what actually went on at the Center. Even more remarkable, though, was that none seemed to grasp what was happening to their patients—namely, that the kind of blindly worshipful dependence that had made Kevin Fitzgerald write a poem calling his therapist God was running rampant among them.

Any psychotherapy professional knew the concept of transference. In strictly Freudian terms, it meant that a patient projected the qualities of a significant figure from his or her past onto a therapist. (This was one reason Freudian analysts remained formal and distant—theory held that transference was vital, so a therapist needed to remain a blank slate onto which a patient could project.) But as more commonly used, it simply meant that a patient came to idealize a therapist. And any professional knew that such idealization happened all the time: The very nature of a therapeutic relationship assumed that the therapist knew more than the (admittedly troubled) patient. Ultimately, anyone occupying such a dependent position would start viewing his or her therapist as larger than life. Most traditional therapists knew it was crucial not to misuse that worship.

The Feeling Therapists talked as if they had some understanding of how transference worked. They knew they encouraged it during Intensives by pushing patients to be dependent on their therapists. They seemed to believe they were being careful not to exploit it: In their 1972 Esalen lecture, they remarked that they had a rule that nobody could be asked to do any work around the Center until he or she had been in therapy at least nine months, because transference made people "want to do things for you. And it's really a bad practice to use people in any way because it takes them away from just being there for themselves." They also seemed to believe that because co-therapy (in which patients played therapist to each other) and Group empowered patients to help themselves, whatever transference existed was only momentary. "At the end of nine months in our therapy," Joe, Riggs, and Dominic said at Esalen, "people are independent of us."

But however good the original intention, that never happened. From the start, the patients who came to the Center were especially vulnerable to transference, for not only were they troubled, they were young, in the midst of the struggle to break away from their parents, and just discovering the terror of being alone in the world. The dismantling during the Intensive of whatever core of self they did have left them almost literal infants desperate for guidance—and the Feeling Therapy credo that therapists could "intuit" true feeling confirmed that their therapists were in fact perfect role models. Even the independence promised by Group was illusory. The hysteria of sluggo often make patients feel more crazy, scared, and confused than ever, and each Group's therapist leader essentially managed its members' lives. It was the therapist who handed out "assignments"; it was the therapist who decided who was doing well and who not; it was the therapist who let a patient know whether or not his or her feeling or bust of someone else was "real." ("Say more about that," a therapist might encourage. Or "Wait a minute; don't talk about him—there's something else going on here, with you.") When it came to determining "reality," it was the therapist's decision that was final.

By the fall of 1974, more than two years after Joe, Riggs, and Dominic gave their Esalen speech, the almost 200 patients at the Center revered and depended on their therapists as much as ever, and the therapists had made no move to disenchant them. Had patients retained some contact with the world outside the Center, perhaps the haze of transference in which they lived would eventually have dissolved on its own. At the very least, the non-Center world could have provided some perspective.

But Feeling Therapy had already decreed that that world was insane. And then, once again the therapy changed, this time in a way that made the outside recede even further and made the spread of unchecked transference even more dangerous. The therapists decided to extend the emotional closeness they felt with each other into a physical one: They formed a neighborhood.

———————

The change had begun earlier that year, when the house Dominic was renting on North Gardner Street in Hollywood was put up for sale. Dominic bought it. The action seemed to give form to the vague idea of "Joe, Dom, and I going off to live together" that Riggs had spoken of at UCI several years before. Since the Center's early days, its "community of therapists" had been spread all over sprawling L.A. But how much *more* intimate and close could it become if, like the Senoi, they didn't have to worry about traffic and rush hour?

Riggs cast his eye on the house next door to Dominic. Dominic's neighbor didn't want to sell her home, but then Riggs left his Doberman at Dom's for a few weeks. The dog howled constantly, as she always did when separated from Riggs, and the woman changed her mind. Soon, Lee moved to the block too. So did Joe.

Gradually, all the rest of the therapists moved nearby as well. Once they did, they began encouraging patients to take the same step. There was nothing chauvanistic about wanting to live with friends, Joe said. It just made sense: "You don't see many dolphins running with sharks and you don't see many cats running with dogs," he explained. "I just like to be around people with whom I don't have to struggle."

The area the therapists had chosen was just north of Sunset and west of La Brea, at the foot of the Hollywood Hills. It was older, run-down, blocks of California bungalows past their prime, tired Spanish-style stuccos with faded red tile roofs, here and there enormous old mansions decaying beneath tired palms. It wasn't a glamorous part of L.A., it wasn't pretty, it wasn't even safe—each night, young hookers in hot pants paraded up and down Sunset, pimps cruised, and about the best you could say was that if you walked alone to nearby Ralph's Market after dark, you *probably* wouldn't get mugged.

Writer Joan Didion, who had once lived there, described it as a "senseless killing neighborhood."

Still, it did offer certain advantages. From there, it was only a ten-minute drive south on La Brea to the Center building. And its very undesirability made it affordable—large four-bedroom homes with generous front porches and formal dining rooms rented for less than $500 a month, which meant that when roommates shared, housing was downright cheap. And perhaps most important, this was Hollywood. No matter how Center people chose to live, no matter how they behaved or what they did, nobody would care. Center therapists and patients began keeping watch over the neighborhood. Now and then, a house would go up for sale or rent, and whenever one did, four or five patients moved into it.

The flier the Center had sent out to prospective patients talked of a program that lasted around a year. By now, some patients had been at the Center for more than three. But as the idea of community took hold, neither they nor new patients nor anyone else talked anymore of end dates. The benefit of getting well was not to leave one's friends but to live among them. Feeling Therapy wasn't simply a therapy anymore—it was a way of life.

Once a week, Laydown. Once a week, Group.

Mary Farrell was getting it again. She was rigid, Catholic; she wasn't fucking. At Riggs's prodding, the whole Group started to laugh at her. Mary wanted to disappear. She was sorry for who she was; she was sorry that her parents and the church had taken her body from her.

"You *confess* your problems instead of *talking* about them," Riggs said. If she wanted to confess, he would help. He took out a crucifix. He'd be the priest. "Say 'I'm a cunt and I'm not sorry,' " he said.

"I'm a cunt," she whispered. She knelt, pressed her lips to the cross.

"Tell the church you won't give in to what it taught you."

"I won't give in."

"Louder."

"I refuse to give in to what you taught me!"

Riggs tickled her. "Enjoy it."

"I refuse to give in to what you taught me!" Mary choked out again. She found herself starting to space out and fought to stay in the moment. Feel what's inside. But at the new Hollywood home she shared with several Center men and women, she retreated to her room. She felt so *bad*. And she was starting to have crazy thoughts. Thinking that Riggs was cruel when his concern was the one thing of which she was certain. Thinking of quitting therapy, which she knew was a sign something was happening inside her. "If you've never wanted to quit therapy," both Joe and Riggs had said, "then we've not gotten to you."

She knew she should tell someone. Admitting her craziness was the only way to get through it. Yet the bust that was sure to come along, the annihilation. . . . Mary shut her bedroom door. She had a secret. A lot of people in the Center kept notebooks in which they recorded what they did in therapy. Mary had something far more personal, a diary. On nights like this, when she was filled with things she couldn't bear, she turned to it. "What's happening?" she scrawled in her big, girlish script. "What are they trying to do to me?" When the words were outside her, she felt better. The thoughts went away. She was able to go on.

"Hey," Lee Woldenberg had said to her approvingly, right after her Group's trip to the desert. "Riggs said you were really tough out there. He said you kicked some ass."

The girl who kicked ass was who she wanted to be. Each time she got busted, Mary could feel herself growing weaker and more confused; when she busted someone else, it was as if her body filled with clarity and strength. She would work harder to be that way always, be tough, like Riggs. This other self would stay on paper, hidden away. No one at the Center would see how far gone she sometimes got. How much it hurt. No one else was ever going to know.

Everything around him was changing, and Russ Gilbert was scared. He'd thought he was settling down after his latest girl-friend moved into the house he shared with his best friend. But after only a few months, the romance crashed and she moved back out. His friend stayed on, but he was beginning to get close to one of the new therapist-trainees, and Russ worried that he was going to lose him as well. Then he and his friend had to move: Over the winter, there'd been a heavy rain, the roof started to leak, and Russ had called the landlady to complain. She told him her own roof was leaking too. Russ was feeling very clear, and he knew he didn't give a shit about her roof, only that he was getting wet. So as a good Feeling Therapy patient, he told her. Said a few "Fuck you's" too. He and his friend got evicted and ended up in a rundown bun-galow court in Echo Park.

But the worst thing was the inexorably solidifying Center community. Everyone he knew was moving to Hollywood, and the idea of doing the same made Russ feel crazy. It was odd. For all Russ maneuvered through the Center social scene, dating, sleeping with women, for all he did OK in Laydown and Group, his inner sense of separation from others had never really gone away. The wall was still inside him, and being part of a *community* would make its presence unbeara-ble. Every day, people would come over to his house and he wouldn't know what to say to them. Every day, he'd watch other people together having a great time and feel shitty and wrong. He didn't know what to do, and it was hard to think—the constant ups and downs of therapy always kept him on the emotional edge. Then, for the first time, he got badly busted. One night, he was sick and missed a meeting with other Center Foundation researchers who were doing tension-reduction experiments. Afterward, Riggs and Werner blasted him off the face of the earth for not being "involved" enough in his work. After the yelling was over, Russ went home and wept until his throat ached. How could his friends suddenly turn on him like that? So they thought he wasn't good enough? He'd show them.

These days, Dominic was driving a Jeep Scout, and Riggs, of course, the Land Rover. Russ had bought a Chevy Blazer to be just like them. When Riggs put an old motorcycle up for sale, Russ bought that too. A few weeks after the terrible trip to the desert where Kevin Fitzgerald got it, Russ went back with a new patient, a guy he knew Riggs really liked. It was a weekday, and the place was empty. They opened the bikes up, roaring up and down, driving like maniacs. Then they headed off in different directions. Russ saw a narrow road leading up a hill and headed toward it, going fast, pushing the bike. The dry wind whipped through his hair. He hit the crest of the hill—and suddenly, there was another motorcycle coming straight at him. There was no room to maneuver, no time even to scream. He woke in the hospital. He'd been unconscious for a week. The doctor told him he'd almost died. There was major cranial damage that would have to be repaired with surgery.

During the weeks Russ spent in the hospital, a revelation came to him, something as unexpected and powerful as his early primal had been. People from the Center kept coming to visit. They rubbed his back, brought him magazines, and let him talk about what had happened to him and how he felt. And one day, when he looked at his comrades Russ felt a huge chunk of the wall inside him crumble. People were *good*, he suddenly saw. Everyone just wanted the same thing—to love and be loved. The people at the Center loved him. Why had he spent so many years trying to keep them away?

The pure simplicity of what he'd felt glowed in Russ's face. Everyone wanted to talk to him about it. Even Riggs got melodramatic, clutching his forehead and shouting, "God, you're breaking through!"

Russ believed he'd found an emotional reference point that would last him the rest of his life. That made him wonder what more there was for him in therapy. Sometimes, when he was alone in the hospital room, he thought of doing something different with his life. But when he imagined the outside world, his mind crowded with bleak images, a desolate, colorless moonscape, people with judgmental, unaccepting faces. He would never find friends like the ones he had here. Then, one day his roommate told Russ that he'd moved with his trainee buddy to a house in Hollywood. They'd taken all of Russ's things with them. It was done, and Russ realized he no longer wanted to fight. When he checked out of the hospital, he too moved to Hollywood.

By the end of 1974, patient households were growing steadily on the Hollywood blocks around the Feeling Therapists' homes, and the first newspaper story entirely about the Center appeared in the radical local *L.A. Free Press.* Feeling Therapy was called "innovative" and "remarkable"; Arthur Janov's name was mentioned only once. Finally, it seemed, the break from the Primal Institute was triumphantly complete. There were more than 200 patients at the Center, more than 200 members of a community who lived and played and worked for a better life together. About two dozen of the men had started meeting for weekly pickup games of ice hockey and basketball. A few people were working together, buying houseplants wholesale and reselling them door-to-door in office buildings. Patients were teaching each other cooking and Spanish; there were plans to start a chorus, theater troupe, and dieter's club. A newspaper, the *Centerfold*, let patients share their poetry, concerns, and dreams, whether they were musicians looking for others who wanted to play or friends who wanted to start a community Yellow Pages, for "the more entwined our lives, the stronger we will be."

New Year's Eve, hundreds of people crowded into the Center building for a huge, raucous party. At midnight, a patient with a camera called for a group photo. Five people leapt in front of him, then ten more joined in, then another twenty, then there were more than one hundred people, all smashed against each other or sprawled on the floor, laughing, waving their hands in the air, shouting "Me! Take me!"

"These are *my people*," the photographer told himself, as tears rose in his eyes. Everyone at the Center knew that feeling. Outside was a society rife with competition, pretense, and lies. Here, in the world Joe and Riggs and the other therapists had created, was a place where the lonely, the scared, the misunderstood, and the confused could finally find a home. There was a special moment in the Center neighborhood each day just after sunset. The air would seem to thin and clear and the urban ugliness of Hollywood recede, until all one saw was a line of tall swaying palm trees leading to hills that blurred into the darkening sky. Even in winter, blooming jasmine laced the wind with sweetness. It was like magic—a promise that the past and its disappointments were falling away, and life was now about to begin.

"We long for our selves," went one poem in the *Centerfold*, written by a twenty-three-year-old carpenter from New Jersey. "The sound of our breathing / The sound of our hearts." On the paper's front page was a special logo—sunbeams radiating from a phoenix. "And he rose from his ashes," the patient-artist had written, "eternally young."

PART THREE
The New World

9

January 1975

Life in the Center community took on the luminous float of
childhood. The days flowed into each other, each the same as
the next. There was no time but the present, nothing that mattered or was worth worry but the effort to get well. Ambition
narrowed: "My three-month goals," one woman wrote for a
Group assignment, "are to lose five pounds, fix up my bedroom with nice curtains and pictures, be with men in a new
way, have more closeness with friends in Group...." Even
speech grew spare as patients reached toward each other in
the "feeling" language they'd learned in their Intensives—
simple statements stripped clean of adult artifice and even
metaphor. "I'm sad," grown men and women told each other,
voices hesitant and grave. "I get confused. I'd like to be your
friend. I'm scared."

Physical survival was easy. Post-Intensive therapy bills
were a high $200 a month, but rent divided among many
roommates was low, and everyone, even the therapists, lived
simply, sharing meals, driving old cars, and wearing jeans.

Anyone could get by working two or three hours a day hustling office plants door-to-door or typing or waiting tables. Those who didn't have careers were unconcerned with establishing them, and those who did often gave them up at their therapists' behests, lawyers and social workers becoming carpenters and gardeners. Being too caught up in intellectual matters and "in your head," it was explained, got in the way of feeling. No one worried—America was flush with money, and there always was another job for the asking if someone got fired for expressing a feeling like "I don't LIKE that!" to the boss or quit rather than have to work overtime on Laydown night. Besides, the community would always care for its own. Center people, Riggs said, were like a flock of penguins: Whenever a penguin was weak or in trouble, it went to the center of the group and the ones on the outside, the strong ones, protected it.

The analogy was easy for patients to believe, for the force and strength of the community were everywhere around them. Being at the Center meant living in the midst of a swirling, tumultuous crowd. Houses were a jumble of mismatched furniture, stereos, waterbeds, and mattresses on the floor, and were jammed to capacity, people sleeping two to a bedroom and, when that wasn't enough, in curtained-off nooks and dining rooms. Since modesty was considered crazy even bathrooms were mob scenes, someone showering while someone else shaved, someone else took a shit, and yet someone else came bursting in, nude and flapping and dying to share some news.

Social life was a constant; any evening could bring an outing with friends, a trip to the movies, a dinner of brown rice and vegetables at nearby Cafe Figaro. Monday there was ice hockey at a rink in the San Fernando Valley; Wednesday, soccer at Santa Monica High School; Sunday, Monday, and Friday, basketball at a local park. Weekends there were camping and surfing trips and big parties, fueled with wine and sometimes a few secret joints, everyone dancing, cocky, and loose.

There was always someone to help fulfill the therapists' encouragement to date, and there was always someone to sleep with, for a date virtually guaranteed sex. Affairs rarely lasted—it seemed impossible for two people to get along when both were concerned only with expressing their own feelings—but that didn't matter; there was always someone else. "Look around," the therapists said. "Experiment." And why not? Any woman could get the Pill or an IUD, and if she was unlucky enough to be the one in a hundred who got pregnant anyway, two years earlier the U.S. Supreme Court had made abortion legal. It was true that unbridled sexuality usually came most easily to male patients—those who'd always had lousy social lives were practically dizzy with their good fortune—but women racked up the numbers too. With the continual connecting and reconnecting, everyone ended up fucking four or five different people each month, and the sounds and smells of sex were everywhere in the packed houses. "Baby, baby," moaned moving naked couples, not even noticing when roommates strolled through the bedroom on the way to the bath. One month a clap epidemic roared through the community; later came crabs.

It was impossible not to get caught up in the closeness of it all, the intimacy and weight of flesh. Soon, it seemed that everyone at the Center knew everyone else as a friend, roommate, lover or ex, as if hundreds of people shared an even greater familiarity than a biological family, for their knowledge of each other was so physical: the smell of hair, the shape and texture of naked bodies, the sounds people made coming. . . .

Now that patients all lived together, life itself had become therapy. Signs with messages generated by some Group or Laydown session hung like artwork in every home's hallways and bedrooms—"I'M NOT CRAZY, I'M JUST LAZY." Whether at home, at play, or in bed, every interaction was about someone being real or not, expressing a feeling or not, confronting or not confronting people who were "defending" or "in their shit."

Even sex required absolute honesty. "That was nice," a man might say, raising his head from between a woman's legs. "At first I had the thought that eating pussy was dirty, but then I went ahead and I really got into it." Likewise, questions of personal taste were fraught with meaning. "I don't like that sweater!" one friend could shout at another. "It doesn't look good on you! Take it off; it's typical of you to wear clothes that don't look good on you! You don't take care of yourself!"

Each week, every aspect of social and sexual life was discussed in Group and assignments for improvement given. If one roommate complained about not getting along with another, the therapist could order them to eat lunch together, talk for an hour daily, or even spend the next week sleeping together in a pup tent pitched in the yard to remind them how much they wanted to be close. And each week, patients made sure to have additional contact with their Intensive therapists or Group leader, dropping by their homes to say hello, calling with updates on what was happening in their lives, getting approval before making serious changes, like breaking up with a lover.

Therapy wasn't easy. Everyone had made sacrifices to come to the Center, leaving hometowns, walking away from good jobs. Everyone was making sacrifices to stay. All were cutting pretherapy lovers and parents out of their lives, either because therapists thought seeing them would make them "crazy" or because their Intensives had left them with too much rage. "Mom and Dad," wrote one female patient, "you're total assholes—Nazi war criminals. I hate you more than I can feel, hate hate hate vomit vomit. . . . You pretended and played a fucking role with me—total assholes *motherfuckers* idiots—I hate you so much—I could kill you, stab you, chop you into little pieces. . . ."

Some women were even giving up their children. For all Feeling Therapy emphasized the importance of childhood feeling, the children that seemed to matter were those the patients had been, not any they had. Actual children took up time and energy; they needed so much. Kids, one therapist told a female patient, were basically "a suck." Besides, others routinely said, you can't be a good parent when you're still crazy yourself.

The assertions met with only halfhearted disagreement. It was hard to go to Laydown and Group and do assignments when there was a demanding child around. And perhaps it was hard for any young woman who'd given birth in the late sixties not to feel a certain resentment about the years she'd spent changing diapers while everyone else was kicking back to smoke dope. The therapists let the women know that that feeling was OK, that this was *their* time, time to discover who they were besides mothers. One patient's toddler went to live with some of her nonCenter friends. Another woman sent her children to live with her ex-husband up north, and one gave her five-year-old twins to her ex-husband to raise in the Midwest. Two more surrendered custody to their own parents.

Therapy wasn't easy, because living from "feeling" was like riding an endless emotional roller coaster—one minute shouting in triumph, the next busted so flat you couldn't move. Things could change in an instant, for there seemed to be no way to ever be sure what was a real feeling. You would come to Group thinking you were happy and the therapist would tell you you were sad. You would say something you thought was reasonable and suddenly people would be cursing and slugging you.

Yet for all its sacrifices and grief—for all its terror—therapy-centered life offered something far more compelling than anything its patients had ever known. After years that had felt empty and meaningless, they were engaged in a struggle of immeasurable importance. And they knew—because the therapists constantly told them—that their willingness to be part of this struggle made them special. Driving home from the Center after Laydown, they might look at the glowing yellow windows of strangers' houses and recall how, in other times, such glances were laced with longing and the desire to be someone else and have another life. Now, the reverse was true. There was nothing better than being here, where every-thing could be said and shared, where life was utterly without restriction. Late at night, after Group, men and women picked over produce at Ralph's Market, their faces twitching with secret smiles. "You don't know," they would think, glancing at the ordinary people around them. "You don't know where I've been tonight. What I've done." And each morning, when they awoke in their crowded homes to the sound of birds sing-ing and familiar voices, when they breakfasted with friends on sunny back porches, when they remembered yet again that *anything* could happen, they were filled with dread and won-der and a nameless thrill. It was like being four years old and today—every day—was Christmas.

Around mid-1975, Center patients got a letter from their ther-apists announcing a meeting in a local elementary school au-ditorium to talk about Group and community. "You know, we're not just in this short-term," Riggs told them there. It was time, he said, to think about real commitment—not just living together but planning for a shared future. That might mean starting a food co-op or other businesses that Center people would own and run so they could all work together and do things the way they wanted. It might even mean buy-ing a parcel of land in the country so someday they could all retire together out of L.A. Riggs smiled. "We're going to grow old together," he said.

Retirement? Old age? Murmurs of surprise, soon fol-lowed by slow nods, passed through the auditorium. It had been a long while since anyone had talked of Feeling Therapy as a finite program, but this was the first time a therapist had flat-out said patients would be at the Center the rest of their lives. But it made sense. There was an old hippie appeal in the idea of starting alternative businesses and pooling money to go "back to the land." And the closer Center patients grew to each other, the more remote and crazy all outsiders seemed. Patients even had a contemptuous name for them, NITs–Not-In-Therapy. There was no reason to live among them, now or ever. Once you had found true community, why leave?

Riggs's talk didn't lead to any dramatic changes. Retirement seemed a long way off, and no one had money to buy country land. But a patient-owned store called Fabulous Furniture, which sold funky items like beanbag chairs, started hiring Center people as workers. A twenty-two-year-old college dropout who was handy with cars began a Volkswagen repair shop in his home's garage. The carpenter whose poetry had appeared in the prior year's *Centerfold* went to work framing houses with a friend. Fledgling electrical and plumbing operations began. And Kevin Fitzgerald, who'd barely been surviving financially on the income of a one-man lawn-mowing service, decided to join forces with a friend to form a gardening company they called Autumn Leaves Enterprises.

The Center's own staff grew too, as the second group of patients chosen to become Feeling Therapists completed training and prepared to go into full-time practice. Riggs's lover, Konni Pederson, was one of the new therapists. Another was Jason Kushner, also twenty-seven, a stocky, hot-tempered dentist from Boston. Phillip Schwartz, a thirty-year-old former New York City accountant, was yet another; so were tall, lean, blond-haired Katie Stendall, twenty-five, and Matthew Lawrence, a dark, husky, 26-year-old from a blue-collar eastern family. Although Konni was only a few months away from receiving a California license to work as a psychiatric technician (a license that would qualify her to hand out medications on a hospital ward), none of the rest had any kind of clinical licenses or training beyond what they'd been taught at the Center. In fact, before the Center none had even thought about wanting to do therapy. And none quite understood why they'd been chosen for this honor; certainly they themselves didn't feel entirely "sane." Even Konni, a former model who had looks that evoked adjectives like breathtaking seemed to have no confidence, inner strength, or sense of herself.

The new therapists were called "junior" therapists. And despite all earlier talk of everyone being equally qualified to help friends, whereas Joe, Riggs, Jerry, Lee, Dominic, Steve, Carole, and Werner—who were now being called the "founders"—were co-owners of the Center and shared its profits, the juniors were paid a low salary. With their addition, the Center was able to admit fourteen rather than eight new patients each month.

The increase was important. Despite the fact that the cost of Feeling Therapy's first three weeks had risen from $2,500 to $3,500, a steady stream of people continued to apply to the Center: In a fragmenting, mobile, lonely society, the offer of friends, lovers, a place to belong, was irresistible, especially to the young. Some newcomers heard of Feeling Therapy through friends; some were patients' spouses who followed their mates into the Center in an effort to preserve the old bonds. The relationships almost always ended anyway, for it usually turned out that pretherapy ties had been built on craziness and pseudofeelings, not real love at all. Or that once both partners began being honest, all kinds of destructive secrets came out, a litany of infidelities, deceptions, and lies that made it impossible to go on. But even after couples who came into therapy together separated or divorced, both stayed. There was pain in that decision, for the Center world was small enough to guarantee frequent sightings of an ex with his or her new lovers. But what other choice was possible? What did either partner have now but a therapeutic quest so important that each had sacrificed the other?

Of course, not everyone who came to the Center stayed. There were always some people who freaked out on the harshness of the Intensive and quit in the first few months of treatment. (In fact, according to Center therapists' own estimates, their therapy had a 20 percent dropout rate, 13 percent in the first month and 7 percent within the first six.) A few left because they were homosexual, and didn't take to the fact that Feeling Therapists, like their primal predecessors, saw this as deeply pathological. Outside, a movement for gay liberation was in full flower; at the Center, therapists talked disparagingly about "fags," and Riggs often did less-than-flattering imitations of homosexual mannerisms. And a substantial number of patients left or were kicked out because their work lives were so erratic they couldn't pay their bills. (Although therapists often threatened to throw patients out of the Center for being "crazy," such expulsions rarely took place.)

But about a third of those people who entered the Center never left. Friends "couldn't afford" to let their friends quit Feeling Therapy, the therapists continually stressed, "We are a source of life for one another." And as the Center population grew, its households spread north, beyond Hollywood Boulevard toward the hills; a few blocks east; four blocks west. . . . In the spring of 1975, the founders even came up with a way to give the neighborhood a real feeling of permanence. One afternoon, they and dozens of patients tore down the garage behind Lee's house to make room for a basketball half-court. The court would be like a community park—everyone could come play and, of course, watch the therapists, so they could learn to "model" the way they interacted with each other.

Some of the founders also showed signs of settling down. Joe and Gina had reconciled and were living together again; their daughter was now nine. Jerry was deeply involved with a new woman, a patient who was sweet and voluptuous but rather meek and quiet, very different from the assertive Linda. Werner and his patient-girlfriend, Julia, had moved in with Riggs and Konni—whose own relationship was so well established that Konni's daughter, now five, had returned to live with them. None of the women patients who'd sent away their kids let themselves think about why two therapists' children were the only ones in the neighborhood. And although it was considered bizarre and scandalous that Joe's wife still refused to come into therapy, no one pointed out that Joe had gone back to Gina, while their own relationships with nontherapy mates always ended up severed.

Style on Gardner Street was changing too. Compared with their colleagues in private practice, none of the Feeling Therapists was earning much in the way of salary—perhaps $20,000–30,000 a year. But they were no longer struggling financially. Dominic decided to remodel his house; a patient who was an architect was doing the job. Other therapists were starting to trim their hair and dress more stylishly. A few bought themselves Mercedes, and Joe Hart zipped around in a yellow Porsche. The unabashed . . . *pigginess* . . . of the cars caused some real discomfort in the community. Some patients even confronted the therapists about it.

"How can you drive a *Mercedes?*" one ex-hippie demanded of Lee Woldenberg.

Lee got mad. There was nothing wrong with liking nice things, he said. Besides, once you took your needs seriously, you knew it was OK to treat yourself well. Buying a good car was one way to do that.

And still the households continued to spread. By now, the other area residents had grasped that something peculiar was happening to their neighborhood. Every time a rental house became vacant or one went up for sale, it immediately filled with a group of strange, hippielike young people who all talked in the same stilted sentences—"I feel *happy*. I'm SAD." And they were so *loud*. At every hour of the day and night, houses exploded with shrieks of "feeling" battles.

"Why don't you *talk*? I *hate* it when you're like this!"

"*You're* the one who's into your shit!"

"Fuck you! Just fuck you!"

"Shut up! I'm sick of your bullshit!"

"You're the one with bullshit! Get out of here! Get out! God, you make me crazy!"

"Ucch, I can't stand *listening* to you!"

"G-o-o-o-d. I *hate* this! I fuckin' *hate* it!"

Neighbors' windows would slam. Sometimes, if the kids

they dubbed "The Screamers" got too loud and it was too late, they'd call the cops. ("Those people are so stiff, so repressed," Center members told each other proudly as the black-and-whites arrived, "so out of touch with their feelings.") Mostly, though, the neighbors shrugged and coped. In Hollywood in the mid-1970s, in a neighborhood where one could walk from Famous Amos Chocolate Chip Cookies to Sindy's House of Joy to a storefront fundamentalist Christian church, and where even the mailman talked about "vibes," people howling "I fucking hate this!" were just one more fact of life.

10

May 1975

At least 50,000 Americans had gone through est training. Transcendental Meditation centers were handing out 30,000 new mantras each month. Actors like John Travolta and Karen Black were lauding writer L. Ron Hubbard's increasingly popular science fiction "religion," Scientology. In airports across the nation, deathly pale young men and women in orange robes accosted travelers, pleading for funds in the name of Krishna; on urban streets, blank-eyed counterparts dubbed "Moonies" hawked flowers to fund the Unification church of Rev. Sun Myung Moon. Anyone interested in quasi-psychotherapeutic improvement could choose from an almost infinite variety of new programs, including actualization, psychocybernetics, bioenergetics, existential analysis, transactional analysis, Rolfing, Gestalt, sex therapy, and Silva Mind Control. Four of the year's top ten nonfiction bestsellers were self-help books.

Midway through the decade, not even five years after 10,000 people were arrested in Washington, D.C., demonstrating against the Vietnam War, the U.S. cultural landscape had changed to a degree that boggled the mind. Widespread concern with the state of society had completely disappeared, replaced by a relentless, burning focus on self. Devotees of the new movements hailed the change as progress. Social critics like Peter Marin, Christopher Lasch, and Tom Wolfe, however, more accurately saw them as symptoms of pervasive despair. Just a month earlier, the war in Vietnam had ended a second, far more humiliating time, as the city of Saigon was taken by North Vietnamese troops and newscasts filled with images of Americans fleeing in total defeat. The price of gas just kept going up, and no one could now forget that at any time, small nations halfway across the globe could send Americans to their knees, begging for fuel. New president Gerald Ford had unconditionally pardoned Richard Nixon, so even those who'd doubted now knew that the rich and powerful were above the law, and two assassination attempts on Ford confirmed to panicked citizens already cheering "vigilante" films like *Death Wish* that on the streets there was no longer any law at all. Americans, Christopher Lasch would write in an essay describing what he called "The Culture of Narcissism," had utterly "lost faith in politics" and in "improving their lives in ways that matter."

Against that lost faith, the promise that serenity was recoverable through a perfected self set off a tantalizing glow. Perhaps the hopelessness so many felt had nothing to do with systemic problems but was a personal issue, solvable through individual effort. Perhaps all unhappiness and failure were self-inflicted and reversal a matter of individual will. It was true that some of the new movements' emphasis on the idea that *everything* was self-controlled sometimes went over the edge. The est goal of "getting it," for instance, meant realizing that "you are the cause of whoever you are and everything that happens to you," and even some of the most stalwart adherents had trouble with the notion that napalmed Vietnamese children and Holocaust victims had "chosen" their fates. Still, in general, the notion of being in charge was such a comforting one. So much of life seemed out of one's control. It felt good to be told it really wasn't.

In the midst of this time of depression and search, the Feeling Therapy manifesto, *Going Sane*, was published by Jason Aronson, a small but reputable house. Its cover was a full-length portrait of Joe, Riggs, and Jerry against a backdrop of deep blue sky. The three men looked happy, earnest, and confident, if a bit slick, with their wide-lapeled suits and open shirt collars. Riggs's old black glasses had been replaced by aviator frames and his hair cut in a currently fashionable shag. There were endorsements from some well-known professionals, including Joe's old mentor, Carl Rogers; psychologist Eugene Gendlin, whom Joe knew from the University of Wisconsin; Esalen Institute cofounder Michael Murphy, an acquaintance of Dominic's; and Steven Applebaum of the Menninger Foundation. "Hart, Corriere and Binder," Applebaum praised, "strive for and often succeed in achieving a sort of super-sonic dimension of feeling compared to which the feeling in other therapies is pallid."

The book's cover and preface—which announced that other Feeling Therapy volumes were already in the works—made it clear that although the founders always said they'd started the Center because they themselves wanted "more" from life, their ambitions had grown. *Going Sane* was meant to reach millions, revolutionize psychotherapy, bring the Center therapists the fame *The Primal Scream* had brought Arthur Janov.

But it didn't. Part of the problem was timing. *The Primal Scream* had had a disproportionately powerful effect because it reached a population largely unexposed to psychotherapy, and any first glimpse of the inner self always carried a special punch. Now, however, the public had been hearing about parental damage and childhood pain for five years, and some of the novelty had worn off. Moreover, as a book, *Going Sane* was rather a muddle. Its claims—that there were only two ways to be, sane or insane, and that "the average housewife in her loneliness and periods of desperation is no different than the fearful manic-depressive of the wards"—were bound to provoke outrage from many traditional therapists. So were replications of some extremely confrontational therapy sessions. In one, a therapist *orders* a male patient, described as twenty-nine and still a virgin, to go out and have sex. When he doesn't, the therapist screams at him, "You're full of crap! . . . It's okay to be a dead virgin?" At the same time, Feeling Therapy lacked the radical simplicity and promise of instant change that made primal therapy and new efforts like est so appealing to the public. Long technical discussions of "the cycle of feeling" were enough to put lay audiences to sleep, and the authors' declaration that therapy was a communal, lifelong endeavor was enough to scare the hell out of them.

But *Going Sane*'s biggest problem was the same one that befalls most first-time authors: lack of publicity. Aronson had released the book utterly without fanfare—no author tours had been arranged, no excerpts sold to magazines, no ads placed in the *New York Times* or the *Los Angeles Times*. The founders, however, knew that their book had an enormous potential market. In recent months, they'd been making periodic forays outside their Hollywood community—teaching a UCLA extension course called "The Freedom to Feel," lecturing at an international psychology conference in Montreal— and whenever they did, they got a warm welcome. At the Montreal conference, for instance, a group of local psychologists were so entranced by the notion of therapeutic community that they made plans to shut down their own practices and come to California to be trained in Feeling Therapy. That meant *Going Sane* would sell if people were made aware of the book. And since their publisher obviously wasn't going to do that, they would do it themselves.

Soon, junior therapist Phil Schwartz, with the help of a few paid patients and several volunteers, was running an in-house public relations firm called Phoenix Associates from a neighborhood back porch. None of the Phoenix staff had done PR work before, yet what they lacked in experience they made up for in enthusiasm. Through the summer of 1975, every Center patient's car sprouted a bright red-orange bumpersticker with the words *GOING SANE*; matching pins adorned their shirts. A simple plan, conceived by a patient who worked as a salesman, and approved by Riggs, ensured that the book would sell: The Center bought back publishing rights and unsold volumes from Jason Aronson, sold the copies to local bookstores, and gave patients assignments to buy them. Linda Binder got the job of seeking out media coverage for the Center, and it turned out that a little effort was all it took. By late fall that same year, thirty Los Angeles and San Francisco radio stations had put various founders on the air, and a number of television stations expressed similar interest.

Later, one would have to wonder if any of the TV and radio hosts who agreed to publicize *Going Sane* had actually read the book. Certainly, none did any serious investigation of its authors. If they had, they might have discovered that although Jerry Binder was listed on the book's cover as a Ph.D., he hadn't yet received his degree. Or that Riggs Corriere, who'd been doing Intensives since 1972, did not have a license to practice clinical psychology.

But perhaps such technicalities were considered irrelevant next to the fact that they made wonderful talk-show guests. At least, Joe and Riggs did. The contrast between Joe's fairness and cool and Riggs's dark intensity was strikingly dramatic, and the familiarity that had developed over their long friendship showed in a flowing give-and-take between them. They completed each other's sentences and cracked jokes, their timing impeccable. And what they discussed on the air was not Feeling Therapy's harsher side but tales of "doctors" who'd learned to heal each other and people breaking down the barriers that separated them—fascinating, catchy stuff. Although other therapists—including *Going Sane* coauthor Jerry—continued to do radio, by the end of the year it was Joe and Riggs who'd appeared on nearly a dozen L.A. and Bay Area TV shows. To many on the outside, they *were* the Center for Feeling Therapy.

More and more, those at the Center were sharing that vision. Daily life in the community had highlighted the fact that Joe and Riggs were different from each other in almost every way. Riggs always seemed happiest when surrounded by crowds of people; Joe liked to spend time alone. Riggs loved the fast-moving brawl of a basketball game; Joe favored golf. Riggs's adored pet was a Doberman pinscher; Joe kept cats. Riggs's lover, Konni—a beauty who was also a junior therapist—was considered a Center "catch," while most patients thought the uninvolved Gina Hart deeply weird. Joe even had some reservations about the new push to publicize Feeling Therapy. "I don't know," he told Russ Gilbert one afternoon. "Personally, I think Riggs is going way overboard promoting this thing."

Yet the old bond between the men was as strong as ever. Most of the other founders traded off who did co-therapy on whom, but Joe and Riggs almost always worked together, and a non-Center UCI graduate student who'd transcribed a tape of one of their encounters for inclusion in *Going Sane* found it so emotionally intense that she could work for only fifteen minutes at a time. The tearful session had ended with an audible embrace and kiss. And to patients, together the two men formed the Feeling Therapy yin and yang. Joe was the quiet, slightly mysterious sage who'd come up with the therapy's theory. Riggs embodied it so perfectly it was as if the Feeling Therapy ideal had been created with him in mind. He was the epitome of forcefulness, loud, vibrant, physical, always ready to speak his feelings without worrying how they'd be received or who'd get hurt. There was a certain humility to Joe, who sometimes went surfing with patients or took guitar lessons from them, readily admitting that they had skills he wanted to learn, but Riggs never seemed to need any patient's "help." (In fact, attempts to confront or contradict him often resulted in a cataclysmic bust.) If no patient quite understood what Joe wanted or was thinking, or even what universe he inhabited, Riggs seemed to have gotten where every patient wanted desperately to go, a place where there were no doubts at all, no fears.

"Riggs, how can you do what you do?" a woman in Dominic's Group asked him one night when he stopped in the therapy room to visit.

Riggs smiled. "I just feel good," he said, "*all the time.*"

All the founders remained powerful people in the eyes of the patients whose lives they oversaw. Each had his or her own fiefdom and identity—Werner as the Center research "brain," Lee as its doctor and "business genius," Jerry as a "thug with a heart of gold," and Dominic as "a small man with a big heart." Patients still imagined them to be both equals and the closest of friends. But the more Joe and Riggs lectured and appeared on TV, the more they told the world what therapy was and wasn't, the more they became the very incarnation of therapy wisdom and power, the more it seemed that it was they who led the other leaders. Patients who heard Riggs poke fun at Dominic, whom he sometimes treated as a comic bumbler, found it hard to remember that Dominic had once been Riggs's teacher. Those who'd come to the Center after 1974 found it hard to imagine that Linda, the media bookings coordinator, had once been a powerful therapist. Even the oldest patients, those who'd been at the Center before the era of Reality Group, had trouble recalling that Jerry—now Joe's graduate student—and Steve, who Riggs sometimes implied wasn't too bright, had once been the only credentialed primal therapists. That they had once been the ones in charge.

11

Mary Farrell sat in the front yard of Riggs's house, a clipboard on her knees, watching a small group of men at work. The sound of humming saws and hammering and the tang of wood dust filled the air. As the late fall sun thinned and shadows grew, she looked at the sky and frowned. She'd been sitting for hours, and the job she'd come to supervise still wasn't done. Her new responsibility was going to be bigger than she'd thought.

Now twenty-five, Mary had spent her whole life passing from one insular world to another: family, Catholic school, UCI, the Center. In her four years in Hollywood, she'd never held an "outside" job. She couldn't imagine why anyone would want one. Instead, she did small tasks for Riggs, such as walking his Doberman; helped the Center Foundation research team keep track of records; and showed Steve and Jerry how to file and organize material for their Ph.D dissertations. Everything she wanted now was at the Center. She'd made some friends, including therapist Carole Suydam. And after fucking a lot of different men—including some therapists—she had a real boyfriend, Jonathan Walker. Jon, tall and attractive, also was twenty-five, and had been raised Catholic in a strict, military family. He'd met Riggs at Kairos, when Jon was sixteen, and immediately become passionately attached to him. Later, he'd enrolled at UCI, where he was now one of Russ Gilbert's colleagues in the psychology Ph.D. program. After nine years of knowing Riggs, Jon still looked up to him, maybe even more than Mary did. In fact, it was because of Riggs that the two were together. The first time Jon asked Mary out, she naturally told Riggs about it. He got all excited. To make sure things went well between them, he gave them an assignment to get help from friends: Every day, they had to meet with one of Mary's roommates and talk about their sex life. It was awful; Mary hated the roommate they were supposed to talk to. And at the time, she hadn't been sure she even wanted to be in a relationship with Jon. Now, though, they were a couple. She was trying to make it work.

The best thing that had happened to Mary was being picked for a third-generation therapist training program—it was like a sign she was starting to get somewhere in therapy. She'd even gone back to school so she could get a master's degree and then an MFCC license. And when, as part of her training, she assisted Jerry in running his Groups, she was even tougher than he was. "You're fucked! You're not living your life!" she screamed, slapping people, beating them with her fists. Patients were afraid of her.

Then—disaster. Mary was so proud of the Center that one week she'd arranged to have Carole, Jerry, and Linda come to Cal State to lecture in one of her psych classes. She couldn't imagine anyone not being entranced by what they had to say. But the other students in the class laughed at the therapists; they booed. The three had been humiliated—and furious at Mary for putting them in such a position. Afterward, it was as if she couldn't do *anything* right; her training leader, Steve, was always accusing her of being "crazy." One day, he blew up. "You're spaced out again!" he yelled. "That's it! You're out of training!"

"No!" Mary had screamed, frozen in terror. A failure this immense—Riggs would crucify her! Steve had grabbed her arm and literally dragged her from the room. For days, she tried to make sense of what had happened but kept having crazy thoughts. "They say I'm insane, but it's really because of that other incident," she wrote in her secret diary. It took weeks of effort—and a lot of Group busts—before she understood just how badly she needed help.

In the summer of 1975, patients had been told to attend yet another weekly group, one in which they'd talk about their dreams. After Mary was kicked out of therapist training, she was further humiliated to be assigned to a Dream Group made up of patients newer to the Center than she. Everyone knew that the longer anyone was in therapy, the "saner" he or she was supposed to be. Still, one evening she'd found herself listening sympathetically as a Dream Group member, Jeff Langley, talked about the trouble he was having with his work. Langley, the poetry-writing New Jersey carpenter, was twenty-four, tall, fair-haired, and attractive. Mary liked him; she'd even dated and slept with him a few times. Now he was involved with a Center woman named Deborah Reiss, who made a living selling plants.

Langley was one of the patients who'd started framing houses after Riggs's talk on building community businesses. He'd worked for a while with two other patients, then gotten his contractor's license. Ever since, he'd been bidding for construction jobs, but was having a terrible time with the nitty-gritty of running a business, getting insurance, keeping books—the kind of organizational detail Mary knew she handled well. "I can help you with that," she'd found herself saying. "I think I ought to."

Jeff liked the idea, so after Dream Group, they came up with an agreement: Mary would work half-time for Jeff. The job would be simple, since Jeff planned to keep his operation small. He wasn't particularly ambitious.

Then, one night in August, four big, muscular men had

tromped into Dream Group looking for Jeff. "Riggs sent us," they said. Later, Mary would laugh whenever she remembered the panicked look on Jeff's face. He'd been sure he'd done something wrong and was going to get beaten up.

But it had turned out that Riggs thought these men were fuckups, crazy loser types who needed to get their lives straight. He'd assigned them to work for Jeff. None of them were trained carpenters, and none of them were thrilled about the assignment. Neither was Jeff. Neither was Mary. But what could anyone do?

To help Langley get his new construction crew in shape, Riggs made him a deal: The founders had torn down all the fences that separated their homes on Gardner Street and now wanted to put up a new fence, one that would surround all four houses. Jeff's men could build it, for practice. If they did, Riggs would help their business expand and grow.

No one questioned what kind of assistance Riggs could give the crew, or what made him a sudden expert on the construction industry, for it was assumed that therapists knew everything. And as the work began, it was clear that this bunch needed all the help they could get. The guys were so inept and inexperienced that they didn't even know enough to wear workbelts with pouches but instead kept stooping to pick up nails from boxes. The job took forever. When they finally finished, however, Riggs surveyed with approval the four-foot-high redwood fence they'd built. They would be starting a new company, he told the crew, Langley Construction. It would be a "family" business, a partnership, in which every worker got a share of the profits. Mary would be the manager and Jeff the boss. The two of them would meet with Riggs every week for guidance.

As Langley Construction struggled to get on its feet, Mary Farrell got a call from the head of another fledgling enterprise. Ron Arliss, a short, husky guy of twenty-two whose full face made him look much younger, was the patient who'd started fixing Volkswagens in his garage the same time Jeff

Langley had begun his framing work. He was a crack mechanic and got so many customers that he quickly outgrew the space. That made him start thinking about what his next step should be. Ron had dropped out of college, and he didn't know whether he should expand his business or go back to school. The choice confused him, so he talked to his therapist, Riggs, about it. Riggs thought opening a garage was the far better solution, especially if Ron did it with other Center people. So Ron and a friend became partners and opened a shop, Slick Auto Service. The trouble was, running an actual business was very different from puttering in a garage. Sometimes things were slow and money got tight. Slick Auto's checking account and books were all messed up. Again, Ron had gone to Riggs for help.

"Mary Farrell's doing a great job for Langley; why don't you meet with her?" Riggs suggested.

When Ron relayed the story to Mary, hearing Riggs's praise of her made her feel good. She also knew that if all Ron needed was to get organized, she could help him a lot. She agreed to meet with him once a week. For $5 an hour, she'd straighten out his books, review his work habits, and make the business run right. Slowly, her shame at not becoming a therapist eased and fell away. She had another role now.

The stark, barricade look of the redwood fence that surrounded the therapists' houses was softened a bit when another patient business, a plant maintenance company, put in flowers and trees. Still, the fence made it clear to everyone—both in therapy and not—that the therapists' homes were an enclave set apart from everything around them. The half-block of homes, permanently joined together, became the heart of the Feeling Therapy community. The place was always crowded and busy, with patients playing basketball, hanging out, or just stopping by to discuss a problem, share news, leave a greeting card that said "hi." Therapists and patients alike called the area the Compound.

Kevin Fitzgerald's gardening company, Autumn Leaves Enterprises, mowed the Compound lawn each week, and whenever Kevin looked at the redwood fence, he found himself feeling jealous of Jeff Langley. Kevin had had big plans for his business, but so far, all it had done was provide him and his partner with poverty-level wages. Still, a lot of good things had happened in the past year. In the late spring of 1975, he'd been taken out of Riggs's Reality Group and placed in one of Jerry's. At first, that had been hard for him. Jerry's people were newer patients, so being stuck with them felt like being demoted. But quickly his feelings changed. He'd always felt specially connected to Jerry, the way most people felt toward whoever had done their Intensive. A lot of patients had therapists who just plain liked them and protected them from other people's busts, and Jerry was that kind of refuge for Kevin. Although the therapist could be a real terror, he never went after Kevin. Instead, he told the others in Group, "Kev's a great guy," and pushed Kevin to be a leader. That turned out to be easy. People always listened to Kevin; since he was the oldest patient among them, they knew he had to be the most "feelingful."

Another good thing: After doing as much flopping around with as many Center women as any horny twenty-four-year-old guy could want, he'd fallen in love with someone in his new Group. Sara Wrightman was twenty-nine, a softly rounded Southern blond. She'd come into the Center early, in 1972. Back then, she'd been married. Once she went into therapy, she and her husband started having real trouble getting along. He came into the Center too, to try to change with her. Of course, they broke up anyway.

Being with Sara was a new experience for Kevin. He hadn't had a real girlfriend since high school, before his bad LSD trip. And Sara was a different sort of person—intelligent, unpretentious, and solid: a woman, not a girl. Until last year, she'd had a career as a computer programmer at a local university. (Konni, who was working with her, told her that the job was spacing her out and if she didn't quit, she'd have to leave therapy.) Kevin felt easy and secure around her. Even when he was feeling most mixed-up, she seemed to think he was a good person.

He himself wasn't so sure—of that or anything else. Since the day he'd been beaten in the desert, something had happened to Kevin. He could barely remember what it was like to speak or act spontaneously. Everything inside him—every thought, hope, recollection—everything he did, and every reaction he had to someone else came filtered through the prism of a single concern: *How am I doing?* My friend looks sad. *What kind of response will help me be healthy?* I feel a little sad this morning. *Is it OK to feel sad?* A constant refrain beat in his brain. *Is this a feeling? Is it the right feeling? Am I doing the right thing? Am I doing OK?*

How am I doing? Kevin tried his hardest to follow every therapy rule. If he and a co-therapy partner were given a specific direction, such as "Tonight, talk about your best friend," he was obsessive about making sure the discussion was long and complete. And he was scrupulous in his responsibility to others. When it came to friends, there was a Center saying, "Save Your Ass." Rather, "Save *Your* Ass." It was bad enough to have moments of personal insanity, but letting someone else backslide was even worse—someone who didn't notice when a friend was spacing out and bust her was sure to get busted himself. That meant it was crucial to keep tabs on people, not just in Group but all the time. Even when one wasn't absolutely sure if someone else was being crazy, there was no time to think about it—it was better to err on the side of confrontation, to bust a friend and later have to apologize, than not to bust at all.

Harshness still didn't come easily to Kevin, who regularly got it himself for being too soft. But, he had his moments, and they always made him feel powerful and good, the way he imagined Riggs felt. They also were one of the few times he felt OK about himself, for though no one at the Center admitted it—or perhaps even consciously realized it—whoever initiated a bust nearly always was declared right. Since everyone knew each other's problems and vulnerabilities, an attack usually had at least a kernel of truth in it, hit *some* nerve, which made it hard for the "bustee" to reject it completely or fight back without getting defensive. And though no one at the Center admitted (or realized) it, that gave the ethic of Save *Your* Ass its most powerful appeal: self-protection. The most sure way to avoid getting in trouble yourself was to go after someone else first. Kevin, like most patients, had learned to spot in other patients the signs of doubt, confusion, or withdrawal that would make them easy pickings. Or he could go after someone who always got in trouble, like Group member Janet Quinn, who had a reputation for being "difficult." Jerry hated her.

"You really seem to be dragging lately," he could say. "What's going on with you, Janet?" There would be her dumb lack of response, then the Group yelling, and Jerry going after her, squeezing her arm, maybe twisting it. The hunted look she got in her eyes, the busted look, no longer was enough to automatically arouse sympathy in Kevin. The violence in Group still scared him, the thought of being punished himself terrified him, but when it happened to someone else, he no longer was sorry.

––––––––––––

At twenty-eight, Janet Quinn had been in Feeling Therapy for three years. She'd never felt so committed to anything as she did to the Center community—not the classes in which she'd gotten A's at Penn, not the antiwar demonstrations she'd helped organize there, not the United Farm Workers with whom she'd spent a summer doing volunteer work. It was ironic, for when she'd originally come into therapy, she'd been looking for short-term psychological help. Like almost everyone else she knew, she'd graduated from college, then gone into an extended, unhappy drift, utterly unsure of what four years of studying sociology had to do with starting a "real" life. For two years, she'd miserably done secretarial work. Then she was dumped by a longtime boyfriend. The crisis, coming on top of her other unhappiness, made her feel genuinely crazy. She quit her job and spent whole days crying. She felt as if she had nothing, and the more she brooded, the more that seemed emblematic of her whole life. She was a fraud, someone who'd always looked and acted "OK" but had never been, inside.

The feeling went way back. All through her childhood, her friends had thought she had everything. Her father was a successful stockbroker, her mother the perfect housewife, baking bread and cookies and sewing all Janet's clothes. The family's suburban home, with its graceful, sunny rooms, had been the envy of all. What no one perceived was the chill in which the Quinns lived, the absence of play and laughter, the nightly dinners without conversation, the two dark, long-haired little girls, Janet and her sister, who spent hours alone in their rooms and were sent to bed without hugs or kisses. Later, in college, Janet had found that that coldness had frozen something in her: While others were able to touch and confide in each other, shout exuberantly, laugh or cry, she remained aloof, her emotions held in rigid check. From time to time, she'd despaired that she was permanently emotionally crippled. As her world crumbled, with the absoluteness of youth she became convinced she was. There was a void inside her that went all the way to her soul. She hadn't been able to afford extended psychoanalysis and didn't want to end up in a mental hospital—which she saw as the main options open to someone breaking down—so going to the Center, which she learned of after reading *The Primal Scream*, seemed a good alternative.

Feeling Therapy had taken her from the very start. It hurt

when her therapist, Lee, started off her Intensive by telling her she was just as emotionally dead as she'd feared. But that day, he also showed her she didn't have to be, pushing her to express anger at her parents, until something in her cracked and she was screaming, shrieking, in rage. She'd never known such intense feelings before and she left the building feeling almost high. The sun was dizzying, colors brighter than before—it was as if her skin had turned inside out until all her nerves were exposed. Her first Laydown was equally powerful. Lee had handed her a doll, and told her to play with it and pretend she was its mother. Janet had held the doll, cuddled it, and stroked its hair and face. At first, she'd felt ridiculous. Then, out of nowhere, an overwhelming sadness shook her. No one had ever held *her* this way. She could feel the pain of loss enter her like something with weight and mass, found herself wailing from the bottom of her heart. As painful as it was, being able to feel, to open up and express herself, was like a revelation.

"I see now that my parents ruined my life," she wrote in her therapy journal as her Intensive ended. "This is my only chance." As the idea of therapy as a short-term effort fell away and the Center community rose around her, she embraced it with her whole being. For the first time in her life, she believed she knew what family meant, what it was to be cared for. Unlike her parents, her new friends, Group members, and therapists took her feelings seriously. They wanted what was best for her. As bad as it was, even getting busted meant someone was paying *attention*. And she was caught up in the seriousness of what they were all after—being part of this effort to create a new world and way of life filled the void inside her to overflowing. She followed all the therapy rules. She no longer saw her parents or old friends or dated NITs. She'd found a job she loved, handling public relations for a television news show, but stopped working overtime when it interfered with spending time with her Center friends. She no longer worried about farm workers or spent hours writing to

Congress to protest this or that. "Save the whales!" Lee had jeered at her once. "Why don't you save yourself?"

Yet to Janet's disappointment, all her commitment and effort hadn't made her a successful patient. There were certain things she couldn't do—sluggo, for instance. The one time she'd been goaded into hitting another woman, she'd suddenly remembered hearing of an experiment in which people gave total strangers painful electric shocks, just because an authority figure told them to. She'd felt like a Nazi. She always felt uncomfortable saying her negative feelings about other people, and when she tried, usually came out with something dumb like "I don't like your hair" that got *her* busted. And though Lee had made it clear just how out of touch with her feelings she'd been, she never seemed to get beyond that point. "Bullshit!" Jerry often screamed in when she spoke up in Group. "That's not what's going on! You didn't do what you had to do this week!"

Now here was Kevin Fitzgerald, a real therapy good-boy, coming after her, catching her off-guard. "Janet?"

"What's happening with you?" asked Jerry.

What was the right response? Janet's stomach ached with tension. *Say something, anything,* a voice inside her urged. *He'll start screaming, but once you're crying, he'll stop and tell you what you're feeling and it'll be all over. Hang on—they know what they're doing, and someday this will get better. . . .*

Hang on: Janet knew she had no other choice. Even the most modest skills the Center had given her—such as the ability to feel real rage, to open up enough to say "I really like you" to someone—were things she had been dreaming of her whole life.

Hang on. No matter how hard therapy got for Center patients, the feeling that came when they were really in sync with the community, that sense of being chosen, invulnerable, supported by the strength of hundreds, was as addicting as any drug. And every day made it more clear to patients that they were part of something important. A new Center venture was flourishing, the Community Training Program, developed for the Montreal psychologists who'd expressed interest in Feeling Therapy after hearing the founders speak. The group was setting up a clinic in Montreal that would be like a Center outpost. The Center's research arm, the Center Foundation, was doing groundbreaking work. It had recently received a $28,000 "grant" from a patient, a thirty-year-old millionaire from a banking family. With the money, the foundation would expand its investigation into the physiological effects of therapy, and finally prove what everyone at the Center already knew: that expressing feelings changed not only people's souls but their bodies. "I'm so lucky to be here," one patient wrote to the parents he no longer saw. "All the tension being released from my body is going to add another ten years to my life."

So much progress was incredible to everyone, and the approach of Christmas brought the urge for a special celebration. One of Werner's Groups came up with an outrageous plan. Daringly, without first consulting Werner, they rented out the ballroom at the plush Century Plaza Hotel, and threw a party for the whole community, an elegant affair, complete with sit-down dinner and dancing. It was a huge success. The event felt almost like a prom, with crowds of young people moving awkwardly in rented tuxedos and formal gowns, and a photographer roaming the floor. But everyone agreed that the best part of the evening was the after-dinner talent show. Anyone who'd wanted to could perform and it was amazing how many Center people had real talent. Two women who'd studied music for years and had once planned to have concert careers played dazzling solos. A woman who'd once *lived* to dance performed a ballet. And some of the entertainment was just plain fun—one guy did a hilarious Nixon impersonation and three others whirled through a complicated dance routine

as they lip-synced to the Temptations. What really made people go wild, though, was one man's imitation of popular "glitter rock" singer David Bowie. Bowie had a hit song,
"Changes," that had always seemed the perfect Center theme,
and never more so than now: They were all changing so fast
the world would never catch them. Changes! The fake Bowie
swayed, the guitar chords crashed out, and everyone
screamed and whistled and threw napkins.

12

In late 1975, Werner Karle, Steve Gold, and Jerry Binder completed and turned in their UCI doctoral dissertations. All focused on the dramatic and positive changes effected by Feeling Therapy. Binder's dissertation even discussed a new "psychodiagnostic tool," the "Process Projective Assessment Instrument," which measured "feeling expressiveness" and had been used to test twenty men and women who were not in Feeling Therapy and seventy who were. The results, which showed that the longer a patient was in therapy, the better he or she did, were scored by five judges, all of whom were in Feeling Therapy. In fact, many of the objective and impressionistic judgments required to make this scoring system work, admitted Binder, could be "intuited" only by someone experienced in Feeling Therapy. The dissertation also included a 113-page individual case study that showed the "rich bounty of sane life" that awaited those who dared to live from complete feeling. The subject of the study bore a more-than-passing resemblance to Steve Gold. Apparently, no one at UCI noticed (or cared): three dissertation committees, each chaired by Joe, approved and accepted the dissertations and awarded the men Ph.D.'s.

In early 1976, the Center went national with the "Associate Program," which offered anyone who was interested in Feeling Therapy but not full-time commitment a way to get involved: For only $25 a month, people could communicate by letter and phone with a counselor who would listen to their concerns and give advice. Because offering therapy by mail was illegal, the Associate Program was called "educational" rather than "therapeutic," though that's exactly what it was meant to be. Nor were all the program's counselors licensed psychologists; many were Feeling Therapy patients who were trained and then paid to write letters.

The founders were reaching out on all kinds of fronts. Therapist Lee Woldenberg coauthored an article that was being published in *Human Behavior* magazine. The Center was publishing a new bimonthly publication, the *Dream Research Newsletter*, which talked about Center Foundation research and was aimed at psychology professionals. Another in-house publication, *The Center Newsletter*, was meant to reach a lay audience. The Center even got its first official logo, drawn by a patient who'd been an art director at a New York City advertising agency. It depicted a group of handsome wolves running side by side, their tails held high. Wolves, patients learned, were the perfect symbol of the Center community, for although the animals were thought of as dangerous, in reality they were intensely social, interdependent beasts that always stuck together.

No one talked about wolves' stability, but in Hollywood, composition of the Center's own "pack" continued to seethe and shift in nonstop upheaval. Households formed, then reformed, as therapists assigned patients to live with people they thought would be "good for them," or broke up roommates who'd gotten too complacent and easy on each other. Couples got together, split apart. A constant game of musical beds went on, even among the single junior therapists and founders: Junior therapists Matt Lawrence and Katie Stendall had started living together. Lee dated one patient, then broke up with her and settled in with another. Dominic's latest companion was Janet Quinn, who reveled in his attention as proof she wasn't so crazy after all.

Below all the Center community's flow and change, one thing remained a twenty-four-hour-a-day constant: therapy. During the year in which everyone had lived together in Hollywood under the ethic of Save Your Ass, it had become an almost relentless presence. It wasn't just that every week patients spent countless hours under the remorseless scrutiny of Group—the effort to feel *never* stopped. From waking to sleeping, patients struggled to keep their "feeling levels" high, doing assignments, "expressing," exercising, not just seeing friends but making meaningful "contact" with them. In kitchens and living rooms, on the sidewalk and basketball court, men and women spent whole days consumed in arguments over who was spacing out, who was falling back; challenging each other; crying. Their minds were never free of a tense, humming buzz—Am I feeling now? Am I doing OK?—and a cold, critical voice that continually passed judgment: That wasn't a feeling! You're not OK. You're fucked up.

"Tell your friends," the voice insisted like a merciless internal policeman, when certain thoughts arose, like *God, I hate this! I want to leave!* "Those are negative thoughts, crazy thoughts. You've got to let someone tell you what's really going on."

There was still tremendous joy in having a life full of friends—patients who got sick, for instance, never had to suffer in solitude, for people always came by to visit or leave gifts. Anyone who felt sad had only to mention it to have two roommates rubbing his back and telling him what a great guy he was; anyone who was lonely could make a phone call and someone would appear to sleep with her chastely, just cuddling and sharing warmth. But constant company had a flip side too, an oppressive weight. It meant there was never any time to *not* be energetic, feelingful, and "on," never any time to mourn or lick one's wounds after a terrible bust, to gather strength before a return to public life. It meant there was never any time to relax, for someone was always watching, waiting to report a slipup to therapist or Group.

Nothing was private in the community; nothing stayed secret. Even in love, Save Your Ass always came first. It was a woman's responsibility to report her mate for sneaking a drink; a man's to tell if he caught his woman breaking her diet. Even Steve Gold had gotten busted for supporting Carole's insanity when it turned out she was smoking, and whenever Matt Lawrence got crazy, his girlfriend, Katie Stendall, let Riggs know about it. A Center relationship also required publicly saying all one's feelings about a lover, even things that could hurt. "I really like her, but I keep thinking she's not pretty enough," a man might confess in Group. "I wish I was with someone who was better-looking." Even when it was determined that such thoughts were just craziness that masked *real* feeling—"You get scared of being close to your girlfriend," the therapist might say, "so you find things about her to criticize"—what had been said would lodge in a lover's heart like a thorn. What made it worse was knowing that everyone else knew about it too. Gossip passed through the community like lightning, until everyone knew everything— whose breasts sagged, whose dick was small, whose boyfriends said she was dry and passive in bed, whose girlfriends complained that he came too fast.

———————

By mid-1976, everyone knew that Mary Farrell and Jon Walker were into their shit. Jon kept thinking he didn't want to be with Mary, but running away from women was part of his crazy process. His Group leader, Werner, wouldn't let him break up. Mary wanted to stay with Jon, but she was pulling her Catholic trip again. The two were always fighting about sex, and their roommates were sick of having to listen to them.

Mary got a new assignment—fuck five nights a week; have oral sex twice. It didn't matter if she enjoyed it; she

should just *do* it. She obeyed instructions, but Jon kept letting
the world know how badly he wanted to get away from her.
He talked about sleeping with other women, even gaped at
the whores who paraded nightly on Sunset Boulevard. Mary
felt ugly, worthless; the rage and humiliation she felt seemed
to color everything she saw in others.

"You're so fucking dishonest!" she shouted at Kevin Fitzgerald during one Dream Group session. "Week after week,
you come in here and you never say anything bad about Sara;
you never say that something's bothering you. I don't believe
it! You're just a liar! Everyone in here is saying you're a liar!"

"Yeah," someone else said, "tell the truth, man."

"I'm really happy with Sara," Kevin said.

"Liar!" someone yelled.

"You're totally spaced out!" Mary said. "You've been
spaced out for weeks. Being with her is really fucking you up."

Kevin was very confused. He'd thought he'd been feeling
happy. "I don't want to stop seeing Sara," he said.

"You *have* to," Mary insisted. "It's not good for you to
be together."

"But—"

"Are you fighting me?" she yelled. "I'll talk to Riggs
about it. Maybe you need to be out of therapy."

Kevin panicked. Mary was Riggs's friend! She really
could get him thrown out! There was only one thing he could
do. "I'm fucked up," he told Sara. "It's not good for me to be
with you."

"Why?" she kept asking, in a voice that tore him up. But
he had nothing to say. Slowly, he walked back home. He had
so many crazy thoughts—that he hated Mary, even that he
hated Riggs. And he had lots of feeling—everything swirled
up inside him, too jumbled to figure out. All he could do was
cry.

———————

Everybody at the Center heard that Kevin and Sara were history. Everybody heard about it when after four months of

steady dating, Dominic abruptly broke up with Janet Quinn. Afterward, Jerry gave her an assignment: To feel how "cut off" she was from others, she could talk only when she went to work and then only about business. The rest of the time, at home and around the Center, she could only make noises. Janet found it unbearable. Trapped in silence, there was no way to shut off her brain. *Why had Dominic dumped her? Was she too crazy? Too fat? Was she dead?* Where Mary Farrell had reacted to attack by getting tougher, Janet just got withdrawn and depressed. Dominic started dating again, and eventually settled down with Linda Binder, but Janet was such a drag to be around that even her roommates got fed up. And no man wanted to date her, for who needed someone with such a bad rep?

Janet slowly fell into "undesirable" status in the community. Nor was she alone. No one talked about it, but everyone at the Center knew that hierarchies had formed among the patients. In part, they were based on tenure—it was almost impossible for a new patient to win an argument with someone who'd been there longer. Even more important, however, was personality. The standards of "sanity" demanded such constant perfection that everyone got busted sometimes, but those who happened to be naturally forceful, athletic, outgoing, and tough were busted far less than others. So were patients who somehow maintained enough sense of self-preservation that they hid occasional failures like failing to do assignments or falling back into old vices like smoking. (Even the most dedicated patients sometimes quietly defied orders. When one woman was busted for paying too much attention to her dog and ordered to ignore it, for instance, she sneaked the animal out for walks in the middle of the night.) And a small group developed a secret strategy that allowed them to stay part of the community they loved without too much grief: They faked it in therapy, not worrying if they'd actually "broken through" or "felt" something, just doing what they were told and saying the right things to keep off the heat. "Don't you see?" one woman begged her roommates. "This is just

like living with your parents! If you can't do what they tell
you, let's agree to lie about it!"

But some patients didn't want to simply stay out of trouble; they wanted to get well. They confessed every time they
did something "wrong," and if they ever tried to lie, they did
it so badly they were caught. And some patients just didn't
possess qualities valued in the Center world—they were small
or overweight or unattractive or stubborn or quiet or weak
and needy. They were the community's losers, and losing became seen as their main problem. If Feeling Therapy was a
program that produced healthy, special people, then by logic
those who couldn't do what therapy required were deficient.
Men and women who'd come into therapy seeking direction
in life, who'd wanted to come to terms with miserable childhoods, who'd just wanted to *feel* more now spent their therapeutic hours dealing with only one issue: their inability to
"make it" in Feeling Therapy.

Once a week, Group.

"Riggs told me I'm a loser," the man scrawled in his therapy notebook. "I am on his lifeboat. What will feel the best is
to row together. When I'm fighting, I stop rowing. I stop helping myself. I forget how much I want help, how good it feels
not to fight.

"Riggs told us if we stay around him he will cripple our
sickness. He will never let us run the show. It is our sickness
against his wellness. He will not let us stay sick."

"Who needs help tonight? Who wants to talk?"

Janet Quinn looked around her and tried to think of what
to say. It had to be something powerful and right-on, something that would start other people talking. Or some cutting
observation of someone else, to deflect attention away so she
wouldn't get slaughtered again. She had to get someone before they got her, for once someone made a criticism, she was
lost. If she argued, they would say she was "resisting," and
everyone else would agree, since officially "resisting" was her
problem.

What could she say? She'd gotten so careful about preparing for Group. All morning, she lay in bed plotting the conversation. She made phone calls to friends, talked to her roommates, had plenty of "contact" with other people so she wouldn't be spacey or dead.

"Janet?"

Jerry's voice came at her. Everyone's eyes followed. It was too late. She was going to get it now. She'd get told to crawl on the floor, take off her clothes, do something awful, and she would do it, she would do it, she would have to do it or she would have to leave therapy, which was death, so really there was no choice.

"Janet?"

Everyone was watching. She had never known dread like this. It was like her whole body had frozen, like her blood was screaming. It was like she was going to die.

———

More and more, it was as if a web was wrapping itself around the Hollywood community, its strands woven of equal parts intimacy and terror. Now and then, patients literally escaped, quietly fleeing the community in the middle of the night. Sometimes people tried to walk out of Group, only to be tackled at the door by friends. "You're trying to kill yourself!" the members of one Group shouted. "You might as well commit suicide!" But most Center patients never even tried to go. It was too hard to abandon the dream of community; there was too much shame in having to admit they'd been wrong to the parents and friends they'd denounced. And leaving evoked far too much fear. After years of therapy, Center patients knew that it wasn't just the world that was insane—they were too. "Without the Center," a therapist told one man who confessed to a masochistic sexual fantasy in Group, "you'd end up dead in an S&M parlor." "Without the Center," a woman was told, "you'd probably become a prostitute."

"Don't you see that you've shut down, gone dead?" a therapist screamed at six friends who took a vacation together and stayed away from the Center for three weeks. "Don't you know that if you don't take better care of yourselves you will not *survive*?"

Patients found such warnings easy to believe, for their lives had come to rest on two foundations: They were so lucky that they got to be at the Center. And they were so fucked that they had to be. After years of busting and turmoil, many no longer trusted anything they felt, no belief, not one impulse— not even the sensations of their own bodies.

"I don't know who this leg belongs to, but it's not mine!" one five-year patient told her roommate one night, her voice rising in almost hysterical laughter as she slapped her thigh. "I don't know whose body this is! But it's not mine!"

13

As patients continued their public efforts to meet Feeling Therapy's impossible goals, different kinds of struggles were going on in the more private lives of the Center's founders. They continually experimented with ways to make their lives more "feelingful"—recently, in defiance of "insane" notions of privacy, Riggs had torn down the walls around his and Konni's bathroom, turning bedroom and bath into one large open space, and two other couples had moved their beds into their homes' living rooms so they could talk more easily at night. But more important (and less visible), the power realignment that had begun with the move away from primal theory and escalated with Joe's and Riggs's appearances on TV was being finalized. In mid-1976, Riggs essentially forced Werner's long relationship with his patient-girlfriend, Julia, to an end. From the Center's earliest days, the two therapists had seemed to share a special, almost brotherlike friendship. A few terrifying times when Werner had had epileptic seizures while playing basketball on the Compound court, patients had marveled at the way Riggs sensed what was happening even before there were visible signs of trouble, rushing to Werner's

side, and catching him as he fell. "Come back, Werner," he'd
call tenderly, holding his friend as he convulsed. But tough,
outspoken Julia had always been a different matter. The strain
that had always existed between them had worsened steadily
in the time they'd been housemates. And when Julia heard
from a relative that her mother in Northern California was
sick and possibly dying and Riggs told her not to visit, she
did the unthinkable: She defied him.

While Julia was gone, she got a call from her Group
leader, Carole, telling her not to come home. She waited two
weeks, then returned, but Riggs wouldn't let her back in the
house, and Werner—forced to choose between lover and colleague—would not override him. "We could leave the Center," Julia begged.

"I've worked my whole life for this," Werner replied.

Defeated, Julia moved to an apartment on the outskirts
of the therapy neighborhood. As Werner began to date new
women, overnight her standing on the community fell. Werner had rejected her; she was obviously "crazy."

Several months later, however, after a co-therapy session
with Linda Binder, Carole had second thoughts about her part
in what had happened and, with Linda, paid a call on Julia.
"I feel really bad about how you were treated," she told Julia.
"There's nothing wrong with you. When I told you not to
come home, I was doing what Riggs told me to do. Linda and
I think it was really sick, and we're going to talk to him and
figure out what's going on."

Whatever the course of that conversation, Werner didn't
take his lover back. Instead, he moved in with the former wife
of a patient—a woman who was fair and pretty, like Julia, but
more docile. And Carole and Linda never did co-therapy with
each other again. Soon, Carole stopped taking new Intensive
patients completely, and it was understood that she, like
Linda, had realized it wasn't good for her to be a therapist
anymore.

Within the community, Werner's breakup and Carole's

demotion seemed just another instance of friends spotting friends' craziness, and stepping in to take care of it. The image of founder strength and solidarity was as strong as ever. But the truth was that by now, almost every founder had been "busted" in one way or another. Dominic and Steve had been publicly derided as "bumbler" and "dull." *Going Sane* coauthor Jerry had been neatly excluded from the book's publicity efforts. For all Werner had apparently agreed to leave Julia, in truth the act had torn his heart—despite his new romance, he regularly sneaked off to be with her. And after Carole stopped doing therapy, even patients noticed that she seemed smaller, somehow, as if something in her body had broken. The only two Feeling Therapists who hadn't ever suffered such busts were Joe and Riggs. And now, as Feeling Therapy evolved yet again, it seemed no coincidence that its new emphasis was pure Hart and Corriere: dreams.

It was time to shift therapy's focus, the two therapists said, because they'd made an important discovery: Freud had been wrong to worry about interpreting dreams' content. Dreams were not mysterious coded messages sent up from the subconscious but simply *pictures of feeling*. There was nothing "normal" about having the kinds of dreams most people did—people had messy, symbolic dreams because they lived messy, symbolic lives. But recent, dramatic alterations in the therapists' own dreams had taught them that when people lived from feeling, dream symbols disappeared. Instead, dreams featured people and situations from the dreamer's daily life. Colors were bright. Feelings were intense. The dreamer was active and expressed him- or herself normally and fully. The dreams made logical sense and were complete in and of themselves. Best of all, often they taught an important psychological lesson, one that needed no interpretation whatsoever. It was as if the nighttime world of dreaming and the daytime world of living connected in one seamless, satisfying whole.

In truth, the two men's "discovery" wasn't new at all. Its

thesis relied heavily on concepts of the Malayan Senoi Indians, who believed in seeking personal power through dream visions, and whom Joe (and plenty of other psychologists) had been studying for years. Moreover, in his doctoral dissertation two years before, Riggs had proposed the idea that Feeling Therapy changed dreams. Even the description "dream maker," which would be the title of the new book he and Joe were writing—this time without Jerry—had been in the dissertation. Why, then, all the fanfare? Perhaps the therapists simply felt it important to always be several steps ahead of their patients. In any case, through the spring of 1976 dreamwork moved to the fore of Center therapy.

It began with the first Centerwide weekend held out of town. For two days and nights (and at extra charge), patients stayed at a USC-owned retreat high in the San Gabriel mountains and did nothing but talk about their dreams and how they could be used to gauge progress made in waking life. The therapists taught them the formula they'd developed to help people make their dreams work for them. It involved four "dynamics." Patients, for instance, needed to examine their "ROLE" in a dream. How active had they been? Were they the center of attention, the star? They also needed to think about "EXPRESSION." In the dream, had they spoken or made noise? Said everything they wanted to say? What about "FEELING"? Were there intense feelings in the dream? Finally, "CLARITY" was important. How vivid was the dream? Was everything in it understandable? Did it make sense?

Each patient came away from the weekend with a set of graphs to be filled out daily. On one, patients measured the quality of their dreams, rating them on how well they'd met each of the four dynamics. On another, they noted each morning whether they were beginning the day in a plus or a minus way. UCI students who'd taken classes in which Joe taught about dreams hadn't known that experimenting with techniques of dream "control," or even just paying attention to their dreams, was bound to change them—they just knew that because of Joe, some powerful and spooky things happened to them at night. "Wait!" one student found himself calling out to a figure in a nightmare. "I know you're from my sub-conscious! What do you mean? What do you want?" Center patients had similar reactions. The more they followed the therapists' instructions, the more their dreams became colorful and vivid. Their dreams were filled with images of the community. Therapists appeared as figures of wisdom and power. *"I am over at R.'s house, watering his plants,"* one woman wrote down. *"He's getting ready to go on a trip and he is busily packing and talking with others. I try to say good-bye but he ignores me and I leave feeling drawn back. Then I am in a car driving to the building where R. works. He is doing therapy in a group. I barge right in and interrupt him. I tell him I am here trying to say good-bye to him. Then R. says to me, 'You are not trying to say good-bye, you're trying to say hello.' "*

The changes struck the patients as further proof that ther-apy was taking them somewhere exciting and new. Any night could bring a moment of change and revelation, the "break-through" dream Joe and Riggs had described as a "snapping between the conscious and unconscious mind." They said all the founders had had one. Dominic's had been the best.

"I was walking down the street," he'd reported. "Every-thing was beautiful. I started looking at trees. The greens of the leaves were intense. And then I realized that this dream was the same one that I had the night before. I turned to run. The way back was becoming brighter and brighter. In every direction I looked there was a wonderful and terrifying bright-ness. . . . I felt ecstatic and terrified. It was so bright I couldn't see. My eyes hurt so much they began to water. Tears started to roll down my face. I felt as if I was in a world of sadness. My eyes were closed and I began to see me. Lots of different me's. I saw all the roles and games I played. I cried more and more. I felt as if I had finally gotten to what I had wanted all of my life. I felt at home inside of myself. I was crying uncon-trollably. I knew I would never be the same. I knew what I had been running from all of my life—me. The more I cried, the happier I became. I was crying and laughing. I was laughing louder and louder. The louder I laughed, the more I could feel my chest expand. Everything seemed familiar. My friends were all standing around. I opened my arms to them shouting, 'Reality. I have found Reality. Reality, welcome to Reality.' "

By the time dreamwork took over the Center, patient Russ Gilbert had nearly finished with his graduate work at UCI. It hadn't been easy. He enjoyed helping Joe teach and doing research experiments, but found writing his dissertation excruciating. Of course, everyone at the Center knew that intellectual work spaced people out. Jerry had scared the hell out of his Group with descriptions of what happened to him while he was writing. "Riggs had to *save* me!" he told the wide-eyed men and women. "I was so DEAD I was nearly *GONE!*" Russ knew that would've happened to him too, without the help of his friends, who regularly stopped in to bring him doughnuts, rubbed his aching neck, and even made him stop work and jog around the block to wake up.

Getting this doctorate would be a good thing for him. After all his drifting and uncertainty, he'd have a sense of accomplishment. And a degree would make him a more important person at the Center. Because Russ worked so closely with Joe, Riggs, and Werner and had known them so long, others at the Center saw him as part of the therapists' inner circle. Russ himself was aware he was not. He wasn't close to Riggs, the way junior therapist Matt Lawrence was; nor had he ever acquired the sharp toughness of people like Matt and his girlfriend and fellow therapist Katie Stendall. And there were times, usually when he was being busted, when he felt the old wall resurrect itself around him, protecting—and isolating—him from the people he loved. The truth was, after all this time, he'd never gained enough confidence to see himself as someone who *gave* as opposed to *needed* therapeutic help. Like most older patients, he was involved in the co-therapy program, trading off playing therapist, then patient, with someone of equal tenure at the Center. But when he was the therapist, he knew he rarely reached the Center goal of letting his own feelings show him what to do or "talking from the heart." Instead, he just imitated the actions and speech of *real* therapists—the founders.

As Russ's dissertation neared completion and his free time increased, he was drawn, with a few other patients who had graduate degrees, into a brand-new training program aimed at teaching how to do Feeling Therapy in a workshop or outpatient setting. Someone at the Center had come up with a new idea, a kind of logical next step to the now-flourishing Associate Program. The Center was making plans to start an outpatient clinic. Joe ran the training, talking a lot about Feeling Therapy, history, and psychological theory. Russ loved the sessions, and the other trainees, who were years out of school, seemed to appreciate them even more, almost to hunger for them. Since being "in your head" had no place in Center life, the hours with Joe were the only time it was OK to talk about something as abstract as ideas. In fact, it was the only time any of these one-time good students even *thought* about such things. None of them ever spent time alone or had the urge to read or write anymore. Besides, some had noticed that a funny thing happened the few times they tried—they couldn't. Their minds kept skipping around; it was impossible to concentrate.

It was during this training that Joe taught Russ and his friends about Trigant Burrow. Joe saw Burrow, a student of Carl Jung's, as an intellectual great-uncle to the Feeling Therapists. Like them, he'd had no use for psychology aimed only at adjusting people to "normality," and like them, he'd traded giving and receiving therapy with several other like-minded professionals. But Burrow's effort, Joe stressed, had gone nowhere, because he'd failed to introduce his ideas to the wider culture. Knowing what had happened to those who came before them affected the Center's own development. After having taken their ideas public through their book, lectures, and talk shows over the past few years, now the founders were going one step further—instead of going to the outside, they would bring the outside to them.

Joe drew a picture that resembled a sales seminar diagram. On it was a funnel. The general public, it showed, might first become aware of the Center's existence through the founders' media appearances and books. A number of those people would "flow" to a deeper level of involvement with the Center, the Associate Program. Below *it* was a series of new programs, just getting started, "Dream Maker Workshops" that would teach the Center's dream theory. The workshops would be roughly comparable to seminars offered by est, Arica, and Transcendental Meditation. Through involvement with the workshops, some people would be drawn even closer to the Center, going through its Community Training Program. And from there, a given number would feed into full-time Feeling Therapy.

Dreamwork was the perfect vehicle for this expanded effort, since dreams were easier for the public to understand than "feelings." "Dreams," Russ wrote in his training notebook, "offer a way of cultural expansion."

All through the spring of 1976, Feeling Therapy's effort at "cultural expansion" grew. Founders gave successful presentations on their theory and work at California State University campuses in Long Beach, Los Angeles, and Bakersfield, and at UC Davis. Riggs, Joe, Jerry, Werner, Dominic, and Steve did TV and radio spots in L.A., Santa Barbara, Bakersfield, Chicago, Sacramento, Dallas, and Fort Worth. In April, the *Los Angeles Times* came calling. Apparently, its reporter never bothered checking the backgrounds of the Center "psychologists" and "counselors" she described as "trim and goodlooking." If she had, she might have learned that Jerry Binder still did not have a license to practice clinical psychology, nor did Riggs Corriere, and that Dominic Cirincione's MFCC license had lapsed. Instead, a laudatory story about the communal life and therapy practiced at the Center ran on the

front page of the paper's "lifestyle" section. Phoenix Associates' *Going Sane* strategy had paid off too. Nearly 11,000 books
had been sold, enough that Dell bought paperback rights. The
students in Joe Hart's classes at UCI were told that nine pub-
lishers were bidding for the right to publish Joe's and Rigg's
new book, *The Dream Makers*. Such competition, they learned,
was unheard of. (Since the therapists' "literary agent" was
actually Phoenix Associates' head and junior therapist Phil
Schwartz, the competition probably didn't really exist.)

As the year progressed and the Center's fame grew, only
one group remained decidedly unimpressed by it, and by Joe
Hart: the social science faculty at UCI. The enmity had been
growing a long time. Some professors had been angry ever
since Joe had turned away from the kind of "straight" research
for which he'd been hired. Many had been appalled by his
embrace of primal therapy and what they considered his ir-
responsibility at urging his students to "feel their pain." In
1971, counselors at the student health service had even reported treating a few kids who said they'd suffered mental
problems as a result. And in the preceding few years, Joe's
"Psychology of Awareness" class had been devoted exclu-
sively to discussing—some said promoting—Feeling Therapy.
Several dozen kids had gone from UCI into the Center, which
looked like outright recruitment, and it was *way* beyond the
pale for a professor to use his students for profit. The department had made its displeasure clear—in the five years since
Joe had gotten tenure, he'd published a number of articles and
a book, but hadn't received a single merit raise.

Thus far, no official action had been taken against him:
No school liked to fire a tenured professor, for it meant hearings, a scandal. But in late 1975, one had broken anyway. That
November, the student newspaper had reported that in order
to get an A in Joe's class, students were being required to
produce research material of possible use to Joe's graduate
students—or write and publish a review of *Going Sane*. A local
Orange County paper picked up the story. An investigation

began and, although Joe denied the report and no formal charges were brought, even those colleagues who still supported him were deeply shocked. What was it about the Center, they wondered, that had pushed an extraordinarily bright, promising scholar to make such a profound ethical shift? Early that spring, Joe and the department reached a "gentlemen's agreement" that he would resign at the end of the 1976 school year. Joe apologized to his nontherapy graduate students for not being able to continue to oversee their work. And he made certain that his therapy students finished up.

As a nonfounder, Russ Gilbert wasn't entitled to the assistance of the six female patients who'd been hired at low wages to help Jerry, Steve, and Werner research, type, edit, and illustrate their dissertations. Still, he turned in his dissertation on time. Then he worried for weeks about it. It was based on temperature, blood pressure, and personality test measurements he'd done on thirty Center patients over a five-day period and was supposed to prove that the longer a patient spent in Feeling Therapy, the less bodily tension and more expression he or she had. The trouble was, that wasn't exactly what the data said; in order to prove his thesis, he'd really had to stretch the numbers. He wondered if Jon Walker and the other Ph.D. candidate had done the same.

But no one questioned Russ's or his friends' work. That spring, three social science department dissertation committees, each chaired by Joe, awarded all three men their Ph.D.'s.

And then it was over for Joe. He was now thirty-nine, and had spent his entire adult life in academia. It would not be easy for him to get a job at another, equally prestigious university. Yet if the realization that he'd given up his profession for the Center grieved him or even gave him momentary pause, he said nothing.

A month later, in July, the Center held its first Dream Maker Workshop for the public at the Beverly Hilton hotel. It cost

$75—at the time, enough to feed a family of four for a week—but a good-size crop of searchers turned out, Associate Program members, people who had friends or relatives at the Center, and those who'd read articles about it. All day, the Hilton's carpeted meeting rooms rang with the sound of people sobbing and cries of "I *want*! I want *more*!" Everyone who attended came away with his or her own dream charts, and a souvenir three-ring binder, the same kind that full-time Feeling Therapy patients carried. It was gray and imprinted with the image of the wolf pack. The workshop was considered such a success that more were planned, including one in Chicago. Around the same time, eight members of a ragtag, unsanctioned primal clinic based in New Hampshire, who'd been corresponding through the Associate Program for six months, came to L.A. to undergo Feeling Therapy Intensives and participate in the Community Training Program. After five weeks, they went home to open a Center outpost as the Montreal therapists had done, this one in Boston. Meanwhile, some positive reviews of *Going Sane* and Center Foundation research papers were published in reputable psychology journals. Media coverage of the Center continued too—Joe and Werner were scheduled to begin a twenty-nine-week run as "The Dream Doctors" on KMET, one of L.A.'s largest FM rock-and-roll stations.

In a lot of ways, it was a summer of celebration. And in the midst of it all, Riggs and Konni got married. With all the sleeping around everyone had done, all the change, heartbreak, and divorce, this was the first time any Center couple had wed, the first time any founder other than Joe had made—or advocated—so permanent a commitment. The ceremony was small and private, but afterward, there was a huge, communitywide party in the Compound. Konni looked radiant, like a queen.

14

It had become clear to Mary Farrell that all her work to earn a master's degree had been for nothing. The founders were never going to allow her to be a full-time therapist. Finally, though, she could accept that. She had another, more important job—running Langley Construction. She and Jeff met twice weekly with Riggs to figure out guidelines for operation, so Langley would be a true *feeling* business. Riggs gave them strict rules: To maintain their closeness, the whole crew had to eat lunch together every day. Mary had to make the lunches, then eat with the men. The crew had to take a five-minute break every half-hour so they could talk and make sure no one was getting spaced out. They had be alert on the job and bust each other whenever doing so was necessary.

And that was the way it went. On construction sites, outsiders would stare, amazed, at the sight of burly, shirtless men dropping their hammers to slug each other and weep. Mary grimaced as she hunkered down on the ground each noontime with her sandwich, the sole woman amid a bunch of men who liked to swear, throw food, and in general act like jerks. But that was OK. What wasn't so OK was that the company wasn't making any money. Nobody on the crew was skilled, plus most of the work the company got was framing custom homes, so the men never established any kind of routine. And it was hard to get much done when you had to stop work every half-hour or deal with the problems caused by doing therapy assignments on the job. One time, a guy had had an assignment to "act like an asshole," and his constantly telling co-workers to "fuck yourself, you ugly piece of shit" caused several near-fistfights. The men on the crew were trying to live on around $2 an hour, less than minimum wage, going home after long days of intense physical labor to wolf down burgers made of "Super Blend," a funky ground-beef-and-soy product that was the cheapest thing sold at the local supermarket butcher counter. Soon, to help, Mary was managing their budgets as well as the company's, telling each man how to juggle food bills, car payments, rent, Group fees. And loan repayments—some were still paying off the thousands of dollars they'd borrowed to enter the Center in the first place.

Day after day, Mary whirled between working with Langley Construction and Slick Auto Service, still doing the occasional odd job for Riggs; attending her own Group, Dream Group, and Laydown once a week; dating; seeing friends; completing assignments; and keeping up her dream graphs. Absolute belief in the Center filled her with power and light. Unlike most patients, she still saw her family sometimes, but the visits were increasingly tense, and she was no longer allowed to spend any time alone with her beloved youngest brother, who was now fourteen—her parents were afraid she'd talk him into joining the Center.

On the job, she found she wanted *more*, and cast her eye on Slick Auto Service. She had done such a great job helping Ron Arliss that his business had really taken off. Almost all his clients were people from the outside who used him just because he was good, and he'd gotten so busy that he'd hired and trained a couple of Center guys. Mary still worked with him, but given what she'd done already, $5 an hour seemed like awfully low wages. She told Ron she'd be happy to keep giving him advice, but in return wanted 1 percent of his profits.

Ron got pissed off and went to Riggs to complain. "I don't want to give up part of my business," he said.

"What Mary's asking is cheap," Riggs told him. "She could get twice that much."

Ron discussed things with his partner. Mary *had* helped them. And they were both afraid of her. She was tough. She was really close to Riggs. They decided to give her what she wanted.

———————

Six Center companies were now in operation—Langley Construction, Slick Auto, Fabulous Furniture, electric and plumbing companies, and a new, three-person accounting firm—and all employed Center members. In fact, therapists often assigned particularly lost or inept patients to work for them so they could learn job skills. Still, they couldn't absorb everyone. Since the Center's start, patients without regular jobs had supported themselves by selling office plants door-to-door. There were a fair number by now who did it regularly. Sometimes they made pretty good money, but other times disorganization screwed everything up: When salespeople went out in small groups, no one knew who was selling where, and the same buildings got hit repeatedly.

One day, Riggs called in Jeff Langley's girlfriend, Deborah Reiss. Deborah, a lanky brunette with a rosy, heart-shaped face, was smart and aggressive—before therapy, she'd been a premed student—and had been making a decent living through plants for several years. "Maybe," Riggs told her, "it would be a good idea to *organize* the plant sellers."

Deborah thought that made sense. It turned out that a male friend of hers had had similar thoughts. The two of them teamed up and put together a "plant class." Each week, they met with the regular sellers, taught sales techniques, and, more important, divided L.A. into territories so people wouldn't run into each other. The strategy was a great success.

The sellers' incomes went up; Deborah and her friend made money on the classes. Pretty soon, thirty people were coming regularly.

While the plant business took off, Kevin Fitzgerald's gardening operation just got worse. He and his partner had spent a lot of money buying a big truck to haul their equipment. Then a whole crowd wanted to work for them, and suddenly they had a crew of ten full- and part-time guys. That would have been fine, except none of them were experienced gardeners, there wasn't nearly enough work for them all, and nobody was making any money. So when Riggs told Kevin Langley Construction needed another worker and he should take the job, he grabbed it. Jeff told the other workers that Kevin wasn't a great carpenter, but had been in therapy a long time and had a lot to add to the group. Kevin knew he was expected to be a leader and tried hard to be a "bust-ass" guy. He was always calling people down off the rafters and yelling at them. "You're spaced out; you're *totally* out of your body! You're going to get hurt!"

Going after his co-workers felt especially good when compared with doing carpentry, which made him feel like a backward child. And it was a way to care for them, just as he did his roommates. Kevin liked the act of *caring for*. A long time ago, when he was just a kid and it was silly to even consider it, he'd thought that he'd really love to be a father. Now, it was hard to see when—if—he'd ever get the chance. "I've been thinking about getting a puppy," he'd said in Group one night.

"A *puppy*?" the therapist said incredulously. "How can you take care of a puppy? You can't even take care of yourself."

———————————

You can't even take care of yourself. For the previous five years, hundreds of Center people had been coupling up and screwing their brains out, but there were still only two children in the therapy community, Joe's and Konni's. A number of women had gotten pregnant, but every one of them had come to understand that she was unprepared for parenthood and should have an abortion. "It's the best thing," Riggs assured the young millionaire who'd given the Center Foundation its large grant when the young man asked for advice after his girlfriend conceived. "You know, my Group at the Center is my family. I don't need any other."

Even women who'd sent away the children they already had never seemed to get "sane" enough to care for them. "I've been thinking I'd like to have my daughter come live with me again," one female patient told Werner.

The therapist shook his head. "No," he said. "You aren't nearly ready for that."

Just four years after Joe, Riggs, and Dominic had proclaimed that Feeling Therapy meant equality for all, it was abundantly clear that some Center people were more equal than others. For all the power imbalances that existed among them, Center therapists' domination over their patients was now absolute. Not only could they order their patients into the most humiliating kinds of assignments and Group performances, but they controlled almost every facet of their lives—where they lived, who they loved, what jobs they held, whether or not they reproduced. Nor did they hesitate to remind patients of that fact. "I gave you your girlfriend," one therapist informed a man. "And I can take her away."

Probably no one who'd known the therapists in their preCenter days would have described them as "bad." Nor was it likely they consciously intended to do evil now. But just as they'd failed to recognize the idealization patients felt for them as transference, the therapists didn't see the degree to which powerful *countertransference*—a therapist projecting his or her needs on a client—had been set loose among them. In fact, there was no way they could have. Since Feeling Therapy theory held that only therapists knew what was a "true" feeling and what was not, whatever a therapist wanted to do *had* to be the right thing. No therapist had to question what made it OK for him to punch one patient or tell another to put her head in a toilet bowl, commenting this was where she belonged. None had to ask himself why it always seemed therapeutically "necessary" that large-breasted women strip in Group; why it was acceptable to get involved with female patients and why, when those relationships fell apart, it was always the women's fault. None had to ask himself why those patients he happened to like were also those he considered therapy "successes."

Patients and therapists were now both caught in the web that bound the Center world, trapped in a closed, self-perpetuating system. The more patients were busted, the smaller and more regressed they got. The more regressed they got, the more they believed in their therapists. The more they believed, the more they told the therapists what they wanted to hear. "I need more therapy," one woman wrote on the "reapplication" to therapy form patients were required to fill out as they began taking part in the co-therapy program. "I believe I wouldn't stay alive without it. . . . Riggs—you are so important to me. When everything is terrifying and awful and I don't believe anyone can help me, I still think I'll make it if I can be near you."

And the more therapists heard how important they were, the more they believed it, too. By Christmas 1976, it seemed natural that every patient make a trip to the Compound, presents in hand, natural that therapists' homes grew piled as high with gaily wrapped extravagant offerings as the palaces of feudal lords. That year, one of Dominic's patients, a talented woodworker, built him a desk. It was a work of art more than furniture, an exquisite creation made entirely without nails, sculpted from a single piece of lustrous wood. Hundreds of hours of labor had gone into it. Carved into one side were the words WELCOME TO REALITY.

15

The Dream Makers was released in May 1977. It was a very different book from *Going Sane*. Although Joe and Riggs said in it that their dream theories represented "a mental health revolution," this book contained no radical pronouncements about the whole world being insane, no official-sounding discussion of "feeling cycles" or pretense of being scientific. It was informal, chatty. There were soap-opera-like accounts of the therapists' lives ("There was no glitter of Hollywood glamour in that therapy room in Los Angeles, only people") and pseudomystical references to the Senoi. And, to help the reader learn to use dreams, there were plenty of exercises that happened to be custom-made for magazine excerpting.

The Dream Makers's publisher, Thomas Y. Crowell Company, made some effort to arrange advance publicity for the book, sending bound galleys to Rollo May, Carl Rogers, and R. D. Laing, among others. None responded. But promoting *Going Sane* had taught the Center founders how to package *themselves* for the media. Now all those lessons went into practice. The *Los Angeles Times* had already run another favorable story about the Center, this one covering its dream research (and misidentifying Joe Hart as a UCI professor), and thousands of television and radio talk-show producers, desperate to fill airtime with interesting guests, proved only too happy to welcome attractive, lively psychologists who could talk about nightmares, wish fulfillment, and what it meant when you dreamed of being chased by a gorilla. In May alone, Joe and Riggs were on twenty TV and thirty radio shows in Boston, Detroit, Dallas, Akron, St. Louis, Cleveland, Cincinnati, St. Paul, and Washington, D.C. Six million viewers saw their appearance with Tom Snyder, and laughed at Joe's "revelation" of his and Riggs's catchy new nickname, "The Butch Cassidy and Sundance Kid of Psychology."

Butch and the Kid! Phoenix Associates had come up with the phrase, and it was the ultimate high-concept sales image. By June, *The Dream Makers* had been selected as a *Psychology Today* Book Club main selection, and the Center theory and way of life were featured on "Good Morning, America." "These people have heeded the advice 'Doctor, heal thyself,' " Geraldo Rivera reported from the basketball court of the Gardner Street Compound. "All of them coexist in what apparently is one big happy family."

In fact, what the Center "family" was doing was changing. In the eight months since Riggs's marriage, therapeutic emphasis on the healthiness of being single and sexually adventurous had gradually been replaced by promotion of monogamy. It was still essential to have sex a lot—at absolute minimum three times a week. But the therapists, all of whom had coupled up, said they now understood the importance of having a deep, intimate, lasting relationship with one person. Groups that once had centered on persuading couples to break up now focused on helping them stay together—sometimes even when they said they didn't want to—or berating single members to find a mate. (Having children, however, still wasn't part of the plan.)

Looking good mattered too. The importance of diet and exercise had always been stressed at the Center, but in the past it had been because movement helped people feel their bodies and because overeating was used as a substitute for feeling. Now, however, the emphasis was on achieving what the therapists considered "ideal" masculine or feminine bodies. Men were ordered to beef up, while women starved to reach slender "target" weights, running endless laps around the therapy community and meeting with fellow patient "diet partners" who told them what to eat and heard confessions of the smallest lapse. Being "responsible" was important as well. Group assignments included making a savings plan. Not having car insurance or failing to pay traffic tickets could bring down a $100 fine. (The money went to a patient's Group leader, who presumably put it in a special account; it was understood that whatever was collected would later be used for something like a Group party.) And being successful at a good—that is, lucrative—job was vital. "I don't want to hear about anyone getting fired for mouthing off at your boss!" announced a junior therapist.

Had anyone been able to step back and consider, he or she might have noticed that in a curious way, Center values were beginning to parallel those of the "insane" society the place had been designed to reject. For something was happening in America. Earlier in the year, there'd been a moment when it seemed that the country was on the cusp of an amazing transformation. Something strange had been in the air, an admission of the deep despair Peter Marin and Christopher Lasch had sensed two years before, an acknowledgment that defeat in Vietnam had changed things forever, and an acceptance of a United States that was less powerful but more human. A new president had been elected, a Georgia peanut farmer named Jimmy Carter, whose style was as simple as Richard Nixon's had been imperial. Even his televised inauguration gala had carried an undertone of terrible sadness, as pop singer Paul Simon performed "An American Tune," mourning "battered souls" and "shattered dreams." There had been a sense of new limitations in the very air of Los

Angeles, as a two-year drought tightened its grip and lawns browned and brush fires turned the sky orange and the desert moved in to reclaim its turf.

Then, suddenly, that looking toward a new future with regret-tinged resignation was gone. In its place came a sharp turn toward the conservative. Thousands of men began reimagining themselves as frontiersmen, buying assault rifles and combat pistols to defend their families against some unnamed holocaust, the more fanatic moving to isolated country homesteads and living as "survivalists." Men and women who'd lived decidedly secular lives suddenly became "born-again" Christians, promoting old-fashioned "family" values. And even more remarkably, a huge number of "baby boomers" were cutting their hair and passionately reembracing everything they'd spent a decade renouncing—ambition, materialism, privilege. A new Manhattan nightclub named Studio 54 gained notoriety solely on the basis of its snottiness— the doormen admitted only the very famous, beautiful, or rich. It seemed that every day, newspapers like the *Los Angeles Times* and the *New York Times* ran an op-ed piece by some "former sixties radical," announcing that he'd found mature fulfillment as a film studio executive or commodities broker and had discovered there was "nothing wrong" with making money. Even *Rolling Stone* magazine left San Francisco for the grownup world of capitalism and commerce in New York.

One could argue that this backlash was just the reaction of spoiled kids who had played at being poor, had finally gotten sick of cinderblock bookcases, and were now ready to reclaim their class privileges. Or that within American history, it was the communal effort and political activism of the sixties that was anomalous. But what was striking was that among those "boomers" quickest to change were a notable number of encounter group participants, of disciples of Arica and est. How could it be that the struggle for inner improvement had come down to endorsement of big salaries and three-piece suits?

At first glance, the conversion made no sense. Yet it had been quite logical. It was the same one taking hold of the Center. And it should have been predictable, for it traced back to the early Calvinists: To believe you have become, by whatever means, a "better person" is to believe you are part of an elite. Yet after a certain point, merely knowing you're one of the "chosen" ceases to satisfy. One's favored status must show. And what is the most obvious outward sign of being special? Why, what else? Being famous, powerful, and above all, *rich*.

———————

A new burst of Center expansion began. More Dream Maker Workshops were scheduled. Each week, the (unlicensed) leaders of the Center's New England outpost ran Dream Groups at the Park Plaza Hotel in Boston. Junior therapists Phil Schwartz, Matt Lawrence, and Katie Stendall applied to the state of California for MFCC licenses (though for some reason, junior therapist Jason Kushner never bothered). The Center Foundation's twenty-four researchers were continually traveling to present papers to a variety of professional organizations. The founders bought an old bungalow on Wilton Avenue in Hollywood so they could rent out rooms to new patients during their Intensives. Most notably, negotiations were under way to purchase a new headquarters, a huge building on Sunset Boulevard formerly occupied by MGM Records and right in the heart of the therapy neighborhood.

To help pay for all this expansion, the therapists were taking increasing advantage of a resource not every similarly ambitious group shared: a built-in supply of cheap labor. A woman who'd trained to be a concert pianist became Lee Woldenberg's secretary. Patients staffed Phoenix and wrote letters for the Associate Program. Others worked for free. The Langley Construction crew sometimes spent off-hours doing odd jobs around the Compound, cleaning out a garage, perhaps, or doing some painting. After all attempts to get celebrities to endorse *The Dream Makers* failed, Joe Hart solicited testimonials from two dozen patients, and, identifying the men and women with their hometown addresses, sent them to his editor as "reader comments." (*The Dream Makers*, a press release from Crowell later relayed, "contains ideas so powerful that readers across the country are reporting that merely reading the book has changed their lives.") Countless patient hours went into working the streets promoting the book: Patients were given small cards printed with advertisements and told to hand them out at grocery stores, tourist spots, and the beach. The Group that passed out the most would win a party at the Compound. And after a dream survey published in the tabloid *Star* drew 10,000 replies, more than one hundred patients spent a dozen hours tabulating them.

The therapists' decision to make blatant economic use of their patients struck at the Center's old ideal of equality in yet one more way. Soon came another blow. Since 1974, when the founding therapists first moved to Hollywood, their homes, and later the basketball court and Compound, had been open to all. One day, however, when patients showed up to play a game of ball, they found the gates around the Compound padlocked. The therapists, it seemed, were sick of having their houses used as common property, sick of being inundated with patients coming around looking for help, with the constant sound of a ball thudding against a backboard. Sure, everyone had helped build the court, but they'd gotten their time's worth.

Patients still were supposed to keep in close touch with their therapists, but after the Compound was locked, going to visit had a very different feel. There was nothing casual about it; patients had to make an appointment or knock and ask permission. They never knew if they'd be allowed in. And Riggs had gotten a new dog, another Doberman, this one named Trucker. Trucker attacked people. He bit.

It wasn't that no one noticed all the changes. *Everyone* hated handing out *The Dream Makers*'s advertising cards. It felt hucksterish; people the patients approached often looked at them with utter contempt. In fact, card passing was so disliked that it prompted rare moments of rebellion. Friends went out together and came to quiet private agreements: Cards meant for tourists at Farmer's Market got dumped in trash cans; those intended for patrons of the Los Angeles Zoo got fed to the goats. No one told and no one got busted.

Not everything seemed so bad, though. No one resented being pushed to get a better job—after so many years of being marginal and broke, the idea of having money was appealing. No woman balked at being put on a diet, for no American woman (Center or not) doubted she was too "fat." No one consciously resented giving time to Joe and Riggs's push for fame, for the more the therapists became celebrities, the more patients felt smart for having chosen them. The closing of the Compound *did* seem strange, but since "good" patients (and skilled basketball players) continued to be allowed in regularly, exclusion could always be blamed on one's own deficiencies.

And some changes were a great relief. Riggs, who'd done Intensives and led Groups for almost six years, was finally getting his clinical psychologist's license. In studying for the exam, he'd learned that experimenting with nudity was no longer as acceptable as it had been in the late sixties and early seventies. Although patients (especially women) still might be told to strip if therapists suspected they were gaining weight, undressing was no longer a regular part of Group. And in late summer, an even more welcome modification came down.

One day, Werner was running Group and busting a male patient for being "dead." Kevin Fitzgerald and a friend happened by. "Hey!" Werner called out to them, "Come in and give this guy a little sensation!"

It was sluggo time. As always, Kevin did the right thing. BAM! BAM! BAM! The next day, almost every inch of the patient's arms and shoulders had turned a frightening black. After that, though the therapists made it clear they didn't care what people did to each other at home, violence in the Center building had to stop. "No more hitting in Group," patients scrawled in their therapy notebooks, some of them almost weeping in relief. "Not ever; no way."

But if individual events and alterations at the Center could be judged as "good" or "bad," its system was simply a given, beyond any question or doubt. After living by Center rules for so long, cut off from the rest of the world, patients no longer even remembered they had choices or that there were other ways to live. "Do *you* know who your friends will be in twenty years?" Jon Walker asked the day he gave a guest lecture to a UCI class run by a nonCenter graduate student he knew. He paused. "We do."

In fact, as if to confirm that there *was* no life outside the Center, during the summer of 1977 an extraordinary thing happened. The year before, a number of patients had left or been thrown out of therapy for not doing assignments and/ or not paying their therapy bills. Now, these men and women voluntarily came back. What the therapists had told them about the outside world had turned out to be true. They'd felt lonely and lost without the community. The uncertainty of life without rules had been frightening. And worst of all, they'd never felt right about themselves. Even when you were away from the Center, it seemed, its voice stayed in your head. You couldn't shake the idea that you'd fucked up badly by leaving, that you were a quitter who hadn't been strong and true enough to stick it out. You were constantly watching yourself, doubting everything you thought and felt. And you couldn't stop fearing that slowly, surely, without realizing it or being able to stop it, you were going insane.

The members of the "Return Group," led by a junior therapist, were considered a new kind of losers. They had it really tough, got assignments like getting down on their hands and knees and begging to be allowed to stay in therapy. Once, everyone had to gain fifteen pounds in three weeks because one of the Return Group members had gotten fat. One woman had to wear a dog collar. But members of the Return Group didn't hesitate to follow orders. This time, they weren't going to quit.

Succeed, fail, elation, bust—the older Center patients kept spinning in the unending cycle that was their lives.

Once a week, Group.

Janet Quinn had been to a birthday party and eaten too much cake and it showed. Jerry weighed her in Group. She was up to 120 pounds, way too heavy for five feet, six inches, and he was furious. She would have to go on a diet and start an exercise program right away. The assignment was to run two miles a day, then work out for another forty-five minutes in any way she chose. Janet had always been athletic; as a teenager, she'd won waterskiing trophies. But now between working, volunteering, and doing co-therapy, she had so little time. After her jog, she'd come back to the house and just do jumping jacks. Up and down she went, over and over, for forty-five minutes, until her legs wobbled and her knees ached.

Kevin Fitzgerald had to find a relationship, *now*. He spent nights leafing through the Center directory, calling up women he hadn't yet dated, taking them out. The evening would go by, then he'd find himself in bed, his body performing, his mind always watching. Three days later, there'd be someone else.

"Isn't there anyone you'd like to go out with?" Jerry sometimes asked in Group.

If a woman Kevin found attractive was around, he'd point.

"Well, *ask* her."

"I'd really like to go out with you," he said. All the time, he could feel Sara's eyes, watching.

Finally, more than a year after things between them had

started to go bad, Jon Walker was allowed to break up with Mary Farrell. He stayed in the house they'd shared; she moved. For weeks, Mary's sense of failure lingered. She made a list of her ex-lovers, titling it "Men I've Let Go." "Why couldn't I let them love me?" she wrote. "It's almost too late for me."

Like many of the other women, Mary had been put on a diet, and at five feet, seven inches was down to 105 pounds, less than she'd weighed since high school. Her cheekbones were sharpening; her tall body was turning all angles and edges; and her health seemed to be worsening. She had strained her back, and it ached constantly. For the last few years, she'd had tension headaches that now became migraines that struck around the time of her period. The pain was excruciating; she would lie in her darkened bedroom, unable to open her eyes or move. In compensation, she got tougher and tougher. She whipped the Slick Auto workers into shape, teaching them to take breaks to talk about their feelings, pushing them to drink protein shakes in the morning the way Riggs said they ought to do. She arranged nap times in the afternoon, set up work hours that wouldn't conflict with therapy, and told Ron Arliss and his partner which patients had been assigned by therapists to work for them. Any violation of the rules resulted in fines.

She came down even harder on the Langley crew. The men needed order, precision. The company owned no heavy equipment, so when wood had to be moved, it was done by hand and the guys were so *slow*. "Hurry up!" she'd scream as one man carried stacks of plywood from one place to another. She brought a stopwatch to the site and sat on a chair, timing him. "You did it faster last time!" The man was twenty-seven and muscular, but the sweat poured down his neck. It was summer in Los Angeles, hot and smoggy, and he was barely earning enough to eat. "Faster!" Mary would scream, Riggs's words ringing in her head. "You can do it! There *are* no limitations!"

Once a week.

In their days as patients, the junior therapists had gotten yelled at and hit like everyone else. Now, power had changed them, the same way it had the founders. Matt Lawrence, who early in therapy had been sweet and sensitive, had become someone who could mock a new patient's "good-boy" smile by bouncing a basketball off his head over and over, until the man's glasses broke. Before nude Groups ended, Jason Kushner had run more than one session that ended with a woman patient having to take off her clothes so he could stare at her crotch. (The patients hated it, but, of course, no one described such actions with phrases like "sexual exploitation"; even Riggs had joked that "looking at pussies" was just Jason's "thing.") But perhaps the biggest change was in Konni. She'd always seemed "ditsy," the kind of pretty girl who made a point of not being too smart. Beneath that, though, had been a sweet vulnerability. There was nothing vulnerable about Konni now. She was the most beautiful woman in the Center, married to one of the two most powerful men. She didn't hesitate to give orders.

Konni's newest Intensive patient was thirty years old, the now-wife of the patient who was a millionaire. And she was pregnant again, and wanted the baby. "You have no life of your own; you just want to live through this child," Konni chided her over and over. "You're not ready to have a child. You'll ruin it." Konni gave her patient an assignment: She was to buy a life-size doll, diapers, a bottle, and enough weights so that the doll weighed fifteen pounds. Then she was to carry it with her everywhere she went. By the third week of her Intensive, the woman had changed her mind about the pregnancy. "I'm doing something for myself," she told her Group. "I'm going to have an abortion." Everyone clapped.

And through everything that happened, the Joe and Riggs media blitz rolled on—to New York, Arkansas, Iowa, Alabama, Kansas, Alaska. The "Merv Griffin Show" that aired nationally on August 25, 1977, marked their fifty-ninth appearance on television.

"Richard Corriere and Joe Hart have devised a simple, yet revolutionary, method of understanding dreams," Griffin told his television audience. He peered at Riggs. "You're a very young doctor," he said.

"Yes," Riggs said, grinning. "A very *smart* doctor."

The sixtieth TV show came the very next night, and was a moment of triumph. "The Tonight Show" was the ultimate in talk shows, and appearance on it a sign that any would-be celebrity had arrived.

"We want people to be able to *use* their dreams," Joe told guest host Roy Clark smoothly, then launched into a line he or Riggs always used, one that always got a laugh: "Freud's *dead*. We want him to rest in peace."

No one could stop Butch and the Kid! Lately, Phoenix Associates had come up with an eye-catching publicity poster based on the nickname. In it, cartoon drawings of Joe and Riggs were captured in the pistol-blasting pose made famous by Newman and Redford. These cowboys, however, were in a cemetery. And they were trampling on the graves of Freud, Adler, and Jung.

In September 1977, the Center for Feeling Therapy moved into its new headquarters on Sunset Boulevard. The building officially opened with a special Dream Maker weekend for the therapy community. Patients walked in the first night and stood still, awed by the change in their surroundings. The new, two-story building was sleek, tasteful, and almost corporate in feel. The carpets were steel gray, the trim chrome. A big wolf pack logo hung near the front door. There were lush plants everywhere. A huge "boardroom" held a massive round table with consoles for the founders. There were individual offices and so many therapy rooms that all Groups could meet in the same place on the same night. Upstairs was an audiovisual department that contained thousands of dollars' worth of equipment. Downstairs were a research laboratory and a huge auditorium, big enough that everyone in the community could gather together.

Patients poured into the auditorium and settled into the new seats. They were rowdy, making noise—Center gatherings were always loud, since people were so expressive. Before them was a raised stage. Jerry Binder appeared on it. Gone was the tacky, wide-lapeled outfit he'd sported on the cover of *Going Sane*. He was wearing a well-cut, expensive-looking three-piece suit.

"We have something at the Center that's bigger than the Irish sweepstakes and bigger than welfare!" he shouted. "What is it?"

Everyone knew *that* answer: "Dream Maker!" they yelled.

"Dream Maker handout card competition!" Jerry corrected.

A junior therapist came onto the stage. He too was wearing a suit and tie. "Once in a hundred years—" he began, then grinned as everyone hooted. "Once in a hundred years, a people rise to a challenge! They are a special breed of people! They are persuasive! They are powerful! They do not stop until their objective has been met and taken!" He laughed and thrust his hand in the air. "You!" he screamed. "You are that people!" Everyone howled and cheered. "In September 1977, there were 20,000 Dream Maker cards handed out!" the junior therapist shouted.

"Yeah!" the community yelled. "All *right!*"

"We have begun a march! A siege! The city of Los Angeles will be ours! . . . You have burned the name Dream Makers into the brains of thousands of people! And they will never forget you. And what's more important—you love doing it!"

Jerry came back and quieted everyone down. "Our flier promised you a great weekend," he told them. "It said that the dream makers of L.A. would be here—and here you are. And we told you that the most renowned psychotherapists in the world would be here—incidentally, they happen to be the people who do your therapy every week. I also told you that we'd have two special guests with us this evening . . . "

Suddenly, the song "Raindrops Keep Fallin' on My Head" came from the loudspeakers.

"Oh," said Jerry, "I believe I hear their theme song. Our guests have done 200 national TV shows. . . . They've had 50 articles written about them; they have a bestselling book. . . . Ladies and gentlemen, I present to you . . . our own Butch Cassidy and the Sundance Kid of contemporary psychology!"

Everyone was standing, roaring, clapping, as Riggs and Joe came out on stage in three-piece suits and cowboy hats. Finally, Riggs shushed them. "You've looked around and seen the building, and it's beginning to dawn on you that we're changing," he said quietly. "We'd like to talk to you about our community. Its birth took place on La Brea. This building marks its adulthood." He balanced himself comfortably against a table. "This isn't going to be a lecture," he said. "It's a visit. I want to talk to you about history, about how we all got to this place."

Out came the familiar tales, the almost mythical family stories everyone knew so well. "You know, when we first started looking for a place, we thought of finding a temporary storefront," Joe said. "But Steve and Jerry said, 'No, we need to get a place we can use all the way.' So we looked all over the city. We finally found the other building, which at the time looked very big. Especially since we didn't have any money. But Steve and Jerry said, 'We're not going to be little very long.' "

"At the start, we didn't know each other well at all," said Riggs. "We all lived in different parts of the city and didn't do things together very much. We didn't have the theory we later developed. And for the first two or three years, it was very bloody for us. We didn't know what we wanted, only that we wanted something more. And that's what we're going to teach over the weekend, now—how to get that something more. We want you to be successful. We *don't* want creeps for patients."

Riggs sat down on the stage steps. "The image this Center has now is very progressive," he said. "It's a new image. That image is spawned from the core of the therapy where therapists work together, they play together, they take care of each other. We want to see that happen more and more and more. So this building evokes new feelings from you. We're going to tell you about new expectations we have of you . . . of how the therapy's changing. There are more things that you're gonna have to do. You're going to have to begin taking more responsibility for the entire community that we have. Not just the community in your Group but in other Groups, and the outside community that you have as well. . . . We've taught you to go inside yourself, and from that inside, we want you to go back outside. So you really become what we call 'dream teachers.'

"We want you to test who you are," Riggs continued. " . . . So when you meet someone, it's not on their terms or their reality, not the continual insanity that is in the world. Because if you do what the world wants you to do, you're going to wind up last. And we don't think anyone in our therapy should be last in anything. You should all be winning. . . . Because you are different. You took all the available information and put it all together and made the decision to come here.

"You've done something that not a lot of other people do. There's not a person here who hasn't been through very, very bad times here. Down and out, your whole mythology of who you are and who you should be was completely blown away. . . . But you're here. And you're becoming experts in an entirely new kind of technology that not a lot of people will ever know. . . ."

"We want you to have a new image of yourself, as a *teacher*," Joe said. "As a person meeting people in the larger community and actually starting to affect what's around us.

Affect what's around us in Hollywood. Affect what's around us in California. And also nationally and internationally. We have very big ideas about responsibility."

"Yeah!" went the cheers. "Yeah!"

"I feel *special*," Joe said. "And I feel that this community is *very* special. When you are able to learn from other people and able to teach other people simple human things about feelings and living together, that's very, very, very special. People are out there waiting to be taught. . . . That's what living is about: being special and spreading that specialness farther and farther out. . . ."

"We have *beliefs*," Riggs added, his face radiant. "We think that anyone who got here is, in terms of evolution, the pick of the litter. You may have a smarter brother or sister or a stronger brother or sister or a prettier brother or sister. But you are the pick of the litter. Because you are here. Evolution usually works that you take a step, then you have a kid who takes another step. We want to fuck with evolution a little bit. We don't want to wait for children. We want you to maximize your own *personal* evolution. When you are a learner and a teacher, you are involved in your own personal evolution. And over the years, you're going to watch us evolve. Things are only going to get heavier and hotter and faster and better. We *expect* to be world-renowned. We *expect* to be rich. We *expect* to be famous. . . . It doesn't make sense to be anything less!"

And the crowd cheered until everyone was hoarse.

PART FOUR
The Circle Dance

16

January 1978

"I made $500 selling plants last week!" a man shouted out to Joe and Riggs.

"All *right!*"

"I made $1,000!"

"Whoo!"

Each Thursday, everyone met at the Center. Co-therapists worked together, some patients coaching their peers, others part of a new program in which experienced patients counseled (for free) those who were newer. Afterward, they all got together in the big auditorium for a "Postgroup" meeting led by Joe and Riggs. It was a rowdy time. Having the whole community gathered under one roof hit like a speed rush, a blast of collective power. Three hundred and fifty people in one room felt like the world.

Anything could happen at Postgroup. Sometimes Joe and Riggs lectured on psychological theory. Sometimes they wanted to talk about people's lives. What had everyone learned that night? What was going on in general? After the fervor of therapy, people were so wired they hummed.

"How're you doing?" Riggs called out to one woman.

"I got a hot, wet pussy!" she shouted. "And I'm ready to go to work!"

"Yeah! Yeah!" the Center men nearly fell out of their chairs.

"How're *you*?" Riggs asked a man.

"I *LOVE* being with my new girlfriend!" he yelled in the classic big, expressive Feeling Therapy voice.

"So what'd ya do this weekend?"

"This weekend?" the man boomed. "Well . . . I *butt-fucked* her!"

"Whoo! All *right!*" the men in the audience howled, while the man's girlfriend flushed and looked furious.

Postgroup was the Riggs 'n' Joe Show, and the two played it to the hilt. Sometimes they picked up on a new "Saturday Night Live" routine and took off: "We are two wild and craaaazy therapists!" Or Riggs would go on by himself, spilling extravagant monologues that were all digressions and jokes—one whole comic riff on whether or not turkeys had cocks. When the evening was over and he said goodnight, it was like listening to a talk show host signing off the air.

Showmanship made the Riggs 'n' Joe Show; their patients loved it. But just below the two men's easy jive was a hard, steadily growing ambition. When the therapists had told the community it was time to reach out and affect the world, they hadn't been kidding.

Intense efforts to promote *The Dream Makers* continued, and the book had sold well enough that Bantam was planning to put out a paperback edition. Short pieces about Joe and Riggs and their dream theory still appeared regularly in high-circulation magazines. In the last four months of 1977, the two had been on twenty-six television shows in seven cities, including three appearances on "Good Morning, America."

Meanwhile, yet another effort had begun to promote the Center itself. After the move to the Sunset Boulevard building, the Center had started holding periodic Friday-night open houses and lectures for the public. Tickets were a few dollars each, and patients were expected to sell them to anyone they could.

And, at Riggs's prompting, several patients had started trying to expand the Center's influence into another, decidedly new sphere—local politics—by forming the ostensibly independent Hollywood West Neighborhood Association. The association's work was fairly low-key, mostly minor attempts to clean up an area that remained hopelessly seedy. But its long-term purpose was more far-reaching. The Center community's unconventional lifestyle made it vulnerable to legal hassles over everything from noise to house overcrowding. At the same time, the Center now virtually controlled a small section of Hollywood. A neighborhood group would enable the community to protect itself and perhaps take future advantage of its geographic dominance by building some real-world political clout.

Then, in the midst of all the promotion and reaching out, Feeling Therapy changed again. On the surface, the alteration appeared minor. For the past few years, Center dreamwork had involved ignoring a dream's content in favor of measuring certain "dynamics" within it—how complete the dreamer's expression, activity, feeling, and clarity had been. Now Joe and Riggs added a fifth dynamic, "contact" with others, and applied the same technique to waking life. The dynamics would provide a kind of shorthand way to calculate therapeutic progress: By measuring how each of the five dynamics was operating in five basic life areas—work, play, sex, relationships, and sleep and dreams—patients could determine if their lives were working for or against them.

But to Joe and Riggs, the change wasn't minor at all. Expanding use of the five dynamics was in fact a jumping-off point for what they believed to be an enormous theoretical advance—they had developed, they told patients, a completely new model of psychology and adult development. At its core was the idea that there was one fundamental reason people were dysfunctional: Their personalities had grown rigid. Personality was formed in childhood, in response to specific conditions. But although the conditions of their lives later changed, people continued to follow old patterns and act in the same old ways. All that made any therapy work was that it forced people to break through their rigidity, to feel and do things differently. In essence, therapy "stretched" parts of the personality. By using the five dynamics, that stretching could be done systematically. Patients could learn readily which areas of their lives were strong and which weak. (For instance, someone might be a superb worker—effective, active, and clear about goals—but a passive, held-back lover.) Just as in earlier days having "feeling moments" enabled patients to recognize their defenses, now areas of strength would be used as touchstones for how all life could be. Weak life areas would then be made strong via "exercises" that pushed patients to break old patterns.

To some extent, Feeling Therapy had always done this. But it had also spent countless hours tracing the source of the old patterns, as well as the feelings that lay behind them. The new program said that wasn't necessary. Helping someone achieve a more satisfying life didn't require understanding *why* the person was stuck in the past; it just involved helping him or her acquire the "skills" to move on. Old-style Feeling Therapy had also held that therapeutic exercises were useless unless done with feeling. The new theory said feeling was beside the point—as long as someone *acted* in new ways, eventually his or her feelings would catch up.

Joe and Riggs called their new theory Functional Therapy. Its intellectual roots, they said, leapfrogged back over psychoanalysis and behaviorism to a midnineteenth-century school of psychology known as functionalism. The early functionalists, influenced by thinkers like Charles Darwin and William James, asked what *function* consciousness served. Was there a practical reason for it?

Their answer was yes. Consciousness, James concluded,

drawing on Darwin's theory of evolution, must have had a biological utility or it wouldn't have survived. In fact, he said, consciousness itself was geared toward evolution of the species. As people's environments changed and new problems arose, consciousness enabled them to choose new ways to react and behave. Consciousness was what guided individuals toward the ends required for their survival.

Through the Center's Dream Maker weekend the year before, the therapists had constantly described the changes wrought by therapy as "personal evolution." But it was a much larger kind of evolution that captivated them now. Darwin had said that adapting to the environment was crucial for survival. According to James, the purpose of consciousness was to help organisms adapt. Because people with weak personality skills were stuck in the past, Joe and Riggs were saying, they had not adapted to their environment. Using the five dynamics and life areas would enable them to do that. The program the two men had developed, then, wouldn't just to teach people how to "feel" more. It would advance *human evolution*.

An outsider would have found it hard to say which was more astonishing—the grandiosity of Joe and Riggs's claim or the fact that the therapists apparently believed it. At the same time, though, these program changes also seemed driven by more practical concerns. By early 1978, thousands of Americans were caught up in a new self-improvement trend, physical fitness. Joe and Riggs described their new theory as being based on a "functional" model, but they had a more colloquial way to discuss it as well: Their therapy was based on a *fitness* model. Just like a sedentary body, an underutilized psyche became weak and flabby. Joe and Riggs's program "exercised" it. The more a personality was exercised, the stronger it got. The result was "Psychological Fitness."

Psychological Fitness was a concept perfect for attracting the general public to the Center. Already, plans were in the works to spin a new series of workshops off the idea. Psych

Fitness theory wouldn't just push humankind further down the evolutionary path; it would complete the job *The Dream Makers* had begun. It would take Feeling Therapy into the mainstream.

———————

As the age of Psych Fitness dawned in the Center community, life changed. Almost overnight, therapy's old chaotic spontaneity disappeared. The first Tuesday of the month, in Group, all therapists announced that month's theme—say, "career"— and all later discussions, exercises, and assignments focused on it. On Thursday, all the co-therapists worked off a written script that spelled out what they were to say and do together, and what lessons were to be learned. Daily, everyone filled out charts and graphs that measured how well he or she was "functioning" and where improvement was needed. Here and there, the new program met with "resistance" from patients who thought it smacked of the assembly line. But the protests didn't last. "Forget the old ways; this is what works!" the therapists declared. "We've discovered how to get you where you want to be *faster*."

Meanwhile, as therapy changed, the ethic that drove the community, the values of the "environment" to which patients were supposed to "adapt," completed the transformation that had started with *The Dream Makers*. "We want you to be successful," Riggs had told everyone that first weekend in the new building. For a long time, the Center had defined that word in its own, radical way—success had meant having "lots of feeling" and being good at spotting and busting "deadness"; it meant being able to express every thought; it meant being vulnerable and able to cry easily. A few traces of the old values remained: Center patients would always get strokes for being loud, aggressive, and domineering. Save *Your* Ass was still a golden rule. But now, many of the characteristics that defined a successful center patient were no different from those defining a successful American. Success meant being attractive and fit, and, for women, thinner than ever. It meant having an active sex life within the bounds of a monogamous, traditional relationship. Above all, it meant giving "100 percent" effort to a job and making lots of money.

Gone were the lazy afternoons of the mid-1970s, when patients hung out together, content to drift and just get by financially. Gone were blue jeans, T-shirts, and clogs. Except for the communal homes, gone were the last vestiges of alternative community. Now, like the rest of the nation, by 8:30 each morning everyone at the Center was dressed and hard at his or her chosen (or assigned) tasks. Patients were back in school studying dentistry and computer science. They were selling real estate, training to be stockbrokers, working on movie studio backlots. And many, of course, were working for Center businesses or the Center itself. They were living the very kind of straight, work-driven life they'd once sought the Center to avoid. They were functioning.

At 4:30 A.M., Kevin Fitzgerald's alarm clock blared and he struggled to wake. No. Already? The sun wasn't up and the bed was so warm . . . He eased over, looked beside him. Like a miracle, Sara. In the eighteen months since they'd broken up, he'd dated and slept with dozens of Center women. Nothing had lasted. Then, one Saturday night, his whole Group had gone out together and he found himself sitting beside Sara. She too was single—she'd been assigned to live with someone for a while, but it hadn't worked out. Talking to her was still easy. He felt himself falling into her eyes, held by her smile. All the old feelings flared. By the evening's end, he knew he was completely in love with her. Probably he had been the whole time they were apart. Lots of people in Group were upset when they got back together; once a relationship had officially been declared unhealthy, people rarely changed their minds about it. For the first time in years, though, Kevin didn't care what was considered "therapeutic." He didn't know much about anything else, but he knew that what he felt for Sara was real. No one was ever going to take her from him again.

He dressed in the dark bedroom of his Hollywood bungalow, eyes aching with fatigue. Sara had been allowed to go back to the computer work Konni had once made her abandon, but he was still working for Langley Construction. In two years, even as inflation climbed into double digits, his pay had never gone up. Because Langley was a partnership, he, like all the other workers, was entitled to share whatever profits it made. But there never were any. New patients who needed work experience constantly got assigned to Langley. All of them had to be trained—and some were so inept that training didn't help—so the men had never become a truly competent professional crew. And because they were always desperate to make money, they underbid jobs and the workload got worse and worse. With everything else Kevin had to do—Group, co-therapy, assignments, house meetings—he was lucky to get five hours' sleep a night. He was always tired. Sometimes he was so tired he wanted to cry.

It was still dark and cold when he left home to go three blocks to the house where the crew met each day before heading out to the job. There, they lined up while Jeff Langley conducted an inspection to make sure everyone had the right tools and gear. "Fuckers! Shut up!" one of the women who lived there always screamed while they knocked around in the kitchen—her Group had decided she was too "private," so for nearly a year she'd been sleeping in the living room. After inspection, they all went out for breakfast together, then on to the job site. The workday began at 6:00 with setup, although the time clock didn't start running till 7:00. Right before 7:00, there was another check-in. All the guys had to talk about what they were responsible for doing that day, so their friends could be alert if they started to get into their shit and slip up on the job. Then time goals for doing work got handed out. There would be breaks every half-hour to make sure everyone was meeting his goal, and if not, to figure out why.

And then, in the milky early morning light, they started. The pace was relentless. Langley Construction was supposed to be the Center's flagship company, one that would show everyone what it was possible to do. Jeff and Mary Farrell wanted everyone going 100 percent, and pushed the crew harder and harder. Kevin and the others could feel the speed-up in their bodies, aching legs and arms, shoulders and backs. Hammer, carry, get the job done. Guys racing to meet their goals got hurt, wrenched muscles, spiked themselves with nail guns. Once, a friend of Kevin's got busted, and a few minutes later his power saw slipped and chewed up ten inches of his leg. Everyone talked about how spaced out he'd been to do something like that.

Hammer, carry, get the job done. "How am I doing?" Kevin thought, heart pounding. "Am I performing? Am I really going *100 percent*?" Tired. So tired. "How am I doing?" So tired. . . . His hand moved up and down; he tried to stay in control, to keep his mind clear. But every day, sooner or later a thought would intrude, someone would say something he thought was stupid, and it was as if he'd fallen into a hole. "What an asshole," he'd think. "I should tell him. But maybe *I'm* wrong, maybe . . . Oh no, I'm getting into my shit. I'd better tell someone. But I'll get busted. Shit, now I'm thinking. Someone's going to look at me and know something's wrong, then I'll get it worse. Stop thinking. But maybe I fucked up by not saying something. I should say something. Should I say something?"

His head hummed, rattled, his thoughts looping around themselves, wrapping tighter and tighter until sometimes, mercifully, everything shut off and his body took over, doing what it had to do while his mind escaped into a sweet, dark place. Sara, women, naked, their legs open, women, needy and wet . . . Three hours passed, then four, and the hammers rang and Mary Farrell yelled "Faster!" but Kevin was gone, off in a world where he was buried in warm flesh and nothing mattered and he just did it and did it and he was strong and in control and he got everything he wanted.

———————

As Center celebration of financial success increased, all the community businesses tried to meet the grade. The plumbers and electricians had a continual struggle—in large part because, like Langley Construction, they were always being given new workers who didn't know what they were doing. Slick Auto, on the other hand, was booming. Its owners, Ron Arliss and his partner, had even been able to buy the land on which they had their shop. And a relatively new company, Plant Power, was the biggest success story of all.

The business had grown out of the weekly "classes" that Deborah Reiss and her friend had developed to teach Center plant sellers selling techniques and keep them from poaching on each other's territory. The simple strategy had been remarkably successful, and each week more of the independent sellers had come for instruction. As the numbers grew, Deborah and her partner got an idea. Plants were "in" these days—every apartment and office had a creeping Charlie in the corner, a tabletop with a pothos ivy or wandering jew. Center patients weren't the only people selling plants door-to-door in Los Angeles; such part-time freelance work also appealed to students, drifters, and would-be actors. One of the biggest groups of nonCenter plant sellers was affiliated with a thriving business called Plant Power. Shrewd and bright, Deborah quickly grasped why Plant Power was doing so well: Whereas all the Center's sellers bought their merchandise from various wholesale outlets downtown, Plant Power bought its *own* plants, then sold them at profit to its sellers. If she and her friend could set up a similar operation, Deborah thought, they could make some real money.

Amazingly, almost at that very moment Plant Power's owners put the business up for sale. Deborah and her friend knew this was their big chance. They took on a third partner, obtained a $50,000 loan, and bought the place. Now Plant Power's old salespeople *and* those affiliated with the Center purchased their plants there. Deborah and her partners also made an informal arrangement to work side by side with two other Center women who ran a plant "maintenance" company: The women had contracts to provide long-term care for the decorative plants most corporations had in their executive offices. Now Plant Power was a full-service operation, teaching sales classes, selling plants, and arranging for their care. Under Deborah and her friend's astute management, it won some big accounts, and the Center therapists took note. Given how serious an operation Plant Power was becoming, they decided it needed their supervision. Werner became the company's unpaid overseer. He set up operating rules, scheduled business meetings and requisite therapeutic confrontations, and told staff whenever one of them was getting "crazy." And if workers disagreed, he had the final say about who was right. Unlike her boyfriend, Jeff Langley, Deborah Reiss didn't find that Feeling Therapy got in her company's way. Plant selling didn't require technical skill the way carpentry did, just persistence and determination. And people trying to earn money to pay for the therapy on which they felt their lives depended made for an incredibly motivated sales force. In the first nine months of operation, Plant Power grossed more than $1 million.

Functioning meant going 100 percent . . . The Center itself continued to grow as a business. The Montreal outpost that had opened in 1975 was still holding Dream Maker Workshops, and had announced plans to publish a French-language edition of the book. Members of the newer New England outpost

were ensconced in a former rug merchant's showroom on Bea-
con Street in Brookline, Massachusetts, running weekly
Groups of their own and regularly sending clients back to L.A.
for Intensives. (A Dream Maker Workshop they'd hosted in
October had attracted 200 people.) Feeling Therapy had even
made it to Europe: A group of German therapists heard about
the Center, enrolled in its Community Training Program for
Professionals, then went home to start a satellite 8,000 miles
away, in Munich. And a new department within the Center,
The Fitness Foundation, was creating four week-long Psychological Fitness Training Programs for the summer and a series
of one-day workshops to be held periodically through the
year.

But perhaps no program received as much attention and
effort as the Center's newly opened outpatient Clinic for Functional Counseling. Riggs was devoting a lot of his time and
energy to training its counselors; so were Dominic, Konni, and
Matt Lawrence. It seemed that for all the founders had emphasized the need for a lifelong therapeutic community,
they'd recently grasped an economic principle familiar to
more conventional therapists: When counseling was restricted
to an hour-long appointment once a week, one therapist could
see dozens of patients, each of whom paid a separate fee. After
seven years of operation, the Center had accumulated around
350 patients. In a fraction of that time, the clinic could serve
thousands.

Russ Gilbert had been thrilled to be chosen as a clinic counselor trainee. Nearly a year after he'd gotten his Ph.D. in psychology, the simple need to earn a living had driven him back
to the aerospace industry and the kind of job he'd entered
graduate school to escape. The clinic was his ticket—not only
out of engineering but into the upper echelons of the Center.
The seventeen other men and women who, like him, had been

picked and trained, would make up the long-delayed third generation of Center therapists. He would be working side by side with Riggs and Joe and the other founders. He'd practically be one of them.

The clinic couldn't go into business without patients, of course, so all the would-be counselors started looking for some. Those who already worked for the Associate Program called their clients. Some people who'd read *The Dream Makers* had written to the Center, asking for more information about its programs; clinic workers called them too. They even made cold calls, like insurance salespeople, to see who might respond.

Rounding up clients was all Russ could think about. Every day, he went to his engineering job, did the least he could to get by, then spent the rest of his time on the phone, hustling. No one bit, though his efforts went on for hours. Sometimes he marveled that he didn't get fired.

Some of the other solicitors were more successful, and a month or so after the clinic opened, Russ was assigned a few patients; he would sneak out early from his engineering job to see them. Although he did have a doctorate, Russ—like most of the other clinic staff, who called themselves "Certified Functional Counselors"—didn't have any kind of clinical license. He didn't worry about that—none of his clients ever asked. Nor did clinic work bring up any of the fears of doing something wrong that he'd always felt when he did co-therapy. At the clinic, there was no way to make a mistake. Unlike the situation in old days, when Feeling Therapy required a therapist (or co-therapist) to "intuit" whether or not someone was feeling, the clinic's ten-month program was spelled out for counselors in an official manual that told them which of the five personality dynamics to cover in what week, what to focus on during therapy, even what to say.

The main goal of the first session, for instance, which focused on "expressiveness," was to create a "bond" between counselor and client. "Tell your client what he can expect from this session," instructed the manual. "Tell him you will be reeducating him to a new way of seeing and experiencing himself. Inform your client that he will be experiencing discomfort, awkwardness, uneasiness, etc. Tell him there will be times he will feel foolish, silly, inadequate, etc. Teach him that these are all *signs* of his own inward changes and deepening."

In virtually every session, clinic counselors were told to move past whatever issues had prompted their patients to seek therapy and instead focus on their *behavior*. "You're talking about your problems and that's fine," Russ would say to a client. "But here, one of the things we learn to do is exercise our personalities. And this week, one of the things we're going to exercise is the voice. I want you to keep talking, but go up one or two notches. Don't talk softly. Talk LIKE THIS. OK?"

"Um, OK," his client said. "I'M NOT FEELING VERY GOOD." With the louder tone, the man's body tensed a bit. His eyes took on a bit of animation.

"Great. Now go back to your old way of talking."

"I'm not feeling very good." The animation was gone.

"Mmm-hmm. Now TALK LIKE THIS again."

"I'M NOT FEELING VERY GOOD!"

"Great! See the difference in how you feel?"

His patient did. As simplistic as it sounded, acting more energetic made most people feel more energetic and seemed magically to lift their feelings of hopelessness and depression, if only for a moment. Such an immediate, dramatic change made clinic therapy seem incredibly potent, and when clinic patients started attending weekly groups of their own, the sense of community they felt further bound them to the program.

In fact, getting patients into the clinic and keeping them there, Russ quickly learned, were the most important parts of his job. Several times a week, Riggs, Dominic, Konni, Matt, or Katie came in to conduct training sessions and business meetings with the clinic workers. The clinicians talked about the patients they were seeing and the problems they were having with them. A lot of times, they got busted themselves for not working hard enough or for being "crazy" in one way or another. (Usually, Russ got it for some old flaw, like being too passive or quiet.) And they spent a *lot* of time talking about recruitment. "Get your people in the door and HOLD THEM," taught Matt. "They must come to sessions. They must come to Psych Fitness Days."

Whenever Russ walked into the Center rooms set aside for the clinic, the place was filled with the sound of eager, cajoling voices. Whenever a prospective client walked in, he or she was immediately set upon by a slim, smiling clinic worker. Per the therapists' instructions, all of them were impeccably and expensively groomed and dressed. People now cared about that sort of thing; even blue jeans had gotten fancy, and no one wore Levis anymore but "designer" brands that cost three times as much. And each clinic worker was simultaneously charming and extremely assertive.

"Let's make a life satisfaction chart!" he or she would order the client. "I'll give you a pen, and you write the numbers. A '1' is a lot of misery; a '5' is pure bliss. . . . Now, predict with me two lines about your future. If you go on the way you're going, . . . what would your future be like? Now, let's draw a line for what your future would be like if you maximized your success here at the clinic . . ."

All the clinic workers wanted clients badly—it was *their* business they were building. And once you had someone's ear, Russ found, it was easy to get him or her to sign up for the clinic. Everyone who came to a Center open house or lecture or who responded to a clinic worker's cold call was sad about something; everyone had a secret hunger. "As long as people want something, you can get them," Matt confirmed. "*You* become what they want. The Center becomes the answer to all their needs." Although all prospective patients were asked to fill out a health evaluation form to weed out serious whackos, virtually no one who wanted therapy was turned away. Gradually, the numbers started adding up, and Russ was able to leave his engineering job and begin counseling full-time.

Now when he looked at his life, he felt a combination of tension and pride. Despite all the years he'd worked to remake himself, the effort still felt curiously incomplete. He remained a rather quiet and passive man. The ideal self the therapists envisioned for him was as vague and elusive as ever.

He had other sources of ambivalence too. He was living with Matt Lawrence, Katie Stendall, and a new girlfriend, Holly Stoddard, a former nurse who now ran Plant Power's maintenance service. He hadn't chosen the relationship. One week, Holly had been assigned to ask him out; then, after their date, both their Group leaders decided they should be a couple. Now he was paired off in a serious way without ever having decided if it was what he wanted.

Still, he liked Holly. And she made a good living, which was helpful. Russ had steep expenses—rent, food, Group— and because the clinic was a fledgling business, the counselors were barely getting paid. Some months, they made nothing at all. That would improve in time, and it didn't bother Russ, not really. Nor did he dwell too long on his failure to change or his doubts about Holly. What mattered was that he'd left behind the scared young patient he'd once been. He'd climbed the Center ladder all the way to the top. He was a therapist.

Once a week.

Some Group nights, it seemed that bringing people to the Center mattered more than anything else.

"Remember your quota for Friday open house," therapists reminded their patients. "You've got to sell at least twenty tickets."

Each Friday, everything ran with cool smoothness, the evening prepared by dozens of patient-volunteers. Cheerful, well-groomed men and women greeted guests, then ushered them to auditorium seats. The lights dimmed. "Psychological

Fitness is as teachable as physical fitness," intoned a male voice as a patient-produced slide show flashed across the screen. "It is the mental health program of the future."

Even in New England, growth was on everyone's mind. Riggs and Jerry visited to tell the outpost all about Psychological Fitness Workshops. One man listened, intrigued. He was a former SDS activist, and teaching personality skills to people who didn't have them struck him as a valuable idea, a real road to empowerment.

"This is great!" he said enthusiastically. "Maybe we could come up with a cheap way to do it and take it to the ghetto, where people really don't know how to get jobs or use their personal power."

Riggs and Jerry eyed him like he was nuts. "No way," they said. "We're gonna charge $1,000 for this."

The man said nothing, but he must have looked disapproving, because Riggs's voice took on a steely edge. "If you don't want money," he said, "you can give yours to me."

Soon, patients began calling familiar phone numbers they'd barely dialed for years. Psychological Fitness theory talked about looking at life strengths as well as weaknesses. That meant taking a new attitude toward family. Once, patients had lashed out at their parents, calling them killers and Nazis. But that had been too harsh. Parents had been caught up in their own old patterns, and whatever they'd done had probably been all they knew how to do. Call them up, the therapists now urged. Tell them about the *good* things they gave you. Try to reach out and help them grow too. The Center's new programs, the lectures and Psych Fitness weeks, offered a perfect way to reconnect.

"Mom? I know it's been a long time, but I've been thinking about you . . . "

Many of the mothers, fathers, and siblings that Center patients had called "fucked" and "dead" were pathetically grateful to be invited back into their loved ones' lives. They showed up for lectures, signed checks to hold places at Psych

Fitness weeks. Not all were thrilled with what they found at the Center or with their relatives' obvious devotion to it, but others found that its appeals touched a sad, empty place in them too. Some joined the clinic. Others went further: By now, eleven patients had brought a sister, brother, or cousin into the Center. One of Riggs's sisters was now a Feeling Therapy patient. So was Joe's brother.

17

Dozens of new patients found their way to the Center during the time of its great expansion. One was twenty-two-year-old Andy Heller. Ironically, Andy, tall and gangly with bright blue eyes, had known about Feeling Therapy for years—he was one of the high school students who'd become infatuated with Riggs at Kairos, all the way back in 1969. After Riggs moved on, Andy had stayed in touch with his idol for a time, though it wasn't long before the diversions of being a teenager—school, parties, girls—became far more compelling to him than therapy of whatever kind. Still, he never forgot Riggs, and in a sense it was Riggs to whom he turned when, in the late 1970s, he found himself in the worst period of his life.

The son of a wealthy, fairly well-known artist, Andy had graduated from high school in 1973 without the slightest idea what to do next. Because it was expected, he enrolled in college but dropped out after only six months, traveled aimlessly through Europe, then finally decided that what he really wanted was to be a painter, like his father. He came home, rented an apartment and work space, and spent two years splashing paint on canvas before admitting in despair that the effort was a total failure. While he was a child and adolescent, before his parents divorced, Andy had observed his father work, his eyes glowing with pleasure and passionate engagement. Andy himself got bored and antsy in minutes. Half the time, he didn't even finish the projects he started, and none of those he did complete were any good. For the first time in his life, he began to hate himself, and the isolation in which he was living made the feeling worse. Most of his old high school friends were long gone, and since he worked at home all day, there was little chance to meet anyone new. He hadn't had a date in so long that he knew his neighbors thought he was gay.

In January 1977, his mother was diagnosed with cancer and Andy gave up his apartment and moved back home to care for her. It was in the midst of this latest crisis that he finally bought the book he'd heard Riggs had written several years earlier, *Going Sane*. He found it brilliant, and immediately joined the Center's mail-order-therapy Associate Program. Coincidentally, six months later, during the summer, an old high school and Kairos friend went into Feeling Therapy. When his Intensive ended, he invited Andy to a Center beach party.

Andy arrived, took one look at the boisterous, attractive crowd, and lost his heart. There were a dozen people partying on the sand, all of them young, slim, and attractive and clearly bound by some powerful tie. They laughed, shouted, threw their arms around each other—he had been alone and lonely so long and these people were like a *tribe*. Andy knew instantly that all he wanted was to join them. By the year's end, he had applied to and been accepted into Feeling Therapy.

Like other patients who entered the Center in its Psych Fitness era, Andy found a new kind of Feeling Therapy. The difference wasn't just a matter of cost—the Intensive alone was now a whopping $4000. It was true that the first three weeks of therapy still focused on attacking patients: "You

have a *dead* life!" Andy's Intensive therapist Katie Stendall
sometimes spit at him. But much of the therapy's physical
brutality was gone—there was no more nakedness, no black-
ened eyes, no arms and legs made purple by sluggo. Over the
past six years, the Feeling Therapists had learned how to
change people without having to rely on such crude efforts.
Brutal psychological attack alternating with moments of understanding and kindness made patients depend on and look
up to therapists and do whatever it took to win their approval.
Constant admonitions that this effort was a matter of life and
death evoked deep commitment. The presence and pressure
of Group and community meant there were rewards for following rules and ostracism for breaking them. In addition,
with Psychological Fitness, patients didn't have to prove
they'd met impossible goals like being "in their bodies"; all
that mattered was whether or not they followed the program.
Where the chaos and terror of the therapy's early days had
made already confused patients feel worse, Psych Fitness's
simple prescriptives seemed to free people like Andy from the
terrible burden of having to make their own decisions. Everything Andy had found unmanageable in his life fell into place
easily when he listened to Katie. At her orders, he abandoned
years of vegetarianism and began eating hamburgers, then
graduated to lifting weights and playing sports. She told him
to stop bitching about "art" and just get a job—and almost
immediately, he found a good one, in the mailroom of a record
company. She told him to get laid—and soon he was fearlessly
asking women out, bedding one after another. Even after his
three weeks ended and he was released to the care of his
Group and the rest of the Center tribe, it was as if he carried
Katie deep inside him. Whenever he started to feel lost or
confused, he would hear her voice, guiding him. "You're just
falling into your old image," he'd tell himself. Then he'd go
through his life areas, looking for what was weak, choosing a
behavior that led toward strength.

"You have the choice of waiting to die or of choosing to

live," Katie had said during his Intensive, and less than six months into therapy, Andy felt he'd gotten more than he ever dared hope. He no longer lived by himself, stewing over what he was or wasn't painting, but with roommates in a big old house at the outer edge of the community. Between therapy, seeing friends, and dating, there was never a minute to spare—sometimes there was so much going on now that he hated having to sleep. And he was never alone. Everywhere he went, even if it was just to Ralph's for groceries or nearby Ida's Coffee Shop for breakfast, he saw someone he knew.

In fact, living in the Center community gave Andy the pleasurable sensation of being back in the insular world of high school. For all the place was supposed to be a united group of friends, it was immediately apparent to him that there were in- and out-groups and specific requirements for being popular. As he had when he was younger, he set about meeting them, became bouncy and personable, the Group clown, always cheerful, bright and *on*. Everyone liked him, even his Group leader, Matt Lawrence, who could be quite tough. He almost never got in trouble.

And beyond the pleasure he took in the community was the thrill of his own personal growth. One night, Joe Hart dropped into Matt's Group. He talked to all the young patients, and offered a piece of wisdom that continually reverberated in Andy. "Don't wait to evolve," Joe said. "Be what you're becoming."

What Andy felt himself becoming was his own dream self—strong, masculine, well liked, confident. One night, at Postgroup, Riggs asked people to talk about their evenings. Andy had spent the time in Group discussing his new life. He felt utterly vibrant and full of feeling. "I have something to say," he called out, standing up. Riggs looked straight at him. Since he'd entered the Center, Andy had barely seen the man he'd so fervently worshiped in high school, but now he stared into his eyes.

"Something really important happened to me tonight."

"Yes," Riggs said softly. He wasn't joking now; his face was loving and intent. "I know."

A sweet rawness opened in Andy, a feeling of having been chosen and blessed. He left the Center with his friends, all of them chattering and hyper. Outside, the smell of warm, sweet chocolate from the Famous Amos cookie store mixed with the scent of fry grease from a Pioneer Chicken stand and exhaust from an endless glowing parade of cars. There was no better place in the world to be. A group of older patients walked by, and Andy watched them covertly. He was a little scared of people like them. They were this school's big kids—they'd been around so long and knew so much. Tonight, though, they were silent, and Andy wondered at the look on their faces. It was not the first time he'd seen it. Sometimes, when older patients were off-guard, something seemed funny about them. They looked tense and edgy. Dour.

Once a week.

Janet Quinn woke each morning to a steady, throbbing pain behind her knees. Each day, she jogged two miles and did forty-five minutes of jumping jacks. With each bounce, the pain sharpened and flared. She refused to acknowledge it. For the first time in ages, she was in love and ecstatic about it, and she was wonderfully, beautifully thin—107 pounds, what she'd weighed as a fourteen-year-old.

In co-therapy, she exulted. "I LOVE being with Jim. I love him!"

Matt Lawrence had replaced Riggs to run Postgroup that night. "Who wants to talk?" he asked.

Janet stood up. "I just want to say again how much I love my new boyfriend!"

Matt looked at her steadily, then shook his head. "Janet, Jim's picked the wrong woman," he said flatly. "You're not good for *any* man."

All at once, Janet's stomach caved in. Being busted in

front of everyone brought such a feeling of nakedness and shame. . . . What was it she'd done? Matt refused to say. But he had been Janet's boyfriend's Intensive therapist. Jim looked up to Matt and valued whatever he said. After that night, he started having thoughts that maybe loving Janet *had* been a bad choice. Janet hung onto him; they worked on the relationship and they stayed together, but the remark was always there, hovering in the air between them. Things were never the same.

Once a week.

Every Postgroup, Riggs would give his rap, tell his jokes. And then, suddenly, his eyes would fix on one particular person in the audience. "Hey, Rachel."

The woman, an older patient, froze.

"It's a good thing Rachel's always on a diet," Riggs announced to the auditorium. "Otherwise, she'd weigh 300 pounds."

The woman sat very still, trying to smile and pretend that she too liked the joke. *In front of 350 people. In front of everyone.*

Or "Virginia," Riggs might drawl. "Virginia . . . Virginia-Vagina." And from that day, Virginia would be Virginia-Vagina to the whole community.

In front of everyone.

Once a week.

"Sara's put on weight," one of Kevin Fitzgerald's Group members said.

"How does that make *you* feel?" someone else wanted to know. "Do you *like* having her fat? Is it attractive to you?"

"No," said Kevin obediently.

"Well, aren't you going to do something about it?"

"I don't like you fat," Kevin told Sara forcefully when they were home. "I'm going to make sure you stay on a diet.

You just do what I say." For a moment, he felt good, really good about himself. He was like Riggs now, controlling the situation, dominant. Sara nodded. The compliant look on her face was pleasing.

Once a week.

Russ Gilbert and Holly Stoddard's roommates Matt Lawrence and Katie Stendall had been invited to move in with Lee and his girlfriend in the Compound. Of course they were going. That meant Russ and Holly would have to move too. Russ wanted to live with a man he'd known since his original Reality Group. Holly was resisting that idea because she didn't like the man's lover. Besides, Holly had her own friends, and she wanted to live with them. Russ didn't like that—his friends were successful patients, and Holly's had reputations for being "crazy," just like she did.

They kept arguing about what to do. Then, in the middle of the struggle, Dominic took over Holly's Group for a week. Holly had dated Dominic briefly. Things between them hadn't gone well.

Russ came into the Group. Holly lay down on the floor. Russ put his foot on top of her. Dominic gave him the words to say.

"Are you my little boo-boo?" Russ asked.

Fury rose in Holly. Normally Russ was a sweet, gentle man. But he always did what he was told.

"Are you my little boo-boo?"

The fury turned to desperation. There was no way to fight back in a situation like this. A therapist had decided she was wrong. Whatever she said would be turned against her.

"Are you my boo-boo?"

Slowly, Holly's insides crumbled. Holly had been raised by an alcoholic mother who'd beaten her, bashed her head against walls, burned her. When someone overpowered her like this, it was as if she were flying back in time, growing weaker and more helpless until there was nothing of her adult self left.

"I'm your little boo-boo," she said.

Russ and Holly moved in with Russ's friends.

During the summer of 1978, shortly after Riggs Corriere got the license that for the first time made it legal for him to be a practicing psychologist in the state of California, the Center held its first week-long Psychological Fitness Training. Parents and friends of Center patients attended. So did the men and women who ran outposts in Boston, Montreal, and Munich, and those associated with a fledgling new outpost, started by a Feeling Therapy dropout who'd never quite cut the cord, in Honolulu.

Around the same time, the founders called a community meeting to reintroduce the idea of everyone chipping in to buy country land so they could all retire together one day. In keeping with the Center's current move toward growth, the new plan was particularly ambitious: The founders proposed setting up a whole series of retirement and recreational facilities—a community gym in L.A. and several country retreats, one in Hawaii, another near a major ski resort, and yet another on a working ranch somewhere in the American West.

More than anything else, it was the idea of buying a ranch that seemed to excite Riggs. His eyes glowed with excitement as he talked about horses and cows, about how great it would be to get away from the congested seaminess of L.A. and live a *real* life, like cowboys. Center patients, on the other hand, loved the idea of having a community gym. All the women who were struggling to lose weight or keep it off were exercising at nearby health clubs. For men, playing basketball remained an integral part of Center life—being psychologically fit meant having an active "play" life and basketball was the "official" Center game—but since the Compound had closed, they'd had to play at the local YMCA. Having a gym would mean bringing all these activities home.

Of course, such big plans required a lot of money. The nonprofit Center Foundation took over the fundraising. A flier announcing the effort circulated through the Center, and although it reassured the community that no one would be excluded from any of the recreation programs for lack of cash, patients were eager to contribute. One turned over a $10,000 inheritance. Another, a successful salesman, offered $20,000. Even those who had virtually no money did what they could. One Langley Construction crew worker who was taking home $1,000 a month and paying out $950 in expenses offered the $50 that remained.

The therapists' new plan showed that they remained committed to the idea that Feeling Therapy should last for life. At the same time, however, it seemed that they were starting to have some ambivalent feelings about their utopian community. There was no question that the Center therapists needed their patients every bit as much as the patients felt they needed them. The therapists were emotionally dependent on patients' adulation; moreover, had they been forced to hire people, even at minimum wage, to do the work patients did for free (running open houses, maintaining the Center's audiovisual library, keeping its collection of scholarly papers filed, and mailing copies to whoever requested them), their business might not have survived. But years of controlling patients and focusing only on their deficiencies had left little room for *respect*. Moreover, the attributes the therapists now declared most valuable—ambition, wealth, success—were those their patients had spent years trying to leave behind. No matter how hard they were working these days, they couldn't possibly catch up with those who'd spent that same period of time in law or medical school or scaling corporate ladders. Worse, after years of weeping, sluggo, and "feeling their craziness," some seemed too whacked-out to even try.

"We *need* each other," Joe and Riggs had said fondly of

their community in earlier days. Now, when patients weren't around, they spoke differently. The Los Angeles Center, they told a reporter for the *Honolulu Star-Bulletin* during a workshop they gave in Hawaii, had two parts. One, the clinic, was outpatient. And the other—the Center itself—ministered to "the seriously ill." The seriously ill: In the new era of Psychological Fitness and Functional Therapy, it seemed that the therapists were starting to be embarrassed that their "chosen" few were a bunch of adults who did nothing but thrash around in endless confusion. Something would have to be done.

For three years, the Center had held special community weekends. The first had been the Dream Maker weekend at Idyllwild. The second was the introduction to the new Center building. In September 1978, after the workshops for the public and outposts, everyone at the Center was called to the third—a special communitywide weekend focusing on Psychological Fitness.

From the start, it was clear that something was going on. As patients filed into the center building, everyone got a number between 1 and 13. No one knew what it was for. The therapists seemed keyed-up, high. They broke everyone up into small groups for exercises that carried a current of hysteria. Go for it! they kept urging patients, until everyone was shouting, screaming, and shrieking at each other. And then, when the weekend was nearly over, when everyone was exhausted, their throats scraped raw and their voices nearly gone, they learned what the numbers they'd been given meant.

Until now, there'd been some shuffling around of patients in Group—here and there, new combinations of people were put together, or therapists took turns in who they led. But for the most part, people had been in the same Groups for years. Their Group members were their friends and roommates. They were supposed to be the people who knew them better than anyone else in the world, to be their families and the rock and foundation of their Center lives.

That was about to change. Which Group patients were in had been based on when they started therapy. From now on, it was based how well they were doing in it. How well they *functioned*. Despite its de facto hierarchies, the Center's chief tenet had always been that its goal was an egalitarian society. In a sane world, Joe, Riggs, and Jerry had written in *Going Sane*, "there would be no artificial class, age, gender, or racial differentiation. There would be no segments of society that were more favored than others." That was over. The numbers everyone had been given marked the new Groups to which they'd been assigned. The Groups were ranked. New patients went to Groups 6 through 13. Older patients went to Groups 1 through 5. No one had to wonder anymore where he or she stood at the Center. The numbers spelled it out.

Andy Heller was in Group 6. (Because newer patients had had less time to succeed or fail in therapy, their ranking was based on how long they'd been at the Center.) Group 6 was led by Matt Lawrence.

Janet Quinn looked at the number in her hand. She was in 5, the lowest of the older patient Groups. Around sixty other people had been classed with her, including several Langley Construction workers and Russ Gilbert's girlfriend, Holly.

"Do you all know why you're here?" its leader, Steve Gold, asked sharply at the Group's first meeting. "You're all losers. You'd better get working and putting out. You'd better start going 100 percent. This is your last chance to make it in therapy. Some of you won't be here in six months."

Group 4 went to Lee. Deborah Reiss was assigned there.

Kevin Fitzgerald and his girlfriend, Sara Wrightman, were put in Group 3. It was led by Dominic.

Werner ran Group 2. Slick Auto owner Ron Arliss was among its members; so were one-time therapist Linda Binder and crew boss Jeff Langley.

At the top of the new Feeling Therapy pyramid was Group 1. Group 1 contained the Center's successful patients, the therapy powerhouses. Group 1 was clinic therapists, like Russ Gilbert. Group 1 was tough business bosses, like Mary Farrell. Group 1 was guys who were good basketball players, who were tall, athletic, and handsome. Group 1 was led by Riggs.

———————

After the Group reorganization, a chill settled over the Center. There was no forgetting anyone's class status, for it was brought home, week after week. Friendships changed, for it just wasn't quite OK to be close to someone in a lower Group—caring for someone less successful implied questionable judgment. Life became frighteningly precarious. Doing well in therapy could bring elevation into a higher Group, but rising required perfection. Every part of life had to be flawless—a good relationship with a mate, a good sex life, good looks, good clothes, a good job making lots of money. You had to complete every assignment. You had to be confident and proud. Above all, you had to avoid ever asking a therapist for real help. Needing help implied weakness. Weakness was failure. And failure meant the public humiliation of a Group fall.

A functional personality, Joe and Riggs had pointed out, adapted to its environment. Center patients who had become adept at adapting to the community's demands now changed again. For some, therapy's new rules were a relief. Meeting concrete goals—Did you do an assignment or not? Did you get a job done or not?—was easier than trying to achieve some nebulous "feeling" state. Out of dedication or fear, others became even more tough and ruthless than Save Your Ass had required them to be, always making sure they looked good, even if that meant bringing down their friends. But some, especially the Center's gentlest souls, those who'd never quite acquired the habit of domination or abandoned the dream of communal equality, watched the transformation around them in disbelief. "No problem!" the friends who'd once shared pain and joy now declared, their faces smooth, smiling masks. "No problem! I'm doing great, man! Doin' fuckin' *great!*"

Once a week.

Group 5, the lowest of the older patients' Groups, was dubbed "Tombstone." It was so big it met in the Center auditorium. The patients sat in the audience. Steve listened and made pronouncements from the stage.

C.'s doing his Jewish wimp-out act. He must *make $600 a week. Work two hours a day for Langley Construction. Work one hour for Plant Power. Run every day. Fuck twice a week.*

R. and L. are forgetting their relationship. I want them to tie themselves together at the wrist with a rope. Stay that way all week. If one of them fades, the other can tug them back.

B. will wear a Band-Aid on her chest every day—over her heart—to remind her that she's damaged . . . .

The criteria for being in Tombstone were simple. You were there because several of your life areas were weak. Your old image was stronger than your new one. You were passive. You weren't close to other people at the Center. You didn't volunteer or participate in Center functions. Failing in Tombstone meant the end of the line. You might be given the "Turkey Award": For a week, you'd have to wear a button that said "All American Turkey," eat turkey one meal a day, and gobble ten minutes of every waking hour. Even worse, you might get demoted out of the therapy community entirely. You could be told to go to the clinic.

Getting out of Tombstone required "persistence" and "good will." You needed to have a major success in at least one life area and the skills to maintain a new image, like "powerhouse." You had to have the ability to affect others in Group. And you needed to talk *up* in Group.

No one wanted to stay in Tombstone, so the Group was all noise and frantic energy, dozens of people trying to show Steve how well and happy and ready to move on they were. One man wrote the Group a theme song, "Tombstone Territory," which everyone sang together each week as if introducing a TV show. "And the love they gave and the love they were shown, they'll carry it with them wherever they roam. . . ."

The members of Tombstone understood that all they had to do was *try*—to pick new images and adopt the necessary new behavior—and their lives would improve. That was the genius of the Psych Fitness program. Did you want to be high-powered in business? *Act* like a businessman! Did you want to enjoy sex more? *Act* like a sex fiend and fuck all the time. There was no excuse not to succeed.

"WE," one Tombstone member carefully wrote in his therapy notebook, "*HAVE NO REASON TO FEEL BAD!*"

If Tombstone was the clamorous rabble, Group 1 was the cool elite. All the other Groups sat on the floor when they met, looking up at their leaders, who had chairs. Group 1 got black leather couches. Some therapy went on in Group 1—the way people lived still got analyzed; there were still busts; and everyone made a point of being expressive and "on." But often, gatherings of Group 1 felt like the meetings of some corporate board. No one screamed for attention. Group 1 members all knew their place. Instead, they listened to Riggs talk about psychological theory, dazzled by the flash and light of his presence. When their leader first walked into the room each week, they got in the habit of standing to applaud.

18

Hundreds of miles north of Hollywood, Congressman Leo Ryan had begun worrying about the changes occurring in another idealistic alternative community, one that had started in his own San Francisco district. The Peoples Temple, founded by a man named Jim Jones, espoused quasi-leftist, egalitarian principles, declaring that its purpose was to prove that people of all different races and backgrounds could get along. Through much of the seventies, it had done remarkably well, being praised by politicians and attracting up to 5,000 followers, most of them black, to its services each Sunday.

But in 1976, *New West* magazine had published an article suggesting that below the Peoples Temple's benevolent exterior were some ugly problems. Some members accused Jim Jones, who was white, of administering public beatings and strong-arming followers into donating money. Jones responded to the charges (and any possible investigation of them) by leading his followers out of the United States and to South America: about 1,200 of them had founded a utopian agricultural community called Jonestown in the jungle of Guyana. Perhaps 900 now lived there, and lately, disturbing rumors had drifted out. Ryan had heard that settlers were virtual prisoners, forced to work dawn to dusk and punished for any slacking. He decided to go to Guyana himself to find out what was going on.

In Guyana, Ryan and a few colleagues toured the Jonestown settlement. Nothing seemed amiss, although six settlers told him they wanted to return with him to the United States. But suddenly, as Ryan's party prepared to board the plane to leave Guyana, someone from Jonestown opened fire on them. Ryan and four others were hit and bled to death on the tarmac.

The day after the shooting, Guyanese troops invaded Jonestown, followed closely by reporters. They found an almost unbelievable scene. After Ryan was shot, Jim Jones had persuaded his followers that their world was crumbling and they had no choice but to die. A wooden vat had been filled with gallons of instant fruit drink. (Most newspapers incorrectly described it as purple Kool-Aid.) The drink was laced with lethal amounts of potassium cyanide and potassium chloride. Then, around 640 adults drank cups of the mixture while 260 children were dosed or had the fluid injected down their throats. Jones shot himself in the head. Every television screen and newspaper front page in America carried images of the result: Paths through Jonestown were choked with corpses. Dead children clutched their parents; dead husbands and wives held each other. And hundreds and hundreds of contorted bodies lay bloating beside a purple-stained wooden vat.

It wasn't only the scene's singular horror that unnerved Americans. Just before the Jonestown mass suicide, there'd been another freakish incident involving an alternative community. In October, a thirty-three-year-old Los Angeles attorney named Paul Morantz had almost died from the bite of a 4½-foot diamondback rattlesnake that someone had deliberately placed in his mailbox. Morantz, it turned out, had recently won a lawsuit charging Synanon, the drug-rehabilitation-program-turned-community, with the kidnapping, imprisonment, and brainwashing of a former member. Only days after Morantz was bitten, two Synanon members were arrested and charged in connection with the attack. (Synanon leader Charles Dederich was later charged as well. All pleaded no contest.) Subsequently, the more the media investigated Synanon, the more apparent it became that what had begun as a utopia had turned into a totalitarian enclave, where members were controlled, beaten, and forced into mass marriages and compulsory sterilizations.

What was going on? Since the early seventies, groups like the Moonies, "Jesus freaks," Scientologists, chanters of "Hare Krishna," and followers of est had been part of the national landscape. The glazed-eyed devotion they evoked had long caused a certain amount of worry; occasionally parents of members arranged for the kidnapping and "deprogramming" of children they claimed had been "brainwashed." But the gothic nature of attack by rattlesnake followed by mass suicide was something else entirely. Involvement with groups that demanded opening the heart and psyche to something new, it seemed, sometimes led to wisdom—and sometimes made ordinary people do unbelievable things. It could turn young men into would-be murderers. It could make people willing to *die.*

News of the attack on attorney Paul Morantz freaked out two sellers from Plant Power. His office was in a building in their selling territory, and they'd gotten to talking to him while making the rounds. They thought he was cute and had invited him to a Center open house. He'd actually come, too, although he'd said little and left early. But few others in the community paid real attention.

The news from Jonestown was different: impossible to ignore. Riggs reacted to it in a typically Riggsian way—by being utterly brash and tasteless. Group night, he kept walking through the therapy rooms with a cup. "Anyone want some Kool-Aid?" he asked.

Other therapists tried to be a little more serious. The en-

tire population of another group that advocated egalitarian-
ism and communal life lay rotting in Guyana. People might
have thoughts. "Do any of you think we're like Jonestown?"
asked one Group leader. A few hesitant hands went up.
"Well," the leader said, looking around. "Is anybody dead?"
Everyone laughed.

"I know you're thinking about what happened," said another. "Do any of you think *we're* a cult?"

In truth, a few patients did have moments of uneasiness.
One man in Group 5 actually went out and bought a book on
cults; he hid it in his room. But for most people at the Center,
the very idea of comparison was insane. Jonestown was
creepy, weird, a subject for bad jokes. "What did one Peoples
Temple member say to the other as he took a drink?" people
asked, then sailed into the tag line of a popular television commercial: "Hey—I coulda had a V-8!"

A cult? Patients shook their heads and went back to their
charts and assignments. What did *they* have in common with
a bunch of black people who killed themselves in a jungle?

———————

Back in the spring of 1978, one longtime member of the Langley Construction crew had reconnected with his family, and
his older brother started spending time around the Center
community. On one visit, he met Mary Farrell. He liked her,
asked her out, and soon they were dating regularly.

From the start, being involved with Ken Lander, twenty-
eight, a tall, blue-eyed sales representative with a slow smile
and dark brown hair that always fell into his eyes, was a whole
new experience for Mary. Because he was a NIT, Ken wasn't
concerned with Mary's place in the Center hierarchy, her reputation, or what she'd done to other patients. Nor did he feel
obliged to bust her if she "fucked up." Their relationship was
loose and easy, and Mary found herself happier than she'd
been in years. For the first time in her life, even sex was rela-

tively simple. "I wish my sex life was as good as yours," one of her roommates said enviously. To her!

There was no way Mary could get serious if Ken stayed a NIT, of course, so she talked to him about therapy. So did his brother. For all that Ken was a laid-back guy, he had his own problems and doubts; everyone did. Soon, he started seeing a counselor at the outpatient clinic. From there, it was only a short step to Feeling Therapy. By fall, he was a full-time member of the Center community, living with Mary.

Still, in important ways her life and Ken's remained separate. All the therapy rules and dictates that so bound Mary just flowed off Ken; even busts never devastated him, for he didn't take anything too much to heart. And he'd kept his sales job, so each day he went off to the outside. Mary, on the other hand, moved deeper into the Center world. Her company management work had become a more complex and important task, and increasingly she was sharing it with Jeff Langley, who after many months of business meetings with Riggs had gone through some changes of his own. The sweet, mellow guitar player had been replaced by a strong-willed, forceful boss who modeled himself on the therapist. At home, Jeff even stood before the mirror practicing being harsh to his employees, so they would learn to fear and thus respect him. He helped Mary keep pushing the workers to do more and more—just as Psych Fitness called for "stressing" the personality to make it stronger, they were stressing the company, taking it to its limits. Mary had big plans for years of expansion and growth. Within the next five years, in fact, she wanted Langley to merge with the Center Foundation, to become part of the Center itself.

Everything seemed to be going smoothly. Then she learned that Jeff's longtime girlfriend, Deborah Reiss, was constantly after him to slow down. "You look awful!" Deborah was always saying. "You have circles under your eyes; you're working too hard." Mary was furious. Who did Deborah think she was? They were *all* feeling the effects of hard work. Mary's backaches were getting worse and worse; every few months, she would be on her knees at the toilet, vomiting, as a migraine sliced into her, a steel arc of pure pain boring through her skull. But that wasn't the point. Building the company was.

She stormed over to Jeff and Deborah's house. "What do you think you're doing?" she demanded.

"What's best for Jeff," Deborah retorted.

Mary got even angrier. "How *dare* you interfere in business?"

"I'm doing what's best for Jeff!" Deborah insisted. She would not back down; worse, she refused to stop complaining to Jeff. But Mary also talked to Jeff, steadily, relentlessly, and soon Deborah came to understand that her love life had a third person in it, one whose influence far outweighed her own. And like the Langley workers, Deborah Reiss began to hate Mary Farrell. Her stomach tightened each time she saw her, tall and sharp, with that blazing hair and those raging eyes. She was like one of Riggs's Dobermans, a human Trucker. Cross her, and she would latch on, all teeth, and rip you apart.

———————

Everyone needed to work harder. All Deborah Reiss's admirable success running Plant Power couldn't shield her from the consequences of interfering with Center plans. Word went back to the therapists about her bad attitude. She was warned in Group to stop going after Jeff Langley. If she didn't, anything could happen. She might, for instance, lose her business.

But Deborah wouldn't lay off. The busts continued, and she continued to fight. Finally, she was demoted from Group 4 to 5. She and Jeff were told to move to a new house. She hated her new roommates; they hated her. Within weeks, things between Jeff and her had fallen apart entirely, and he told her he didn't want to be involved anymore. Devastated, Deborah moved out of the house. Some people from Group 5 took her in.

Afterward, Jeff could work as many hours as he wanted. Soon, he was moved up to Group 1. While Deborah grieved, he started seeing a new woman, a younger patient who worked as a beautician. She was a pretty girl, sweet and supportive and very feminine. Everyone said she was good for Jeff.

Work harder. The Slick Auto employees were putting in longer and longer days. One of them threatened to quit. He really didn't want to be an auto mechanic, he said. He wanted to go back to college and study music.

"You're running away from your real life!" his Group leader, Lee, blasted him. "If you're gonna live your life like a baby, then you should *be* one." He gave the mechanic an assignment. For the next several weeks, he had to wear diapers and eat only baby food. He couldn't have sex with his girlfriend. He was to sleep in a cardboard crib.

It took a lot to upset Center people, for everyone had seen his or her friends ordered to do things that were embarrassing and painful. But there was something unbearable about the sight of a grown man in diapers. Some of the mechanic's friends made a point of avoiding him entirely while his assignment dragged on. At least he would be spared the humiliation of being seen, and they the deep terror that seeing him evoked. The mechanic did his assignment, and when it was done, he went back to dressing in adult's clothes. And he returned to work at Slick Auto.

Work harder. In weekly Groups, recruiting efforts intensified. Talk of money and success was nonstop. One five-year patient, a former hippie, started freaking out. Why were friends stepping on each other to get ahead? Why did no one even *mention* the word "feelings" anymore?

"Help me!" he pleaded to his former Intensive therapist and Group leader, Jerry Binder. "I don't feel like I can be human here now. I don't feel like I can talk from my heart."

"That's so stupid!" Jerry exploded. "*Anyone* can talk from the heart! It's not enough for you anymore!"

And still, neither he nor any of the other older patients left the Center. If their first years they'd been held by confusion and the promise of community, now there was just too much at stake. To leave the Center would mean being cut loose from every mooring and tumbling in free-fall in empty space. Everyone lived in Center houses with Center roommates. They all had Center jobs. All their friends were at the Center; the men or women they loved were at the Center. To go would be to start over, in a foreign land, alone. It was too late to leave, for finally, what the therapists had said all along had become literally true: There was nothing on the outside. There was nowhere to go.

———————

In May 1979, *Psychological Fitness* hit the bookstores. In content, it was Joe's and Riggs's most insubstantial work yet, all exercises, anecdotes, and platitudes. The majority of the book was devoted to a three-week self-help program, "21 Days to Feeling Good." Quizzes allowed readers to analyze their five life areas to determine if they were "life athletes," "weekend athletes," or "spectators." "Do you enjoy work?" readers were to ask themselves to determine their level of "work fitness." "Are you financially successful, according to your own standards, in your work? Are you successful pursuing your chosen career?" Activities to promote improvement—like "Think of the most successful person you know in your business [and] imitate his or her most efficient work attitudes" were described as "mind jogging." Mind jogging was "just like physical jogging," explained Joe and Riggs. "You do it at a pace that is comfortable for you. The more that you do it, the more fit you become."

The book, released at a time when self-help tomes like *How to Get Everything You Want out of Life* shared the bestseller lists with the ultra-successful *Complete Book of Running*, was clearly meant to be commercial. Once again, though, Joe and

Riggs felt they'd been stiffed by their publisher, this time Harcourt Brace Jovanovich. Between the purchase of *Psychological Fitness* and its release, their original editor had left the press and the woman who'd taken his place didn't seem overly enthusiastic about it. Harcourt was planning to print only 10,000 copies and restrict promotional efforts to the West Coast. The publisher's indifference exacerbated other disappointments. Joe and Riggs had been angling for a regular spot on "Good Morning America"; it hadn't come through. They had also been trying to convince locally published *Playgirl* magazine to hire them as columnists; that hadn't happened either.

But as it had two years earlier, in-house Phoenix Associates stepped into the breach, coming up with its own promotion and sales plans. Some of them were ambitious to the point of being ridiculous. The Center could let *Psychological Fitness* fail entirely, then buy back all rights and self-publish and distribute it, went one (rejected) proposal. In the end, though, Phoenix adopted the strategies that had worked so well in the past. One drew on something Joe and Riggs had that other authors did not—a built-in captive audience. All clinic clients were advised to purchase copies of *Psychological Fitness*, and Center therapists made sure their Group members did the same, assuring them that they needed to read the book to "get more" out of Group. Patients were even given directions for buying: Older and newer Groups were to make their purchases during different weeks and no one was to buy more than two or three books at once, so it wouldn't be obvious that the sales had been arranged. Finally, all patients were to shop at large chain bookstores and ask for *Psychological Fitness* by name.

Phoenix's second promotional effort involved calling on a familiar Center friend, the media. Joe and Riggs were still getting a lot of public attention for their dreamwork: *Savvy*, a new magazine aimed at "professional" women, approvingly dubbed their theories "sandman psychotherapy"; in an article comparing men's and women's dreams, *Ms.* cited Joe's research. Not only was *Psychological Fitness*—both the book and the concept—perfect for excerpting and talk-show segments, but Joe and Riggs had so often been called "doctors" and "experts" that they'd acquired a solid patina of legitimacy. (*Ms.* erroneously identified Joe—who hadn't been at UCI for three years—as a "psychologist at the University of California.") The *New York Daily News* featured a "Test Your Psychological Fitness" quiz, and the *San Francisco Chronicle* ran a feature article on the fitness concept. Joe and Riggs, wrote the *Honolulu Star-Bulletin*, were "a couple of easygoing guys from Los Angeles" who might be "onto the biggest thing to hit psychotherapy since Freud kicked cocaine." A short piece on the theory of Psychological Fitness went out over UPI, reaching thousands of subscribing newspapers. The book got a brief but favorable review in the *Los Angeles Times Sunday Book Review*, and was mentioned in *Gentleman's Quarterly*, which featured a photo of Joe and Riggs shooting a basketball. *Mademoiselle* bought a *Psychological Fitness* excerpt.

Radio and television stations started calling again, and Joe and Riggs went on the air in Cleveland, Chicago, Baltimore, New York, San Diego, San Francisco, Portland, Seattle, L.A., and Washington, D.C. And if the two men had always appeared smooth and at ease before the cameras, these days they looked something else as well: positively prosperous.

Money was rolling into the Center. Profits from the Center for Feeling Therapy corporation (which derived its income from Intensive and Group fees) were shared by its partners, the founders; by 1979, the corporation was grossing more than $500,000 a year. Money was coming in as well from the Fitness Foundation (which ran the Psych Fitness days and weeks). Fees paid by those attending groups in Hawaii, Boston, and Montreal were worth another $125,000 a year. The clinic was worth about $500,000 annually and was still growing. And in 1979, the Center Foundation, which was nonprofit but legally allowed to pay founders' salaries, would take in about $1.4 million.

As the Center became successful, its founders, in true "functional" fashion, had changed their images to fit the new "environment." Within a year, Riggs would claim to be earning $100,000 annually, with the other founders not far behind. In March, they'd spent around $800,000 for their dreamed-of country retreat, the Dollbaby Ranch, a 200-acre cattle ranch seventy miles northeast of Phoenix. And they'd expanded their belief in the rightness of "treating themselves well" in terms of material goods. These days, they were shopping at Bijan, a Beverly Hills clothing store owned by an Iranian immigrant that was so self-consciously "exclusive" customers had to make appointments just to get in the door. Bijan clothing was more than a bit slick and tacky—class as interpreted by the hard-core nouveau riche—but it held one very specific appeal: It was stupendously expensive. Buying suits off the rack at Bijan cost more than having them custom-made, over $900 (in 1979 dollars). And anything that cost so much, the founders seemed to believe, had to be the best.

These days, the best was what the founders wanted, what they seemed to feel they deserved. The Center they had begun from scratch was flourishing beyond their wildest dreams. Through the year, articles on Joe and Riggs had appeared in newspapers ranging from the *Chicago Tribune* to the *Seattle Post-Intelligencer,* and national magazines like *Vogue* and *House & Garden.* Center Foundation researchers had delivered seventeen papers at professional conferences. Harcourt had promised to publish yet another book, *Dreaming and Waking,* a more technical version of *The Dream Makers. The Functional Analysis of Dreams,* a version of Riggs's dissertation, was going to be printed as a research monograph. Manuals on Functional Therapy and long articles on the functional approach were in the works; so was a huge follow-up to *Going Sane,* called *More Sanity.*

For eight years, the Center founders had basked in the worship of patients in a closed community in which they made the rules. For the past four, they had enjoyed as well the adulation of a media that defined who was considered "important" in American culture. Any doubts they once might have had about themselves, their theories, or the heights they could scale were gone.

"Prepare for your call when you're trying to place articles about Joe and Riggs," Phoenix Associates' desk manual instructed its workers. "The image you want to convey (not say) about them is that Dr. Richard Corriere and Dr. Joseph Hart are the Freud's [sic] of today. They are future Nobel Prize winners. They are out to take over the field of psychology."

At the founders' urging, the junior therapists also began shopping at Bijan. Nine hundred dollars was a stiff expense for them—a whole month's salary—but they too needed to have the "look" of success. Then the clinic workers went upscale: Russ Gilbert went out and bought a $500 suit. Since he was earning only around $700 a month, with $200 of that going for Group, without the money Holly brought home he wouldn't have been able to survive. In fact, some of the other clinic workers *weren't* surviving financially. On their days off, they joined the Plant Power sales force and lugged plants door-to-door for cash. Their credit cards were charged to the limit.

But the clinic itself was looking more swank. The founders had bought an old house next door to the Sunset Boulevard building and restored it, so counselors could see clients in their own space. And, they were assured, there would be more money for everyone as the patient load grew. "The most important thing now is RECRUITING!" Matt and Dominic lectured when they held clinic business meetings, and Russ and the other workers were always on the phone, hustling. *More* was an insistent hum in the air. Get *more*—and that meant not just actual numbers of clients but their type and quality.

"We are *target marketing*—for a specific type of client,"

Matt emphasized. "We want the work-oriented client—who can pay!"

Get more. The refrain also echoed through the Center. Each week in Group, therapy shared time with—sometimes even gave way to—talk about expansion and book sales. Everyone was doing what he or she could. Janet Quinn, who worked for a television show, produced a segment on Psychological Fitness. Sara Wrightman donated four volunteer hours to working at the Center each week. Andy Heller helped set up the Center building each time there was an open house. And if occasionally patients had feelings of "resistance" at being asked to give up yet more precious time, they were quickly squelched. Donating time, recruiting friends to programs, they were told, was *good* for them—it was a way to become more a part of the Center itself. *Get more.* The push paid off that summer, when perhaps a thousand people attended each of the two $1,000 Psych Fitness weeks open to the public. Afterward, a number of those who came signed up for counseling at the clinic. Members of the Boston and Montreal outposts also came west for a Psych Fitness week, both paying additional fees.

The last week of Psych Fitness was for the Center's own community. "We have a limited time here and we will die," Joe and Riggs exhorted their patients, who had paid hefty extra fees to hear the message. "In the time we have, we want to function as fully as possible. . . . *We* can add to mankind's future. . . . We can show all other human beings how they can be by being who *we* are. . . .

"Take up the mantle of power! We *must* be powerful."

19

September 1979

Fall hit Southern California with the usual apocalypse—Santa Ana winds, brushfires, a brutal smog attack. In the crackling dryness, the Center community exchanged its summer high for the normal routines of Group, co-therapy, dates, house meetings, exercise. And basketball. This year, a whole formal league had been created. Everyone was involved; there were six women's and twelve men's teams, divided into A and B leagues. Every team had a name, a coach, and a captain; there were scheduled practices and games played before spectators at a nearby community center that were refereed by men from outside the Center wearing regulation striped shirts.

The games absorbed even more scarce time, yet a lot of patients truly loved them—especially the seriousness of the contests. The therapists had their own team, the Wolf Pack, which was good but not great. Lee had two bad knees, and for all Riggs adored and promoted basketball, he wasn't nearly as skilled as he liked to think he was. He was big but clumsy, and his in-your-face aggression meant the refs were always calling fouls against him. Some of the patients were better players—particularly one who was six feet, four inches and a former collegiate star. The patients were well motivated too. Playing basketball was one of the few opportunities they had to really let loose. And it was about the only time they could challenge a therapist and actually hope to *win*.

With the formalization of the basketball league, fundraising for the community gym picked up again. Just building a basic facility would cost $1.5 million, patients were told. But for an additional $250,000, they also could have handball and racquetball courts and showers. Another $250,000, bought a lit tennis court. Another $500,000 added spa and exercise rooms, an indoor pool, and an electronic drive range. And for $500,000 beyond that, they could have a soccer field.

That added up to $3 million—a lot of capital for a private group to raise. Doing so would have required that every single person in the Center community lay out $8,500, a figure that represented the yearly gross income of a number of them. Even the $4,200 apiece it would have taken to build a basic structure was beyond most people's means. But the idea was dazzling. Some patients already had contributed money to the gym fund. Now more gave what they could—and for some, it was a lot. One patient offered $12,000.

Mary Farrell watched the late summer and early fall pass from bed. The back trouble that had plagued her for the past year finally had become crippling and required surgery. Afterward, she spent weeks at home, trying to do business while in traction. A dog slept near her feet; she was a Doberman pinscher, a recent present from Riggs.

Mary was living in a new home, a small bungalow, and she loved it. Not so much because of her roommates. Two were fine—a clinic counselor with whom Mary was close, and the counselor's boyfriend, who ran the plumbing company.

But the other couple, who'd been assigned to be together, never got along, either with each other or with Mary, with whom they'd also been assigned to live. Still, the house was on North Gardner Street, on "therapists' row," near the Compound. Joe Hart himself lived next door.

The Compound was looking better than ever. Many of its houses had been painted and spruced up. Over the summer, in fact, Langley Construction had done a massive remodel of Riggs's home—at a discount, of course. Now the place had a bright, polished look, and was so stylish that Riggs even talked about trying to get a spread on it in the *Los Angeles Times* Sunday "Home" magazine. The Compound's common yard looked almost like a commercial recreation area, with a Jacuzzi, barbecue, and pool, as well as a "rec" room with skylights and a Ping-Pong table.

The Compound had also been enlarged to include adjoining Sierra Bonita and now contained seven houses. Jeff Langley lived in one of them with his new girlfriend, three clinic counselors, and Riggs's personal secretary. Three junior therapists and their girlfriends shared another house.

Mary was aware that Jeff and not she had been picked to live in the Compound itself. But she was *close*. She and her roommates had a kind of mini-Compound—next door were three Langley Construction workers, including Ken's brother, and all of their girlfriends. The two houses shared a common yard with a home on Sierra Bonita, where Russ Gilbert and Holly Stoddard lived with another couple. The mini-Compound made Mary feel as if *finally* she was moving ahead in therapy, hovering on the cusp of the long-promised world in which the distinction between therapists and patients disappeared and everyone could just be friends. She had Ken now, her home, her place. Life was about to get good.

Then, not long after Mary had gotten well enough to be back on her feet, she got a panicked call from her parents. Her adored younger brother, Billy, now seventeen, was missing. One day, he'd gone off and just not come home. He seemed to have simply disappeared. Mary was terrified. Billy wasn't the sort to run away from home, and if he had, surely he would have called *her*. Something terrible must have happened to him.

Weeks dragged by without word. "Something's wrong," Mary told Riggs anxiously. "Something bad's happened."

Riggs said that was a crazy thought. "That's your family talking," he said. "Your fatalistic Catholic outlook. I have a feeling he's OK. In fact, I know he is."

Mary clung to Riggs's strength and certainty. But then her parents called again. Billy's body had been found at the bottom of a gravel pit. He was dead.

Mary's whole body went cold with pain. Her parents had been so worried she'd recruit Billy to the Center that she'd barely been allowed to see him in four years. But she'd known that when he was grown and no longer had to obey, he'd come to her. She'd been waiting for that day. And now it never would come. God, she would never, never see him again! Her brain whirling, her back throbbing, she rushed down Gardner to the Compound. Everyone but Katie Stendall was away, playing basketball.

"My brother's dead!" she said, and broke. Katie held her, crooning, while she cried.

Soon, the other therapists came home. Mary told them the news, and Riggs thought for a moment. "Meet me at the Center," he said. "Bring Ken."

At the building, Riggs led Mary and Ken to the audio-visual room, and took them through a therapy session on death, loss, and grief. "You're sad; just let it out," he said tenderly, and Mary wept and wept until at last the anguish inside her seemed to loosen and ease.

A lot of people at the Center heard what had happened to Mary Farrell's brother. As much as they resented Mary, they felt sorry for her. Kevin Fitzgerald's throat closed when he heard the news. He would never forgive Mary for coming between him and Sara. Still, what had happened was a tragedy, and it made him think back to the early days of the Center. Mary had been so young and different then, no power-broker, just a scared, schitzy little hippie with wild hair and a pretty face. Whatever else had gone between them, she had been his friend. He could tell her he was sorry.

At Mary's house, a roommate turned him away at the door. "Riggs says it's best that Mary not see people now," she told him. "It will take away her feeling."

Inside, Mary mourned. All her brother had wanted was the family back together, and now it would never be complete. Still, when her mother called to tell her of the funeral, it was therapy that came first. Her friends had advised her against going—she was too tired and weak from surgery, and being around her family would just make her crazy.

"You're not coming?" Her mother's voice caught at the news. "We're going to say a mass," she said.

"Billy wouldn't want that," Mary said brusquely. Her mother was silent. Then Mary told her about the special session Riggs had given her. It had been filmed. Riggs was going to take the film with him when he lectured professionals on the East Coast, to demonstrate how Feeling Therapy worked. Other people would see from it that Feeling Therapy could help them handle their pain.

"The film was good," Mary said. "It was a really good, special thing about Billy dying."

Over the wires came the muffled gasp of her mother's shock, her quick, sucked-in breath.

Ever since the Center founders had purchased the Dollbaby Ranch in Arizona, they'd started making regular trips there during their time off each month. Janet Quinn heard about the trips and nursed a secret fantasy. She'd always dreamed of living on a ranch, and this was her chance. Soon, the therapists would realize who she really was—not a "difficult" patient at all, but the most vibrant and charming person in the whole Center. They would take her to Arizona with them, ask her to stay. She would live in the sun, among the therapists forever.

In reality, she couldn't even get out of Tombstone.

The demands of Tombstone filled every minute of Janet's free time. She was supposed to volunteer as much as possible at the Center and spend dozens of hours with other people in her Group, to show she was developing deeper community ties. She had endless assignments, like being a servant to other people in the community for an hour or two each day, so she'd learn humility. "Can I help you?" she'd ask anyone she met. "Can I do something for you?"

If she could learn to be humble before the community, Janet was told, she'd learn to accept her need for it. Then she'd be open to its help. But as always, Janet found herself unable to get with the program. She didn't feel *good* about therapy right now. Matt Lawrence had nearly destroyed her relationship with her boyfriend by telling him it was wrong to be with her. Her assignment to Group 5 had made several old friends back away from her—they knew it wasn't "functional" of them to want to spend time with a loser. Her whole life made her feel limp and depressed, and it showed.

"Chickenshit!" she was blasted in Group. "I'm tired of your wimp act!"

Janet would try again to be cheerful. Fail. Finally, Steve blew completely. "I'm sick of your depression," he said flatly. "I'm not going to give you any more help. I've had it."

Janet sat very still. She was thirty-three years old now, and had been a failure for seven years. Seven years of always being busted, her Group yelling, Dominic turning away, Jim filled with doubts. She couldn't take it anymore. If Steve gave up on her now, she'd be a loser the rest of her life. She'd never get to the ranch.

"Tell me what to do," she begged.

And with that, to the nods of everyone else in Tombstone, Steve gave control of Janet's life to someone else in the Group.

"What should I wear today?" Janet would ask her overseer each morning. "How should I fix my hair?"

Day after day . . . "What should I eat for lunch?" Janet would ask. "Should I go running this afternoon? What should I cook for dinner? What movie should I go see? Should I have sex tonight?"

Week after week . . . "Should I go to the supermarket now? Should I put gas in my car? Should I brush my teeth?" As Janet listened and followed orders, the tension inside her began to dissolve. There was no more need to think anymore, to worry about making decisions. Someone else knew what was best for her—all she had to do was obey. It was so easy. Not fighting felt so peaceful and good.

Gradually, the struggle that had raged so long inside Janet calmed, and into the space it opened flowed the goodness of therapy. All the therapists asked, she finally understood, was that people accept what they gave. It made so much sense. Janet abandoned the television job that had once seemed so important, and took a new position, as a Center secretary. In Group, she grew so hard on anyone who screwed up that other patients became afraid of her. Their fear fed her feelings of power—she was a success now. One night, at home, with no remorse at all, she slugged someone.

While patients like Janet Quinn dreamed of the idyllic lives they might lead at the Dollbaby Ranch, others at the Center had more mixed feelings about the place's purchase—for instance, some of the junior therapists. As the Center had grown, as the founders' salaries surpassed standard professional levels, the juniors started having trouble understanding why they were still getting paid like janitors. It was true that Center employees had always gotten poverty-level wages. But most of those workers, people like the secretaries and the head of the write-in Associate Program—who was earning around

$7,000 a year—were *patients*. They understood they were lucky to do what they did. In addition, most Center employees were women, and these days, men were supposed to be a Center couple's major breadwinner. And the clinic workers, who at best made around $8,000 yearly, were also patients and riding on the promise of future riches besides.

But junior therapists like Jason Kushner and Phil Schwartz had been doing Intensives and leading Groups for nearly five years. They didn't see themselves as patients anymore. They were therapists. It just didn't seem right to them that one set of therapists earned roughly seven times more than the other, especially when apparently the Center was flush enough to shell out $800,000 for a ranch. And a few said so.

The founders were outraged. "You're crazy!" they blasted them. "You have a chance to be part of something great and you're bitching about *money*? You're really fucked up! You're really acting out!"

That seemed to end the protest. Certainly, none of the juniors publicly mentioned that there was a blatant contradiction in the founders' promoting financial success *except* for their own employees. Yet an edge of resentment lodged inside some of them and sometimes flared into outright anger when they looked at their puny paychecks. "It's not fair," they whispered to themselves. "It's *not* fair."

The Langley Construction crew members were also less than thrilled with the Dollbaby. The founders had big plans for the ranch. One was to continue raising beef cattle there, with the profits going to support the Center Foundation. Although none of them had the slightest bit of ranching experience, they let the Dollbaby's regular crew go, figuring they could handle the business themselves. The other plan was to improve the Dollbaby, so it could be used for Center recreation. Even though Center patient businesses like Langley Construction were private enterprises, it seemed natural that their employees would help with that work, either in trade for business advice from the therapists or for free.

The patients who accompanied Jeff Langley to work in Arizona had no complaints—they got paid the same salary no matter where they were. But those who expected a break from the Los Angeles grind were sorely disappointed. The Dollbaby was rural and isolated, about ten miles from the nearest town, and bordering undeveloped national forest land. There were parts that were pretty, with trees and meadows, even a small creek. But most of the ranch was in hard, high mesa desert country, dry, barren, and hot. And the crew, who slept in a cowboys' bunkhouse just down the road from the ranch's main house, were expected to *work*. Each morning, they were up by 6:00 and laboring in the dry heat to build a horse and cattle arena so the Center could hold rodeos. At 2:00 P.M., there was a rest break;, then work continued into the evening. When they weren't building the arena, the men baled hay, doing it Center style, 100 percent effort, seeing how fast they could go. A week went by, and it was clear that being at the Dollbaby in the country was no different from being at the Center in L.A. The work never stopped.

Whenever any of the Langley men went to the ranch, those left behind worked harder than ever: The crew had to meet its usual goals with fewer people. Kevin Fitzgerald's days ground on, steady and relentless—the alarm clock blaring, the early morning walk, the hammers ringing, the noontime break. Each day, a female patient Mary Farrell had hired delivered lunch to the construction site. One of the crew's employment benefits was having their monthly therapy bill paid by the company; free lunch was another. But the sandwiches, fruit, iced tea, and cookies were a mixed blessing. Everyone got the same thing to eat, no one had a say in what it was, and if your sandwich had mayonnaise and you didn't like mayonnaise, that was just too bad. The truth was, all the men would have preferred that Mary forget the lunches and just give them more money. They were earning so little. Once, a crew member had had an assignment to bring weekend lunches to a friend who was laid up with pneumonia. He couldn't do it, because he just couldn't afford the extra food.

Kevin wolfed down his sandwich fast. After lunch, everyone got to take a fifteen-minute nap, and he craved sleep more than he did food. His body ached for it. As soon as his eyes closed, he went down and under. After fifteen minutes, an alarm clock went off, and its buzzer yanked him awake. His first minutes were always filled with disorientation and terror. "Where am I?" he'd think, heart pounding. "What's happening? What's wrong?"

And then, bam!—he was up and moving again. The afternoon wore on until his brain grew almost paralyzed with fatigue. Then, when the day was done, all the men gathered together to rate their performances on the job. Had they gone 100 percent?

"I was only 65 today," one man confessed.

"*Why?*" Jeff demanded.

"I don't know."

"Well, why didn't you say anything about it? You seemed like you were all right."

"Yeah, but I was thinking about my girlfriend all day."

"You fucking *what*? You'd better talk about it tonight! Isn't someone here in Group with him? You make sure he talks about this!"

Like not having your work belt prepared in the morning, not having the right nails and screws, going less than 100 percent didn't just mean getting busted; it meant getting fined. The fines weren't big, but when you were broke, every little bit hurt. There was one guy in particular, sweet, rather passive, and excruciatingly honest about his limitations, who always had to pay. Sometimes he had virtually no paycheck left. Mary Farrell took the fine money and bought the rest of the crew pizza with it.

At home, Kevin grabbed a shower, then went off to the Center. Dominic's Groups could be awful, interminable. Everyone was allowed to drone on and on, and when someone was fucked up, there were no savage, instant-destruction busts, just an endless raking over the coals. Mondays and Wednesdays were co-therapy; after therapy, at 10:00 or 11:00 P.M., he and his roommates had dinner together—they had to make sure they spent sufficient time visiting and being "close." Around midnight, bed. Going 100 percent meant sex at least three times a week. No matter how tired . . . It wasn't the feeling but the behavior that mattered. Just *do* it. Almost instantly, he was asleep, and after what felt like no time at all, it was 4:30 A.M., and the alarm was ringing again.

"You stick to your diet," he ordered the still-dozing Sara as he left, his voice firm and full of authority. "You eat only what I told you to eat."

———————

In the new Psych Fitness–era Center, perhaps nothing was altered from the early days as much as the status of women, who were now clearly second-class. The change had been coming for several years, gradual but inexorable. Whatever the ostensible justifications, both female founders had been stripped of authority. The only women who now held any real power were Katie Stendall and Konni Corriere. Yet theirs was power of a lesser sort. Katie was a tough woman, fit and athletic and unquestionably hard-assed when she did therapy. But she was still a junior therapist—that is, someone chosen and allowed to practice by the male founders. And as much as Konni wielded her clout, she softened it with a hyperfeminine style, clouds of blond hair, a soft, breathy voice. When it came to her relationship with Riggs, there was no question who was boss.

The absence of true female leaders meant there was no one for women patients to "model." Even more important, there was no one to do therapy on male founders and possibly get them to consider that some behavior they prescribed for female patients—for instance, being very thin and earning less money than their mates—might have roots not in therapeutic insight but in old-fashioned sexism. Moreover, in recent months the therapists' prejudices had gotten solid reinforcement from changes in the wider culture. Not even a decade after the rise of the women's movement, an antifeminist backlash was passing through the country. A small but virulent antiabortion effort was thriving. Arbiters of American style were happily proclaiming a return to "feminine" fashion— that is, uncomfortable high heels and overtly sexualized get-ups. A pinup poster of actress Farrah Fawcett, all tousled hair and erect-nippled breasts, was selling millions of copies.

The idea that "sane" men and women were equal—like the pretense that there were no class divisions between Center patients—vanished completely. Center women were still supposed to be "therapeutically" strong, loud, expressive, and always—*always*—hungry for sex, but they were to be strong *feminine* women who supported their men and put them first. "Women are powerful when dominated by their men," one leader flatly told his Group. "Otherwise, they are just lonely. Nothing more." And in appearance, Center women were as pretty and delicate as flowers. Almost all were on rigid diets, with the penalties for slipping immense. A woman who didn't lose weight might have to wear a swimsuit to Group so the leader could keep tabs on her body. She might be forced to *gain* forty pounds so she could really "feel her fatness." As usual, no one at the Center spoke up in protest. The women were well trained in the habit of unquestioning obedience. Center men too knew better than to ask questions; besides, in a way they didn't dare acknowledge, the change felt good to them. All those who had power at the Center dominated those below them. Now, they, who'd always been at the bottom, had people even *more* powerless to order around.

Clothed in floating dresses of silk and crepe, their hair

sculpted by expensive cuts and their skin glowing with coats
of carefully applied makeup, Center women served their men
huge platters of food, then settled in with their half-cups of
cottage cheese and single hardboiled eggs. Stay hungry for
months, especially when you're working hard and not sleeping much, and a trembling weakness grows, a bottomless
need. Sometimes the women went half-crazy with it, drove off
alone to stuff themselves or hid in the kitchen to gorge on
cookies and bread. Some taught each other how to avoid the
consequences. After the binge, a quick finger down the throat
brought the calories back up in a choking rush of acid. The
women got thinner and thinner. When their periods stopped,
they told themselves it was the price of living such intense
lives. Publicly, they never mentioned it.

20

"The worst thing that could happen in therapy," Riggs told Group 1, "is that it isolates you from the competitiveness and life-and-death struggles that really go on just outside the walls." It was a declaration that would have been unthinkable just a few years earlier, when competitiveness was considered insanity. But the more time the therapists had spent in the outside world, the more intrigued with it they seemed to become—and the more determined to bring it back into the Center with them. Suddenly, patients were expected to read the newspaper each day, to be able to discuss current events in Group. When militant Iranian students captured the U.S. embassy in Teheran and held Americans hostage there, Matt Lawrence even encouraged his Group to express their anger about the situation. "Nuke and pave!" Andy Heller, the liberal son of an ex-Communist father found himself shouting gleefully. "Nuke and pave!"

The point of understanding the outside world, however, wasn't to reintegrate with it. It was to conquer, and on two fronts. The first, of course, was psychology—eventually, the Center would take over the field. The second was business.

Through his involvement with Langley Construction, Riggs—who'd never had a corporate job in his life—had become intrigued with the business world. He wanted all the patient businesses to become far more serious enterprises—to show everyone what those who were superior could do. Center companies, he said, should have worldwide influence.

For that to happen, every business within the Center had to operate under the same system he'd devised for Langley Construction. (No matter that the company still wasn't showing a profit.) That meant every business needed the guidance of Mary Farrell. During the years she'd helped run the construction company, Riggs had taught her his formula for business success—everything from how to set up books to requiring that everyone eat lunch together. Now she would teach that formula. Jeff Langley would become her partner, and the two would perform management in a more formal way.

In the late fall of 1979, after weeks of planning meetings with Riggs, Mary and Jeff began offering their services to all the patient companies—a business they called "Professional Advisory Training," or PAT. The offer wasn't welcome, for most business owners didn't think they needed advice. But refusing wasn't an option. Mary and Jeff were in Group 1; they worked hand-in-hand with Riggs. Grudgingly, the plumbing and electrical companies hired them. Almost immediately, working conditions deteriorated, hours increased, wages were cut to the bone. And what galled the business owners most of all was what all this misery cost them: Mary and Jeff paid themselves salaries by taking 25 percent of each company's profits.

Slick Auto co-owner Ron Arliss had been thrilled about his shop's success. He had a constant stream of customers and seven good employees—all of them Center patients—that he'd trained himself. Although his company wasn't earning that much by outside standards, it was enough to pay him around $25,000 a year, a lot more than many of his friends earned. When he went to work each day and listened to the sound of gunning engines and clattering machinery, he felt proud of what he'd created.

When Jeff Langley asked to meet with him, Ron's antennae went up. He'd seen what happened to companies when Mary and Jeff went to work with them. And the size of their fee! He agreed to meet with Jeff; he had to do that. There was no way to be prepared for what Jeff said.

"Your business is failing," Jeff told him flatly. "You're in trouble. Your employees are unhappy. They're about to walk out on you."

Ron was so dumbfounded he could hardly speak. "I—I don't see that!" he managed.

"This isn't just what I see," Jeff assured him. "Riggs sees it too. And if you want to get anywhere, you'll let PAT manage you."

"I don't want to do that!" Ron said.

Jeff looked at him steadily, and said he wanted to remind Ron of something. If he didn't take PAT's services, the therapists would no longer consider Slick a good place for their patients to be employed. Ron knew what that meant. It would only be a matter of time before all the workers he'd worked so hard to train would quit. He would lose everything.

Ron went to Riggs, who told him not to be so upset. Ron should trust Mary and Jeff, he said, for he, Riggs, had trained them himself, carefully monitored everything they did, and would never let anything bad happen to Ron. With help, Ron could be rich! Why was he fighting to maintain absolute control of a small business when it would be better to have partial control of a huge one?

And so Mary and Jeff went to work for Slick Auto, in exchange for 25 percent of its gross labor billings. Although wages stayed the same, the men had to come in earlier, stay later, and work Saturdays. And when one worker tried to spark a rebellion for better pay, Jeff Langley fired him.

Once a week.

"By being at the Center, we accept a reality different from our own," Matt Lawrence taught his Group. "We agree to the reality here—that the therapists know more than the patients. We all become reflections of what they want or picture for us. We all stay here because persisting in believing our own perceptions makes us nuts. . . . When our own perceptions don't work, we are forced to depend on and trust the therapists that another reality does exist. We need to perceive the therapists as all-knowing, right, good—they agree to be that for us because we have to depend on them."

————————

Basketball season ended. A patient-team whipped the therapists' Wolf Pack for the league championship. There was supposed to be an awards ceremony, but the therapists seemed testy and nothing was scheduled. Finally, the patients gave up and bought a trophy for themselves.

Through October and November, Joe and Riggs made their usual fall trip to the East Coast. They lectured to good-size crowds at the New School for Social Research, the University of Montreal, Rutgers, and SUNY Geneseo; they appeared on TV in New York City and Boston. Their talk was still clever, the Riggs 'n' Joe Show as smooth as it had ever been. On the surface, everything between them seemed to be fine.

Yet somehow, sometime, tension had started to develop between Butch Cassidy and his Sundance Kid. And back in Los Angeles, clinic workers were shocked when first Matt Lawrence, then Riggs himself, intimated that there was something wrong with Joe. He wasn't, they said, fitting in with the rest of the therapists.

At the clinic, an already frantic pace was getting even faster. Russ Gilbert worked from 7:00 A.M. to 11:00 each night. *Find clients, recruit them, bring them in.* "Referrals are how our business stays alive," emphasized Matt. "Clients *want* our help."

Bring patients in; hold them. Men and women who came to the clinic had been sold a finite course of therapy. But, counselors understood, there was no reason to *ever* let a good, paying client go. After the Phase I clinic program came Phase II. If a clinic counselor did his or her job, a client would stay in therapy forever.

Bring patients in; hold them; work harder. "Clearly, the only reason we don't have time is because we're inefficient," chided Matt. "The more work you do, the more concentrated you become, and the more fun it is! YOU HAVE TO DO WHAT IT TAKES!"

Behind closed doors, when he was with his patients, Russ, like other clinic counselors, allowed himself to care about them, to try to give them something more human than a printed therapy program followed by rote. But he never could afford to cut them any financial slack, even if their lives weren't going well. Having a client who couldn't pay implied that a counselor wasn't doing his or her job properly. "Think of your clients as your *investments*," Matt urged. "You're not making friends here. Think of everyone as meeting your personal needs for money."

Andy Heller had been promoted into the publicity department at the record company where he worked, and was making more money than ever before in his life. He was working harder as well, or at least trying to. The older patient who did his co-therapy had been ordered by Katie Stendall to "make sure Andy succeeds at this job." The co-therapist then assigned Andy to work at least sixty hours a week. Actually, the job really didn't call for that much time, but Andy knew he couldn't contradict a co-therapist, especially someone in Group 1, so he padded his hours by bringing *Billboard* magazine home each weekend and reading it very, very slowly. At least the long-hours assignment wasn't as bad as the time the co-therapist ordered Andy to dress for work in a suit and tie— this at a company where everyone wore gold chains and snorted coke in the bathroom! People had looked at him and *laughed*. Andy complained to Katie, and she busted the co-therapist for being "unrealistic." He loved her for that.

Andy was high on his new career success, high because he'd left his first set of roommates and moved in with some even better friends, high because he'd found a steady girl-friend and she was going to move in too. (She was a NIT, but Andy was already working to change that.) Then he got a call from his mother: Her cancer, in remission for two years, had come back. Andy phoned her doctor, who explained the situation bluntly. There was no hope. His mother was dying.

The first time his mother had gotten sick, Andy had dropped everything to care for her. He couldn't do that now— didn't want to. He had a life of his own, and he needed to live it. His mother didn't complain when Andy declined to move back home to be with her—complaining was never her way— but Andy himself felt guilty. His Group leader, Matt, assured him that he'd made the right choice. "She needs," he told Andy, "to take care of her own life."

Matt suggested that therapy at the clinic might help Andy's mother deal with her feelings about her illness, and the two of them had some wonderful sessions together, where they talked about death and cried. But aside from that, he hardly saw her. The twenty-minute drive from his house to hers, then to the hospital, seemed harder and harder to make.

The night his mother finally died, Andy was in Group. Katie came in specially to help him deal with his feelings. Everyone nodded approvingly while he wept.

"I'm so lucky," Andy told friends for weeks afterward. "I'm so lucky I have the Center to help me through this."

"No matter what you have done," Riggs told the whole Center softly one night at Postgroup, "you are loved, and have been loved, for some time, persistently."

Nothing could stop Janet Quinn's ascent up the therapy ladder. She said and did everything by the book. Steve was very pleased with her. Just before Christmas, she and six other Tombstone members were promoted to Group 4.

"It's easy to go to Group 4," Steve told the rest. "Struggling drains the shit out of you."

Kevin Fitzgerald was now twenty-eight. He had been in Feeling Therapy for eight years and had loved Sara Wrightman, now thirty-three, for many of them. Like other Center women with steady relationships, she'd taken his name as if they were married. They wanted to make it real.

When Kevin told his Group leader that he wanted to get married, Dominic looked pained. The Center had a few married couples, men and women who'd come to therapy together and somehow managed not to divorce. But no couple who'd met at the Center—except, of course, Riggs and Konni—had married. Dominic gave Kevin an assignment that would help him and Sara see if it really was time to take so serious a step. Once a week for the next year, they were to ask their friends to write and perform a mock wedding ceremony. They would see what feelings that brought up in them.

Kevin bought Sara a diamond ring, but they didn't use the word *engagement* to describe it. And each week, the two of them made sure to do what Dominic asked.

"We have a wedding assignment," Kevin would tell friends. "Will you marry us?" Everyone was sweet about it. Week after week, roommates and Group members officiating, they exchanged vows.

The woman who'd had to carry a doll through her Intensive, now thirty-three, got pregnant again. Her husband went to his Group leader, Matt Lawrence, and asked if this time she could please, please have the baby.

"Absolutely not," Matt said.

In December, the seventies drew to a close. Colored tinsel brightened by sun swayed across Hollywood Boulevard, and every newsstand was filled with papers and magazines vainly striving for analysis of the years that had gone by. What coherence could be given to a decade that began with students slain protesting a war and ended with cult members killing themselves? At Christmas, yet another cascade of presents filled the Feeling Therapists' homes: art, food, clothing. Riggs got a $400 bottle of French wine. The Center secretarial staff received bottles of inexpensive imitation champagne. They were grateful to be remembered.

On New Year's Eve, everyone in the Center community came to a party at the Sunset Boulevard building to see the eighties in. There were wine and champagne, dancing, yet another wonderful talent show. The woman who'd planned to be a concert pianist and now did secretarial chores for Lee

Woldenberg played Chopin—then broke everyone up by flipping up her skirt to show she wasn't wearing underwear. The burly, macho Langley crew, dressed to the teeth as Greenwich Village gays, did a lip-sync of the Village People, singing "YMCA."

But that night, the most popular act was a patient-band who declared themselves to be even cooler than Group 1— they were Group *Zero*. Group Zero was dressed as another currently popular band, a group of art students who called themselves DEVO, which stood for the opposite of the Center's effort, *de*volution. Everyone cheered as they took the stage, and their guitars and drums began pounding out a steady, driving beat. No one considered too seriously the idea of devolution, for this was, after all, just a joke. Only dead, discredited Freud might have raised an eyebrow, or commented that there are no jokes or accidents. . . .

———————

Or perhaps so would have Joe Hart. All through the latter half of the year, his unhappiness had grown. Some discontent stemmed from the Center's new corporate focus, but more profound doubts seemed to nag as well. One week, he'd posted a piece of paper on his home's front door. On it, apparently per an "assignment" of his own, he'd printed his "negative" or "crazy" thoughts about the Center. "The dogs will take over the cats," Joe had written. "The Center does not accept children. Individuals cannot survive here."

Then, in November, Joe had read a *Los Angeles Times* article about the U.S. hostages that were being held in Iran. Several, who'd been released, had made statements that supported Iran's policies. This was hard for Americans to understand. Some speculated that the men had been tortured or subjected to some sophisticated brainwashing.

The article's author put this theory to psychiatrist Louis West, head of the UCLA Neuropsychiatric Unit, and an expert

on brainwashing. (He had studied and written about the reactions of American fliers held prisoner by the Chinese during
the Korean War, Dutch civilians held hostage by Moluccan
terrorists in 1975, and Patricia Hearst.) But getting prisoners
to speak well of their captors didn't require any sort of sophisticated techniques, West explained. All that was required
was a combination of factors he called "DDD." Prisoners had
to be *debilitated* by fatigue, malnutrition, or physical abuse.
They needed to be made *dependent*—isolation forced a prisoner to depend on his guards for everything. And they needed
to feel *dread*—not knowing what would happen next or when
their captivity would end. Given the DDD combination, two-
thirds of any given captive group would ultimately come to
do, say, and believe whatever they were told. And when captors had absolute control of prisoners, this could happen in a
very short time. The hostages who'd spoken in support of Iran
had been held for three weeks before their release. Three
weeks, West said, certainly was long enough.

Three weeks—the exact length of a Feeling Therapy Intensive. In December, Joe had written to Dr. West, asking to
see all his publications on the subject of brainwashing, hostages, and prisoners of war. When the papers arrived, they
detailed eight basic components that, under conditions of
DDD, could produce "forceful indoctrination," or what was
commonly called brainwashing:

- Captors had to require prisoners to obey trivial demands, such as following minute rules and schedules.
  Such obedience gave the prisoners the habit of compliance.
- Captors had to demonstrate their omnipotence over
  their prisoners, thereby suggesting that resistance was
  futile.
- Captors had to offer unpredictable indulgences, rewards for compliance, unexpected kindness, and
  promises of better treatment. This provided positive
  motivation for obedience.

- Captors had to threaten their prisoners with punishments like isolation and change in treatment. These threats would produce constant anxiety and despair.
- Captors had to degrade prisoners in various ways, deny them privacy, and impose demeaning and humiliating punishments. This made resistance more threatening to self-esteem than compliance.
- Captors had to control their prisoners' environments.
- Captors had to isolate prisoners into small groups that developed an intense focus on the self.
- Finally, captors had to induce exhaustion, which weakened prisoners' ability to resist.

Was it possible for someone as bright and introspective as Joe to have read the list and not heard frightening echoes? Joe didn't talk publicly about the information, why he'd requested it, what he thought about it, or what he meant to do with it. In January, he went with Riggs on yet another publicity trip, talking about Psychological Fitness on radio and television shows in L.A. and San Diego. In February, the two men went to San Francisco, Seattle, and Joe's hometown, Portland. But after nearly nine years of pouring his heart and soul into the Center, Joe had quietly begun sending out résumés to universities.

And then something happened. Later, rumors would go around the Center that Riggs had ordered Joe to do something he didn't want to do. It would be said that the order had to do with his wife, Gina—the only adult Joe loved more than Riggs. And Joe said no.

In late February, Joe accepted a teaching position at USC, abruptly withdrew from the Center for Feeling Therapy, and left the neighborhood. He explained nothing to patients. No one followed him. Even his own brother stayed behind.

There was no official announcement of Joe's departure. The other founders bought his house, and four clinic workers and trainees moved into it. Joe's decided to take some time off, the therapists told their Groups. He's going through some personal changes. He needs to be alone. Don't try to seek him out, don't talk to him. Lct him be.

"It's best that Joe go because the community wasn't working for him anymore," Riggs told Group 1.

"I'm *angry* that he left," Russ Gilbert said.

"Aaah, what do you care?" Riggs replied.

"I don't," Russ answered dutifully, but it wasn't the truth. So long ago—it was almost ten years now—it had been Joe and Riggs *together* who'd started him on the road that led him here. It had been Joe's wisdom coupled with Riggs's strength, the power of the love he felt between them, that showed him there was more to life than his own locked-off ways.

He said nothing. No one else did either; it wasn't the Center way. Nor did it occur to patients to think for a moment about the wolf pack logo gleaming near the Center's front door. For years, the therapists had compared the Hollywood community to wolves, animals that were social, gregarious, and always stuck together. What the therapists never said was that wolf packs had a distinct social order. Some were dominant; others submissive. Some followed; others led. And among wolves, there could be only one dominant male.

Yet deep inside them, an uneasiness began. Joe had been the Center's father and theorist. He'd been the one to move beyond Janov to create the very world in which they all lived. He'd talked of community as a life source and of the outside world as a bleak, insane hell. And now Joe had turned his back on the community and left it. No matter how Riggs tried to gloss over that fact, it did not make sense.

PART FIVE

The One Ring

21

February 1980

Rain came to central Arizona as it can in the desert, in a sudden torrent. Heavy dull silver sheets pounded the ground; inches fell in minutes, far too much for the parched earth to absorb. Dry washes changed to streams, then streams traveled downhill, swelling into rivers that rose and turned violent, lifting and tossing and taking whatever stood in their paths.

The flash-flood waters raced through the Dollbaby Ranch, sweeping heavy machinery into gullies and trapping cattle in the hills away from their food. The cows were already weak and sick. On their last visit, the Langley Construction crew had baled hay for them, and the men had done it without knowing what they were doing. The hay had been damp. Clumped in bales, it molded, and sickened the cows that ate it. Now, caught out on the range, the ranch empty of the experienced hands who might have known what to do for them, they began to starve.

The therapists, who were at the ranch, made an emergency call to Jeff Langley. Within hours, he and two of his workers were on their way to Arizona. Amid the downpour, the men tried to save what they could, hooking winches to trucks caught deep in moving water and pulling them free.

But there was nothing they could do for the cows. They were beginning to stumble and fall, and when a cow went down, it was the end. Desperately, the men propped up the animals on sawhorses, even tried bottle-feeding them. It was too late. One after another, they died. As the rain finally eased and the waters receded, the Langley men, feeling trapped in something surreal and grotesque, wrapped chains around the dead beasts' necks. With a tractor, they dragged the corpses to a ditch, heaped them in a pile, and soaked them with gasoline. And as the cows began to burn, a terrifying stench filled the damp desert air—the smell of death.

"No one else cares about what happened to the cattle," Riggs told Group 1 emotionally. "No one *cares*."

That was only partly true. Most Center patients had never even been to the ranch and so had no reason to be concerned about what happened there. But more to the point was that no one in the community had the energy to worry about dead cows. No one had time.

In the weeks that had passed since Joe's departure—still undiscussed and unexplained—the very air around the Center seemed to have changed, its molecules spinning with a manic electricity. More new programs for the public had appeared, taken hold, then multiplied. Now, in addition to a once-a-month open house, the Center offered a whole series of Psych Fitness introductory courses for the public—"Relationship Fitness Training," "Intellectual Fitness Training," "Work/Career Fitness Training." There were weekend "Family Fitness" days, special presentations of Psych Fitness theory at hospitals, a special open house just for Catholic priests. Matt and Konni were spending far more time training the clinic counselors in sales techniques than in how to do therapy, and the 18 counselors now treated 406 outpatient clients. As the numbers rose, another batch of Center members were chosen to become clinic counselors. There was no time to give them long-term training. Would-be counselors who needed master's degrees got them from mail-order diploma mill colleges, passing around and sharing copies of some already written theses. Acting clinicians who had legitimate licenses offered to sign statements that the trainees had worked thousands of supervised hours so they could get their MFCC licenses right away.

Meanwhile, all the Center's old programs continued to thrive. Hundreds of people were involved with Groups and workshops at the Center's Montreal, Boston, Munich, and Hawaii outposts. Another outpost was beginning in San Francisco. Associate Program counselors still corresponded with far-off clients. New patients still were coming to the Center for full-time Feeling (or Functional) Therapy, paying Intensive fees that had risen another $500, to $4,500. Not even a decade after its birth, the Center had become the ultimate psychological conglomerate, and it was on its way to becoming an empire.

Carrying the expansion forward required a growing number of patient-employees, and caught up in the momentum, they worked harder and harder. In the gray-and-chrome Sunset Boulevard building, Janet Quinn, dressed in a sleek skirt and nylons, sat at a tiny secretary's desk trying to complete chores that could have kept two or three people busy. Activity whirled around her. The Center receptionist not only greeted people and billed patients but answered a ten-line switchboard servicing three different programs and made travel arrangements for the founders. At noon, she rushed home to share a "family" lunch with all six of her roommates, everyone cooking, eating, cleaning up, and getting back to work within one hour.

After the business day ended, there was Group, co-therapy, volunteer work, an ever-increasing number of assignments, league basketball for both men and women. Time had to be set aside for "contact" with roommates and friends, for buying clothes to look nice, for doing exercise, for having sex at least three times a week. There wasn't a minute to spare. Everyone had to go 100 percent. Everyone's life had to be perfect.

Excellence was Riggs's new buzzword. "You're going to teach the world excellence," he announced at Postgroup as shivers of excitement ran through the community. "We are the next step on the evolutionary development of human beings!"

Excellence meant doing everything hard and to win. "Be aggressive!" Riggs would scream at the women's basketball team he coached, the one made up mostly of therapists' girlfriends and called the Black Widows. "Punish them!" Excellence meant rooting out any last vestiges of the old sixties ways, for they smacked of hippie "sensitivity," weakness. Even a habit like eating health food had to go. "You want to eat bean sprouts more than you want to be with your friends!" Riggs sneered at one man over and over in Postgroup, while everyone looked on. "It's weird. *You're* weird."

Excellence meant being "beyond therapy," like the members of Group 1, whose main function these days was to serve as role models for the rest of the community and plan social events like movie screenings and parties. Excellence meant there was no more time to waste in moving up a Group level. "You're like dogs, loyal," longtime Tombstone members were told. "But if you don't make yourself noticed, you'll be left behind. Your friends are gonna go up and you'll still be here." Each week, members looked at each other in measurement and suspicion, turning away from friendships with people they actually liked in favor of those who had a chance to get ahead. Excellence meant wealth, excellence meant success, excellence meant power, excellence meant domination.

The ex-hippie who'd told Jerry Binder that he couldn't

talk from his heart felt trapped in a nightmare. His friends, even the girlfriend he loved desperately, had been transformed into hard-polished success machines, robots sucked dry of humanity. And when he tried to tell them what was happening, they reported him for "resisting." The man fell to Group 4. "Keep this up and you'll lose your friends," its leader, Lee, told him. But who could pretend to be proud and successful when he or she was dying inside? One day, Riggs dropped in to visit Group 4.

"I hear you're still resisting," he told the man.

"Yeah, I am."

"You might as well be out front with it," Lee said.

The man cracked. He leapt to his feet and stalked toward Riggs until they were inches apart. "WHAT GIVES YOU THE RIGHT TO RUN PEOPLE'S LIVES THIS WAY?" he shrieked. He thrust out a fist, middle finger extended, and shook it violently. "WHO THE FUCK DO YOU THINK YOU ARE?"

Riggs flinched, then looked him in the eye. "Maybe you *do* belong in Group 5," he said quietly. He took the man's arm and led him to the auditorium, where Tombstone met. "Here's someone new for your Group," Riggs told them all. "He's the biggest loser I've ever seen in my life."

Group 5. After the fall, the man's girlfriend left him. His roommates asked him to move out. Kevin Fitzgerald was one of only two or three friends who didn't cut him off. For a few weeks, the man shuttled from place to place, a pariah. Finally, Deborah Reiss and her latest roommates—all of them considered failures already—took pity on him, and took him in.

After that, who would be courageous—or foolish—enough to risk rebellion? *"I'm* doin' great, man!" Group members assured their therapists, lest there be doubts. "Doin' fuckin' great!" And around the Center's Hollywood neighborhood, local residents noticed that the odd, scruffy kids who'd lived among them for six years, the ones they'd called "The Screamers," had changed. They were older now, and more clean-cut, always sleekly and tastefully dressed. Mercifully, they were quieter. But there was a disconcerting new strangeness to them, to the cheek- and collarbones that jutted too prominently, the glitter in their eyes. Everyone's lips were permanently pulled back in a wide, desperate grin. The Center's neighbors had a new name for Center patients. They called them "The Smilers."

As the founders' desire to conquer the world grew, some of them came to Mary Farrell and Jeff Langley with a plan. They wanted to try the ultimate Southern California business venture, real estate speculation. They would buy land, build a house on it, then sell it for profit. Mary and Jeff agreed to be the contractors.

The land the therapists bought was in upper-middle-class Pacific Palisades. Mary and Jeff hired all the crews to do the building work. The deal went down, though Mary and Jeff screwed up a set of numbers for a bid and got busted badly for it. Even after the spec house was sold, bringing the investors a 25 percent profit, the therapists stayed mad. Riggs and Lee told the two they'd done such a shitty job that they didn't deserve their contractor's pay. Lee even called Mary nothing more than a "glorified secretary."

A glorified secretary? Mary had the terrible feeling that she was losing her power in Langley Construction. Riggs was spending more and more time talking only to Jeff, making business decisions into which she had no input. Then, one day he informed her that there'd been a long-standing misconception about the company. Langley Construction didn't belong to all the men who worked there; it belonged solely to Jeff Langley. Riggs had never meant that the workers should be partners, just profit-sharing employees.

Mary's face flushed with rage. "That's not *true*," she said. It wasn't fair! Not just for the men but for *her*. Since the day the fence went up around the Compound, she'd worked hard to build this company. It belonged to her too!

It had been a long time since any Center woman had tried to assert her will, and though the battle raged for weeks, the outcome was predictable. Whenever Mary disagreed with Jeff about something at work, he told Riggs she was "fighting" him. Riggs got angry and called her a bitch. Deep inside, Mary knew that was a warning to soften and retreat. But she'd been trained to be tough; she wouldn't let go. Finally, the bust came.

Thursday night, Group. "Go get Ken and the guys who work for you," Riggs said, his voice mild. She pulled Ken and the rest out of their own Groups and brought them back.

"Come here," Riggs said. He led Mary to the front of the room, then turned to the men. "Mary is insane," he said flatly.

Mary felt as if she couldn't breathe. Her boyfriend was there watching, all her employees—some of them were really low patients, only in Group 4!

"Mary's in horrible shape," Riggs continued. "She's desperate. She's dangerous. Can't you see it?"

"Yes," the men nodded, one after another.

"From now on, all of you, when you see her acting too authoritarian at work, you step in. Stop her."

After that, it was impossible to get anything done. Whenever Mary gave a crew member an order, he'd balk. "Hey, you're acting really harsh! . . ."

Then, within days, another bust, this one aimed at her relationship with Ken. She was too dominant with him; it was unnatural, a danger. A special "marital intensive" workshop had been developed for Center couples who were "in trouble"; she and Ken would be the first to go through it. It would last a week and cost each of them an extra $500.

Mary began her first session with an exhausted dread. She and Ken were separated and assigned to two different counselors. Mary's was a woman who normally worked in the clinic. Years ago, she and Mary had been friendly, but she was different now, her face set with determination, her eyes icy clear and hard.

Her attack was immediate. "You're in dangerous shape," she informed Mary. Indicting words poured out. "Authori-

tarian." "Domineering." "Macho." "Look at you!" the counselor hissed, gesturing at Mary's jeans and unmade-up face.
"You're so unfeminine! You look like an old man. How do
you think that happened? Do you think Riggs made you that
way?"

Mary thought about the years she'd spent overseeing the
construction crew. "Yes," she said.

The counselor exploded. "You're turning on the only person who's ever loved you!" she screamed. "Look at you! Look
at the way you dress! Look at your hair!"

On and on. She was fucked, she was bad, she was wrong.
Mary felt herself collapsing inside. After all these years, she'd
never learned to protect herself from a bust like this, to keep
what was said from shredding the most vulnerable places
within her. The first day became a blur, faded into the second.
Then she and Ken were together in a room. Both counselors
were yelling. Mary was too dominant. Ken was too passive.
Things would have to change. And then it was the end of the
third day, and the two of them got an assignment to help them
feel the imbalance in their relationship.

"You," the counselors told Ken, "go home and put on an
apron. Wear it all night, and wait on Mary. Mary, you sit in
bed and tell him what to do. You can sleep for three hours,
but Ken can't sleep at all."

Of course, Mary did as ordered, and sat in bed calling
out for water, for food. But inside, her stomach churned with
the ugliness and humiliation of it—herself the bitch barking
orders, Ken's sweetness turned to this mockery of groveling
docility in a frilly apron. She truly loved this man, he loved
her, and they were killing it.

And then it was day four. Mary met with her counselor,
alone; then it was time to work with Ken again. She stumbled
and slowed as she was led toward another therapy room. They
would make Ken break up with her for sure. She couldn't take
this. She began to weep.

The counselor turned around and looked at Mary. For an

instant, her face changed, fell into its old, more gentle lines. "Come on," she said softly. "It's not that bad."

"Yes it is," Mary sobbed. She had to get out of here, get away. But there was nowhere, and even if there had been, she couldn't just walk away. She couldn't abandon her companies. And despite it all, she could never, never leave Riggs. She was bound to him; he was inside her like her own bones and blood.

That day, the issue of sex came up—or rather, the fact that Mary, tired from her long workdays, wasn't making love as often and as long as Ken wanted. Who fucked for only a few minutes? They got another assignment, to go home and have sex every hour on the hour for exactly seven minutes. In, out, in, out, what had once been so good became unbearable, in, out, in, out, sometimes Ken would come, sometimes not, sometimes Mary would get up to put in contraceptive foam, sometimes not. In, out, after a few times it started to hurt, in, out, scraped and sore, in, out, burning, raw, in, out, and awful, it was awful. And everything was ruined now.

At the end of the week, the two counselors went to work rebuilding Mary and Ken's new relationship. Ken was taught a new way to behave. From now on, he was to call Mary "Toots" and not let her get away with being pushy. "Boss her around," the counselors said. "Put her in her place. And whenever she gets hyper and needs slowing down, you pick her up in your arms. Don't put her down until she feels right to you."

Mary had her orders too. After the marital intensive, she called Ken "Fred Flintstone." She proudly linked her arm through his wherever they were. She called him "my hero" a set number of times each day. Each evening, she greeted him by loosening his tie and kissing him on the cheek. (Since Ken actually got home first, he kept his tie on so Mary could loosen it.) She gave away all her jeans and pants to one of the Center secretaries and wore only dresses, plus jewelry and full makeup. She went to each of Ken's basketball games. Ken bought all her clothes, and each day she asked him what to wear. If there was anything she wanted to do, she asked his permission. She still did her work and kept the businesses running smoothly. She was harder than ever on those below her. But with the men above, she kept her place.

Since 1975, the men who worked for Langley Construction had considered themselves its partners. After Mary's bust, they were given a paper to sign, affirming that they relinquished claims to the company for which they worked. Dully, all of them did.

In the spring of 1980, Jeff Langley and Mary Farrell, manicured and made-up, legally incorporated PAT and set up operations in a small apartment in back of a house on Sierra Bonita. The two met regularly with Riggs and then with the owners of all the patient businesses, teaching them bookkeeping and filing systems, setting up employee schedules, and gathering data about operations so they could plot out strategies for future growth. Whatever advice Mary gave, whether it was instructing Slick Auto owner Ron Arliss where to hang fire extinguishers or telling a newly-hired Slick secretary that Arliss needed to be busted a few times each day, it was always followed. And when PAT changed its arrangement with Slick Auto, not only taking a percentage of profits but awarding itself 10 percent ownership of the business, there were no overt complaints—no one crossed Mary. The patients whose work lives she oversaw knew nothing about what happened to her behind closed doors, only that she visited Riggs constantly at his house and that he was always praising her.

"Mary's really great," he'd say. "She can really run those companies." And they knew the zealousness with which she enforced his orders. Anyone who made trouble at work paid for it later, in Group—thanks to Mary, word always got back.

Quickly, PAT's own staff grew. Jeff formally disbanded what was left of his construction company—most of the men were worn-out and suffering shoulder and back problems anyway. Two crew members who'd gotten their contractor's licenses stayed in the construction field, but PAT hired some of the others and put them to work as management overseers at PAT companies. (Like those of all PAT employees, their wages would come from the profit percentage client companies paid.) Two other Center patients went to work as PAT secretaries. Another was hired to do bookkeeping chores at Slick Auto and the plumbing company. Yet another prepared the twelve ice chests of sandwiches that went out to worksites each day.

Then, with its own structure in place, PAT roared through the Center, sweeping up any companies not yet under its wing. It took over a fledgling patient-owned insurance company and set up a schedule for its owner that plotted out every hour of his day. It took over a two-man advertising agency. It took over the furniture company. Finally Jeff and Mary cast their eyes on the most profitable Center business of all, Plant Power.

Like Ron Arliss at Slick Auto, Deborah Reiss and her partner wanted nothing to do with PAT. Deborah was especially antagonistic—Jeff was the man who'd broken her heart and Mary who she held responsible. So PAT went to work through Deborah's partner. He was in Group 2, and Werner started busting him. He resisted. The busts intensified. One week, the partner really fought back, calling Riggs a Nazi and Werner his "lackey." It had been several years since sluggo was officially outlawed, but that night it resurfaced. The man had suffered severe shoulder problems for years, had even gone through surgery, and that was where his furious Group beat him, beat him in outrage—*a Nazi?*—beat him to drive the craziness out of him, beat him until he was black-and-blue and couldn't lift his arms. Soon afterward, he realized he'd been wrong, about Riggs and about management of Plant Power. He moved up to Group 1. And, along with Mary and Jeff, he was made a legal partner in PAT.

"We're working under PAT now," the man told the Plant Power workers one morning when they came to the office. "We're reevaluating the whole company. Meanwhile, I'm changing your jobs."

Kevin Fitzgerald was brought in to Plant Power as manager. He had no idea what he was supposed to do, and so each day, he just . . . watched over things. Kept tabs. It was all right with him. He wasn't so tired anymore. He had been moved up into Group 2, and after eight years of their therapy, the therapists seemed to think he was getting better. "You've really matured," they said. At home, his roommates, who were only in Group 5, looked up to him.

Russ Gilbert's girlfriend, Holly Stoddard, was told she was not doing well enough to keep her old job as partner in the firm's plant maintenance operation and so from now on would be a retail manager, earning $800 a month rather than $1,600. Despite the fact that Deborah Reiss had started Plant Power and cosigned the original loan, she was demoted to salesperson. Her salary also dropped, from $1,250 a month to $850.

The profit percentage that poured into PAT's coffers paid Mary and Jeff each $50,000 a year. Deborah was furious enough to visit PAT's office. "I can't live on my new salary!" she complained to Mary.

Mary looked at her without sympathy, then had Deborah break down her monthly expenses. Rent, food, therapy, clothes . . . Pet medicine? Deborah had a fourteen-year-old dog with a chronic illness that required costly medication. "You need to rearrange your budget," Mary said. "Your dog's real old. Probably you should have her put to sleep."

Deborah stared at her, speechless, then walked out. Mary had destroyed her relationship with Jeff. Was destroying her business. Now: *Kill your dog*. She was a monster. Deborah kept the dog. After her salary was reduced, she started going into debt.

Several weeks after the night of seven-minute sex during her marital intensive, Mary missed a period. A test confirmed the pregnancy. She was thirty years old now, still deeply in love with Ken, certain she wanted to spend the rest of her life with him. But pregnant! She couldn't even let herself think of whether or not she wanted a child. She couldn't have one. It was impossible. She'd get crucified just for letting this happen. Numbly, she made plans for an abortion.

"No," Ken said. "I want this baby."

"Please don't talk like that," Mary pleaded. "Don't tell anyone. We can't. There's no way they'll let us have it."

Ken wouldn't listen. He wanted to get married and be a father. He dreamed about the baby. "I want this," he wrote in a letter to Konni, who'd been his Intensive therapist and now led his Group. "I want this child."

But Mary went ahead and did what she had to do. After the abortion, a pelvic scan showed an apparent mass in one of her fallopian tubes. She was rushed to emergency. It was evening by then, so Ken had to leave her there. Mary understood. It wouldn't do for him to miss Group.

"Mary's in emergency," Ken told Konni.

She merely looked at him. "Sit down," she said. "How'd it go, *Daddy*? Did you bring it back in a bottle?"

The scan was a false alarm, and within days, Mary was back at work. In addition to companies, she was managing twenty patients' monthly budgets now. With Jeff, she traveled to Montreal, Boston, and San Francisco to lecture satellite clinics on the "Methodology of Excellence"—the PAT program for business success. "Always ask: 'Am I producing?' " she announced, sleek and confident-looking in a $900 Alan Austin black gabardine suit tailored down to fit her now-ninety-five-pound body. "If not, then you are costing your business money. . . . Make work as rote as possible. Make days and weeks the same, and it will be easier to take on more. The more successful you are, the more time you will have. Being confused is what takes up time."

22

Another new Center program began. "Executive Fitness" was aimed at teaching executives to become better managers through using Psych Fitness principles in the workplace and had a solid aura of mainstream legitimacy. The *Los Angeles Times* detailed the program in its "lifestyle" section. The Center even obtained a $19,000 contract to run training seminars for the city of Los Angeles's Department of Water and Power.

The Center Foundation's *Dream Research Newsletter*, in its fourth year, expanded to cover all behaviorally related sleep issues and publish the work of nonCenter academics. More Psychological Fitness weeks for the public were planned for the upcoming summer, and therapists regularly urged their Groups to "set goals and go after" the people they wanted to bring to them. It was a blow when Harcourt Brace Jovanovich decided not to publish *Dreaming and Waking*, which was written by Joe, Riggs, Werner, and Lee. (It shouldn't have been a surprise, though; the manuscript was little more than a remix of *The Dream Makers* and Riggs's Ph.D. dissertation.) But the therapists turned to self-publication, and afterward, the usual promotion effort began. Butch Cassidy was gone, of course, but Sundance took on a new partner, his old fellow graduate student and leader of Group 2, Werner. The two men did TV and radio shows in Los Angeles and Massachusetts, and Phoenix Associates scheduled a local "Day with the Authors" that would give the public a chance to meet the two men (and buy books).

Pressure at the clinic intensified yet again. Russ Gilbert and his colleagues were even given quotas of people to bring to the upcoming Day with the Authors. "When you're talking to people, keep in mind how *you* love listening to Riggs and Werner," a bulletin directed them. "Tell them that this is like hearing Freud speak. . . ."

Client load at the clinic continued to rise, and visions of what the future could bring were wild and sweeping. "We want to have thirty-eight clinics in L.A. in the next ten years," Matt Lawrence told the staff. "We want 4,000 people in each of them, and we're going where the highest-income families are." A whole new plan for organization of the clinic structure was being set up, he explained. The clinic's home office would remain in L.A. Riggs would be based there, working on therapy theory, and the business itself would be run by Matt, who'd oversee development; Dominic, who'd be in charge of quality control; and Konni, who'd be in charge of training. Reporting to them, in other cities across the nation, would be ten regional directors, each earning $200,000 a year. Ten branch managers would earn $100,000 each. Ten executive directors would make $60,000, and counselors would earn $40,000 each. The whole system would have a projected yearly gross of *$1 billion.*

Anyone who looked past the dollar signs might have noticed that the new structural plan showed how power lines were being redrawn within the Center now that Joe was gone. Lee continued in his old role as the therapist who kept watch over business in general, but clearly Riggs was the man in charge. It was his friend and roommate Werner who'd taken Joe's place on the media circuit. Matt Lawrence, his protégé, would occupy a position of enormous importance. So would Dominic, who'd been his mentor (although he was below Matt), and his wife, Konni. Steve Gold (a founder, Ph.D., and recent recipient of a state of California license in clinical psychology), would be responsible for training staff in other cities *under* Konni. *Going Sane*'s coauthor, Jerry, was not even mentioned.

But no one in the clinic could see anything but the promise that one day, all their current sacrifice would be richly rewarded. Giddily, the clinicians chose their turf, dividing the nation among them. "I want New York!" voices cried out. "Hawaii's mine!" The staff room looked like a war room, with maps and a ten-year plan for Center growth covering the walls. Riggs placed markers on those cities the Center had already penetrated—just as Freud himself had once tracked the spread of psychoanalysis.

Jon Walker, who now dressed and wore his hair just like Riggs did, set out with a fellow clinic counselor to found another outpatient clinic in Southern California. One clinic counselor with a Ph.D. made plans to teach a course through UCLA's extension program and bring one-third of her students into the clinic. Clinic workers approached anyone who came to a Psych Fitness Workshop or Center open house, their faces welcoming, their smiles sincere. And they kept a tight rein on the patients they already had, refusing to let them walk away. Anyone reluctant to make long weekly drives to Hollywood was excoriated as "lazy." Was someone having trouble meeting the clinic's weekly fees? "When people tell you 'I'm too poor,'" Konni instructed in her soft, breathy voice, "tell them it's an investment—financially and emotionally—for them to take out a loan."

Ron Arliss was sick about his business. Recently, Jeff Langley had started "borrowing" Slick employees to work at the ranch. "I just need them for a little while," he always said, but then the men were gone for weeks—still on Ron's payroll. How was he supposed to run a repair shop when he didn't know how many workers he could count on?

"Don't worry," Jeff reassured him. "We want to do something to make it up to you. We can reimburse you for the wages you're paying your guys. Or, as a trade, Lee and Riggs will give you their time, special time, to counsel you in business so you can go further." Ron said nothing. "That," Jeff added, "is what I recommend you do."

"OK," Ron said. "Sure."

Somehow, though, there was never time to meet with Riggs and Lee. There was never time for anything. Life at Slick was no longer fun. Each day, Ron, his partner, and their secretary had to show up at 5:45 A.M. and spend fifteen minutes together "visiting." At 6:30, the shop opened. Each hour, there'd be a five-minute break so workers could report on what they'd done and determine whether or not they'd met their time goals. They learned to do "eye checks"—looking in each other's eyes to see if they were "clear" or not. Failure to meet time goals, to have clear eyes, all resulted in fines. In fact, workers got fined every time they made a mistake of any kind. It was completely humiliating; besides, given how little they were earning, the men couldn't afford it.

And the money that was hemorrhaging out to PAT! Ron had paid almost $30,000 by now, per Mary Farrell's demand, all of it in cash. Once, he'd delivered a whole briefcase of money to Jeff Langley's house.

Ron had no respite from his misery at home, where he was living with someone he didn't love, a troubled incest survivor whom the therapists had decided would be the woman with whom he would "make it." His only release was basketball. His league team this year, the Wizards, was one of the Center's best. Ron himself was too short to be a great ballplayer, but he could be tenacious as hell. When he played defense against the therapists' Wolf Pack, no one could score.

After one of those games, he got busted. "You're out of control; you're losing it!" he was told in Group. "You can see how crazy you are when you play ball. The only reason the ref doesn't call fouls on you is that you're short. But someday you're going to hurt someone."

If the therapists said he was crazy, Ron knew he had to be. But he couldn't help it; he found himself having some doubts. And so, the next time he played, he checked with the referee. "Are you giving me breaks because I'm short?" he asked, explaining the situation.

"*What?*" the man said. "Nah, I wouldn't do that. You know what, man? They're just sore losers."

It was strange to hear someone talk about the therapists like that. It didn't give Ron negative thoughts but the vague outline of thoughts, the blurred beginning of something . . . Something odd.

The Wizards won the league championship, but again, there was no celebration of the victory, no trophy. Meanwhile, at Slick, the men kept working, everyone pressured, strained, and broke. The plumbers, the electricians, the Plant Power staff were strained and broke. All through the Center, people were strained and broke. Sometimes Janet Quinn found herself secretly wishing she were one of the patients at the lowly clinic. At least they got to go home and relax.

But if the clinic patients had time to relax, its counselors did not. Those who were in Group 1 were working on less and less food, for Riggs had instituted a rigid diet program. Each week, Group members stripped to their underwear for weight checks. Those who didn't meet their goals got fined. And all of them felt a cold steel band of relentless pressure wrapped around their guts.

"Recruit" was their mantra; "recruit." There were more than 500 patients in the L.A. clinic now, but that still wasn't enough. Sometimes Konni or Matt would announce a contest, with the person who brought in the most new patients winning a prize like tickets to a Lakers game. But more often, the clinic workers were penalized for failure. Anyone who didn't get a potential client to sign a contract, anyone who lost an existing client, or anyone who couldn't bring a lost client back got busted, screamed at in staff meetings, humiliated, and torn apart. Or there would be yet another fine to be paid to the clinic worker's regular Group leader. Sometimes it was as much as $200, more than a week's pay.

Recruit. Jon Walker and his girlfriend and two other clinicians were not only counseling patients but driving hundreds of miles around Southern California, lecturing anywhere Phoenix Associates could get them an audience, still trying to find a site for a new clinic. Finally, they were able to set up a program in Newport Beach, a fabulously wealthy community only a few miles from UCI. The four began holding weekly Groups in the "Sailing Suite" of the Newport Beach Marriott. The *Los Angeles Times* covered the opening.

Now the four had to make a regular sixty-mile drive between Los Angeles and Orange counties. And keep up their lecture schedule—they were trying to start yet another clinic in Claremont, which was fifty miles inland from both Newport and Hollywood. And keep seeing their own clients. And keep up with their own therapy Groups and assignments. There was so little time that often they wrote their lectures in the car while commuting. Yet no matter how hard they worked, it seemed the clinic still wasn't successful enough to pay them more money.

———

Money. Money. Increasingly, the thought of money was getting under the skins of the junior therapists. Perhaps as much as Riggs, they'd been horrified by the death of the cattle at the ranch, but for a very different reason. The deaths were just one more fuckup among many, one more *expensive* fuckup. "Just act like a rancher and you will *be* one," the founders seemed to believe, following their own Psych Fitness advice.

But the truth was, none of them knew what they were doing in Arizona. They'd spent more than $40,000 buying two bulldozers to move sand at the ranch, without it ever being clear if these purchases were really necessary. Then some of the equipment had been left out in the rain until it rusted. Now cows had to be replaced. According to the founders' original plans, the ranch was going to make money. Instead, it was swallowing it. And it was money that the juniors knew could have gone to them.

Since early 1980, the juniors had been going to the ranch regularly, and there, much about their own position in the Center had become painfully clear. As if it were simply a given, Werner, Lee, and their girlfriends each took bedrooms in the ranch's comfortable main house. Matt and Katie slept there too, in a screened-in front porch. The master suite, with its own private bath, went to Riggs and Konni. The rest of them slept down the hill, jammed together in the communal cowboys' quarters. And although time at the ranch was supposed to be time off, Riggs was always after them to work, waking people up at 5:00 A.M., for instance, to build a corral.

The more the junior therapists noted the discrepancy between how they and the founders—especially Riggs—lived, the more pissed off they got. They were making $13,000 a year, while Riggs got around $100,000, plus a number of perks— the subsidized remodeling work done by Langley Construction, the $4,000 souped-up dune buggy Slick Auto had given him for his birthday, the services of Mary Farrell, who watched his house and did errands while he was gone. The juniors were sacrificing to buy their expensive clothes, while Riggs's Bijan wardrobe was paid for by the Center because it was a business necessity that he present the proper image when he lectured or went on TV. For all the responsibility the juniors carried, the founders still treated them as underlings.

The juniors spoke up once again. Once again, they were busted for "acting out." Once again, they backed off. But this time, their anger did not subside. For the first time in their years at the Center, the juniors knew with certainty that they were being told they were "crazy" when they were speaking the truth, and with that knowledge, the self-policing they'd practiced so long lost its power. With the exception of Matt, Katie, and, of course, Konni, they began to talk openly to each other. Whenever a junior had doubts, he or she said something to a colleague. And whenever one junior said aloud, "Something's not right here," the others had a new response. They didn't bust. They didn't talk about "negative thoughts." They said, "You bet."

23

July 1980

If the founders had sensed the unhappiness building within their community, perhaps they would have tried to stifle it by clamping down or to diffuse it with pay raises or some special reward. But they didn't. Some, like Jerry and Lee, seemed exhausted, depressed, and burned-out themselves.

So instead of handling matters at home, during the summer of 1980 all thirteen founders and juniors and their mates left town. Part of their time away was spent on an extended road trip, during which the therapists ran this year's Psych Fitness weeks at all the outposts. But even after the business was done, the therapists didn't come back. Quietly, privately (later saying they didn't want their patients blindly following their example), all the established couples—Carole and Steve, Dominic and Linda, Matt and Katie, and Jerry, Lee, and their girlfriends—got married. And eventually, they all met for a long vacation at the ranch. In the end, the therapists stayed away for nearly two months. It was a pivotal decision. For the first time in nine years, their patients at the Center were left on their own.

In the therapists' absence, Group 1 ran the Center. They took their job seriously and got right to work planning a big Centerwide "Olympics" for the fall. (President Carter's order that America boycott that year's Moscow summer games to protest a Russian invasion of Afghanistan had disappointed everyone.) Each week, they led Groups, just like therapists, and each week, a few of them hosted a Postgroup lecture for the whole community. Mary Farrell and Jeff Langley spoke on the Methodology of Excellence. Jon Walker, Group 1's star basketball player, and a clinic counselor taught about sex. "It should be simple and easy," they said. People were "biologically wired for it"; according to Riggs, sex was "like shaking hands."

Another trio, a woman and two men, taught about family values. Marriage was the "ultimate commitment," they said, a relationship in which each partner profoundly changed the other. Women, for instance, changed from independent to submissive—they made conscious and deliberate choices to give in to their husbands. Having children was a different matter, though, an ex-Langley worker pointed out. People thought kids were "cute," or that having one would fulfill them or make them "successful" as adults. In truth, childrearing was a full-time job. It required time, money, and sacrifice, and created major upheaval. And patients' parental abilities directly parallelled their psychological profiles. Anyone prone to fighting with a spouse, for instance, would be likely to punish a child.

The community listened and dutifully took notes. Younger patients were dazzled by what they heard; Group 1 members were heroes to them. But some older patients were irritated. Over the years, they'd spent tens of thousands of dollars on therapy at the Center, and now their money wasn't even buying time with therapists. They knew that none of the people lecturing had any special training in what they were talking about. Even more troubling, there was such coldness to some of what they said. Kevin Fitzgerald recoiled as he listened to his former co-worker, a man with no children of his own, talk about babies in a way that made them sound like nothing more than parasites. In truth, his line was no different from the one the founders had given all these years. But it *sounded* different. Without the founders' slickness and style, without their charisma and magic, Feeling Therapy's beliefs looked ugly.

As the weeks went by, therapy changed in other ways too. Group 1 members were less brutal than therapists when they led Groups. Nor did they inspire the same fearful idealization, for to older Center patients, people in Group 1 were essentially peers. Group was less terrifying. Without terror, life was far less controlled. The repression under which patients had lived so long eased. And as it did, so did their regression. They began to feel better—more capable and adult, more able to act and make decisions. And happier. It was nice not to go after each other all the time, people admitted to each other. It was nice not to be afraid to go to Group. It was nice— it was nice living without the therapists. "I wish," some patients daringly whispered to each other, "that they'd never come back."

The new ease spreading through the Center eluded the clinic workers. They were too much a part of the therapy hierarchy, too invested in identifying with the therapists to turn away from them. And even in the therapists' absence, they were too scared. The fact that the founders and juniors were gone didn't excuse them from meeting their recruitment goals. But the summer of 1980 was a terrible time to get people to commit to weekly therapy bills. Inflation was up to 11 percent and interest rates 18 percent; people were hurting and angry.

The clinic workers tried all the recruiting techniques they'd been taught, even came down hard on their new trainees, but still new clients did not come in. Jon Walker and his three fellow clinicians were working so hard to get their Newport clinic off the ground that all of them were pale and sallow, their eyes ringed with dark circles. From Hollywood to Newport to Claremont . . . They were so tired. They were so *poor*. They often had to struggle to scrape together money for gas. The sleek, expensive clothes they wore to convey the right image of the Center smelled because they didn't have the money to get them dry-cleaned.

One day in August, after the clinic workers lectured at a potential clinic site about how wonderful it was to be at the Center, living among friends and sharing therapy, work, and basketball, a man rose from the audience. "I just want to know one thing," he said. "If you guys have such a great life, how come you look so sick?"

All four clinicians had tried to ignore the remark. But its truth lodged somewhere inside them, and between it, their exhaustion, and all the hours they spent together on the road, away from the Center, something was set free in them. Slowly, they began admitting aloud how unhappy they were. And there, in the privacy and safety of the car, there was no one to "correct" them, answer their "thoughts," or tell them they were misperceiving reality. Instead, they agreed on some basic facts. They hated being broke. They hated what they were doing. They hated everything about therapy.

Only one thing had kept any of the clinic counselors going—the therapists' promise that toward the end of the summer, they could come to the ranch for some time off. In late August, they arrived in Arizona exhausted and depleted, imagining days of relaxation and comfort. Instead, they discovered, they would be sleeping outside, in tents. And even here they were awakened daily at 6:00 A.M., the women to toil in the ranch's garden, the men to put up lights, bale hay, and do construction for hours in the blazing heat. Riggs strode among them, beaming with contentment. "Isn't this all great?" his smile seemed to say.

It wasn't great. On some days, the clinic women got to go horseback riding or swimming in the creek; a few took walks or just stayed in their tents. Toward the end of the stay, everyone got together to put on a rodeo, complete with barrel races and a barbecue. But Russ Gilbert, like most of his colleagues, felt awful. Instead of the letting down he'd anticipated, once again he'd had to perform. It wasn't just the physical labor he minded; it was the continued pressure to be that perfect therapy self, smiling, proud, *right*. Like the rest of the clinic workers, he went back to Los Angeles as tired as when he'd left. And even more resentful.

In September, as soon as the founders, juniors, and clinicians got back to Los Angeles, the Center went straight into its special "Fitness '80" program for the community. It was called "The Three-Day Week"—at the Center, now even a week went by twice as fast. Riggs had all kinds of new concepts to teach: "Perpetual Set Theory," for instance. Every person, he said, had a "set" and perceived reality based on it. But it was possible to change that set, to change *how* you perceived and, as a result, *what* you perceived. "The major conflict we have is biologically adapting to our environment while living in our memory of the past!" he pronounced. "You think if you remember something, it must have value. But mankind progresses by *replacing* memories."

As usual, the community wrote the ideas down. Or tried to. But this was odd stuff, psychological theory that danced on the edge of Orwellian doublethink. And some of it didn't even make *sense*.

No one complained—or even consciously understood there was something to complain *about*. As always, what Riggs said sounded good while he talked, his personal magnetism infusing the words with power. And the fact that Riggs said anything had always defined it as right. But the summer weeks the patients had spent without the therapists, the brief easing of the regression in which they'd lived so long, had opened a space for an unconscious awareness to grow. It was there that some noted how profoundly Feeling Therapy theory had changed since Joe's departure. Joe's ideas always had been far-out and radical, and, in recent years, also openly commercial. But there had always been a certain amount of intellectual solidity to them. There was so little substance to what they were hearing now, that some patients quietly put down their pens. On paper, Riggs's ideas lost their force. Trying to take hold of them was like grabbing air.

In late September, after "Fitness '80," came the Center Olympics. It was held in a park set in the dry brush and steep red rock of Malibu Canyon, and Group 1's planning made it a perfectly organized, choreographed event. Everyone in the community got a special commemorative T-shirt, and all kinds of athletic contests, from serious cross-country races to egg rolls, were organized. Every Group (but 1, the hosts) composed a competitive team; the therapists had a team of their own. Every event was scored and timed. There was a huge picnic lunch of delicious barbecued chicken and beef.

Andy Heller began the day feeling like a king. He'd finally persuaded his girlfriend to go into full-time Feeling Therapy, and he himself had moved up a Group level. He could not believe the joy that was his life. All his doubts and worry were gone, all his confusion. He had never felt so powerful. When it was time for his own competitive event, the swimming pool inner-tube relay race, his team was losing. Andy threw himself into the pool. "Go!" a friend shouted from the sidelines. "Make every stroke count!"

Something exploded inside Andy, imbuing him with a strength he'd never known he possessed. He moved faster and faster, until he passed the team that was winning, passed better swimmers. His teammates were screaming as he won the event—and a medal—for all of them.

Afterward, he collapsed at the side of the pool. It was fifteen minutes before he could catch his breath, and he was exhausted the rest of the day. And yet feelings of strength and utter transcendence kept surging through him; his happiness was evident to everyone who came near. When the day's awards were given, his team came in second, behind only the therapists. Andy was shocked and thrilled to receive a special individual medal, for "Most Feeling." He looked at the community around him, the tribe that he had longed to join and that now had unconditionally declared him a prized member. He had never felt prouder to be one of them. He knew with all his heart and soul that they were the vanguard of the human race.

———————

Within days after the Olympics ended, a newer patient told some of his friends a story. The therapists' team had won enough events that they were the overall Olympic champions. But the only reason the therapists had won, the patient said, was that during the cross-country race, Lee had run across a field rather than around it, and come in first. The patient had mentioned this to the therapists and been busted for it. But he knew what he had seen. And here and there, word of it reached other patients and left them with a sour feeling. There was only one way to understand what had happened. The therapists had cheated.

Only weeks later, the third basketball season began. Word came down that due to injuries on one patient team, everyone would be reshuffled. With the reorganization, the Center's best player, Group 1's six-foot-four ex-collegiate star, was made a member of the therapists' Wolf Pack.

For two seasons, patients had won the Center's basketball championships. With their new addition, however, the Wolf

Pack would be unstoppable. Patients' sourness grew. Whether it was therapy or sports, it seemed, the therapists always had to come in first. They always had to be number one.

As the fall wore on, the grueling pace picked up again. Even eighty-hour weeks weren't long enough to get everything done. Relationships were crumbling under the constant pressure, and each week more couples were ordered into $1,000 marital intensives. One weekend that fall, patients from the Center's Hawaii satellite came to L.A. for a special session. The former community member who'd started the satellite couldn't believe his eyes. The loose, hip crew he remembered looked like members of some fundamentalist church. All the men were burly and macho. All the women were skinny and wore dresses and lots of makeup. They reminded him of characters in a movie he'd seen about suburban men who replaced their wives with compliant robots; they looked like "Stepford Wives." *Tired* Stepford Wives. During his visit, there was a big party at the Compound.

"How come there are no kids here?" one of the Hawaii women asked.

"Riggs will tell us when we can have children," an L.A. patient answered.

Riggs will tell us. The placid acceptance in the words chilled the man from Hawaii to the bone. When he went back to Honolulu, he quit the satellite.

PAT continued its march through the Center. At Riggs's order, Mary Farrell and one of the Newport Beach clinicians became co-therapy partners; Mary knew she was to use the opportunity to work her way into reorganizing the Newport satellite. Jeff Langley began doing therapy on the employee of a successful businessman in the hope it would give PAT an inroad to the boss. With Riggs, Mary and Jeff started making plans to bring companies associated with the outposts in Montreal and Boston under PAT, and they continued giving individual L.A. patients advice. For $125 an hour, they told one man to buy a $200 watch and briefcase, post his work goals at home, and always dress flawlessly. A wealthy patient who'd come into the Center with writer's block got a program that included having his front teeth fixed, imposing a "writer's style" on his house, and buying $23,000 worth of Bijan clothes.

Since everyone knew that Riggs oversaw Mary and Jeff, these words of wisdom had to be coming from him—which meant they had to be right. But Center patients who had solid business backgrounds were beginning to have their own "negative thoughts." They'd had no trouble believing the therapists' claim to knowledge when it came to matters of the psyche—they themselves had known little or nothing about therapy. But they *did* know business—enough to see that the founders' grasp of commerce was roughly equivalent to what they knew of ranching. When one of them had casually mentioned to Riggs that he could save money by buying office supplies wholesale, he was astonished at the naïveté of the therapist's response. "Really?" Riggs gasped. "Where can you do that? Write it down!" The doubts even reached within PAT itself: Deborah Reiss's former partner was quietly instituting changes in the way things were being run at Plant Power. "This isn't the way Riggs and Lee do things," Kevin Fitzgerald protested.

The man took him aside. "You say anything about this and I'll deny it and you know they'll believe me," he said. "But Riggs and Lee don't know shit about business. I'll leave it at that."

"There was a major loss of revenue during July and August," Matt Lawrence castigated the clinic workers. "It is not an organizational problem; it is a *commitment* problem."

Fines came raining down. Three workers were penalized $100 for not completing their caseload analysis. One paid another $500 for losing clients. And the recruitment push began again, this time to get people who'd completed one clinic program to reenlist on a track that ultimately would lead them into the Center itself.

"Graduates of Phase I will be given to certain therapists," said Matt. "A minihierarchy will be established among us so the better therapists will get the Phase II clients. Look," he added, "accept the business hierarchy that exists. Don't get bitter about it. It's just part of what *is*."

But the clinic workers *were* bitter. Jon Walker's girlfriend was having constant nightmares in which the doors were ripped off her home and she was robbed. Some were so exhausted they were physically breaking down—one woman was having episodes of bleeding from the rectum.

And some of them were starting to be very afraid. After their time at the ranch, the clinic workers had been invited into Center staff meetings, to sit side by side with all the founders they'd considered virtual gods. But there in the staff room, it was clear that the founders weren't equal. Riggs ran the show, and he exerted a frightening power over the others. "Everyone who wants to be making $200,000 a year, raise your hands," he might say, and there would be a founder, with his two hands in the air, like a child. When Riggs went after some of the therapists, they seemed to turn into scared little boys.

One clinic counselor panicked. "We're just like Jonestown," she thought. "Riggs is our leader. We'll do anything for him." During co-therapy, she told her partner, a fellow clinician, her thoughts. For all his anger at his own situation, this was too much. "Those are crazy thoughts," he said. "You should talk to Dominic about them."

So the counselor talked to Dominic. "I must be insane. I keep thinking we're like Jonestown," she said.

"That *is* insane," Dominic agreed. The real problem was that she wasn't close to her boyfriend. The next Group, he busted her boyfriend for not taking care of her.

But the woman's thoughts didn't go away. Nor did the Newport clinicians' anger. Even Konni—who herself was suffering from tinnitus, a ringing in the ear often caused by stress—sensed there was a problem. Something in Riggs was veering out of control. "Talk to Riggs," she urged the clinic workers. "Share your feelings. He needs people to be responding to him."

"Talk about *what*?" Russ Gilbert wondered dully. The idea of even mildly criticizing the therapist was so unthinkable that it was as if his brain shut down.

Riggs seemed wound more and more tightly. He was juggling an increasing number of projects, working with a new clinic trainee on another book, lecturing, dealing with PAT and business, drafting theory papers. His Group 1 lectures were getting more far-out. One night he'd be talking about society and history and how by reading a stack of *Time* magazines backward chronologically he could understand how people thought. Another, he'd give out an article by a historical philosopher like Toynbee, then analyze and criticize the writing, pointing out the flaws in thought. He seemed to think he was beyond any limits now, any rules, even his own: The man once so adamant about avoiding drugs, tobacco, and caffeine, anything that got in the way of pure feeling, spent all day in his office drinking cappuccino. At Postgroup, he stood before the community holding a can of Coca-Cola.

"Wow," Konni told the co-therapists one night, shaking her head as she read, then passed out, the programs Riggs had written for them to follow. "Your dad's really out there this week. He's on the moon."

Through the fall, overt grumbling spread through the ranch. "This is like the army," Steve Gold once said bitterly. He watched Riggs zoom by on a motorcycle. "There goes the general."

Outright defiance grew among the juniors. Being packed into the cowboys' quarters together and away from the main house freed something in them. Men and women sat together on the porch at night, drinking wine and joking—joking, even, about Riggs. If one of them had been busted that day and was wearing the requisite "I'm fucked" look, others committed an unbelievably radical act: They mocked it. Riggs and his busts were "nothing, nothing," the juniors told each other. "We're having a great time!" When one of them would have to go to the main house for something, he or she always returned as soon as possible. "You know what?" came the breathless reports. "They're not having any fun over there!" And as the days passed, it began to dawn on the juniors that for all Riggs's talk about community and closeness, he himself seemed utterly alone. He had subjects and patients, he had sycophants and professional colleagues, but he had no *friends*.

All the juniors' anger and doubts hardened into conviction. Something had gone very wrong at the Center. Back in Los Angeles, they began holding meetings at their homes. Some of the exhausted, edgy clinicians attended. Even Carole Suydam Gold came to one. She talked to the juniors about her own situation, told them about the way she'd been "de-foundered" years earlier. The others listened, forgetting Carole's second-class status as "fallen" therapist. They didn't bust her. Instead, they were sympathetic.

Work. Perform.

"I don't need to think anymore," Riggs told Group 1. "I'm just . . . out there."

In mid-October, he and Werner flew to New York to lecture once again at the New School. While there, both men did radio shows and Riggs talked about dreams on "Good Morning, New York." He returned home blazing with excitement. "I haven't slept for four days!" he told everyone at Postgroup, his cheeks bright red. "I'm high, 'cause life is so exciting. I'm just gonna keep going till I drop!"

Work. Produce. Some patients were beginning to crack. Mary Farrell's migraines were getting longer and closer together. The secretary who worked at Slick Auto had the excruciating headaches too. One of the Center's secretaries went off her diet and started bingeing uncontrollably. A woman Janet Quinn had known in Group 5 turned up on her doorstep. She was thirty-one, sweet but emotionally fragile. The Group had been pressuring her, and she'd crumbled and been kicked out of her house. "Janet, I want to tell you something," the woman whispered, her eyes wide, her voice strange and high. "I think . . . this whole thing . . . is crazy. I think . . . this whole thing . . . is nuts."

The next Janet knew, the woman was on medication. Then her family was called in. One night, when Janet came home from work, she was gone. Back home, her family had her institutionalized.

Work. Work. While some patients were too consumed to think of anything but survival, among others, defenses weakened by exhaustion allowed questions to surface. Questions like, What exactly were they all doing here? Why were they all paying $200 a month for a therapy that was teaching them to act like corporate managers?

Questions like, Where were they going? Were they really going to be together in Hollywood forever? Once that had sounded OK, even appealing. But it had been one thing to sign on to such a plan at the end of the sixties when you were young. The sixties were over now; the *seventies* were over; and many Center patients were well into their thirties. They were getting tired of "growing" and changing all the time, of fighting and upheaval. They were tired of sharing crappy houses with ten other people and moving five times a year. They were tired of asking permission for everything. They wanted to get married and have children. They wanted to live like adults, to run their own lives—and they were beginning to suspect that the therapists were never going to let them.

"You know," a seven-year patient said to her Group 1 boyfriend one night when they were walking around the neighborhood alone, "in the town where I grew up, my parents weren't the wealthiest people or the most powerful. But they were respected, and they were equal with the other people in town. I don't see how we're ever going to get there. When does this become a true community? When will we be equal?"

The question was the kind of heresy that once would have provoked rage. But this time, her boyfriend didn't bust her. Nor did he know what to say.

———

News came of another animal death at the ranch—Riggs's beloved Doberman, Trucker. The official word was that Trucker had been bitten by a snake. Riggs wept like a child when he talked about it in Group. But another story quickly made its way around the Center community, one whose resonance haunted the exhausted older patients and clinic workers. The story was that Riggs had taken Trucker out with him on a horseback ride in the late fall heat, that he was going fast and hard, that even after the dog got tired, he wouldn't slow down. That the dog had died because he had been run to death.

24

In late October 1980, Kevin Fitzgerald finally completed the "marriage assignment" Dominic had given him the year before. He went to the therapist with a notebook recording each of the fifty-two separate "wedding" ceremonies that had been performed by their friends. Dominic was speechless. Perhaps he'd never figured Kevin and Sara would actually do the assignment. Perhaps he'd forgotten all about it. But he nodded his permission, and Kevin and Sara were married in their home. This ceremony was mostly written by therapists.

Around the same time, Konni Corriere paid a call on her old lover, Dominic. Riggs, she said, was out of control. He was unbearable. She couldn't stand it anymore. She needed help.

The founders and junior therapists went out to the ranch for several days, leaving Riggs (and his ally, Werner) behind. In their absence, clinic workers began talking back to Riggs. He was furious. "Wait until my friends get back," he told Mary Farrell. "They're not gonna like this."

But at the ranch, the therapists were coming to a different conclusion. They did not seem to understand the depths of their own corruption, the responsibility they bore for what the

Center had become. They did, however, see that Riggs seemed to be cracking up. And they believed they knew why. One of Feeling Therapy's prime tenets was that no one could stay sane without getting regular therapy. But no one—except maybe Joe—had ever been able to do real therapy on Riggs. Even for the founders, the absolute certainty and control he projected was too frightening. In the early Center days, whenever Linda Binder had worked with Riggs, she'd looked up what the therapist before her had done in his session and just copied it. The men had done no better. Riggs had even bragged to Group 1 that "I know what my therapist is going to say before *he* does."

For years, the therapists had berated their patients for the insanity of living out of images rather than feelings. But, they now believed, Riggs was the one who was living an image. He had to be brought down, humanized. He had to be busted.

It was his old teacher Dominic who took him on. The private sessions went on nearly a week, and when they were over, Riggs's swagger was gone. His face was drawn, his eyes sunken. He could barely talk.

There was no way he could run a Group in this state, so the founders decided Jerry would go to the regular Group 1 meeting with him. People in Group 1—and a few of the other higher-level Groups as well—would be brought in on what was going on. They would be told that some changes were being made.

On Tuesday, November 4, while the outside world watched Ronald Reagan elected president, Center patients came as usual to the Sunset Boulevard building for Group. The evening went normally in Groups 6 through 13. There was no mention of trouble in Group 5. In Group 4, Lee told his patients that things at the Center had been too hard and harsh of late. From now on, life was going to be easier. In Group 3,

Dominic counseled several couples on their relationship problems. Then, about fifteen minutes before the evening's end, he paused.

"I don't know if any of you have noticed," he said, "but Riggs has been working hard and is getting stressed-out. We think maybe he's working more than he should and he's losing his focus. It's not good for him, and we're going to have him take a rest for a while and not lead Group, so he can focus on himself. We're going to take good care of him."

A few eyebrows went up. *This* was new. Still, Dominic hadn't sounded terribly upset. No one worried much.

It was different in Group 2. No one had ever seen Werner the way he was that night, nervous, flippy, *scared*. "I have a lot to tell you people," he said. "There's been a lot going on." And then suddenly, he began to do something no one had ever heard a therapist do before: He apologized. Things at the Center had been too hard. People had been pushed too much. It just wasn't right, and he was sorry, so sorry. . . .

Suddenly, Dominic came in the room. "Things aren't going to be so tough here," he said. "We're not going to be doing such heavy busting. And Riggs and Werner have been overworking. They're tired. They need some therapy of their own to get back on track."

Riggs and Werner publicly declared in need of therapy? A shock wave passed through much of the Group. But a number of Group 2 women worked at the Center or were junior therapists' mates—they knew of the upheaval at the top. And they snapped.

"You're fucked up!" the clinic's administrative secretary shouted at Werner. "You're crazy!"

Werner stared at her blankly. No one had ever talked like this to a therapist before.

"Respond!" screamed a junior's wife and the Associate Program director. "Say something! Respond!"

Werner started to cry. "My life isn't right . . ." he wept.

Kevin Fitzgerald stared in amazement. He had come to

Group ready to talk about how happy he and Sara were to be married, glad that for once he had something good to talk about. And now . . . People were yelling at Werner! They were saying the kinds of things no one was allowed to say! And Werner was falling apart! Something began to move deep inside Kevin, like geologic plates along a fault line. Everything he'd agreed to do and become for the past nine years had been built on the assumption that the therapists knew more—*were* more—than he. And now he was being told something else: Not only weren't Riggs and Werner infallible; they were *crazy*. That couldn't be true! But there was Werner, right in front of him, trembling, weeping, practically on his knees. There was no denying that reality. Kevin's mind shuddered and shifted, realigned: He looked out onto a changed world. A feeling shot up from within him, something unexpected, like indignation, even anger. Words began to spill out. "You always said there was something wrong with me for not getting into heavy busting!" he told Werner and Dominic. "You made me think there was something wrong with me all this time! There's nothing wrong with being sweet! There's nothing wrong with *me!*"

Down the hall, Jerry led Riggs into Group 1. The star basketball player automatically rose to his feet and started to clap, then noticed no one had joined him, and stopped in confusion. He looked at Riggs. He seemed like a different man, weak, confused. His shoulders were sagging, his eyes dull.

"Riggs has been having a hard time," said Jerry quietly. "He has a hard time making friends. He'd like to hear what you think of him. Give him some feedback."

"Um, I'd like to thank you for helping me get a work-study class at UCLA," ventured one man.

"I don't like it when you yell," mumbled someone else. "But I'd really like to be your friend."

There was a silence. Then, again, it was the women—the starved, underpaid, forced-to-be-submissive women—who cracked.

"I *HATE* YOU!" screamed a clinic counselor. "I hate the

way you called me 'cow'! I hate you for calling me a 'beast'! You're fucked to women! You're a pig!"

Heads jerked around as if touched by live wires.

Now Carole Suydam Gold was exploding, rage in her eyes. "You ran over Steve!" she screamed. "You treated him like dirt!"

Then Jerry's wife was screaming too. "You screwed Jerry! You shit on him!"

Linda Binder Cirincione had come in from Werner's Group. She too was raging. "You played all the therapists off against each other!" she yelled. "You always made fun of my sex life! You always thought *you* were sexy! You're not! Konni says you're an asshole! She says you treat her like shit! You treat *women* like shit! I trusted you! I did everything you said and you raked me over the coals, you broke up my marriage, you made me feel bad about myself! I didn't do anything to deserve that!"

Riggs said nothing. His eyes looked like dark, empty pits.

"I hate you!" shouted the woman who was junior therapist Phil Schwartz's wife. "At the ranch, I tried to tell you something and you told me I was nuts! You pushed me down! You *spit* on me!"

Russ Gilbert looked at his idol in amazement. This guy, he thought, this guy . . . is an asshole.

Jon Walker spoke up, striving for calm. "I have to tell you, I feel really bad about the way I did my Ph.D! We made things up in our dissertations! We made things *up*! We weren't looking for the truth!"

"Lots of my employees hurt their backs and legs working so hard," said Jeff Langley. "There's something wrong!"

"You've been running a plantation here!" yelled the basketball player.

"You hit people and throw them against walls because you have no idea how to do therapy!" shouted a Newport Beach clinician. "All you know how to do is beat people up!"

Inside Russ, years of feelings he hadn't even realized

were there rushed to the surface and broke free. "You didn't *have* to bust me like that on the research project!" he found himself screaming. "I blame *you* for that motorcycle accident! I blame *you* for all that busting in the desert!"

God, what was happening? Mary Farrell sat white-faced and dazed as the world shook and turned upside down. Nausea pulsed through her; she started to cry. In a panic, she turned to the man on whom she'd always depended. "Riggs, I'm so confused," she said in a small voice. "No one ever loved me the way you did."

There was no answer, no response in Riggs's dead eyes. One man rushed from the room and vomited outside the door.

Jerry tried to speak in a business-as-usual voice. "I appreciate your feedback," he said. "Next week, we'll keep talking—"

His wife cut him off in disgust. "Jerry, you missed the whole point!"

Now another patient spoke up. "It's finished," he said. "It's over. I'm out of here. I need a cigarette."

Lee appeared at the door. He was holding a meeting at his house right now. Riggs would go home, but everyone else had to come. He was almost frantic. None of the founders had come even close to anticipating the explosion that had just occurred. Everything they had was at risk.

"Don't throw out the baby with the bathwater," he kept urging everyone who came to the meeting. Yes, many things at the Center were wrong, maybe everything was wrong, but it could be made right. Everyone was talking at once; no one knew what to do. They'd have to get together again tomorrow.

Mary went home, reeling. The house was strange—all her roommates had heard different stories about what was going on. One had heard Dominic talking about "changes." One had seen Werner fall apart; one had called Riggs a pig. In Group 13, Ken had been told that everything at the Center was great.

Confused, dizzy, sick, Mary fled to her room. Her brain echoed with the screams of Group 1, with Lee's pleading, with

Dominic's voice. And with the words of her marital intensive counselor. Just after Group, as they were all leaving the room, she'd grabbed Mary's arm. "I'm sorry about what I did to you," she said. "You were right; it *was* Riggs who made you the way you are. I'm really, really sorry."

———

News of what had happened in Groups 1 and 2 leaked into the community unevenly. Some patients heard nothing; some tried to deny anything was going on. Kevin Fitzgerald's Group 5 roommates came home worried only about getting their assignments done, shaking their heads in disbelief when he tried to make them see that their world was unraveling. But finally, his words began to sink in, and the shock spread to them too. Kevin went to the kitchen, got out a bottle of wine left over from his wedding, opened it, and all of them started to drink.

———

"Riggs is fucked!" Russ Gilbert told his girlfriend, Holly. Rage and anguish poured off him like heat. "He's fucked! I hate him!"

Holly listened, torn. Riggs had been her Intensive therapist, and the bond she felt to him had never been broken. Now, one of the two men she loved most in the world was raging against the other.

"I've gotta talk to Riggs," she said.

At the Compound, therapists walked around like zombies. Konni was locked in her room. Riggs was sitting very still on the living room couch.

"I love you," Holly told him. "I'm going to stay here with you."

Riggs started to cry. "I'm sorry," he said. "I didn't know that I was pushing people too hard. In my family, I was told you keep doing things until you get them right. That's all I know. I didn't get paid much money when I worked at my parents' restaurant. You're supposed to work real hard and then there's a payoff at the end. That's what I was taught."

Holly thought he sounded scared. "I miss my mother and father," Riggs whispered. "I want to talk to them, but I haven't been very nice. I'm afraid."

"I'll sit with you," Holly said. "Go ahead and call." She held his hand as he dialed.

"Mom? Dad?" Riggs sobbed. "I'm scared. I'm alone and everything's bad. I'm sorry. If you let me, I'll come back to work for you in the restaurant. I'll do anything."

By Wednesday morning, reports of what had happened in Groups 1 and 2 spread to the Center businesses. Everyone showed up at Plant Power, but no one could work and the phones kept ringing. No one knew what was happening, but the smell of revolution was in the air. That afternoon, Dominic called Slick Auto. The company secretary couldn't understand what he wanted, except that he seemed afraid that Ron Arliss was going to sue him. The Center had its own rules, Dominic said, and they all needed to stick to them. . . . But by now, the Slick Auto secretary had heard about the night before. Something in her too had wrenched free.

"Dominic, there aren't any more rules," she snapped. "Not *your* rules." And she hung up on him.

Back at the Center, chaos reigned. All the founders (including Riggs), juniors, and clinic counselors had been in meetings for hours; yelling and shouting kept coming through the walls, and the secretaries didn't know what to do. All the therapists but Riggs and Werner were right in the middle of treating a new set of Intensive patients, but no one was taking care of business. Normally, no mere employee would dare breach the sanctum of the staff room, but today wasn't a normal day. The clinic and Center secretaries marched to the room and broke in.

"We can fix this," one of the clinic counselors was saying. "We can save the business."

The clinic secretary was horrified. "What do you mean *the business*?" she demanded. "People's lives are at stake!"

Lee's voice took on a patronizing Group-leader tone. "The Center for Feeling Therapy is a for-profit corporation," he said with exaggerated patience. "The Center *Foundation* is nonprofit."

"No!" she insisted again. "You're talking about corporations and I'm talking *souls*!"

"Good, he's bullshitting you and you didn't fall for it," said Jerry. He turned to the rest of the therapists. "This is where we've gone wrong. We have to start listening to the patients more."

Suddenly, Ron Arliss and his partner were at the door shouting about the tens of thousands of dollars they'd paid to PAT. Someone tried to silence them, but other founders said no, they wanted to understand. They seemed to have been told nothing about PAT's operation and practices. Then owners of other businesses taken over by PAT rushed into the room too. "Where's our money?" they were asking. "What's happened to our money?"

Where's the money? The question hummed in the air. The Center had been making a fortune on its clinic, all its programs—where *was* it? One secretary had been looking through the books, and there were things she didn't understand. Where had the money gone?

And then the awful answer came out: It had been spent on the ranch. The tens of thousands of dollars patients had donated to build a gym had been deposited not in a separate fund but in the Center Foundation general account—and then taken and used to maintain the ranch. Riggs had appropriated

$1 million in Center income—and spent it on the ranch. All the money that could have been spent paying clinic counselors decent wages—even the fines for losing clients that had decimated already tiny paychecks—had gone, instead, to the ranch.

The counselors sat, stunned. All those endless, exhausting days, the phone calls and pressure, the voices insisting *"Recruit,"* their poverty. . . . For what? For Riggs's cowboy dreams. For *nothing*.

With the revelation, something seemed to break inside the therapists. Admissions of the ambivalence and guilt with which they'd been living began pouring out.

"You know, Riggs had a hit list for which patients to bust!" exclaimed Phil Schwartz. "It got so bad I'd just tell people, 'If Riggs asks, tell him I busted you.' "

"We're the ones who create the relationship problems for people by working them so hard!" said his wife. "Then we make them pay $1,000 for an intensive to solve the problem! It stinks! I'm tearing up the checks I have!"

Then the confessions turned to anger, and right there, in front of patients, the Center myth of solidarity and harmony at the top crumbled, and the therapists were shouting that they too had been busted and humiliated and kept from having children, that they'd been hit, hurt, ridiculed, dominated. And for all of it, they blamed Riggs.

"You would never let *me* be on TV!" Jerry Binder shouted at him. "You broke up my marriage to Linda!"

"I went to his house; I tried to confront him!" cried Matt Lawrence. "He beat me up! He tore all the buttons off my shirt!" He turned to his wife in a fury. "You'd always tell on me!" he yelled. "You sent me to Riggs like meat to a butcher!"

"I think some patients may sue us," Lee said.

"No, I don't think anyone will sue," the clinic secretary reassured him.

Lee shook his head. "I know there will be lawsuits," he said. "*I* feel like suing."

The meeting ended, but it spilled out into the Center building and no one could stop talking. Janet Quinn sat at her desk, astounded as the compulsive recriminations and confessions swirled around her for hours. The therapists were falling from their pedestals; a hierarchy she thought was cast in stone was crumbling to dust right before her. It was like a miracle, an act of grace. Now everything would be all right. "Oh *good*," she thought. "I won't have to feel bad around them anymore. Now we can just be friends."

But through Wednesday evening, what had been revealed in the staff meeting was traveling with different effect through older patient networks. Money had been taken from the gym fund, friends told each other. Money had been *stolen*. The fact hit like a sledgehammer to the skull. It was one thing that no one had ever reached the dreamy end point of sanity the therapists had promised. That goal had been vague and elusive, and failure to reach it was something a patient always could blame on him- or herself. But money was hard and absolute; when a dollar had been taken, it was theft—there was no other way to see it. And if the therapists had stolen money, they were not the good men they had always claimed to be. With the realization, a tiny chink opened in the haze of idealizing transference through which patients had always viewed their leaders.

That was all it took. Through the opening poured all the feelings of doubt patients had so successfully repressed the past few frantic years, and all at once, the transference shattered. If the therapists were not good men, everything they'd said and done was open to question. If they had lied about money, perhaps everything else they'd said was a lie as well. What had they all been doing here, then?

Through the night, the doors of older patient houses opened and men and women began to walk the streets. Scenes from the past played like slide shows in their heads: All the terrible things that had been done to them. All the terrible things they had done to others. "I'm sorry," patients cried, clutching at each other. "God, I remember when I busted you! I don't know why I did it. I'm so sorry, I'm so sorry."

Angry groups gathered before the homes of Jeff Langley and Mary Farrell. The therapists were bad men and these were their footsoldiers. For years, they'd driven people to work for nothing while they lived like royalty. PAT had been paid a fortune, and no one had accounted for that money yet. *Where was it?*

"I'm gonna sue you!" Ron Arliss was screaming. "I'm gonna sue!"

At Kevin Fitzgerald's house, people gathered in a living room still surreally wreathed with wedding flowers and ribbons. Wine bottles were opened again; men and women drank, trying to make sense of their lives.

"Goddamn it!" one man shouted. "I've been a plumber for five years! I never *wanted* to be a plumber!" A sudden shock of awareness raced through the room; switches flicked "click" in a dozen heads. That made *sense*. This was a man who should be in graduate school. Why *was* he a plumber?

"That time when I was so fucked up," someone else confessed, "it was 'cause he made me take my clothes off and busted me so bad. . . ."

"Was *that* what he did to you back then? Was *that* why you were so upset?"

"I know, I know," someone else chimed in. "He did that to me, too. . . ."

Another shock, more clicks. More wine. The people in this room had known each other for years. They had revealed their childhood stories to each other, shared their bodies and sex lives. But they had never before talked honestly about how they felt about what happened to them at the Center. Everyone thought he or she was the only one who had doubts or didn't "get it"; everyone had imagined himself or herself alone in failure and felt a private disgrace in being humiliated and busted. But now it was clear that everyone had been busted. Everyone had been scared and hurt. It was not because they were bad people. It was because they were part of a bad *system*.

God, what had they all been doing here? What had they done?

The clinic secretary who'd stormed the staff meeting raced home from Kevin's and started packing her bags.

Suddenly, her roommate was tugging at her arm. "You can't go!" the woman pleaded. "You can't! Stay with us!"

The secretary froze in terror. Center people had always told each other not to leave the community, for keeping friends here was considered the most loving thing you could do for them. But the familiar words sounded so different now, like something out of a horror movie—pod people from *Invasion of the Bodysnatchers* grabbing at humans, ghoulish voices moaning "Stay... stay...." A veil seemed to fall from the secretary's eyes, and she looked out with terrible clarity on the past eight years of her life.

"Oh my God," she thought, "I've been part of a mass hallucination."

Back in the flower-draped living room, Kevin Fitzgerald drained his glass and looked around. His head rang with liquor, yet through the pounding in his ears, one fact stood out, stark and true. The therapists had lied. What they had built here had been built on a lie. He was done with it.

He turned to one of his roommates. "You know what?" he said. "I'm not going back to therapy."

"You know what?" she answered. "Neither am I."

––––––––––

Early Thursday, word went out that instead of Laydown/co-therapy, there would be a communitywide meeting at the Center that night. All morning, people streamed in and out of the building. Andy Heller, who, like most newer patients, had heard only vague dark rumors about trouble, came by on his lunch hour. The place was bedlam. All around, therapists were weeping—*weeping*! Andy had never seen any of them look so destroyed. He found Katie Stendall Lawrence. She was crying almost hysterically. When Andy saw that, he saw his world crumble, and he too began to sob.

"I didn't know what I was doing with you!" Katie wept. "I had no idea! I totally failed you!"

"No, Katie, no!" Andy cried, grabbing her hand. "That's not true!" He held the sobbing woman tightly, his insides churning with fear.

The afternoon veered toward anarchy. People kept coming in, screaming, and with each hour the therapists looked more broken. "I'm sorry you got ripped off," Katie told a secretary, then gave her her own diamond ring in compensation.

"Even *I* didn't understand the therapy assignments I was making up," confessed Matt Lawrence.

Another staff meeting was called; someone had to decide what to do with the center's new Intensive patients and the clinic clients. Some of the clinic counselors still wanted to practice, but was that wise? In the middle of the debate, Mary Farrell rushed in.

"Ron Arliss is threatening to sue me. What the fuck are you going to do about it?" she demanded.

"Stop," Riggs said, speaking up for the first time. "We haven't done anything wrong. Just stop."

But what was happening could not be stopped. Word that gym fund and Group fine money had been stolen kept spreading through the community. By the time evening fell Thursday and all 350 patients arrived at the Center building, there was ugliness in the air. Anyone who'd held power at the Center was fair game for attack. Mary Farrell fled home to hide. Panic spread among the founders. Werner collapsed on the floor, his body jerking in a grand mal seizure while Riggs cradled his head in his arms.

"I want to call a lawyer immediately," one founder said, terrified. "I could go to jail for what I did here. I don't want to go to jail and get butt-fucked by some convict!"

In the big auditorium, where Tombstone normally met, the clinic counselor who'd been the first to scream at Riggs in Group 1 was on stage, trying to lead an organized discussion of how the Center was going to change. Upstairs, founders sat in chairs in their therapy rooms and men and women poured in to confront them. For nine years, these men had held absolute power, had told their patients who they were and what to do and never, ever allowed them to talk back. Tonight, the tables were turned.

Deborah Reiss, raging, broke, sought out Lee, her long-time Group leader. "I sent you a birthday card every year for *eight years!*" she screamed. "Where was *my* card? Where was anything you did for me? I hope they *do* put you in jail, Lee. I hope they burn you."

"You're really gone!" a patient screamed at Jerry Binder. "You've lost it!"

"Riggs told me I wasn't a very good therapist," Jerry said, and then he was sobbing loudly, his face looking ravaged and broken. . . .

In still another room, Werner, now recovered from his seizure, was backed up against a wall, surrounded by yelling patients. "I'm scared," he called out, tears running down his face. "I'm really scared!"

But the bulk of the rage was saved for Riggs—once the ideal Feeling Therapy man, now the symbol of all the Center's betrayal. In the therapists' private staff room, with its expensive couches and tables, he sat flanked by Dominic and Russ Gilbert, while patient after patient came in for the attack. Everything he had ever said and done for nine years was coming back at him all at once.

"You hurt me!" one man screamed.

"I trusted you; I believed in you," charged a woman.

"You convinced me I couldn't take care of my child; you told me I would commit suicide if I left, that I would harm my child. Riggs, you're sicker than me. You need help."

"You're acting out," Riggs said.

"Shut up," hissed Dominic.

"But listen, they're just—"

"Shut up!" shouted Russ. "You sit down, be quiet, and listen for a change."

Riggs slumped back in his chair. His eyes were red-rimmed, vacant.

"You fucked me over!" a woman screamed.

"You made my boyfriend into a basket case!" shouted another.

"You busted me! You made my husband and me break up!"

"You took away my job!"

"You made me move out of my house! You took away my best friend!"

"You're an asshole! How dare you have treated me this way!"

Tears welled up in Riggs's eyes, but the crowd jeered.

"What about all the money I had to pay PAT!" Ron Arliss screamed.

"Where's the money?" The others took up the cry. "What bank accounts do you have? How much money is there in them? Where's the money? *Where's the fucking money?*"

In the auditorium, Matt, Katie, and Steve Gold had taken the stage, clinic counselors around them. Patients twisted and moved in their seats, as feelings swept through them—confusion and fright among the newer patients, gusts of rage in the rest. "I know I did a lot of things wrong," Matt tried to say, "but I never did anything really—"

"What about the time you hit me?" someone screamed. "What about the time you threw me against the wall?"

"You made me take off my clothes!"

"You called me a slug!"

Matt started to cry and nod. "I know there are grievances. Things will change. I didn't mean for it. . . . The clinic is a sham. I never meant it to be this way. . . ."

Kevin Fitzgerald looked at his wife, Sara, and the friend who'd come with them. It was like the earth splitting open: A therapist was admitting to all of them that therapy was wrong.

"But what about how they helped us?" A woman who'd been huddled with the other new patients on one side of the room came forward. "I don't care that you've done things wrong," she told Matt. "You haven't done anything that we can't go past."

"Shut up!" an older patient shrieked, his face contorted and red. "You don't *know* what they've done! You don't *know*!"

"You made me break up with my husband!" someone else screamed at Steve.

"You made me have an abortion!"

Janet Quinn clutched the arms of her seat in terror. Something was happening that the Center could never get beyond. What would she do now? How could she live without the community?

Andy Heller sat stunned. A friend collapsed to the floor, sobbing. "Don't take away my Center," he wept. "It's my whole life!"

The rage broke like waves, receded, rushed back in higher and higher.

"You beat me!"

"You humiliated me!"

"I didn't mean—" Matt began.

"BULLSHIT! BULLSHIT!" Patients' faces turned dark red; their spit-flecked lips pulled back in furious grimaces.

"You *motherfucker*s! You ripped off my life!" A man raced

to the wall, grabbed a fire extinguisher, and tried to wrench it free to throw. A fistfight broke out between two other men.

Suddenly, Kevin Fitzgerald was afraid. There were hundreds of people in the room, each filled with years of suppressed fury, and the air was charged with madness and murder. He looked at Sara, their friend. The women were rigid with terror.

"Let's get out of here," he said, and the three of them fled.

"I can't feel my heart," Konni said over and over as a clinic worker led her away. "I can't feel my heart."

And still the screams continued, all that had been boiling in so many patients exploding in a surge of triumph and pain. All the years they'd been at the Center learning to "feel," there had been so much patients had *not* felt. The true depth of each hurt and humiliation had been blocked out, explained away as "defense" or "craziness." Everything had been made endurable by the belief that it had a higher purpose. But now the truth stood out, stark and terrible. Everything they'd done in the Center's name—the horrible things they'd said to parents, the children they'd abandoned or aborted, the marriages they'd ended, the unwanted sex they'd had, the time they'd spent in poverty and confusion—all of it had been for nothing. It was not outsiders who were "reasonably insane," whose good-looking exteriors masked the fact that they were dead inside. It was them. It would take years to fully feel or understand, but that night, some Center patients caught the first glimpse of themselves as they truly were—no master race, but a wretched group of overworked men and starved women, exploited, lied to, robbed of their youth. And they knew one thing with a certainty most had not felt in years: It was over.

A patient making his way down one of the Center building halls ran into Dominic.

"I hate you!" voices screamed from nearby rooms. "I fucking *hate* you!"

"Hey," the patient said to the therapist, "welcome to reality."

PART SIX

Going Sane

25

November 6, 1980

Devastation. All night, the Center neighborhood was like a war zone, lights blazing everywhere, house doors unlocked and standing open, groups of patients roaming the streets, screaming with rage, embracing, apologizing, crying. Rumors leapt from block to block: Bags of money had been delivered to the Compound in the middle of the night; Riggs had Swiss bank accounts; the ranch had been no more than a slave labor camp. People turned on each other, then themselves, overcome with horror at what they'd done and become. "If I'd been in the Third Reich," one die-hard Group 1 member told his girlfriend in anguish, "I'd have been a Nazi."

The Center was gone—it was gone because it had been corrupt and crazy. A few clinic counselors got together and called Joe Hart. "Why didn't you tell us what was going on here?" they demanded.

"You wouldn't have listened," was all Joe said. "You wouldn't have believed me."

Joe knew. The story made its way through the community.

Until now, patients' fury at Riggs hadn't touched their memories of Joe, the soft-spoken sage and dream father. But his words changed everything. *Joe knew, and he saved himself but left us behind.* "The ball-less wonder of the world!" one woman would cry in fury even years later. "These were people's *lives!*"

The Center was gone. For his own protection, Riggs was sent to spend the night with his parents in Orange County. The other therapists retreated to their homes, huddling behind closed curtains. They had nowhere else to go. The Center was gone; it was *over.* The realization hit everyone again and again with a rush of disbelief, the clammy vertigo that follows a 3:00 A.M. phone call announcing an unexpected death. What never seemed possible had actually happened. In only seventy-two hours, the whole world had changed.

Amazingly, the very next day some of the founders tried to go back to their Intensives. Clinic counselors stopped them, and the Center's newest crop of patients' therapy was over. The clinic counselors called their own clients to tell them the clinic was closing; the Newport Beach counselors did the same. Calls went out to Boston, Honolulu, Munich, and San Francisco, and within days, those satellites closed down. Members of the Boston satellite, who in recent months had been recruiting and working as hard as anyone in L.A., went to talk to a lawyer. Those in Montreal—who, unlike the others, had had legitimate therapy licenses all along—decided to go into practice for themselves (though presumably using different theory and technique). By the end of the week, the Center building was closed, its front door secured by a padlock.

Patients living in the Hollywood neighborhood spent their time veering between confusion and grief, joy and rage. Unmistakably *real* feelings swept through them like constantly changing winds. Many of those who'd been most committed to the Center now hated it the most, cursing the therapists, calling anyone not equally angry a Bodysnatcher "pod." Others wrestled with terrible ambivalence, unsure if the therapists' confessions meant they had known all along that they were doing wrong, unable to believe they had. And some could recall only what they'd loved about the community and saw its end as a terrible tragedy. "We'll keep things the way they were," they told each other. "We'll have our own Group. We'll stay together."

But even those who tried to hang on to Center ways could not. And for most, as the old rules and restrictions fell away, the world took on a dazzling openness, the soul a sweet lightness, as if suddenly freed of a great weight. Then that sweetness changed to pain, for feeling free brought home the reality of having been jailed. Then pain gave way to overwhelming fear—after years of being told what to do, no one was sure of anything. Patients quietly engaged in ordinary pursuits like taking baths suddenly found themselves paralyzed with the fear that they were "going dead." Every relationship was open to question and change. Roommates kicked roommates out of houses; "friends" allowed to say what they really thought revealed they couldn't stand each other, then each turned around and got close to people they'd shunned because of their Center ranking. People grabbed other people's possessions and vanished. Engineered love affairs fell apart overnight, men and women who'd lived together for years mumbling hasty good-byes, those who'd genuinely been in love left devastated as their partners disappeared. Some of the newly single turned to each other, and new affairs began.

For weeks, the aftermath of revolution raged. Chunks of garbage landed in the therapists' yards, their phones rang with anonymous calls, bricks crashed through car windshields, packages of dogshit arrived in the mail. Patients plastered Compound homes with eggs, and someone scrawled graffiti on the redwood fence: "Methodology of Egg-celence." And each night, the windows of patient homes were filled with small red lights that were the glowing tips of dozens of once-forbidden cigarettes as small groups gathered in living rooms, drinking and debating, reminiscing and mourning, trying to understand the enormous change that filled their minds and tore apart their hearts and even took over their bodies. Just two weeks after the night the Center ended, several women who hadn't had their periods in years once again began to bleed.

Kevin Fitzgerald kept going to work at Plant Power. So did almost everyone else on staff; they didn't know what else to do. But they were all too dazed to function very well. One day, Kevin found his boss, Mary Farrell and Jeff Langley's PAT partner, crying uncontrollably. He told Kevin about the night he'd been beaten in Group 2.

Kevin himself was on the verge of losing it. Sara was calm, but things were different for her. She'd had a life before the Center and, for the past few years, an outside job that allowed her to hold on to one small piece of herself; she'd never even told her co-workers about the Center. But Kevin had gone into primal therapy at nineteen—he was being thrown out of the only adult life he'd ever known. On one level, he was furious about it, joining friends on egg-throwing runs and screaming "Fuck you!" whenever he saw a therapist drive through the neighborhood. It felt great, though sometimes the absurdity of it hit him hard. People had stolen nine years of his life and he was throwing *eggs*?

But right below his rage was an overpowering terror. Everything he'd trusted as solid had shifted. The world he thought a good one was bad. The self he believed was real had turned out to be someone else's projection. He was thirty years old, and he felt no different from how he'd felt at nineteen. None of the problems he'd brought into therapy had been solved. He had no profession, no sense of himself, no place in the world. In nine years, he hadn't learned anything except how to be a Feeling Therapy patient. At least once a day, all that piled up on him, his fear mounting until he was wailing and sobbing his heart out.

Sara was patient with him. But one day, a co-worker at Plant Power took Kevin aside. "You have to stop crying and get your life together," she told him sternly. "You have something now that you haven't had in years: You have the ability to think."

Kevin tried to take hold of the words, to make a plan. Then Plant Power started going under. In retrospect, it was inevitable. The business had been dependent on a willing, dedicated patient labor force to maintain sales. But now that the Center was gone, people didn't see any reason to spend their lives selling plants. Those who did no longer felt obliged to buy them from Plant Power. Quickly, it became clear to Kevin that he had no professional future at the company. And he was starting to hate living in the old neighborhood, surrounded by bad memories. Nothing good would happen to him until he got out. He and Sara leased out their half of the house until it could sell, then packed and moved to the outskirts of San Diego.

Plant Power slid into free-fall. Sales plummeted; debts grew. It could not be saved. Holly Stoddard abandoned her share of the business. So did Deborah Reiss, who had begun it—and whose name was still on its bank loan note. Neither had anything to show for years of eighty-hour workweeks. Within months, the once-thriving business was bankrupt.

The furniture and electric companies managed to keep going. At Slick Auto, Ron Arliss and his partner spent weeks working out their new relationship. Though it was clear they'd never be best friends, for the time being their partnership would survive.

Every day, Ron woke with the feeling that he'd been released from a prison he'd never understood he was in. He ended the relationship he hadn't wanted abruptly, even brutally, ordering the woman out of his Hollywood house. And he gave Jeff Langley hell about all the money he'd paid PAT. Jeff acted remorseful, swearing he'd do whatever he could to get the money back. Then he split the neighborhood. Although later the Center's attorneys would send Ron $2,000 to reimburse him for the work his crew had done at the ranch, the $60,000 he'd paid PAT was gone forever.

But finally, the repair shop was his again. An attorney who represented PAT returned the 10 percent interest in the business Mary and Jeff had awarded themselves. Almost all Slick's mechanics stayed on duty; they needed time to figure out what they were going to do with their lives. Ron reduced their hours and put them on commission. Mechanics' pay doubled and tripled; sales and profit both went up. Sometimes Ron would make bitter jokes that he'd paid PAT $60,000 just to learn how to get up early and feel tense. But now the tension was dissolving. The higher pay made everyone happy. And being together helped everyone get through this hard time. Sometimes the mechanics would do the old "eye checks" on each other, giggling. Or "I don't *like* the way you put that car on the hoist!" someone would declare, his friends roaring as his voice took on those loud, distinctive therapy rhythms. "I don't *like* the way you did the last tune-up! I just wanted to tell you that."

––––––––––––

For days, furious people filled Mary Farrell's living room. Now that there was no Center, her power too was gone, leaving only a thin, haggard woman to whom anything could be said.

"In the real world, you *never* would have become this important!" one woman flung down in scorn.

"I *pity* you," spat the former Slick Auto secretary. "I never want to be like you."

"What's happening?" Mary wept over the phone to Riggs. "What did I do?"

"You didn't do anything wrong, Mary," came the familiar soothing voice.

There was no way Mary could believe that. One of her best girlfriends had stopped speaking to her; people she barely knew were shouting out their loathing. And each day, former Langley Construction workers turned up at the house, strong, burly men who were so angry that Ken stayed home from work to make sure she didn't get hurt.

"You bitch!" the men screamed. "You bitch! I want my money!"

But there *was* no money. What PAT had collected from companies like Langley was a "fortune" only in the context of the Center, where so many were earning poverty wages. Out of it, Mary and Jeff had paid salaries to themselves, their partner, secretaries, bookkeepers, and sandwich makers. The little left over in the Langley Construction account Mary gave to the overly honest worker who'd been fined all the time. But she couldn't give him back all he'd paid. It was gone.

"Bitch! I want my money!"

Mary clung to the shreds of the life that was evaporating around her. Then one night, not long after the Center's fall, she went down the block to visit Carole and Steve, purposely waiting until after dark—if she was seen talking to therapists, people would hate her even more.

"Riggs fucked me over," Steve was ranting that night. "He made me think I was stupid! All I ever wanted was to do therapy. I'm a therapist! I didn't want a Ph.D.! I never wanted a goddamn community! Why did I allow it?"

"I want to ask *you* something, Mary," Carole said in her soft voice. "Last month, you busted Steve really bad. Do you remember? I want to know why you did it."

"Riggs told me to," Mary said.

Carole got a pitying look on her face. "You really did things because Riggs told you to? Mary, for the past year, none of us did *anything* Riggs told us. We knew he was crazy."

Mary's stomach dropped. All the time she'd been building PAT, all she'd done to others in its name, all that had been done to her—the other therapists had known it was crazy and said *nothing*?

Carole turned out the porch light before Mary left, so no one would see her go. In the dark, she turned to the therapist.

"You know," she said, "Riggs really did use me."

"Face it," Carole replied quietly, "we all had our slaves."

By the end of 1980, like a universe that had lost its gravity the Center community began to break into pieces and fly apart. "You people are stupid," Riggs told a clinic counselor when she dropped by the house to tell Konni she was moving out of the neighborhood, and to say good-bye. "You're stupid to let this happen."

But there was no stopping the exodus now. One by one, junior therapists too left the neighborhood. Then the founders started to move on. Most stayed in Southern California, but Riggs and Konni took off for a long vacation in Aspen, Colorado. The money patients had donated to the gym fund was returned to them. The ranch was put up for sale and ultimately sold for around $1 million. The Center building itself went for more than $2 million.

Caught up in the impulsive need to take action that gripped everyone, Andy Heller proposed marriage to his girlfriend, then moved with her to the house his late mother had left him. Mary Farrell and Ken Lander rented a small house in West L.A. Janet Quinn and her boyfriend also took an apartment on the West Side. Russ Gilbert and Holly Stoddard ended up in the San Fernando Valley. America was in a recession, so it was a bad time to sell real estate, but "For Sale" signs sprouted through the neighborhood; as soon as a place sold, its occupants took off. Most couples stayed in Southern California, while those who came out of the Center single went home, to the South and East, to Northern California and the

Midwest, to see if anything remained of the lives they'd abandoned.

No one really knew what was happening or what to do. And in all the anguish and confusion, hardly anyone noticed that the end of 1980 brought two final ironies: Just weeks after the Center's fall, John Lennon, the man whose embrace of primal therapy had been responsible for bringing so many patients here, was shot and killed by a deranged fan in New York City. Flowers piled up in front of Lennon's Manhattan apartment, where day after day, weeping crowds gathered, men and women mourning so many lost dreams they couldn't even sort them out. The next month, Ronald Reagan, a man who epitomized everything sixties movements had promised to defeat, was sworn in as president of the United States. To the outside world, it was clear that an era had ended. But to Center men and women, everything fell by the wayside against the immense task they all faced of trying to salvage their lives. Of trying to pick up pieces that were still breaking apart.

26

The former Center members entered the world like children in adult bodies—not the radiant, open children of the seventies ideal, but broken kids straight out of abusive homes, emotionally raw, afraid, angry, distrustful, unsure who to be unless they were told, and so used to second-guessing themselves that some could barely construct a coherent sentence. Faced, in addition, with nearly overwhelming logistical tasks, like simultaneously finding new homes, friends, and careers, and buffeted by continuous emotional upheaval, by early 1981 many began physically breaking down. Some people were half-crippled by constipation; others had diarrhea. Some had headaches and insomnia; some were wildly euphoric, some were paranoid, some so depressed they could hardly get out of bed. Women whose eating habits had been warped by years of enforced diets found themselves caught in bulimia's vicious circle of bingeing and purging.

Because a number of those who got sick were friends and ended up seeing the same Beverly Hills internist, the doctor heard enough about the Center to see a connection between it and the symptoms he was treating. His patients were not only

ill but desperately confused. They needed badly to talk to
someone about what had happened to them. He'd heard one
expert on destructive groups speak recently at the County
Medical Society, and put in a call to him. He was a psychiatrist
who also headed the UCLA Neuropsychiatric Institute—and
he was the very man who'd written the articles on brainwashing that Joe Hart had read shortly before he quit the Center,
Dr. Louis Jolyon West.

Dark-haired, genial, and comfortably round enough to
make appropriate the nickname "Jolly," West knew little of
the Center for Feeling Therapy. But he'd spent enough years
studying cults and "nonprofessional psychotherapies" like
Transcendental Meditation and est that he found the few details the Beverly Hills doctor recounted depressing but not
particularly surprising.

"I'm not taking any new patients now," West told him.
"But if you bring your people here some evening, we can have
a seminar. No fee, just some education."

Word of the upcoming "seminar" spread through the
Center patient networks, and, to West's amazement, the February night it was held nearly fifty people showed up at
UCLA, crowding into a room meant for no more than a dozen.
"Why don't you just tell me what happened," West said quietly. For nearly three hours, the men and women before him
talked frantically, almost compulsively, about their years at
the Center, as if confirming to themselves that what they remembered had really happened.

"I think . . . I got slugged in Group," someone said.

"You did," someone else chimed in. "I saw it happen."

"Yes." Now a third person spoke up. "It happened to me
too."

"And I saw it happen to *you*. . . ."

"I got busted," said a woman, "and I had to crawl with
my face pressed against the rug in front of everyone, and I did
it until all the skin had rubbed off my nose and I was bleeding. . . ."

The men and women in the room were at a fever pitch of emotion, weeping, gritting their teeth. And they were all terrified: For years, they'd been told they couldn't survive on their own—without the Center, what would keep them from going insane, just as the therapists predicted? Clearly, one night of talk wouldn't be enough to help them. West scheduled a second meeting, and in the days before it took place read a number of the Feeling Therapists' publications, including *Going Sane*. He found them absolute nonsense, especially the idea that everyone in the world was insane except those in Feeling Therapy. It was incredible to him that such theory had been published, even well reviewed, although he knew that kind of thing could happen when people did each other professional favors out of personal loyalty. It also happened, West thought, because people were ignorant. In recent years, psychotherapy had spread well beyond professional and reputable boundaries. Anyone could call himself or herself a therapist, and those who did could get away with anything.

About thirty people came back to UCLA for West's second seminar, and they brought more than a dozen new people with them. This meeting had more focus: Patients didn't just want to tell West stories; they wanted him to make sense of them. Was it possible they'd misinterpreted what had happened at the Center, seeing it as worse than it was?

"I learned a lot there," several people insisted. "It wasn't all bad."

"No experiences are all bad," West assured them. "You can grow from going through any experience, even if it's from the bonds you make with other people going through it with you."

"But weren't the therapists respected scientists?" someone demanded. "Didn't they make really important discoveries?"

"No," said West.

"Isn't Richard Corriere considered the most brilliant person in the field since Freud?"

"No," said West, "he's not. The ideas you were taught aren't generally accepted in the mainstream of scientific psychology. And the procedures to which you've been subjected aren't considered acceptable among reputable psychologists." He began to tell them about characteristics common to groups he'd studied. They all had a charismatic leader. All had a "revealed word," a set theory or doctrine that defined them. All placed significant emphasis on power and raising money. And all set rigid boundaries between those who were inside and those who were out—outsiders were not to be trusted. "You've been part," said Louis West, "of what I call a cult."

A *cult*. The word redefined what had happened at the Center from "mistake" to systematic, deliberate exploitation. Ex-patients' rage grew. And two men and two women, all of whom had been roommates, decided to take specific action. For all that they too were reeling in pain and confusion, certain facts were becoming clear to them. They'd been mistreated by men who'd identified themselves as medical professionals. These same men had apparently misused money. The Center was over now, and they were living in the real world. And in the real world, people who'd been victimized had recourse.

The roommates talked to the Los Angeles district attorney's office, whose staffers didn't seem to think what had happened at the Center warranted criminal prosecution; after all, no one had been physically forced to stay there or to give money. They began calling Los Angeles newspapers and television stations. They learned there was a state regulatory agency, the California Board of Medical Quality Assurance—later to be renamed the California Medical Board—one of whose prime functions was handling complaints from patients who thought they'd been mistreated by licensed practitioners. And they started looking for a lawyer.

———

Attorney Paul Morantz, now thirty-six, wasn't completely surprised when, in early 1981, he got a phone call from a man and woman who wanted to talk about filing a civil lawsuit for damages against the Center for Feeling Therapy. Morantz still remembered the evening he'd spent at the Center Open House in 1978, not long before the Synanon-ordered rattlesnake attack that nearly killed him. He'd gone because the young plant sellers who'd invited him had made the Center sound so *unlike* Synanon. But once there, the active recruitment of patients and deification of founders he'd seen had let him know it really wasn't. He'd slipped away, saying nothing—in his experience, it was useless to criticize a cult to dedicated members. But now, as he heard the full Center story, he began to think he'd been there that night for a reason.

It wasn't that he wanted to take on another cult lawsuit. After the rattlesnake attack, he'd filed a civil suit of his own against Synanon; before it had settled, it had eaten up five years and destroyed a relationship with a woman he loved. Moreover, suing the Center would be a big, complicated bitch of a case. Besides having to prove all the wild things his would-be clients claimed happened, he'd have to show that hundreds of people hadn't freely chosen to stay in therapy for years but had instead been coerced through thought control processes. Morantz believed utterly in the power of thought control to change people, and the Center's structure seemed to have all its classic elements. Still, charging "brainwashing" was a long shot, for not everyone felt the same. Moreover, most Center people were stone broke. Taken on contingency, the suit promised years of effort with a nebulous chance of payoff.

But Morantz was fascinated. The people he'd talked to seemed credible and the abuse they'd described outrageous. There was part of him that saw practicing law as a kind of moral crusade, a way to show those who exploited others that they couldn't get away with it. And there was a *big* part of him that just loved to battle—to get knee-deep in the shit and fight his way out.

He took the case.

News of the fledgling lawsuit was passed around California, then beyond, to wherever patients had scattered. Those who mourned the Center's loss were infuriated. Others just didn't want to hear about it; the idea of suing the therapists was too great an acknowledgment that their betrayal had been deliberate. But some people began contacting Morantz. A small number found themselves other lawyers. And dozens started registering complaints with the medical board.

Through the spring of 1981, media coverage of the Center collapse picked up too. The *Los Angeles Herald Examiner*, then L.A.'s second-string paper, had run the first long story in January, a juicy exposé filled with tales of beatings, forced abortions, and seductions by therapists. Afterward, the *Los Angeles Times* started following the case, and by July, its "lifestyle" section, which had run several adulatory pieces on the community, would print a long narrative on the "dream" that had "gone sour." *New West* magazine also ran a short article. But the local CBS news affiliate provided the most high-profile coverage—a five-part series that ran in May 1981. It featured more than a half-dozen patients recounting incidents of stripping, abortions, sluggo, and other brutality, and weeping as they mourned the years they'd lost in Feeling Therapy. Others ardently defended the Center as "a bold effort for human contact and social success." Ron Arliss and his partner, their faces hidden in shadow, discussed PAT's involvement in their company and Riggs's control of PAT. And Louis West blasted the Center therapists. "I can't say they weren't sincere," he said. "But if they weren't sincere, they were *stupid*. . . . The things that these people were led to believe were not true. And the so-called science that was preached to them as justifying the procedures they went through was *phony*." Full-page ads heralded the series in the *Times*'s television section. It had the sensational name "Cult of Cruelty."

By the time "Cult of Cruelty" aired, the California Board of Medical Quality Assurance, based in Sacramento, had received nearly fifty complaints from patients who alleged that they'd been beaten and abused in a therapeutic cult. It was an astonishingly high number, and two Southern California investigators were assigned to talk to them. Then, through the weeks, the numbers of complainants kept growing—ultimately, the investigators talked to some ninety people and obtained written sworn statements from them all, almost a thousand pages' worth.

Clearly, something very strange had occurred, but it wasn't clear what it was or even how it should be handled legally. The medical board was part of the licensing division of the state attorney general's office. (Another division, for example, oversaw licensed building contractors.) And the board itself was further broken down into two different divisions. One oversaw physicians; the other, nonphysician license holders, such as clinical psychologists, social workers, and MFCCs. Any actions brought by the BMQA were considered civil, not criminal, matters, although anyone found guilty of misconduct in a board administrative law hearing *could* be punished—either by having restrictions placed upon a license or by its outright revocation.

A typical BMQA case was a fairly simple one—one or two patients accusing a doctor or therapist of some sort of malfeasance. In the Center matter, however, nearly one-hundred patients were leveling charges at more than a dozen professionals with all different kinds of licenses: Lee was an M.D.; Joe, Riggs, and Steve were clinical psychologists; and Werner, who'd been licensed as a psychologist's assistant while at the Center, had obtained his own clinical license shortly after it closed. Jerry, who'd taken and failed the written exam for clinical licensing while the Center was still operating, was licensed as a psychologist's assistant. Dominic, Carole, Phil Schwartz, and Matt and Katie Lawrence all had MFCC licenses. Konni was a licensed psychiatric technician. (Former therapist Linda Binder Cirincione and junior therapist Jason Kushner had never had any professional licenses, so there was nothing the board could do about them.)

The statements complaining patients had written were given to "peer experts" for evaluation. Those dealing with Lee, for instance, went to psychiatrist Norman Brill, founder of the UCLA Neuropsychiatric Institute and Department of Psychiatry. Those against Joe, Riggs, Steve, and Werner went to Margaret Singer, a licensed psychologist who'd studied thought reform programs since 1952, researched U.S. cults since 1975 (in the process, treating hundreds of ex-cultists as patients), and served as chairperson for the American Psychological Association Task Force on Deceptive and Indirect Persuasive Techniques.

The experts all came to the same conclusion. It was true that the actions being judged had taken place during an extraordinarily open, experimental time. But certain acts—like hitting a patient—were *never* OK. In fact, a number of the things patients alleged therapists had done could be considered "grossly negligent," a standard for evaluating whether a medical licensee could be disciplined. The BMQA took its investigation of the therapists a step further, sending the work that had been done so far to the attorney general's office in L.A. The papers came to Deputy Attorney General William Carter.

If Paul Morantz, with his attractive, tanned face, toned body, and T-shirts, resembled a beach boy, Carter, in his mid-thirties and a graduate of USC law school, looked every inch the government servant—wire-frame glasses, nondescript suits, neatly trimmed brown hair, and reddish mustache. His office, in the unfashionable mid-Wilshire section of Los Angeles, was downright drab, all file cabinets and institutional-oatmeal-colored carpet. Although he'd been handling cases for the medical board for more than six years, most of his work had been routine medical malpractice. He had no real experience dealing with psychologists or offbeat groups, and although he was of the age to have been aware of primal therapy, he'd never heard of the Center.

As he began to review the sworn statements Sacramento had sent, he could barely believe what he was seeing.

"Sluggo" therapy? "Assigned" sex? And how was it that despite all the abuse they alleged had occurred, so many people had stayed at the Center? The last question bothered him a lot. It might mean that even if their allegations turned out to be true, the Center patients were too disturbed to make competent witnesses. Gradually, Carter began seeking out and talking to the people who'd written what he'd read. Still others heard that he'd been given the case and sought him out. To his amazement and relief, although the men and women he met were angry, depressed, and confused, they were definitely not nuts. With each day, Carter became more convinced that awful things had taken place at the Center for Feeling Therapy and that there was a case to be made against its therapists.

In June 1982, Paul Morantz filed a $95 million suit against the Center's founders and junior therapists on behalf of nineteen former patients, charging they'd been defrauded, brainwashed, and physically and emotionally abused. Sara Wrightman Fitzgerald was one of them; among the others were the man who'd been ordered to live like a baby, a Langley Construction worker, and three women who'd sent away their children. Within six months, a number of other patients, including Janet Quinn, would join the suit, and ten other actions would be filed, until some fifty-two people were suing the Center.

The number of ex-patients who were either suing the Center or complaining of malpractice (not to mention those still making crank calls to the founders) might have clued the Center therapists that a lot of people were very upset with them. But if patients expected their former therapists to repeat the confessions and mea culpas made during the days of the Center's fall, they were wrong. Professionally, most seemed to have simply picked up and gone on with their lives. Jerry and Werner set up shop together in Orange County: Werner saw private clients and conducted "stress management" courses for the Huntington Beach Police Department, while

Jerry continued to work toward his own license, passing his orals in June.

Riggs and Konni spent some time in Colorado, then made plans to return to L.A. so Riggs could start a private therapy practice. (Riggs was also hoping that his friendship with a former Center patient who was now in the entertainment field would lead to a job as a talk-show host.) Joe continued to teach and counsel at USC, publishing a stream of papers that showed his intellectual interests had remained basically unchanged: "The Significance of William James's Ideas for Modern Psychotherapy" appeared in the Fall–Winter issue of the *Journal of Contemporary Psychotherapy*; essays on "functional psychology," sports psychology, and Trigant Burrow showed up in an edited anthology.

In fact, for the first half-year after the Center's end, it seemed to live on like a beast that didn't know it was dead. More than a month after the fall, the city of Los Angeles paid a junior therapist $5,500 to put on a one-day Fitness Foundation seminar on "The Keys to Productivity" for 140 government officials. In the spring of 1981, an old article written by Joe, Riggs, and Werner showing that, with increasing time in Feeling Therapy, patients shifted toward a "self-actualizing" profile appeared in the journal *Psychotherapy: Theory, Research, and Practice*. The magazine *Psychology Today* still marketed Psychological Fitness self-help tapes.

But as negative publicity increased—news of the Morantz suit, for instance, went out over the UPI wires—the therapists found carrying on harder and harder. "In terms of publicity, this is a new experience for me," Joe Hart's shaken supervisor at USC told a reporter from the campus paper the week "Cult of Cruelty" aired. "It has never happened where a colleague of mine has been accused of such things, let alone in the television media." Thanks to some angry ex-patients, copies of the *Herald Examiner* and *New West* articles on the Center also found their way to Joe's faculty co-workers. Afterward, although Joe's teaching evaluations for the first semester of 1981 had been considerably above the average for the social science division, he was told he was no longer welcome at USC. He applied to smaller, less prestigious Chapman College in Orange County; was turned down; and ended up at the University of Redlands, a small private school one-hundred miles east of L.A., on the edge of the Mojave Desert.

After the Center stories broke, Riggs decided not to come back to L.A at all but to divide his time between Aspen and New York City. But when he tried to set up partnerships with therapists in private practice in those cities, they too received copies of articles about the Center, and backed out. Steve and Carole left Southern California and moved to a suburban small town on the East Coast where Carole did secretarial work and Steve taught part-time at a local college. Lee and his wife moved to the Midwest, where he had done his residency. There, he went back to work as an M.D., in radiology—a specialization that didn't require doctor and patient to have any personal contact.

But the therapists were not about to take these setbacks lying down. Although they'd quickly settled a lawsuit filed by the Boston outpost—offering members just enough to reimburse them for therapy fees they'd paid over the years—through their attorneys, they denied every charge made in "Cult of Cruelty." They'd never ordered people to strip; never used brainwashing techniques; never encouraged, condoned, or permitted physical abuse or violence; never forced anyone to do *anything*. Riggs denied involvement in PAT. And not only did they also deny all the allegations Paul Morantz made in his lawsuit, they filed one of their own: a class action suit against virtually everyone who was suing them, as well as Ron Arliss, his Slick Auto partner, Louis West, and 200 unnamed "Does." They had been defamed, they said, by the lies patients had told the media, and they were seeking damages of $50 million.

Paul Morantz stepped in to defend his clients from the therapists' lawsuit. Ron Arliss and his partner's defense was picked up by an attorney hired by their business and home-owner's insurance company. Louis West sought his own representation. At first, all the founders were represented by the Century City law firm of Wildman, Harrold, Allen, Dixon, Barash & Hill—one partner had known Lee Woldenberg since they were camp counselors together—but before long, Lee hired his own attorney, and Jerry and Werner another. Jason Kushner, Phil Schwartz, and Matt and Katie Lawrence all had their own attorneys. The lawyers lined up, their meters running. The Center had ended, but the fight to decide who was to blame for what had happened there—and who would pay—had just begun.

27

Shortly after they left the therapy neighborhood, Janet Quinn's lover left her. "I need to be on my own," he said. Numbly, Janet found her own apartment and a job to pay the rent, then sank into a miasma of misery. Her home was gone. Her boyfriend was gone. The community without which she was doomed was gone. And when, finally, she found time to see a doctor about the pain she'd had for years in her knees, she learned that her health was gone too: The nightly running and jumping jacks she'd done trying to stay thin had caused permanent damage. There would be no more running for her, no more jumping, dancing, or waterskiing. "You'll never," the doctor said flatly, "be able to do more than walk."

Loss piled on loss. In February 1981, she attended the two seminars given by Dr. Louis West. In some ways, they were a relief. West was an important person, respected in the world, and he didn't believe she and the other patients were terminally crazy or doomed without Feeling Therapy. In fact, he thought therapy had hurt them. But his definition of what the Center had been devastated her. A *cult*. She'd left the second seminar stunned into breathlessness, more depressed than ever. She had given her heart and soul to the Center because she believed it was something special and that it made her special as well. Instead, she had been no more than a Moonie. She had spent eight years of her life in a cult, and she'd never even known it.

Through the months after the seminars, she stayed in daily touch with a number of other Center people. Some called to gossip; others were after something deeper. Slowly, new friendships took hold. A man Janet had seen as another Group 5 failure turned out to be acutely intelligent, warm, and supportive. A Group 4 "loser" to whom she'd once been kind out of pity proved smart, literate, and loyal. But between friends' calls and visits, life was a vast, silent strangeness. In the morning, Janet got up alone in her boxy stucco apartment and went off to work in the secretarial pool of a large architectural firm. She typed, she had lunch, she came home. She knew it was a life like anyone else's, a normal life. But it didn't feel normal. She didn't know how to act outside the Center. In the world, you didn't say things to people like "You're fat again! I hate it!" But what *did* you say? What did you do on a date if you didn't talk about feelings, if it wasn't a given you'd end the evening fucking? Sometimes, caught in traffic, she sat staring at the faces in cars around her. What were all these people thinking? How did they feel? She had forgotten everything.

Worse: She had forgotten herself. Even if the Center's teachings were wrong, she no longer could separate them from what she believed about herself. "*I'm tired of your wimp act!*" she heard therapists bellowing and "*Jim's picked the wrong woman. Janet, you're not a good woman for any man.*" Were any of those things true? Was she a wimp, a bad woman? And if she was not who the therapists said she was, who *was* she? Dimly, she recalled that once she had been different, but it was as if there were something physical inside that kept her from reaching that person, a wedge that cut her off from who and what she'd been before therapy. She couldn't remember what she'd thought and wanted, couldn't recall her own dreams and fantasies, the way she'd looked at and felt about the world. Even decorating her apartment was hard. She would spend hours in department stores staring at furniture, just trying to remember what she'd liked before people told her how to think. Sometimes memories would come in little flashes—yes, before the Center, she'd favored country pine! She'd liked sofas that were tan, fabric that had a pattern! The tiny clues only made it pathetically clear how far she had to go.

She was broken on the outside, broken on the inside. She was thirty-four years old and had wasted years of her life and ended up with nothing. There were times Janet just wanted to die.

But she held on. She had given up her body and soul, but she was determined to get them back. She took the referral names Louis West had given out at his seminars, and began searching for a therapist who could root the Center out of her. And when she heard about the investigations the BMQA was conducting and the lawsuit Paul Morantz had filed, she grabbed at the small piece of her old self the news reawakened—the activist. She filed a complaint against Jerry for the damage his exercise program had done to her knees and began calling William Carter regularly, offering to help him in any way she could. She joined Morantz's civil suit, and when she filled out an Interrogatory that asked "How do you think you were damaged?" something clicked deep inside her. Janet looked at what she'd written, a chronicle of bust after bust, assignment after assignment, and for the first time, she understood what had happened to her during eight years of Feeling Therapy. It wasn't her fault. People had done things to her that had broken her down further and further until she was the wreck she was now.

Anger surged, and with it, hope. Once, she had marched against the Vietnam War, worked for the United Farm Workers, fought injustice. Now, she would fight for herself.

There was no way Kevin Fitzgerald was going to get involved in a lawsuit. He'd supported Sara's decision to sue completely, but dealing with things in a straightforward, determined manner was Sara's way. As soon as the two of them left Hollywood, she immediately stopped dieting and regained her natural roundness—and her period. She got very clear that she was angry about the Center. She yelled. She filed suit. It wasn't that Kevin didn't share her rage—like his wife, he'd filed a complaint with the BMQA, and he had absolutely no patience with former friends who found justifications for what had happened at the Center or shied away from using the word *cult*. And he knew that suing meant potentially winning a lot of money that God knows he and Sara could use.

But he also knew that lawsuits went on forever, and he would not give the Center any more years of his life. People he knew who were suing practically begged him to change his mind, which made Kevin even more adamant. He loved the other ex-patients who were his friends now, people he'd come to naturally, in relationships that weren't tainted with the memory of busts or therapeutic scrutiny. He literally hungered for the times each month when he and Sara met with them in someone's living room. All of them had a visceral need to talk about the Center again and again, to mourn and pass gossip, to tell stories and rage. Even people who'd moved far away traveled to come to them. Talking about the Center was like letting out poison, but it could be done only with people who'd understand.

"Yeah, yeah," they'd shout, pounding the arms of chairs, "I remember him doing that! That son of a bitch! No wonder we were fucked up! It all makes sense now!"

"I had this dream," someone would say. "I was in Group, and Riggs came in, and I stood up and said, 'This isn't right! I don't want to be here! I'm leaving!' "

Dreams, as Joe and Riggs once said, are pictures of feel-ings. Everyone in the room cheered. "I had that dream, too!" they cried. "Wasn't it great? Didn't it feel *righteous!*"

But for all Kevin loved his friends, he was not about to let them tell him what to do. People had been telling him what to do for nine years. He would not sue. He would not even *begin* to consider seeing a therapist to deal with the confusion and terror that still plagued him. He would find his own way to heal.

The first order of business was finding a job. After years as a failed gardener and inept carpenter, Kevin had virtually no skills, so he turned to the work he knew anyone could do: selling plants door-to-door. It was an astonishing experience, and not just because there was no one in his face all day screaming, "You're spaced out! You're gone!" It had been so long since he'd spoken to people outside the Center about anything more meaningful than buying gas or groceries. Now, as he made his rounds, he talked to his customers endlessly—about girls, the weather, sometimes politics or things that were more important. And it turned out that the people he'd once derided as NITs weren't crazy; they were *nice*. They laughed at his jokes, even when they were lame. They listened sym-pathetically. They acted as if he was a really neat person. His amazement at normal human interaction sometimes amazed *them*. "Where're you from, man?" one guy asked. "*Mars?*"

Kevin found a lot of life amazing. He no longer lived in seedy Hollywood but a clean suburban development of pastel homes with Spanish red tile roofs. Every day, he had conver-sations with neighbors that didn't have to be emotional or heavily laden with meaning. And without Group and co-therapy and house meetings and volunteer work, he had so much *time*. There was time to run errands, time to read or sit for hours and watch TV. There was so much time he didn't know what to do with it all. He and Sara joked to their friends that they were "modeling" their cats—sometimes they just spent whole weekends lying in bed.

They also started working to reimagine their own relationship. The love they felt for each other had flourished despite, not because of, the Center, but their daily lives had always been run by therapy rules. They had to find new subjects to discuss, ways to tune in to each other's desires, so they could have sex when they both wanted it, not to meet a three-times-a-week requirement. And Sara immediately let it be known that the dominant way Kevin had behaved at the Center had to go. She simply wouldn't put up with it if he acted superior or started ordering her around.

Everything had to be rethought, remade. Like everyone else he knew, at times Kevin felt half-drowned with the immensity of the task he faced and sorrow over all he'd lost. When he felt worst, when sorrow turned to rage over the theft of his life, he found himself wishing he'd had a gun during the Center's last days and killed all the motherfuckers. He could have pleaded—good joke—insanity. He probably would have been in and out of jail in a few years.

But things weren't going to be so simple. The small steps he was taking would have to be enough. As the family he'd rejected welcomed him back, Kevin took a good look at his brothers and sisters. They hadn't gone into therapy, but they weren't the same people they'd been when they were young. They'd experimented with life, reacted to it, changed in response. It struck Kevin with a deep sense of truth that you couldn't force people to change, as the Center had tried to do. Change was something far more slow and gradual. It came from inside.

Each morning, Kevin's alarm clock rang at a human 7:00 A.M., he and Sara had a quiet breakfast together, called a quick "hello" to neighbors, then went off to work. Each day, he reached out and slid his hands along the outlines of his new life until it felt real to him. The Center voice still rose in him frequently, loud and insistent. "You're going dead!" it warned. "Work harder, feel more, this isn't good enough!" Kevin couldn't stop hearing the voice, but he knew where it came from, and no matter what it said, he refused to listen.

In September 1983, the state attorney general's office filed formal accusations against Lee, Joe, Riggs, Steve, Werner, and Jerry, citing more than seventy specific examples of mistreatment from the complaints of seventy-eight patients, most of whom had been at the Center in excess of five years.

"——— was pressured into undressing by therapists' threats . . . and commanded to masturbate in front of her therapist 'because her talking was criticized as masturbation,' " William Carter wrote, the bizarreness of the stories a strange contrast to his bland, matter-of-fact tone. "——— was referred to as a 'pig.' . . . ——— was threatened he would end up in a mental institution if he did not obey his therapy instruction. . . . ——— was beaten until he was bruised and bleeding. . . . ——— was 'very directly and powerfully' convinced to undergo an abortion. . . . ——— was repeatedly subjected to 'racial slurs and derogatory remarks about blacks and Jews.' . . . ——— was engaged in sexual relations with her therapists, although she had specifically sought therapy due to perceived sexual problems. . . ."

What had happened at the Center? After two years of looking into the matter, Carter had come to the same conclusion as Paul Morantz. Although patients had been led to believe that in Feeling Therapy, caring, trustworthy therapists would help them with their problems, he wrote, instead, the therapists had "instituted and participated in a systematic social influence process and an enforced dependency situation which fits the recognized criteria of brainwashing."

The six therapists were formally accused of committing fraud; misrepresentation; gross negligence; unprofessional conduct, including patient abuse; the unlicensed practice of psychology; and aiding and abetting the unlicensed practice of psychology. Former patient Jon Walker was charged as well; although neither a founder nor a junior therapist, he had worked at the outpatient clinic and held a clinical psychologist's license. Similar accusations were soon filed against Carole, Dominic, Matt, Katie, and Phil Schwartz. And the state asked that every license in question be revoked.

Once again, the therapists denied everything. The state's charges, Lee's attorney, Arnold J. Stone, told the *Los Angeles Times*, were based on the accusations of a small number of "disgruntled" patients already involved in a lawsuit. Other attorneys filed objections, saying that the accusations made against the therapists were so indefinite that they couldn't prepare adequate defenses against them. The founders' work lives went on. In 1983, Joe Hart even published a new book, with Plenum, a reputable academic press. *Modern Eclectic Therapy: A Functional Orientation to Counseling and Psychotherapy*, wrote a *Los Angeles Times* reporter who apparently didn't read his own paper, focused on a new concept, "psychological fitness." A library journal that reviewed the book recommended its purchase for both graduate and advanced undergraduate libraries.

Nearly three years after his first clients' phone call, Paul Morantz was immersed in exactly the kind of life-absorbing struggle he'd sworn never to get involved in again. His client list kept growing. A few patients who'd filed suit against the Center and were represented by other lawyers had settled their cases—reportedly, in some instances for as shockingly little as a few thousand dollars. But those who wanted to go after bigger money jumped to Morantz and his co-counsel.

Each new client meant going through a new discovery, the process in which each side, by subpoenaing and reviewing relevant documents, tries to determine what the other is presenting as the facts of the case. Each new client meant holding a new deposition, the taking of sworn testimony prior to trial, with both sides' attorneys and a court reporter present. Because they dealt with the same basic issues, the civil suit filed by patients and the libel suit filed by therapists were joined for deposition and discovery. That meant around seven lawyers, more than a dozen defendants, and fifty plaintiffs were involved in everything that happened. Even though all parties agreed to limit each deposition to four days, nearly a year would be devoted to that process alone.

Meanwhile, re-creating and understanding the Center world was proving a grueling, emotionally draining task. Again and again, Morantz was struck by how damaged were the people he saw. Even nonsuers he contacted as potential witnesses were in terrible pain. Some said his phone calls gave them nightmares. They didn't want to testify—they didn't want to talk about the Center at all.

But documents spoke. Like Richard Nixon, the Center therapists had been so convinced of their own place in history that they'd had patients keep records of everything. And, as they had Nixon, those records were now being used against them. Boxes of files were piling up in Morantz's home, three-ring binders filled with Group and lecture notes, graphs, dream and personal diaries. There were cassette tapes of Intensives and Groups recording moments like a woman groaning in pain as a therapist bent back her fingers and a distraught woman being persuaded to strip as men in the Group shouted "Yeah! Take your clothes off!"

If there was no smoking gun to be found in the Center case, there already was an accumulation of damning detail. In October 1983, just a few weeks after the state filed its charges, the first two patient plaintiffs were deposed. A month later, Morantz and the therapists' attorneys held their first settlement conference. Morantz rejected what the therapists offered; in December, the offer tripled. By the spring of 1984, two women agreed to settle; seven more patients would follow through the next year. Each time a patient settled, the therapists dropped him or her from the libel suit.

But the rest of the complaining patients held fast. They wanted more money. The therapists refused to budge, and the united defense they presented in the civil suit, the libel suit, and the BMQA action did not crack. They had done, they said, absolutely nothing wrong.

28

Five ex-Center men who'd become friends after the fall were making up for years of therapy-mandated austerity with a second adolescence. They called themselves "The Buds" and met on weekends to play music in one guy's garage, laughing themselves sick singing twisted lyrics about their old therapists. When they weren't singing, they were partying hard, snorting coke, spinning out on psilocybin, and drinking themselves shit-faced at Hollywood nightclubs, where they chased women and got into fistfights with tattooed two-ton bouncers.

The woman who'd worked as the Slick Auto secretary had cast off her Center self by starting to play piano again (something the therapists criticized as "too private"), pushing her silk dresses to the back of the closet and wearing only "tough" clothes—cords, T-shirts, and flannel tops from L. L. Bean. An ex–Langley Construction worker had gone back to smoking dope and living like a hippie. A few patients who'd made no money for years were racing after "power" jobs. And, given the Center's educated population, more than a few were trying to come to terms with what had happened to them through intellectual effort. They were reading classic books on brainwashing—Robert Lifton's *Thought Reform and the Psychology of Totalism*, Edgar Schein's *Coercive Persuasion*. Those who'd gone back to school in search of new careers were producing a series of papers on the Center. Janet Quinn was one; her master's thesis was about thought control. The patient who'd been advised to buy Bijan clothes to unblock his writing did extensive interviews so he could write a book on the Center's rise and fall—after nine months, he stopped, paralyzed by writer's block.

Yet for all patients' efforts to understand the Center experience or just get past and forget it, no gathering of old acquaintances went by without some reference to it. "Watch out," someone would jokingly chide a cigarette smoker, "I'm gonna tell Riggs on you!" "Be quiet while I read these cards!" the guest of honor at a birthday party might order his friends with mock severity. "I need to have my feelings."

It was hard not to think and talk about the Center, for it was still there in so many ways—few of them funny. Differing positions on what had happened destroyed a number of friendships. And while some patients came out of the Center with mates they cherished and careers in which they were happy to continue, others were finding that what they'd forsaken for Feeling Therapy was irrecoverable. There was no way to undo years of family estrangement, no way to bring back missed Thanksgivings and Christmases or to reconcile with parents who'd died before the Center's end. There was no way to bring back marriages destroyed a decade before. There was no way to jump-start a career put on hold for years, no way to feel, at thirty-five, the burning energy and ambition of a twenty-five-year-old.

There was no way to bring back children who had been let go. Toddlers sent to live with their fathers or grandparents in the early 1970s were nearly grown; the chance to share their childhoods was forever lost. Fetuses aborted would never come to term. Childbearing years that had passed were irretrievably gone.

There was no way to undo the toll "pushing it to the max" and "going beyond limitations" had taken on once-vigorous young people's bodies—the carpal tunnel syndrome and back trouble that plagued Langley Construction workers, the bulimia that continued to afflict women who'd been on rigid diets, the commonly suffered "chronic fatigue syndrome" that doctors said could be brought on by years of sustained stress.

And perhaps worst of all, there seemed no way to recover the self-trust that had been lost. Everyone who'd been at the Center carried the memory not only of having been hurt but of hurting others. Everyone bore the responsibility for not having said no to it all. And the more newspaper and television reports told the Center story, making what had happened there sound both wild and utterly incomprehensible, the more guilt was joined by shame. If the Center's madness was clear to everyone else, how had those who were there missed it so completely? It was one thing for Center patients to read books that discussed the abstract process of brainwashing and another to be able to look back on what they'd said and done and believed without feeling like unspeakable idiots.

How could they ever forgive themselves? And having made a mistake this big, how could they ever trust themselves again?

Like Kevin Fitzgerald, many ex-patients couldn't bring themselves to seek professional help dealing with their pain. The very word *therapy* set their teeth on edge. But some, like Janet Quinn, took the chance and searched for an ally among mainstream psychologists and social workers, often choosing those who specialized in dealing with former cultists. (By the early 1980s, there was enough public awareness of the damage caused by cults that some organizations—for instance, Jewish Family Services—had set up special "cult clinics" to help ex-members.)

Therapists who didn't know much about the Center were horrified by what they heard—one psychiatrist referred to the place as "the camps." Like Louis West, however, while they were ashamed and disgusted by what had been done in the name of psychotherapy, they weren't that surprised. In 1982, an article in the professional journal *Psychotherapy: Theory, Research, and Practice* had revealed the existence of five other American "psychotherapy cults"—close-knit, incestuous groups of fifteen to seventy-five members held together by idealization of a therapist—some of whose dynamics were eerily similar to the Center's. Not only did therapists fail to maintain professional boundaries, treating their friends, lovers, employees, and colleagues, but, said the authors, "they did not consider their patients' idealization of them to be a transference, to be understood as part of the treatment, but used it to encourage submission, obedience and adoration."

Still, therapists found helping Center people tricky. Many of the problems they faced were typical of ex-cultists—depression from losing a sense of purpose; regret over lost time, innocence, and self-esteem; loneliness; sexual conflicts; difficulty with complex thinking and making independent choices; guilt; and the pain of no longer feeling part of an elite. In one sense, they were lucky—people who left groups that still existed often also felt guilty about leaving and for a long time continued to hear the voice of some "master" in their heads, urging them to go back. Although their therapists now professed innocence, at least Center patients had once heard them admit they were wrong. At the same time, they had a problem other ex-cultists did not: Understandably, most found it extremely hard to trust the one group of people who could help them—therapists. Some ex-patients, who expected all therapy to be like Feeling Therapy, were so terrified on counseling appointment days that they vomited from tension or fell into the old habit of seeing friends beforehand, so "contact" would keep them from "going dead" and saying something "wrong." Others fled any counselor whose methods seemed at all experimental—even those who suggested something as innocuous as hypnosis for relaxation. Many angrily rejected treatment that involved either writing off the whole Center experience as irredeemably awful or learning to accept what had happened and move on. "I don't want to accept it or forget it!" a former member of Tombstone shouted at his therapist. "I was ripped off! I don't want to *ever* not be angry about it!"

What worked for ex-Center members, discovered Nancy Weiss, a young Los Angeles social worker who ultimately treated twenty, was giving patients what Center therapists had taken away from them: control. "I consciously created a relationship that wasn't authoritarian or in the least bit mystifying," she later recalled. "I promised them I wouldn't keep any secrets, that I'd share whatever I was thinking. I validated their experience by listening to their stories—they all had to tell their stories a lot. I just let them talk, and I shared my own feelings about what they said. Sometimes I cried with them; sometimes I cried for them."

To ease patients' self-doubt, therapists like Weiss also helped them recall and acknowledge the positive, legitimate reasons they'd stayed at the Center. They hadn't been completely nuts to remain—people *had* learned how to open up and share their feelings with each other; they'd felt togetherness, the joy of community. Then, slowly, the therapists helped patients separate out the Center's good from what had been damaging, and cast the latter away. It was painful and took time, this slow excavation of self, but the new therapists kept chipping away until at last patients began to feel themselves again, to reach the place where they had begun.

———

Three years after its fall, hardly a day passed that Andy Heller didn't think of the Center, a hard knot of mournfulness in his chest. He still could see his old Hollywood house, hear his roommates shouting "Yeah! Feelin' GOOD!" He still could picture himself hitting up the stores along Sunset for a fast-food dinner and running into four or five Center friends no matter where he went. He remembered the joy of seeing Katie every week, the sound of Riggs's voice, closing Postgroup with that talk-show host flourish—"That's it, everyone, good-night. . . ."

Every memory hurt, for each made clearer the life he'd lost. It wasn't that there was anything *wrong* with what he had now. He still lived with his Center girlfriend—now his wife— in his late mother's house, which renovation had transformed into a sleek, handsome place of white walls, big windows, and sanded, polished floors. In 1982, they'd had a baby girl, whom Andy adored with his whole heart—watching her emerge, wet and red at birth, had been the transcendent experience of his life. He'd been promoted yet again within his record company's publicity department, which meant he got all the free albums, cocktail party invitations, and passes to concerts and screenings that went with a "glamour" job. His wife had got-ten her MBA and a corporate job, so between them they did pretty well. They bought furniture and clothes, went out to restaurants, took nice vacations. It was a perfectly decent life. But after what he'd known, the *ordinariness* of it!

A lot of his Center friends had scattered, some around Southern California, others to distant states. Two people from his old Group were suing the Center, and Andy had stopped speaking to them. As far as he was concerned, those involved with the lawsuit were scum. How dare they claim they'd been abused and imprisoned at the Center? Everyone had chosen to go into therapy, chosen to stay!

There were some Group friends he still saw, but not as often or for as long as in the old days. Relating outside the Center could be strange. One night, he'd gone out drinking with a guy from Group. Reagan came on the TV in the bar, and Andy, who was a little drunk, let loose. "Fuck you, pig. You Republicans don't care about anyone else."

"Shut up!" his friend exploded. Andy looked at him blankly. "*I'm* a Republican. I think Reagan is right. I *like* him."

Andy could only shake his head. Jesus, a Republican. For three years, he and his buddy had talked in excruciating detail about their parents, their defenses, the precise mechanics of their sex lives. They'd known everything about each other— except small things like where they stood on how they saw the world.

About once a month, he wrote to Katie through her lawyer. A few times a year, she'd answer, short, cryptic letters whose only return address was a post office box number in another state. "Matt and I are happy" was all she said. "We're finally resting. For the first time, I feel rested."

For all their flatness and lack of detail, Andy treasured the letters, for each one brought back his connection with Katie, and beyond her, the Center—brought back the hope that its way of life was still possible, and some future awaited him besides . . . this. . . .

It was as if the Center had picked him up and stretched him like a rubber band, taking him beyond anything he'd ever imagined for himself. But then it had let go, and with every moment, he was snapping back further and further. Only a few years ago, he had been charming and outspoken, brash and aggressive, a man surrounded by loving friends and a proud part of a vanguard society that would shape history. Now he was just a twenty-seven-year-old husband and father, successful, pleasant, and well liked, but essentially timid and passive, a typical American who drove a compact car and went to work and came home at night to fight with his wife and play with his child in ordinary, suburban isolation.

Once, he had been a hero, a king. Now he was only himself.

The Center's end left Russ Gilbert so dazed and disoriented that days went by when he wasn't even sure he was really awake. His last days in Hollywood were a nightmare. Because he'd been a clinic counselor and in Group 1, people had been really hateful, yelling at him, calling him a "pod." Then he got into an enormous fight with a roommate over selling their shared Hollywood home, and when it was over, he and a man who'd been his friend since 1972 had stopped speaking forever. He and Holly ended up renting a house in the Valley. Weeks went by, and Russ spent his time either dull as a sleepwalker or shaking with electric bolts of terror. Suddenly, he had no job, no world, a ten-year past that made no sense. Some of the clinic workers who had licenses or academic degrees decided to set up their own private practice, primarily with patients they'd been seeing at the Center. They were *not* going to be following the Center formula, and Russ thought briefly of joining them. But counseling in the real world meant spending the time and effort to get a license, and after the Center, the idea of being a therapist wasn't so appealing anymore.

Holly took charge. Unlike Russ, she wasn't consumed with the need to understand what had gone wrong at the Center and why. They'd figure that out later; right now, they had to go on with their lives. She wanted to get out of L.A., find some place where life was a little easier, so they could buy another house, maybe have kids. They settled on Santa Cruz, found a plain cabin that backed into a wild hillside. Holly went to work building another business, a small catering company. They needed money. And so Russ found himself, as if by rote, moving back into an old, familiar world: He drove to San Francisco and found work as an aerospace engineer.

By 1982, the year Russ and Holly got married, Holly's business was taking hold, vegetables were coming in in the cabin's small backyard, and a few new friends had been added to the old Center standbys who still called or sometimes even came to visit. But thoughts of the Center continued to fill the inside of Russ's head with noise and confusion. Night after night, he replayed its history, trying to find the place where the fracture began. He simply could not believe that the therapists had set out to screw their patients from the start. He remembered the summer of 1971 and working with the therapists on the La Brea building, all of them certain they were about to make discoveries that would change the world. He remembered Joe's soft voice talking about dreams and growth; the tenderness in Riggs as he reached out a hand, saying, "I know how much you hurt." He was convinced they'd meant to do well.

But then what had happened to his life? How had he ended up here? A fury would come up in him when he looked in the mirror and saw, despite all the therapy, the same mild, reserved guy he'd always been. It was there when he walked into work each day, to the kind of dead job he'd worked so many years to leave behind. Most of all, it was there when he looked at Holly. He knew she was a good woman. There were times she brought up a gentle feeling in him, an immense tenderness. But on the days when he couldn't stop thinking how his life had slipped beyond his control, all he knew was that he'd never picked her to be his—she'd been *assigned* to him by therapists. The knowledge made her the emblem of everything that had gone wrong. How could he possibly love her? How could he even know if he did? He hadn't chosen her! He hadn't ever been allowed to make a choice!

Holly bore with him as he lashed out. Ironically, given all the times Center therapists had busted her for not being "compliant," her true problem was the opposite: A former battered child, all she wanted was to please. She took in whatever Russ said, watched his moods, tried to change. But by 1984, she broke. "I've decided to leave you," she told Russ, her body rigid with pain. "I love you, but you aren't able to love me, and I'm tired of that. I think I'm a great thing for you, and all you see is that you didn't choose me."

Russ stared at her as once again all he knew threatened to fall away.

"I *do* want you!" The words burst out of him. "I *do* choose you!" For an hour, they cried and held each other.

It wasn't as if that day healed things between them—the unnatural way Russ and Holly's relationship had begun would haunt their marriage forever. But afterward, Holly was less afraid of displeasing Russ and he was less critical of her. And with the change, the amorphous feelings inside Russ shifted too, hardening into anger that had a new focus. It wasn't Holly's fault that the normal human pleasure of falling in love had been taken away from him. Other people were responsible for that—and for a lot of hurt. Perhaps they hadn't meant to do it, but they had. And afterward, they'd never even made the human gesture of an apology.

Within a year, along with Deborah Reiss, who had been driven into personal bankruptcy by the failure of Plant Power, and seven others, Russ contacted Paul Morantz and joined the lawsuit against the Center.

All through the first months of 1981, Mary Farrell's hair fell out in handfuls. Migraines hit almost weekly. Letters kept coming from PAT company owners demanding money, and she waited in terror for lawsuits. Even after they failed to materialize—perhaps the business owners were too disoriented to file or simply wanted to move on—she stayed scared. In May 1981, she and Ken got married. Before they did, she had him sign a premarital agreement to keep their property separate, just in case. It would take two years of work to dissolve PAT, to untangle it from the companies it had once controlled.

But cutting this last tie to the Center was a good part of Mary's life, a relief like the mindless ease of whole nights spent eating potato chips and watching sitcoms with Ken, no one yelling at her or making demands. Only a few friends remained from the old days. Too many people remembered too much. For a while, she talked regularly to a clinic counselor; for a while, Carole wrote. She and Ken saw Jeff Langley and his girlfriend, but then they got married and moved up north. The first Christmas after the fall, a card had come from Riggs. "We tried" was all it said. Mary didn't answer. She didn't want to see Riggs or speak to him. She didn't want to think about him or the Center ever again.

Her world now was Ken and, ironically, a few women she'd sought out from her days in Catholic school. And her family. Her parents had welcomed her back into their lives without hesitation, though they wrestled with questions about who Mary had been for so long.

"Why did you say . . ." her mother often began a sentence the first year after the fall.

"What?"

"Why did you scream at me about not breast-feeding you? Mary, it wasn't that I didn't want to. I had problems with my nipples. I *couldn't.*"

Oh God.

"Why did you say that awful thing when Billy died?"

"What?" she whispered.

"You told me about a film you made where you talked about it. As if it mattered more than he did. You said it was a good, special thing about him dying."

Mary's stomach clenched. She remembered the words, but who *had* she been when she said them? She had been used so badly, and at the time, it had felt like such love. . . .

"I don't know why I said that—I don't know about any of it," she said. "I'm sorry. Please don't tell me any more right now."

Blank out the Center. Forget it. "C'mere, Toots!" Ken called out one night.

Mary's fists clenched. "Don't you *ever,*" she screamed, "call me that name again!"

Blank it out. Forget it. Mary took a temporary job in the construction industry, then one teaching small children to swim. She watched people she met carefully and tried to ape their behavior. They were normal. She would be normal too. Her twenties blurred into nothingness, years she knew had passed but could not really remember. But the migraines still came, problems with Ken over sex, nightmares. In one, she had to marry Riggs. Sometimes she was just running through streets, trying to get away. A voice kept saying, "What do you mean, 'It's over'? It's not over."

One day, in the spring of 1984, one of her few Center friends called. She wasn't involved in the lawsuit against the Center, but she knew a lot of people who were.

"Mary, someone just phoned me," she said. "Listen. The therapists are suing a lot of people for libel. Their lawyer really wants to talk to you. They need your help. And it might be something that will make you start feeling better."

Mary fought the idea for days. She couldn't stand the thought of being on a witness stand admitting all the things she'd done. She didn't want to look into the eyes of the people who hated her.

And then she turned on the news. A sensational criminal case was enthralling L.A. For the past year, dozens of children at the McMartin Preschool in nearby Manhattan Beach had told investigators that they'd been molested and sexually abused by their teachers. This month, a county grand jury had indicted seven people on 115 separate counts of abuse. (All would later be acquitted.) Mary found herself caught up in the TV report. The children, lawyers were alleging, had kept what had happened secret from their parents, in some cases for years, because they'd been afraid to say anything. Mary's heart started to pound. It sounded so familiar. Kids made to fear their families. Kids told not to fight back or tell. . . .

The next afternoon, she watched the news again, tuning in to the longer reports on cable. Suddenly, she was thinking about the Center. *They tell you you can't tell, and you believe them, until pretty soon you really can't. You become part of what they're doing.* An eight-year-old boy was revealing his story on screen. *The therapists are suing a lot of people. They need your help.* If a little boy could be brave enough to step forward, so could she.

She looked up Paul Morantz, made the call. "Are you the lawyer who's suing the Center?" she asked.

"Who is this?"

"Are you?"

"Who *is* this?"

Mary took a deep breath. "Mary Farrell."

Even through the wires, it sounded as if Morantz was leaping out of his chair. "Jesus! I've *got* to talk to you!"

Reluctantly, Mary agreed to a meeting—just a short one. But as Morantz started asking questions, all the recollections she'd so carefully blocked out rose in her like a tide and rushed out. She found herself telling Morantz not only about PAT but about herself. It was all coming back—old busts, sex assignments, the marital intensive, the abortion. She left the lawyer's house in a daze and woke the next morning crippled with the worst migraine she'd ever had. When it finally eased, for the first time in years she opened her Center diaries.

"They say I'm spaced out and insane, but it's really because of this other incident," she read. "Why are they doing this to me?" Then, just a few weeks later: "I'm really crazy. I need help."

She looked back further. "Riggs said I really kicked ass in the desert. . . ."

Further: She remembered Irvine, the desperation of a lost, scared young girl who worshiped her teachers and believed whatever they said. She remembered Joe's class, LSD, the journey to the farm, herself in a rainy landscape striving toward some elusive goal. And she heard words she'd discounted at the time, those of Riggs's own brother-in-law, there in the distant farmhouse. *"Watch out for Riggs,"* he'd said. *"He's dangerous."*

It was as if her brain had cracked open. She picked up the phone, called Paul Morantz.

"Can *I* sue?" she asked.

Morantz and his co-counsel conferred. More than three years had passed since the Center's close. The statute of limitations for suing had expired. But there were provisions that stopped the clock in cases where people didn't remember what had happened to them or understand they'd been injured. Clearly, that was true of Mary. They took her case.

Soon afterward, Mary filed her own complaint with the attorney general's office. And she took her notebooks, her Group notes, all she'd recorded of Riggs's theories and speeches, the information she had about PAT and how it worked, and gave it all to Morantz and told him everything she knew.

29

By mid-1985, the patients' civil suit against the Center had been going on for nearly four years and the therapists' defamation suit against the patients for three. Seventeen different law firms were involved, and although a February 1986 trial date had been set for the civil suit, only half the depositions had been done. Nothing moved. The therapists fought everything. (At one point, they even tried to have the judge overseeing the civil suit recused, accusing him of bias, prejudice, irrationality, and unjudicial conduct.) After the deposition of Mary Farrell, who knew all about PAT and could verify the truth of statements the therapists claimed were defamatory, the attorney defending Ron Arliss tried to have the defamation suit dismissed. But the therapists wouldn't budge on that either. For all that the bad publicity about the Center had disrupted their careers at first, most seemed to have recovered and gone on, even flourished. Steve and Carole had come back to Southern California. For a while, Carole had run a counseling center (the place later closed); Steve was practicing therapy and writing. Joe had moved from the University of Redlands to California State Polytechnic University, Pomona, just east of L.A., where he was director of the student counseling center. And Riggs, who now called himself a "personal coach," had established therapeutic practices in Aspen and Manhattan. Some of his patients were individuals; he was also hired by companies to give advice to executives on dealing with stress and management issues. He was even at work on a new book.

Then, that spring, for the first time a rift opened in the therapists' united defense. Nearly three years earlier, Jerry and Werner had left the law firm representing the other founders and hired their own attorney, Louis Marlin. Marlin now took a hard look at the therapists' defamation suit and decided it was bunk. The things patients had said to the media were opinions they had the right to express. Besides, the more he reviewed the facts of the Center case, the more he believed what they'd said was either true or close to it. He said as much to the other therapists' lawyers at Barash & Hill. In return, Marlin would later say, the attorneys admitted that the defamation suit was being used as a "weapon" against the plaintiffs in the civil suit, a way to get them to dismiss their claims. The attorneys, Marlin also said, admitted that this was also a way to keep Dr. Louis West from talking more to the media or being used as an expert witness in the civil suit. He was furious. By filing a groundless suit, he felt, the therapists' attorneys were making their clients vulnerable to charges of malicious prosecution. By June, he would file a request to remove Jerry's and Werner's names from the defamation complaint. They would not be part of this anymore.

Around the same time, Matt and Katie Lawrence broke. The lawyer who represented all the MFCCs came to William Carter with a proposal: Matt and Katie would voluntarily surrender their licenses if the state would agree to let them reapply later. Carter forwarded the proposal to the BMQA, which rejected it. He was disappointed, and so contacted the Lawrences' personal attorney with another idea: He'd be lenient with the Lawrences if they'd testify against the other therapists.

Matt and Katie agreed. They were, said the second attorney, "remorseful and guilt-ridden" about what they'd done and wanted to "prevent the sort of abuses which occurred [at the Center] from ever happening again." Outraged at what they called an "unauthorized communication" with the Lawrences, Riggs, Steve, Joe, Werner, and Jon Walker asked for an order recusing the entire office of the attorney general from further involvement in the case. It was denied, the denial appealed, and the appeal denied. The deal with the Lawrences fell apart. But Matt and Katie agreed to speak honestly in their civil/defamation suit depositions in return for not being sued beyond the limits of their insurance coverage. The wealth of information they'd provide couldn't help but build the patients' case. When Matt testified, he broke down and wept. He seemed so anguished by what had happened at the Center and the part he'd played in it that even opposing attorney Paul Morantz found himself in tears.

At the therapists' request, the judge had ordered the depositions taken in the civil suit sealed—an unusual but not-unheard-of ruling—so no one outside the case was allowed access to the transcripts. Attorney General William Carter would never learn what Matt Lawrence had revealed. But by now, he'd amassed 3,700 pages of sworn statements, transcribed investigation interviews, and investigation reports detailing abuse at the Center. He was ready to begin trying the therapists. The hearings would be divided according to licenses. Jerry, a psychological assistant currently in the process of applying for full licensure, would have his own hearing, as would Lee, the M.D., and Konni, the psychiatric technician. The MFCCs—Dominic, Carole, Phil, Matt, and Katie—would be tried as a group. So would Joe, Riggs, Steve, Werner, and Jon Walker, the psychologists.

Out of the hundreds of patients who'd complained, around sixty were being prepared to testify in court. All were volunteers, ready to face therapists against whom they had specific grievances—those who'd done their Intensives or forced them into something particularly humiliating or harmful. Carter had subpoena power but had decided not to use it. Given the issues on which the case focused, people who testified would be put through a lot. Their medical histories would be made public, including the problems that had driven them to the Center in the first place. And since the goal was to prove that the Center had been abusive, people would have to talk about the most unpleasant and embarrassing moments in their lives. He refused to force anyone to go through that. Janet Quinn and Sara Wrightman Fitzgerald were among those who agreed to speak against Jerry. Janet would also be testifying against Lee, as would Deborah Reiss. Mary Farrell and Ken Lander were set to testify against Konni. Mary, Deborah, and Kevin Fitzgerald would speak against Joe, Riggs, and Steve.

Carter spent hours preparing his witnesses, letting them get comfortable telling their stories. Unlike Morantz, Carter wasn't the kind of lawyer who got emotionally involved with his work. Still, he couldn't help being stirred by his witnesses. He didn't think he'd ever worked with such intelligent, articulate people. And he couldn't help feeling sorry for them. No matter how he thought about it, he just couldn't understand why the therapists had done what they did.

In late September 1985, Jerry's hearing began in a cramped, nondescript room in a state office building in downtown Los Angeles. According to standard BMQA procedure, there was no jury, only an administrative law judge, who would render the verdict. Janet Quinn was the first patient to testify. Conservatively dressed, her olive skin subtly rouged and her long black hair combed back, she looked more like a self-assured young career woman than a troubled psychotherapy patient or cult victim. Which in some ways she was: After a long period of counseling, Janet had gotten a master's degree and teaching credential and now taught emotionally disturbed children. But her composure was hard-won. She'd been up since 5:00 A.M. and had gotten to the courthouse an hour early. Even so, her first few minutes on the stand were scary. She looked out into the small room, and there, just feet away, was Jerry. After four years, he seemed both achingly familiar and terribly strange. He was just an ordinary man, yet for years he'd had the power to make or destroy her life.

Her veins opened to a flood of adrenaline. That was what she'd come to talk about. Yes, she told William Carter, because she was "overweight" she'd had to strip in Group. Yes, Jerry had told her she was "too negative . . . emotionally dead." Yes, she had been "busted" on many occasions. Yes, he'd convinced her that her past life had been a total failure. . . .

Jerry's eyes were tearing. He blew his nose. For an instant, something moved in Janet's heart. She was hurting him, and she couldn't help it—she was sorry. Then she thought about her ruined knees, and the feeling was gone. Never run, never dance, never ski. Fuck him. And she looked away and just continued to talk.

Jerry's trial lasted fifteen days. A clinic worker told of being pressured to give up her young children. Sara Wrightman Fitzgerald talked about sluggo therapy and the time she and Kevin had been broken up and she'd been "assigned" a boyfriend. There was silence in the room as one woman recounted a sexual encounter with Jerry, then her Group leader. Afterward, she'd been so distraught that she was told she was acting "crazy." The woman's older sister was an institutionalized schizophrenic, and she'd always been afraid that one day she too would lose her mind. Jerry, who knew this, had given her an assignment: To "feel her craziness," she was to go to a state mental hospital and tell the staff she was thinking of admitting herself.

A number of people spoke in Jerry's defense. A psychologist with whom Jerry and Werner currently shared an office said he thought Jerry was a good therapist—and reminded the court that standards in the 1980s were more conservative than they'd been in the 1970s. Several former patients also took the stand. "I think Jerry had good, real heart," one said earnestly. "He wanted a better life for his patients. He had a vision for them. *I* feel better today because of the Center."

Jerry himself denied everything. He'd never had sex with his patients. He'd never told anyone to give up her kids. He'd never pushed people to hit each other or ordered them to strip or exercise. He'd never taken action to cause anyone psychological or emotional harm. He really didn't know, he said, why the Center had ended.

The arguments didn't work. On December 16, 1985, Administrative Law Judge P. M. Hogan ordered Jerry's psychologist's assistant license revoked and his application to be a psychologist denied. Jerry appealed, but by the following summer, the appeal too would be denied, and the revocation made final. He would never practice as a California psychotherapist again.

For four days in December 1985, then seven the following July and August, another administrative law judge heard testimony against Konni Corriere. A former patient said she'd been instructed to leave her children, ages four and eighteen months, with her estranged husband, and later, told to ask her mother to adopt them. Mary Farrell and Ken Lander repeated Konni's comments following Mary's abortion. And the court heard the story of the woman who'd had to carry a doll during her Intensive until she agreed to terminate her pregnancy. Within two years of the Center's fall, she'd had a child—and she was pregnant again.

Konni denied that any of these things had happened as reported. But in October 1986, Judge Marilyn L. Nelson, citing incompetence, gross negligence, and patient abuse, forever revoked her state license to work as a psychiatric technician.

Lee Woldenberg's hearing ran through January and February of 1986. There was testimony from a man told to wear a T-shirt that said "DOG SHIT," from a man called a "neurotic Jew," from the man ordered to wear diapers and sleep in a crib before he agreed to go back to work at Slick Auto.

Janet Quinn spoke again too—among other things, about how Lee had turned over her therapy sessions to an unlicensed fellow patient. Testifying was harder this time. She'd gotten to the courthouse late, without time to compose herself. And while she was clear about her rage at Jerry, Lee had been her Intensive therapist. Despite everything, she still had feelings of love for him. Then the defense attorney went after her hard. Didn't you say on your application that you needed therapy because you'd had a homosexual affair? he demanded. Isn't this the letter you wrote after several years in therapy explaining how you'd improved and why you wanted to stay in therapy? Janet flushed as he started reading and she heard her own sentences, her proud use of the new therapy language she'd learned. "Fuck," it said, "cunt," "tits." "Aren't those your words?" the attorney asked.

Of course they were, but how could she explain they really weren't? After Janet left the stand, she burst into tears. She felt crazy, dirty, and humiliated. After all this time, the Center had gotten her again. Soon she was crying so hard a friend had to drive her home.

Like Jerry and Konni, Lee denied all charges against him. He also had patients speak up in his support. "In therapy, I could let it all out, especially with Lee," one man said. "He really knew what he was doing."

Administrative Law Judge Milford A. Maron disagreed, and found Lee guilty of unprofessional conduct that included gross negligence and aiding and abetting the unlicensed practice of psychology. His medical license was ordered revoked. However, the judge proposed that the revocation be stayed, and Lee placed on probation for ten years, if he agreed to certain conditions: He would limit his practice to radiology; obey all state and federal laws governing the practice of medicine in California; submit to the medical board quarterly declarations stating his compliance with the conditions of probation; comply with its probation surveillance program; appear in person for interviews upon request; and notify the medical board of any departure from and return to California.

The medical board refused to accept this recommendation and revoked Lee's license completely. He appealed, and the appeal was granted. He was allowed to keep his radiology practice, but he would never be a psychotherapist again.

The dominoes were falling. In early 1986, one month before the patients' civil suit was to go to trial, the therapists' attorneys approached Paul Morantz and the opposing sides finally began talking realistically about a settlement. Everyone would gain by bypassing court—save the cost of a six-month trial, avoid the inconvenience it would cause dozens of plaintiffs and defendants who lived out of town, and perhaps most of all, spare everyone the humiliation of a very public trial. Hammering out the terms of the settlement and wording of the agreement was no easier than any other part of the lawsuit had been—it took more than six months. As part of the condition of settlement, the records of the case—the depositions taken, documents assembled, briefs and interrogatories written—were sealed. Paul Morantz agreed not to represent any other claimants against the Center therapists.

The settlement figures were sealed too, but numbers leaked out. According to the *Los Angeles Times*, the therapists had agreed to pay their former patients just over $6 million. As the checks were cut, charges were dropped against all the patients the therapists had sued for defamation. All, that is, but Ron Arliss, his partner, and the one nonpatient being sued,

Dr. Louis West. The therapists had offered to drop their suit, but only if the three men waived their right to sue back for malicious prosecution. They refused.

Paul Morantz ended up well paid for his five years of work. The patients split their share of the money, based on a formula that factored in how long they'd been at the Center and how much damage they'd sustained there. Those who got the most received around $150,000 to $200,000. Paying that money didn't personally hurt the therapists, since the settlement, along with a reported $4 million in defense costs, was paid by the Center's insurance policies. The founders walked away with whatever profit they'd made from the Center, as well as from the sale of its Hollywood buildings and the ranch. Nor was what patients received enough to really compensate them for what had happened—$100,000 valued each year of youth lost at the center at less than $20,000. But nothing could make up for those losses, and $100,000 *was* enough to send an ex-Center patient with no career back to school, enough to buy some security, enough to make it possible to purchase a decent home, even in overpriced Southern California. Even more important was its symbolic value. In America, those who paid monetary damages to others were those society judged as having done wrong—$100,000 was justice.

As the civil lawsuit was being settled, the attorney general's office made its final preparations to begin hearings against the Center's five clinical psychologists, Joe, Riggs, Steve, Werner, and Jon Walker. And finally, one of the founders broke ranks. It was Werner.

Werner's attorney and Attorney General William Carter began to talk about a deal. Werner would waive his right to a hearing and sign a stipulation admitting to many of the allegations against himself and the other founders. In return, although the state would revoke his license, it would stay the revocation and put him on probation for ten years, with some strict conditions: He'd be suspended for a year, then have to pass an oral clinical exam before resuming practice, and he'd have to provide free psychological services to a charity for twenty hours a month for three years, complete a clinical training program approved by the medical board, take an annual educational course on ethics for ten years, periodically undergo a psychiatric evaluation by a doctor appointed by the medical board, and, if necessary, undergo treatment. And he would never engage in solo practice.

Werner agreed. "At all times while I was a therapist at the Center for Feeling Therapy, I had a belief that I was helping my patients," he wrote in his stipulation. "However, events as they progressed resulted in the therapists at the Center instituting and participating in a systematic social influence process and an enforced dependancy [sic] situation which greatly effected [sic] the ability of our patients to act independently and to control their own lives. As part of the purported therapy at the Center for Feeling Therapy, therapists used racial, religious, and ethnic slurs, physical and verbal humiliation, physical and sometimes sexual abuse, [and] threats of insanity."

And then he began to inform on his former colleagues. He was aware, he said, that Steve had criticized a woman for being a bad mother and said her therapy would be successful if she put her kids up for adoption. That Steve told a patient-couple they needed to have frequent intercourse for their therapy to be successful. That Steve struck patients and ridiculed one for being a "loser."

He was aware that Joe had convinced a patient to have an abortion, that he had struck a patient, that he had told a patient she was insane. And he was aware that Riggs had aided and abetted his wife, Konni, in the unlicensed practice of therapy; used his position as a therapist to coerce Kevin Fitzgerald into working for Langley Construction; told the woman required to carry a large doll that she needed an abortion for her therapy to be successful; ridiculed patients for being Jewish; humiliated patients by calling them "crazy"; and struck patients during therapy.

But if William Carter expected Werner's admission to prompt the other founders to also give up and confess, it did not.

30

By the time hearings against Joe, Riggs, Steve, and Jon began on March 3, 1986, local newspapers were calling the BMQA action against the Center the "longest, costliest, and most complex psychotherapy malpractice case in California history." All along, some ex-patients in addition to those testifying had attended the various hearings. Now, as action focused on the two men considered Feeling Therapy's leaders, the numbers increased. Since everyone knew who'd be speaking and which stories they'd tell, these proceedings wouldn't have the flashy drama of prime-time TV law—there would be no last-minute surprise witnesses or attorneys pounding tables and crying "Isn't it true, sir, that *you* were there?" Everything would be slow and technical, long and drawn-out—in fact, hearings against the four psychologists would take place intermittently for the next year. But there was something appropriate about this very ponderousness, for it belonged so clearly to state authority.

Throughout its history, the Center had compared entry into its community to an initiation into another way of thinking and being. But in truth, it had been something more. With their Intensives, patients had passed from normal society into a whole new *world*, one entirely defined by the therapists. It was they who said what was and wasn't feeling; it was they who decided what was and wasn't love; it was they who were well, and everyone else who was sick. With their claims of innocence, they were trying to preserve that world even now. The men on trial, said defense attorney Larry Watts in his opening arguments, were not villains at all but innovative therapists who'd developed unconventional techniques to treat "lost souls"—young adults caught "between the radical peace movement of the sixties and the yuppie generation of the seventies and eighties" and consequently "uncertain of their place in society." All the complaints about the Center were merely the distortions and fantasies of extremely troubled men and women—everything from "outright lies" to "such extreme exaggeration as to be totally unreliable."

But the state believed the Center's patients, and through it, a very different ritual was taking place, a ceremony of judgment, reintegration, and excommunication. As patients stood up to speak, as they heard their peers' stories accepted as the truth, the society they'd left was taking them back in. And it was the therapists who were being cast out.

Kevin Fitzgerald was one of the first to testify. Nearly thirty-five years old now, his once-wild dark curls trimmed and tamed, he was broader than he had been in his Center days, calmer, more solid-looking and self-assured. Over the past few years, he'd moved from selling plants to starting and building a successful business of his own, a small housepainting company. He and Sara had bought another home, a large, comfortable place in northern San Diego County. And they finally had a family—a year earlier, at thirty-nine, Sara had given birth to a son. They were planning to have another child as soon as possible.

The stories Kevin told the full hearing room were straightforward. He had received weekly therapy from Riggs at a time when Riggs had no license. Riggs had told him he was a failure and a loser and had sent him to work for Langley Construction.

"How many hours a day did you work for Langley Construction?" William Carter asked.

"Around thirteen hours a day."

"How much were you paid?"

"Sometimes as little as $4,500 a year."

Kevin looked at the therapists in the room who sat in their chairs, not allowed to contradict him. A lightness came over him. This was wonderful. It was like—it was like finally having a true Group: He was telling the truth, and someone was listening.

Mary Farrell, now nearly thirty-six, testified the next day. Long-haired, still slender, but no longer so gaunt, she'd been through two years of therapy with a psychologist who specialized in treating women abused by therapists and had slowly come to understand how being brutalized by her father as a child had primed her for unquestioning loyalty to another dominant man. She'd also read every book on brainwashing she could find and had a grasp on the mechanisms of what had happened to her at the Center. That didn't mean she was over it. She was still tormented by migraines, nightmares. And Feeling Therapy continued to wield a destructive power over her marriage to Ken. Every gathering with his family was an ordeal, for Ken's brother, who'd worked for Langley Construction, and his wife had never wholly forgiven her for her part in PAT. Just hearing about the Center made them furious. "Don't bring us up, don't mention our names," the wife had hissed when she learned Mary was involved in the Morantz lawsuit. "We won't get involved." Sex continued to be a problem. Perhaps hardest of all, Ken didn't seem able to understand why Mary didn't just get on with her life. Mary still loved Ken; she thought he was one of the sweetest, most decent men she'd ever known. But she wasn't at all sure their marriage would survive—if any that carried a similar burden of history could.

Her heart was beating fast as she took the stand. She'd been afraid to come to court at all, afraid to run into other patients who still hated her, very afraid of what she might feel when she saw Riggs. Her therapist had told her earlier to be on guard, for when she saw him in a vulnerable position, she might feel sorry for him. Just in case, she'd asked Paul Morantz to go along, for support.

The story Mary told was of the Group where Riggs had played priest and she'd knelt and renounced her past with a scream of "I refuse to give in to what you taught me!" In cross-examination, the defense tried to make the craziness seem all hers, focusing on the conflicts she herself had admitted about her Catholic upbringing, and asking about all her LSD trips. She didn't fall apart. And she glanced at Riggs only once. He was heavier than he'd been years earlier, his shaggy black hair cut short and slicked back in a corporate cut. He wore a gray pin-striped suit and was making a great show of taking notes. She had loved him once. Whatever she felt now, it wasn't that. She looked away, and never looked back.

Through March, seventeen other former Center men and women took the stand to tell their stories or confirm what others had said. Jewish patients recounted being called "kike" and "Jew boy." A woman testified to being "assigned" to have sex weekly by Steve Gold; one of the men she'd then slept with was Riggs. A couple recalled a similar assignment, to have sex each day. Another woman recounted having dated and slept with Joe Hart. Deborah Reiss described how Steve Gold had told her she was a "fighter" and needed to lose weight to become more "fragile" and "feminine." After her weight dropped to 101 pounds, she stopped menstruating and developed pneumonia.

Several women recounted being pressured to have abortions. A man told how he'd been wrapped in plastic, tied up, blindfolded and gagged by Riggs, and left alone to listen to a tape of his own voice because he was "a nobody with no personality." Another said Riggs had punched him in the back, kidneys, and stomach for more than half an hour because he'd complained he was "bored" during therapy.

The state's expert witness, psychologist and thought reform authority Margaret Singer, went through each recounted story, pointing out how and why what had been done represented "an extreme departure from the standards of practice of psychology." "The goal of psychotherapy," she testified, was "to help patients learn skills in thinking and in control and proper expression of feeling and in getting along with others so that therapy can *end*." Instead, the Center had used brainwashing techniques to manipulate and control patients for their own purposes. "It was," she said, "a cult."

A chastened Werner Karle took the stand to confirm that. He admitted having ridiculed patients, calling them "stingy Jew," and "crazy"; he'd abused patients, struck them, threatened them, had sex with them. Feeling Therapy, he said, involved "patient brutality in a cult setting practiced largely by unlicensed individuals."

Then, through April and May, and from July to September, the defense made its case. Every story patients had told was either reinterpreted as a therapeutic intervention proper for dealing with an extremely troubled person or dismissed as a lie. Women were not pressured to have abortions; they were simply counseled in a way that was "considerate, thoughtful, and beyond criticism." Steve denied he'd assigned a particular couple to have sex. Rather, he had performed a kind of marriage counseling, suggesting that a patient and her boyfriend make "daily loving contacts" with each other. He'd never told Deborah Reiss to diet. Joe flatly denied he'd had sex with a female patient. He'd never ordered anyone to get an abortion. No one had ever pressured patients to donate money to the Center.

Riggs took the stand for a week in July. Patients sat quietly in the audience as he explained that everything that had been said about him was wrong. Stories of beatings and other humiliations came from troubled people who had faulty recall, a tendency to exaggerate, or a lack of insight into the techniques of Feeling Therapy. The man who claimed he'd been punched in the back, kidneys, and stomach, for instance, was a depressed alcoholic with schizoid tendencies. Another man who'd complained about being hit suffered from "a borderline personality disorder with hysteric tendencies." The man who said he'd been wrapped in plastic suffered from "borderline personality with periodic delusional states" and had imagined the whole event. He had never told Kevin Fitzgerald to work for Langley Construction. He had played priest to Mary Farrell not to mock her religion but to help her stand up for what she believed to be true regarding her choices in life. He had never practiced psychology without a license, he said, but acted only as a supervised psychological assistant to Joe Hart.

Several patients who still felt the Center had been a positive experience testified in support of the therapists, as did two experts. One, Dr. Albert Marston, a former director of clinical training at the University of Wisconsin and USC, had himself experimented with Feeling Therapy programs for a short time. Incidents like Mary Farrell's kneeling before a crucifix were entirely appropriate therapeutically, he said. In a kind of psychodrama, Riggs was helping Mary explore some of her long-held inner conflicts about Catholicism.

The other defense expert, to the surprise of many, was a true luminary in the field of psychology. Dr. Perry London, a former director of university clinical training programs at USC and Harvard, and the author of a classic text on therapy and ethics, had worked with Joe on some research projects in the late sixties, and now spoke up for his former colleague. The American Psychiatric Association, he said, currently had identified 417 different psychotherapies being used in practice, at least 30 of which involved confrontative techniques. Psychology was no exact science, but an approximate art. And because there was no professional consensus on either the theory or practice of psychotherapy, it was extremely difficult to evaluate particular psychotherapeutic interventions in terms of some abstract "standard of practice." Thus, he said, there could be times when using deprecating language to a patient, provoking him or her into a confrontation with parents or other significant figures, or even requesting disrobing in a session could be therapeutically appropriate. Simply detailing events that had taken place at the Center wasn't enough for anyone to judge whether or not the therapists had exercised due professional care. Nor was the pain patients recounted proof of anything. That came with the territory. "If it's not painful," London said, "it's not therapy."

In September 1986, a long break was announced in the medical board hearings, with testimony scheduled to resume early the following year. Three months later, in December, Werner Karle, whose epilepsy Arthur Janov claimed primal therapy had cured, suffered a grand mal seizure while on a ladder fixing the roof of his Orange County home. He fell backward, hit his head and died.

The funeral was small and quiet. A big photo of Werner skiing was propped near a closed casket. People from the assembly came up to stand before it and reminisce about Werner. Most of them were people Werner had met long after the Center's fall. His old friend and roommate, Riggs, didn't come to the funeral. But Jerry was there, as were Steve, Dominic, and junior therapist Jason Kushner. Word of Werner's death made the rounds of the ex-patient networks. Some people felt sorry. Whatever else he'd done, Werner had been the only founder who'd made a confession or shown any remorse. One woman in particular grieved: Julia, the girlfriend Riggs had pushed Werner to break up with so many years before. Like Werner, she'd been happily married to someone else for years. But the bond between her and Werner had outlasted Riggs's orders, and ultimately, even the Center. They had continued to stay in touch and had seen each other the week before his death. Neither had ever fully let go.

Toward the end of 1986, forty-two patients who'd decided not to join the original civil suit against the Center changed their minds about suing. Since as part of the settlement agreement Paul Morantz had said he would not represent any new Center clients, they found their way to Bob Burlison, the attorney who'd been defending Ron Arliss in the defamation suit. Six years had passed since the Center's fall, so the statute of limitations for suing had expired. But Burlison found an archaic code of civil procedure that held that time clocks stopped running when a defendant moved out of state. Since both Riggs and Lee had been living outside California, they still could be sued. He filed the papers.

In early 1987, the state began trying the center's MFCCs. Carole spent four days on the stand; then she, Dominic, Phil Schwartz, and Matt and Katie Lawrence quietly gave up and voluntarily surrendered their therapy licenses.

In February, the hearings against Joe, Riggs, Steve, and Jon resumed, and continued on through March. Closing arguments were filed in May and June, and in August, Administrative Law Judge Robert A. Neher handed down his decision. It was sixteen years since the summer eight young rebels left the Primal Institute with hopes of saving the world, and hundreds of kids trailed after them, in hope and in faith, in love and in desperation. According to its own plans, by now the therapy community should have tripled in size. The clinic should have been earning billions of dollars. More books of theory should have been filling the shelves, and Riggs's and Joe's faces gracing the covers of *Newsweek* and *Time*. Instead, everything was gone. And what had been was being judged in the harsh language of law.

''Respondents' assertion that they developed a 'client

centered' therapy is deceiving and untrue," wrote Judge Neher in a passionate, angry, twenty-three-page decision. "They developed a 'therapist centered' therapy in which therapists were allowed to, and did, vent their own emotions on patients and acted out their own feelings on patients who were in a subordinated, dependent, and susceptible state. . . . Through clever networking of each other and manipulation of their patients and by use of threats of insanity, ostracism, rewards, punishments, and a litany of coercive actions, the respondents demanded and received the obsessive devotion of a large group of fearful, dependent, and relatively powerless young people, to themselves and their system.

"The respondents developed and enjoyed the seat of power in a cult; that it was a psychological cult or cult of personality rather than a religious one is certain, but by any definition it was a cult."

Jon Walker was placed under five years' probation, with restrictions on his practice comparable to those set up for Werner before his death.

It was different for the others. None of the therapists, wrote Neher, "display any remorse for, or indeed any understanding of, the damage or potential for damage of any of their actions. There is no question that if the opportunity arose, they would repeat the acts or similar acts."

With that, citing gross negligence, incompetence, patient abuse, false advertising, misrepresentation of professional qualifications, fraud and deception, and aiding and abetting the unlicensed practice of psychology, he forever revoked the California psychologist's license of Stephen Gold, and that of Joseph Hart, and of Richard Corriere.

Childhood's End

November 1990

During eight years of Ronald Reagan, then two of his former vice-president, George Bush, the national embrace of materialism that began with the rise of disco and Studio 54 became a kind of delirium. As programs for the poor were cut, unions broken, and factories closed with barely a whimper from the middle class, a new figure rose to prominence: the "young urban professional" who made at least $100,000 a year, spent it all on clothing, condo, and car, and always wanted more, *more.* "Greed," went a much-quoted line from a movie of the times, "is good." And through the decade, like a relic of another time, legal fallout from the Center for Feeling Therapy dragged on.

To the astonishment of attorney Bob Burlison, the lawyers defending Riggs and Lee in the second mass patient lawsuit started the whole process of meetings, depositions, and discovery again. It wasn't until 1989 that they settled—according to rumor, for just over $1 million. Around the same time, the therapists' defamation suit against Ron Arliss, his partner, and Louis West was finally dismissed. Immediately, both Ron and his partner sued the therapists' law firm for malicious prosecution. Both men later settled, for a reported several hundred thousand dollars each. In 1987, eight former clients sued Paul Morantz, claiming they'd gotten less money than others involved in the first lawsuit. A few years later, that suit too settled. And the therapists' attorneys filed their own suit against the Center's insurance carriers, for refusing to pay their fees.

By the end of the 1980s, the world that had given rise to the Center had indisputably changed. The growth center Kairos was long defunct. Carl Rogers was dead. Although primal therapy was still in existence, it was hardly the great social force it had once been—the Primal Institute was now located on a nondescript West L.A. street and rented unused rooms to small businesses and free-lance writers. Its founder, Art Janov, however, retained his belief in its principles. By 1990, he was completing another book, *The New Primal Scream*, and several years later, when a fanatic religious group barricaded itself inside a compound near Waco, Texas, would propose in a newspaper editorial that the glue bonding any cult member to a leader was the neediness of unexpressed primal pain.

The Center's own staff had scattered. Many clinic counselors had obtained the necessary licenses and become practicing therapists with conventional practices (although one regularly appeared on late-night TV to hawk "subliminal influence" self-help tapes). Junior therapist Phil Schwartz, who married his Center girlfriend, was once again an accountant. Jason Kushner returned to dentistry. Matt and Katie Lawrence lived for a time in Nevada, where Matt worked as a stockbroker. The two had a child, then reportedly separated, and dropped from sight.

Lee Woldenberg continued to practice radiology; he and his wife had two children. Dominic Cirincione found a new career in personnel management. His wife, Linda Binder Cirincione, became a life insurance salesperson. Their child was born in the early 1980s.

After losing his psychologist's assistant license, Jerry Binder went to work for the plant maintenance company his patient-wife had begun. The couple adopted a child.

Steve Gold and Carole Suydam Gold and their children made their home in California. Carole returned to social work, then gave it up, switching careers several times. Although Steve no longer practiced psychology, he found work related to the field.

In January 1988, five months after he was stripped of his psychologist's license, Joe Hart requested reassignment from Cal Poly Pomona's student counseling center. He was named director of the school's academic advisory center. "His work here has been exemplary," a supervisor said that year. "What happened, or didn't happen, [at the Center] was years ago."

Joe remained married to his college sweetheart, Gina, and to the few patients who stayed in touch with him, enigmatic as ever. Exactly what Joe had hoped to find through Feeling Therapy, what piece of himself had been left sufficiently untouched by it that he could sense its madness, why he left without sharing that understanding with others, and how he now interpreted what had happened at the Center were still a mystery. So were his feelings about his one-time best friend and soulmate. Although some of the founders stayed friendly even after the BMQA hearings ended, as far as anyone knew, Joe Hart never spoke to Riggs Corriere again.

For a long time, Riggs and Konni divided their time between Aspen and New York City. In 1987, a year after her psychiatric technician's license was revoked, Konni, identified as an "Aspen psychotherapist," was quoted in a major women's magazine criticizing the role model offered by Snow White on the fiftieth anniversary of the Disney movie. "Snow White is about how a good little girl grows up to be a *big* good girl," Konni said. "She depicts dependency 100 percent. She takes no control over her own life." Within a few years, Konni would show that she herself was no sleeping princess. Her long marriage to Riggs ended, and she returned to Southern California, where rumor had it she went back to school.

Riggs, who now went by the name Richard, established permanent residence in a high-rise, high-security building on the Upper East Side of Manhattan. New friends found him charismatic and charming. In 1986, William Morrow published his new self-help book, *Life Zones*, which drew heavily on Psychological Fitness concepts and was dedicated to Bruce Springsteen, Tina Turner, and his mother and father. During a break in the medical board hearings, he flew back to New York to talk about it on CNN, which in 1981 had done its own report on the Center's demise and the abuses that had occurred there. He was introduced as a "prominent psychologist." By the decade's end, he had expanded the effort to "help people perform at their best" that he'd originally called "personal coaching" into a new business, "Corporate Counseling." Although he called what he was doing "consulting" rather than "therapy," there was every indication that's exactly what it was.

None of the founders ever spoke publicly about what had happened at the Center; no one but Werner ever publicly admitted he or she was sorry or that what had been done was wrong. Perhaps the therapists maintained silence on their lawyers' advice, or maybe they themselves were afraid that admitting culpability would open up the door to more litigation. Or perhaps it was too painful for them to face in public the ugly secret the Center had revealed about them: that they were people who, when given unlimited power over others, were capable of the worst.

It was hard not to imagine that at times the therapists faced that part of themselves—that there were nights when they lay rigid and awake, recalling their own cruelty and grieving for the extent to which they'd abandoned all they'd once stood for. It was hard not to believe that some broke down in other ways, pouring out their guilt and anguish to a mate or friend. But there was no way to know—ironically, the fact that nearly all had lost their licenses meant the state no longer had any control over them and couldn't require, for instance, that they get therapy themselves. So there was no way to be sure the founders hadn't just buried the ugliness they'd glimpsed in themselves deep inside, in the hope it would never have another chance to surface. Even more frightening, there was no way to be sure any of them had fully grasped the seriousness of what they'd done. In a professional newsletter profile, Jerry identified himself as a former "environmental psychologist," and said his last job's main problem had been "lack of feedback." And Riggs seemed to have lost the trace of repentance he'd displayed during the Center's final days. "He still felt pride in what he'd done at the Center, but felt people couldn't take what he'd had to offer," said an old friend who visited him in New York. As far as she could tell, she added, he was the same old Riggs. The night she visited, a woman came by. Riggs was totally wrapped up in her, and his old friend wasn't sure whether the woman was a friend or a client. "I think he gets close to the people he works with," observed the old friend. "I think he gets involved in their lives."

Ten years after the Center's fall, its former patients still longed for the apology it was clear would never come, for the absolute closure it finally could bring. But most were trying to let go of their rage and obsession, for in the end, staying angry at the Center seemed just another way of staying controlled by it. Finally too, patients were able to acknowledge that in its early years, some good had been done there, that for a time it was a place where childhood wounds were excised, where the emotionally closed learned to open up and love, and where those in real despair were given hope. They could remember moments of exaltation during the middle years, when they had a fleeting glimpse of the joy of true community. The Center was where many had found husbands and wives and formed friendships whose intimacy and intensity still drew notice.

"Where'd you guys meet?" people were always asking the group of men who called themselves "The Buds."

"Where'd we meet?" they'd echo, howling. "In a mental institution!"

One by one, former Center patients moved back toward the middle class. Former auto shop owner Ron Arliss became a wealthy stockbroker who now voted Republican. Deborah Reiss found a new career as an interior decorator, though the bankruptcy into which Plant Power's failure sent her remained on her record, making it impossible to get credit and keeping her on the financial edge. Center patients became doctors, lawyers, businesspeople, art directors, real estate agents, economic consultants, social workers. One by one, they bought houses. Those still young enough had children. One by one, they moved on.

Yet the Center remained inside them, an event, like a war, after which nothing would ever be quite the same. The Center had made it clear that human nature, which once seemed so perfectable and benevolent, also held real evil. They had seen it in what the therapists had done; worse, they had seen it in themselves. When the Berlin Wall came down in the fall of 1989, ex-Center members thought they appreciated, more than most Americans, the feelings of liberation surging through East Germany. But they also believed they understood a darker part of that country's history. Looking back, patients knew there had been moments when they'd glimpsed the insanity that was taking place at the Center—moments when it was clear that hitting was brutal, not therapeutic; when someone told "You're crazy" was in fact speaking the truth; when they themselves had hurt someone else solely because they'd been told to do so. And yet they'd said and done nothing, for it was one thing to spot a wrong and quite another to have the courage to go against the crowd and try to stop it. Like Germans of the 1930s, instead of challenging an evil system, they'd simply accommodated to it, doing and accepting whatever was necessary to survive. It was that knowledge patients would have to face for a lifetime in their own dark nights: awareness of their own moral fallibility. And even more terrifying, many believed that had the Center not ended, they never would have had the strength to leave.

─────────

After a decade out of Feeling Therapy, Andy Heller no longer hated those who'd sued its therapists. If all the stories he'd heard over the past few years were true—and the medical board's decision suggested they were—then the Center had been wrong. Worse than wrong, evil. When he looked back now, Andy saw a lot of things in a different light. One week, home sick in bed, he reread *Going Sane* and *The Dream Makers*. They struck him as rubbish. And when he recalled the self-righteousness with which he'd ignored his own mother as she was dying, he wanted to pound his head against the wall in remorse and shame.

At thirty-five, Andy found it hard to remember the desperation over what to do with himself that had driven him to the Center. Everything had turned out fine in the end. In 1986, he'd lost his job at the record company and had started a small but successful freelance graphics business from his home. Finally, he was an artist—perhaps not a great one, not as talented or celebrated as his father, but good enough.

And yet, and yet. . . .

Shortly after the BMQA hearings ended, Katie Stendall's letters to him had stopped, and her lawyer refused to provide an address or even forward mail. "Leave her alone," he said. "She wants to put that part of life behind her." Despite everything, the idea of never hearing from Katie again filled Andy with terrible grief. Strange as it seemed, for all he condemned the Center intellectually, he knew he would never stop loving and missing it in his heart. It had given him something the outside world never had, and never would. He would never find another tribe. It was an insane thought, but if one day the phone rang and a familiar voice told him it was time to return to Group, there was a good chance he would go.

———————

In Santa Cruz, Russ Gilbert, nearly forty-seven, finally put away his grief over the Center the way he and Holly had packed up their papers, notes, and cassettes from those days for storage. In 1989, two years after he and Holly had a child, the two of them had become interested in a new kind of therapy, "reevaluation counseling." Russ had been wary of involvement in any group at first, but what he learned won him over. The program, which said that nonprofessionals could help each other work out problems just by listening to each other, involved pairing off with someone—just like the Center's co-therapy. But the resemblance ended there. This counseling was emphatically nonauthoritarian; partners were supportive of each other, never critical or harsh. And everyone was encouraged to take note of what was going on in the world, to use his or her mind as well as emotions. In this new counseling, Russ talked about the Center over and over until the memories of those years lost their terrible power and became just another set of things that had happened to him.

Now, although he still didn't accept the idea that the Center had been flawed from the start, figuring out just what *had* happened wasn't so important to him anymore. It was time to move on. Unlike other Center people, he hadn't lost faith in alternative ways to live. He and Holly were toying with the idea of moving even farther out of the mainstream than Santa Cruz, some place where they could own more land, leave the city behind. One day, he hoped he'd make it out of engineering and back into some kind of healing. Both people and the planet Earth, he felt, had a long way to go.

It took almost eight years after the Center's end before Janet Quinn fully felt like herself again. In the fall of 1988, the parents of one of her students accused her of racial discrimination and the school started a formal investigation. Although she knew she'd done nothing wrong, Janet had to hire a lawyer; she was put on probation, and her classroom behavior carefully monitored. Janet fell apart. Suddenly, it was as if she was back at the Center—watched all the time, never sure if what she did or said would be considered OK. Every morning, she woke in tears.

She went back to the therapist she'd seen years before, and went through everything all over again. Even after the discrimination charges were dropped, and both her probation and the classroom monitoring ended, her therapy continued. And finally, as she painstakingly separated what she'd been taught at the Center from what she truly felt and believed about herself, the wedge inside her dissolved. Finally, she could connect with her own core.

After that, the Center receded. She retained the few good things it had given her—friends, the ability to express herself emotionally, the way she once had dreamed. And she would always carry in her mind and body memory of the damage it had done. But she no longer cared to spend time sorting out the *why* of what had happened. There were other, more important things to do. At forty-four, it was too late to have children, but there was still time for a good, loving relationship with a man. And there was still time to carve out a meaningful, fulfilling life. Back when she'd come to the Center, she'd been paralyzed with confusion over what that meant. Now it seemed so simple. It had nothing to do with establishing utopian enclaves or following "perfect" systems. Ironically, it meant coming back to all her old sixties values. At home, she diligently recycled trash, conserved water, avoided using chemicals on her lawn or in her kitchen. At school, although she knew she couldn't save all her kids, she worked hard for those she could help. She treated people fairly, made a point of always being honorable and honest. If the Center had taught her there would always be evil in the world, she would do her best to add to what was good.

Her divorce from Ken Lander nearly four years old, Mary Farrell lived alone, with the Doberman pinscher Riggs had given her, in a tiny cottage north of Santa Barbara. She had never recovered her health; migraines still came with merciless regularity, sometimes as many as six in ten days. Because of them, she'd never really recovered her life either—being sick so often had made it impossible to ever get a career off the ground. Her circle of friends remained tiny, circumscribed. She still avoided everyone from the Center days, and new friends were hard to make. Before she could truly get close, she needed to talk about the Center so that people would understand who she was. And it was such a hard story, so emotionally exhausting to tell. Often people didn't understand. Some were harsh and judgmental, contemptuous of anyone who'd been part of a cult. Others just didn't buy the idea of brainwashing. Sometimes it was easier just to be alone.

At thirty-nine, she had spent as much time trying to undo Feeling Therapy as she'd spent in it. The job might take the rest of her life. She could no longer be sure she'd ever have a real profession, ever have a chance for normal, pleasurable sex, ever get another chance to have a child. She might never have any of the things that would have been hers if, at eighteen, she'd been directed to an ordinary counselor and a very different road. And there was nothing she could do about it. That each day of her life be a tiny bit better than the last was so much less than she'd once hoped for, but now, it was all she could ask.

On weekend nights, thirty-nine-year-old Kevin Fitzgerald could not look around his house, its living room floor covered with kids' books and toys, without feeling the overwhelming sense of having been blessed. He and Sara had a second child now, a daughter, and were hoping for a third. The depth of the love he felt for his wife and children sometimes took Kevin's breath away. Being a family man was an unequivocal joy. Finally, he believed, he had all he'd ever really wanted.

The Center was long behind him now. It had been two years since his last Feeling Therapy dream. When he saw friends from the old days, they talked about different things— their kids, politics, interest rates. He could barely believe they'd once spent hours—days—analyzing the nuances of every interaction and feeling. It seemed absurd now, not only a boring way to live but one that was selfish and narrow. One day, several years ago, when he'd been up in L.A. attending the BMQA hearings, he'd made a detour back through the old neighborhood. On his way out, he'd stopped at a local convenience store for a soda.

"I used to live here," he told the guy behind the counter. "What's it like these days? Are those people who used to scream all the time still around?"

"Oh Jesus, you heard them too?" the man replied. "No, thank God. No one could stand them. They'd come in here at night and offend everybody. They were in some kind of therapy and said they were interested in feelings but they never paid attention to anyone else's, that's for sure."

Kevin stood still at that, his body rigid with shame. He paid for his soda, left, and never went back.

These days, his interests were the opposite of what they had been in the seventies, wider and sweeping. He wanted to hear about everything going on in his employees' lives and what his children's babysitter had to say. He listened to the radio, consumed the daily paper. Being part of the world and knowing what was happening in it felt real and human.

He knew that in some ways the Center had changed him forever. He was harder and more cynical than he might otherwise have been. He had absolutely no tolerance for being manipulated or treated badly by anyone. And he was always a little on guard, for he knew now that the world included people who used others for their own gain. But in many ways, that seemed like a good thing to have learned. He and Sara were saving all their old Center papers so one day they could show them to the kids and tell them the story too. They even made a point of not hiding the past from new friends. "Sara and I met when we were in a cult," he'd told neighbors. The funny thing was that even in this bland-looking suburban subdivision, no one was shocked. Maybe it was because of their ages. Sometimes it seemed that whenever you sat around a dinner table with people in their thirties and forties and talked about the 1970s, it turned out that *everyone* was living in a commune or following some religion or doing huge amounts of drugs. Back then, everyone was into something weird. The Center was his.

But that kind of weirdness was over for him. Even after the disaster primal therapy and the Center had turned out to be, his mother retained her faith in "growth" and was always sending him the latest books on psychology and self-improvement. "Give me a break," he finally told her, and in the margin of her latest offering drew a funny-looking flower with only two petals. "The incomplete, imperfect flower," he wrote next to it, "opens its petals to the sun just as well as the rest."

No, he wasn't perfect. He wasn't ever "100 percent." And that was OK. *He* was OK. The feeling wasn't one he wanted to shout about, the way he would have at the Center. It was just in him, a knowledge burning deep in his core that he loved Sara and the kids, that he was basically a decent guy. There would always be people after something more than that; there was even a joke among ex-patients—"There's a seeker born every minute." But not him. The truth was, he never wanted to "improve" again as long as he lived.

November 6, 1990

On Election Day, a cold front moved through Southern California. Temperatures stayed in the sixties and the sky was filled with clouds until a late-afternoon wind kicked up and cleared them away. Less than half the region's registered voters even bothered going to the polls; everyone was feeling discouraged and cranky. The United States was hovering on the brink of war with Iraq for reasons many thought had to do more with improving presidential image than with punishing Saddam Hussein's invasion of Kuwait. Meanwhile, the country and even the Golden State were caught in the grip of a long recession.

In Orange County, UCI was celebrating its twenty-fifth birthday. Brightly colored banners hung from all the campus lampposts. The school had changed radically since the late 1960s: Spindly trees had grown lush, new buildings had mushroomed, and the number of students had more than tripled—many of them refugees or children of refugees from the Southeast Asian country in whose name the campus Bank of America had been burned so many years earlier. No one in the social science department noted the day that marked the tenth anniversary of the Center's fall. There were only a few professors left who even remembered Joe Hart and Riggs Corriere. None of their students knew about Feeling Therapy; had they known, probably none would have understood why the idea of "living from feeling" had once had such power. Nineties kids didn't feel entitled to happiness and fulfillment the way their sixties predecessors had, for the world they inhabited didn't lend itself to such idealistic fantasies: The politics they knew were not a force for change but a source of corruption; drugs didn't give visions, they ruined lives; sex killed. There was little time to dream when you were focused on economic survival, and even if you wanted to, there was no place to go. The nearby fields where cows had once grazed and kids smoked dope at night, imagining themselves a wild, limitless future, had vanished under townhomes and shopping malls. Irvine, the planned city that would avoid the mistakes of the past, sprawled outward, overpriced, graceless, covered with a blanket of smog.

In Hollywood, the streets around Sunset and La Brea were different too. Urban renewal had swept through in the 1980s, replacing small businesses and restaurants with enormous crowded mini-malls. The old Center building housed a video company. In the eastern blocks of the old therapy neighborhood, nearly all the houses had been bulldozed and replaced by modern high-rise condominiums. West of Vista Street, where homes were intact, gentrification had transformed once-run-down bungalows into glowing paragons of Craftsman cottage charm, all varnished wood floors, beveled glass, and landscaped lawns, with selling prices of over $400,000. On the 1600 block of North Gardner Street, several sat behind a tall redwood fence, weathered now to a soft reddish gray.

Ten years after the Center's fall, the remnants of the fence that once marked off the Compound was the only visible relic of the hundreds of people who'd occupied this neighborhood for six years; the only reminder of the hopes crushed here, the devastating, needless loss. And it was the only tangible sign of an even greater tragedy.

A moment of real possibility existed in the late sixties and early seventies when millions of men and women, yearning for a world more fulfilling than the one they inhabited and a way of life that was not so grim, cut-off, and lonely, paused for a moment and looked inward. Widespread gaining of psychological awareness could have been of huge benefit to a culture created by men almost entirely ignorant of their own inner workings (and everyone else's). Widespread use of therapy—particularly a therapy that grasped the basic human need for joy and transcendence—might have changed millions of lives. And had therapeutic insight been added to the political awareness of the times, used with the understanding that it was also necessary to continue tackling nonpsychological problems like poverty, war, racism, and sexism, American society itself could have been transformed. A whole new model of adulthood might have been created, one in which connection to one's inner self went along with connection to the public world, in which a responsible grownup could also be one who was spontaneous, joyful, and fully alive.

But there was almost no way the therapies spawned by humanist psychology could have given birth to such a vision. The central thesis that made humanism so optimistic and appealing—that everyone had a healthy self waiting, intact, beneath layers of social conditioning—also made it profoundly isolationist, for in essence it said that the true self existed apart from the world. By this logic, there was no point in working to change society, for once everyone was "self-actualized," it would happen automatically. Like those hippies who believed that politics and economics were less important than "consciousness"—and that if everyone took LSD, the country would be altered overnight—humanism suggested that therapeutic self-awareness wasn't merely a step toward social change; it was all it took. It was an idea embraced by a culture frustrated with an outer world that had not proved amenable to quick fixes, and taken even further by the therapies (and quasi-therapies) humanism spawned.

By 1990, it was possible to look back at those therapies and make a long list of the ones that, like Feeling Therapy, had gone wrong in one way or another. Through the 1970s, Esalen suffered a rash of suicides; by 1979, the institute's management was taken over by a young Englishwoman who claimed to be a "channel" for a group of 8-million-year-old, mass-energy entities from the star Sirius. Rajneeshpuram, the one-hundred-square-mile Central Oregon "model city" built by 600 followers of Bhagwan Shree Rajneesh, where human potential movement therapies like Rolfing and bioenergetics were a vital part of life, collapsed in 1984: One of the commune's leaders had turned into a virtual dictator, who among other things, tried to poison local officials opposed to the Rajneeshis taking control of county government in an upcoming election. In 1988, newspapers detailed a scandal within the Movement of Spiritual Inner Awareness, whose estlike "Insight" trainings had attracted some 100,000 participants. Some MSIA members left the organization, alleging that its leader, best-selling author, John-Roger, had seduced a number of male followers and responded to criticisms with poison pen letters and death threats. (John-Roger denied these allegations and no legal or law enforcement actions resulted.) In 1989, a child custody battle focused attention on the Sullivanians, a longtime New York City therapy community, which, critics said, had evolved into an authoritarian cult that was virtually enslaving some 200 members. In early 1990, a longtime employee of est guru Werner Erhard sued for wrongful discharge, claiming that she was fired when she opposed policies that forced employees to work more than twelve hours a day, six days a week. Several other followers filed supporting declarations, charging Erhard with using abusive tactics to enforce obedience. (Within a year, two of his daughters would tell reporters that he had abused them and their mother physically and emotionally, calling him "a total control monster.")

The high disaster rate shouldn't have been surprising. No therapeutic relationship is ever one of equals, for therapy is based on the assumption that the therapist knows more than the patient. It's also a given that a patient must accept both this inequality and dependence on the therapist in order to be helped. But inequality and dependency should be temporary, conditions a patient enters for brief periods of time, then sheds as he or she resumes life as an adult. Human potential movement therapies that emphasized "letting go" of the outer

world, however—whether those like the center which advocated the formation of a separate society or those like est
which affirmed some version of "You are the cause of everything that happens to you"—made such a resumption impossible, for they denied the moral and social responsibilities that
are the hallmark of true adult life. And by that denial, they
made inequality permanent. Their promises to deliver total
harmony and bliss appealed to a wish that is essentially infantile—for perfection and union with a powerful parent; their
emphasis on living in a state of unintellectual openness and
vulnerability encouraged adults to literally become children.
Rather than providing a new model of adulthood, such therapies popularized—and millions embraced—a very different
ideal: *regression*. Ultimately and ironically, they ended up re-
creating the very kind of system most people enter therapy to
escape—a destructive family that infantilized everyone involved. Children-patients remained perpetually dependent on
those they saw as having "the answer," unable to grow or
move. Parent-therapists felt free to act out, for given too much
power, they lost track of their own boundaries and came to
believe they were the center of the universe, and others only
extensions of themselves.

By the 1980s, the fact that a lot of 1970s therapeutic experi-
mentation had gone over the edge was clear to the mainstream
professional community. The 1980 American Psychological
Association Code of Ethics, for instance, reestablished some
professional boundaries, prohibiting therapists from treating
anyone who was a relative, friend, employee, lover, or student. (Which also meant therapists shouldn't hire their patients or try to turn them into friends.) In 1989, nearly two
decades after psychologists debated the possible benefits of
sleeping with their patients, California governor George
Deukmejian—joining lawmakers in Minnesota, Wisconsin, Il-

linois, and Colorado—signed a bill making any psychiatrist, psychologist, licensed clinical social worker, or MFCC who engaged in such behavior guilty of a *crime*. He was supported by nearly every professional mental health organization in the state.

But with the exception of Jungian James Hillman (whose book title *We've Had a Hundred Years of Psychotherapy and the World's Getting Worse* says it all), no professional publicly examined or condemned the deny-the-world premise underlying the therapies that became so popular during the seventies. Nor was there acknowledgment of how deeply the seventies culture of regression became embedded in the larger society. It was no coincidence that the decade ended with the election of the ultimate father figure, Ronald Reagan—a soft-voiced man who said not to worry, for he would make everything all right. It was no coincidence that the years that followed saw the rise of "yuppie" values, with their emphasis on materialism and acquisition—their cry of "Buy, buy, buy" no more than a mantra of released infantile greed. (And, of course, all those years of human potential movement emphasis that everyone was responsible for his or her own life took care of any guilt feelings that unrestrained getting-and-spending might provoke: Obviously, anyone who was poor or unsuccessful just hadn't *tried*.) Even into the 1990s, as the real world reasserted itself in the form of serious economic crisis and the shallowness of the preceding ten years was being loudly denounced, at a deep emotional level, Americans still refused to grow up. Instead, tens of thousands of men and women began immersing themselves in the study of their childhood wounds without ever placing much emphasis on the idea of going *beyond* them—in essence, declaring themselves permanent victims rather than actors with independent will, identified by the telling name "adult children."

Twenty years after the first "encounter" groups, workshops, "primal" screams, it was clear that a therapeutic movement that had promised to change the world had instead abandoned it. Rather than expanding human "potential," it had instead encouraged people to become smaller. And it was clear that a nation of children (wounded and otherwise) had never really grasped the true lesson of the rise and fall of the Center for Feeling Therapy—that for all its appeals, in the end, regression offers no redemption. For while children may be fresh and pure, wide-eyed and without guile, they are one thing above all else: They are powerless.

———————

It is that lesson which reverberates during one last trip to the former Center neighborhood. Walking the streets, it's easy to recall the old days, for at twilight the area takes on the same dreamy stillness it did so many years ago, hills and palms growing sharp against the glowing sky, air turning a rich dark gold. Yet if this hour in this place once promised rebirth, now it urges a different kind of start. The memory of what happened here catches in the mind like a harsh whisper, an echoing song: a warning to aging kids of the white middle class how painful it is—and yet how necessary—to move out and into the world, to finally leave childhood behind.

Sources

A significant percentage of the material in this book was derived from personal interviews with former patients of the Center for Feeling Therapy as well as those who had more tangential contact with the Center and its programs and therapists. Material also came from Feeling Therapy patient notebooks, diaries, audio- and videotapes, transcripts of lectures and presentations given by Center therapists, Center brochures, newsletters, fliers, and business meeting notes. Court and Board of Medical Quality Assurance records were used as well, as were dozens of newspaper and magazine articles and television shows covering the Center, both before and after its fall.

Works written by Center therapists were also used extensively. They include the following:

Books

Corriere, Richard. *Life Zones: How to Win in the Game of Life.* New York: William Morrow, 1986.

Corriere, Richard and Joseph Hart. *The Dream Makers: Discovering Your Breakthrough Dreams.* New York: Funk & Wagnalls, 1977.

Corriere, Richard and Joseph Hart. *Psychological Fitness: 21 Days to Feeling Good*. New York: Harcourt Brace Jovanovich, 1978.

Hart, Joseph, Richard Corriere, and Jerry Binder. *Going Sane: An Introduction to Feeling Therapy*. New York: Dell Publishing, 1975.

Hart, Joseph, Richard Corriere, Werner Karle, and Lee Woldenberg. *Dreaming and Waking: The Functional Approach to Using Dreams*. Los Angeles: The Center Foundation Press, 1980.

Dissertations

Binder, Gerald Michael. *The Discovery of Personness: The Assessment of Feeling Expressiveness*. University of California, Irvine, Ph.D., 1975.

Corriere, Richard Joseph. *The Transformation of Dreams*. University of California, Irvine, Ph.D., 1974.

Gold, Stephen David. *Experience and Expression: A New Approach*. University of California, Irvine, Ph.D., 1975.

Karle, Werner. *A New Orientation for Sleep Research: The Alteration of Sleep Patterns in Psychotherapy*. University of California, Irvine, Ph.D., 1975.

Book Chapters and Papers

Corriere, Richard et al. "Application of the Process Scoring System to Waking, Dream and Therapy Reports." In *Journal of Clinical Psychology*, July 1978.

Hart, Joseph T. "Dreams in the Classroom" (1969)

Hart, Joseph T. "Worknotes for an Integrative Psychology" (1970).

Hart, Joseph and Richard Corriere. "Abreaction, Feeling and Satori" (1973).

Hart, Joseph. "Beyond Psychotherapy." *New Directions in Client-Centered Therapy*, ed by J. T. Hart and T. M. Tomlinson. Boston: Houghton Mifflin, 1970.

Hart, Joseph, Richard Corriere, and Werner Karle."Functional Psychotherapy." In *Handbook of Innovative Psychotherapies* ed. R. Corsini. New York: Wiley Interscience, 1980.

Karle, Werner, Richard Corriere, and Joseph Hart. "Psychological Changes in Abreactive Therapy: I. Primal Therapy." In *Psychotherapy: Theory, Research and Practice*, 1973, vol. 10, no. 2.

Karle, Werner, Richard Corriere, Joseph Hart and Lee Woldenberg. "The Functional Analysis of Dreams: A New Theory of Dreaming." In *Journal of Clinical Psychology*, January, 1980.

Karle, Werner, Lee Woldenberg, and Joseph Hart. "Feeling Therapy." In *Modern Therapies*, ed. Virginia Binder, Arnold Binder, and Bernard Rimland, Englewood Cliffs, N.J.: Prentice-Hall, 1976.

In addition, a number of other written sources were used. The first list is of those which provided background information. Sources of facts and quotes directly cited in the text are listed according to the number of the page on which they appear.

Back, Kurt W., ed. *In Search of Community: Encounter Groups and Social Change*. Westview Press, 1978.

Herink, Richie. *The Psychotherapy Handbook: The A to Z Guide to More than 250 Therapies in Use Today*. New York: New American Library, 1980.

Hougan, Jim. *Decadence: Radical Nostalgia, Narcissism, and Decline in the Seventies*. New York: William Morrow, 1975.

Kovel, Joel, M.D. *A Complete Guide to Therapy: From Psychoanalysis to Behavior Modification*. New York: Pantheon, 1976.

Lifton, Robert Jay. *Thought Reform and the Psychology of Totalism: A Study of "Brainwashing" in China*. New York: Norton, 1961.

Lowen, Alexander. *Bioenergetics*. New York: Coward, McCann & Geoghegan, 1975.

Ofshe, Richard, Ph.D., and Margaret T. Singer, Ph.D. "Attacks on Peripheral versus Central Elements of Self and the Impact of Thought Reforming Techniques." In *The Cultic Studies Journal*, Vol. 3, no. 1, (1986).

Reich, Charles A. *The Greening of America: How the Youth Revolution is Trying to Make America Livable*. New York: Random House, 1970.

Roszak, Theodore. *The Making of a Counter Culture: Reflections on the Technocratic Society and Its Youthful Opposition*. New York: Doubleday, 1968.

Rubin, Jerry. *Growing (Up) at Thirty-seven*. New York: M. Evans, 1976.

Schein, Edgar. *Coercive Persuasion: A Socio-psychological Analysis of the "Brainwashing" of American Civilian Prisoners by the Chinese Communists*. New York: Norton, 1961.

Schur, Edwin M. *The Awareness Trap: Self-Absorption Instead of Social Change*. New York: Quadrangle/The New York Times Book Company, 1976.

Streiker, Lowell D. *Mind Bending: Brainwashing, Cults and Deprogramming in the '80s*. New York: Doubleday, 1984.

Tart, Charles, T., ed. *Altered States of Consciousness: A Book of Readings*. New York: John Wiley & Sons, 1969.

West, Louis, M.D., and Margaret Thaler Singer, Ph.D. "Cults, Quacks, and Nonprofessional Psychotherapies." In *Comprehensive Textbook of Psychiatry/III*. Baltimore/London: Williams & Wilkins, 1980.

Wolfe, Tom. "The Me Decade and the Third Great Awakening." In *The Purple Decades*. New York: Farrar Straus Giroux, 1982

PART ONE

page 16   *"Executive secretary of the American Psychological Association":*
Perry London, "From the Long Couch for the Sick to the Push Button for the Bored." *Psychology Today*, June 1974.

"a cripple psychology and a cripple philosophy":
Duane Schultz, *A History of Modern Psychology* (New York: Academic Press), 1975.

page 26   *"Sensitivity training":*
Martin L. Gross, *The Psychological Society: A Critical Analysis of Psychiatry, Psychotherapy, Psychoanalysis and the Psychological Revolution* (New York: Random House, 1978), p. 304.

"and an AA alumnus":
Jane Howard, *Please Touch: A Guided Tour of the Human Potential Movement* (New York: McGraw-Hill, 1970), p. 133–5.

page 27   *"a new dedication to life as art":*
Jay Stevens, *Storming Heaven: LSD and the American Dream* (New York: Harper & Row, 1987), p. 209.

"Maslow's election":
Walter Truett Anderson *The Upstart Spring: Esalen and the*

American Awakening (Reading, Mass.: Addison-Wesley, 1983), p. 159.

"*going to Esalen alone*":
Howard, *Please Touch*, p. 21.

page 28   "*in terms of changing the whole world*":
Ibid., p. 36.

"*Award for Best Documentary*":
Ibid., p. 25.

"*Intensive group experiences*":
Ibid., p. 19.

page 37   "*his world exploded*":
Sam Keen, "Janov and Primal Therapy 'The Screaming Cure.' " *Psychology Today*, February 1972.

"*I can feel*":
Arthur Janov, Ph.D., *The Primal Scream: Primal Therapy, the Cure for Neurosis* (New York: G.P. Putnam's Sons, 1970).

page 41   "*Janov showed me how to feel my own fear*":
The Rolling Stone Interview, *Rolling Stone*, January 7, 1971.

"*a million-seller*"
Jon Wiener, *Come Together: John Lennon in His Time* (New York: Random House, 1984), p. 143.

page 42   "*the sleazier the better*":
Albert Goldman, "Can Primal Therapy Return Happiness?" *Vogue*, September 1, 1971.

page 47   "*Primal therapists could sense it*":
Janov, *The Primal Scream*, p. 392.

page 52   "*demonstrating the therapy's success*":
Goldman, "Can Primal Therapy Return Happiness?"

"*stories practically wrote themselves*":
Albert Goldman, *The Lives of John Lennon* (New York: William Morrow, 1988), p. 385.

page 53   "*Sixty case studies*":
Goldman, "Can Primal Therapy Return Happiness?"

page 54   "*dangers associated with encounter groups*":
Irvin D. Yalom, M.D. and Morton A. Lieberman, Ph.D., "A Study of Encounter Group Casualties," Archives of General Psychiatry, Vol. 25 (July 1971), pp. 16–30.

"*3,000 applications each month*":
Goldman, "Can Primal Therapy Return Happiness?"

"more people prepared for reality":
Francis X. Clines, "Mysteries of the East off Central Park,"
New York Times, October 8, 1971.

page 55   *"In California . . . Werner Erhard":*
Flo Conway and Jim Siegelman, *Snapping: America's Epi-demic of Sudden Personality Change* (Philadelphia: J. B. Lip-pincott, 1978), p. 26.

"that Janov's therapy had cured him":
Arthur Janov, *The Anatomy of Mental Illness: The Scientific Basis of Primal Therapy* (New York: G. P. Putnam's Sons, 1972), pp. 144, 158.

PART TWO

page 69   *"200,000 copies of* The Primal Scream*":*
Goldman, "Can Primal Therapy Return Happiness?"

"people had primals":
R. D. Rosen, *Psychobabble: Fast Talk and Quick Cure In the Era of Feeling* (New York: Atheneum, 1977), p. 136.

"tens of thousands of requests for therapy":
According to *Psychology Today,* February 1972, the Primal Institute was receiving 2,000 to 3,000 therapy applications every month.

page 72   *"faking their Primals":*
Gross, *The Psychological Society,* p. 281.

page 92   *"get into one's fear, pain, instability":*
Todd Gitlin, "John Lennon Speaking," *Commonweal,* Sep-tember 1972.

page 93   *"overthrow by force and violence":*
Janov, *The Primal Scream,* p. 102.

"a fat 15-year-old guru":
Andrew J. Edelstein and Kevin McDonough, *The Seventies: From Hot Pants to Hot Tubs* (New York: Dutton, 1990), p. 111.

"an ex-speechwriter":
Fred Gardner and Lynn O'Connor, "The 'Inner Peace' Racket," *The Second Page,* Summer 1973.

"going back to his body":
R. D. Rosen, *Psychobabble,* p. 7.

page 95 *"you're still not talking":*
Mary Beth Ayella, "Insane Therapy: Case Study of the So-cial Organization of a Psychotherapy Cult," unpublished Ph.D. dissertation, UC Berkeley, 1985.

"you're a wimp!":
John Hochman, M.D., "Iatrogenic Symptoms Associated with a Therapy Cult: Examination of an Extinct 'New Psy-chotherapy' with Respect to Psychiatric Deterioration and 'Brainwashing,' " *Psychiatry*, November 1984.

page 103 *"whether therapists should go to bed with patients":*
Michael Glenn and Richard Kunnes, *Repression or Revolu-tion? Therapy in the United States Today* (New York, Harper & Row, 1973), p. 82.

"the wisdom and ethics of therapist-patient sex":
Perry London, "From the Long Couch. . . ."

page 113 *"a senseless killing neighborhood":*
Joan Didion, *The White Album* (New York: Simon and Schuster, 1979), p. 15.

PART THREE

page 124 *"fraught with meaning":*
Ayella, "Insane Therapy," p. 198 .

page 132 *"At least 50,000 Americans":*
Peter Marin, "The New Narcissism," *Harper's* October 1975.

"John Travolta and Karen Black":
Edelstein and McDonough, *The Seventies*, p. 112.

"quasi-therapeutic improvement":
R. D. Rosen, *Psychobabble*, p. 27.

"the year's nonfiction bestsellers":
Christopher Lasch, "The Culture of Narcissism," *New York Review of Books*, September 3, 1975.

page 159 *"probably become a prostitute":*
Ayella, "Insane Therapy," p. 227.

page 179 *"six million viewers":*
Edelstein and McDonough, *The Seventies*, p. 214.

PART FOUR

page 201 *"ends required for their survival"*:
Schultz, *A History of Modern Psychology*

page 227 *"All-American Turkey"*:
Ayella, "Insane Therapy," p. 194.

page 228 *"how well and happy . . . they were"*:
Ibid, p. 193.

page 235 *"live your life like a baby"*:
Ibid, pp. 191–192.

page 263 *"The article's author put this theory"*:
Lois Timnick, "Sophisticated Brainwashing Unnecessary Expert Says," *Los Angeles Times*, November 26, 1979.

PART FIVE

page 272 *"You're like dogs, loyal"*:
Ayella, "Insane Therapy," p. 196.

page 285 *"as Freud himself had once tracked the spread of psychoanalysis"*:
Jeffrey Moussaieff Masson, *Final Analysis: The Making and Unmaking of a Psychoanalyst* (Reading Mass: Addison-Wesley, 1990), p. 182.

PART SIX

page 359 *"encourage submission, obedience and adoration"*:
Maurice K. Temerlin and Jane W. Temerlin, "Psychotherapy Cults: An Iatrogenic Perversion," *Psychotherapy: Theory, Research and Practice*, Summer 1982.

"Many of the problems they faced":
Margaret Singer, Ph.D., "Coming Out of the Cults," *Psychology Today*, January 1979.

page 367 *"children at the McMartin Pre-School"*:
John Crewdson, *By Silence Betrayed: Sexual Abuse of Children in America* (New York: Little, Brown, 1988), p. 138.

EPILOGUE

page 392 *"neediness of unexpressed primal pain"*:
Arthur Janov, "A Craving for Love, Cradle to Grave," *Los Angeles Times*, March 28, 1993.

page 406 *"mass-energy entities from the star Sirius"*:
Jeffrey Klein, "Esalen Slides off the Cliff," *Mother Jones*, December 1979.

"Rajneeshpuram"
Frances FitzGerald, *Cities on a Hill* (New York: Simon & Schuster), 1986.

"a scandal within the Movement of Spiritual Inner Awareness":
Ramsey Flynn, "Insight Out," *Washington City Paper*. December 7–13, 1990.

"the Sullivanians":
Phoebe Hoban, "PsychoDrama: The Chilling Story of How the Sullivanian Cult Turned a Utopian Dream Into a Nightmare," *New York*, June 19, 1989.

"est guru Werner Erhard":
"The Sorrows of Werner," *Newsweek*, February 18, 1991.

page 408 *"California governor George Deukmejian"*:
Susan Diesenhouse, "Therapists Start to Address Damage Done by Therapists," *New York Times*, August 29, 1989; Deborah Klinger, "Criminalizing Therapist Sex," *LA Weekly*, October 6–12, 1989.